CHINA'S WINDOW ON THE WORLD
TV NEWS, SOCIAL KNOWLEDGE
AND INTERNATIONAL SPECTACLES

THE HAMPTON PRESS COMMUNICATION SERIES
Mass Communication and Journalism
Lee B. Becker, supervisory editor

CHINA'S WINDOW ON THE WORLD
TV NEWS, SOCIAL KNOWLEDGE
AND INTERNATIONAL SPECTACLES

TSAN-KUO CHANG

UNIVERSITY OF MINNESOTA

WITH JIAN WANG AND YANRU CHEN

Printed in the United States of America

Library of Congress Cataloging-in-Publication Data

Chang, Tsan-Kuo
    China's window on the world : TV news, social knowledge, and international spectacles / by Tsan-Kuo Chang ; with Jian Wang and Yanru Chen
        p. cm.
    Includes bibliographic references and indexes.
    ISBN 1-57273-419-1 (cloth) -- ISBN 1-57273-420-5 (paper)
        1. Television broadcasting of news--China. 2. Zhong yang dian shi tai (Beijing, China)--History. 3. Television broadcasting--China--History. I. Wang, Jian. II. Chen, Yanru. III. Title.

PN5367.T4 C595 2002
070.1'95--dc21

                                                                    2002024147

Hampton Press, Inc.
23 Broadway
Cresskill, NJ 07626

To Linn, James and Alex

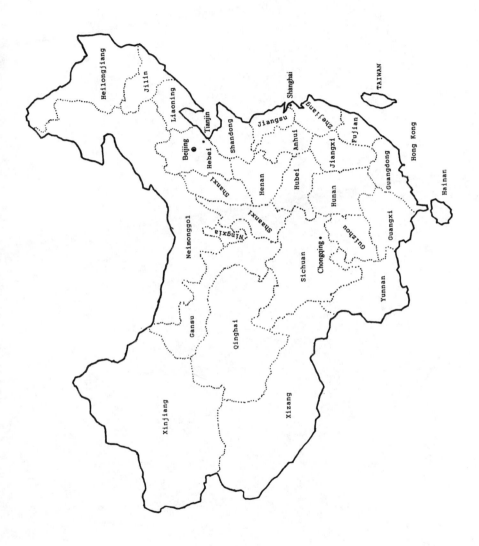

CONTENTS

ACKNOWLEDGMENTS

It is a daunting task to document the form and content of China's window on the world, especially when its television landscape has been fast changing at both the national and international levels. Without the help of many individuals and organizations in data collection and manuscript preparation, this project would not have taken off in the first place. The book started 10 years ago when I received in July 1992 a contractual award from the East Asia & Pacific Branch, Office of Research, United States Information Agency to do a comparative study between China Central Television (CCTV) and *People's Daily* in the People's Republic of China and ABC in the United States. It was the first time when Chinese and American national television news networks were systematically compared on a relatively large and longitudinal scale.

The month-long set of actual CCTV newscasts provided by the USIA in mid-1992 was significant. For one thing, it captured the evolving Chinese sociopolitical changes at a time when the pace and scope of economic reforms picked up momentum in China following Deng Xiaoping's inspection tour in the south in January 1992. Chih-Hsien Chen and Jian Wang assisted in extensive content coding, data analysis and the painstaking summary of texts. Their attention to detail and excellent analytical skills made my work much easier. After the USIA report was submitted in late 1992, I continued to examine the data within a variety of perspectives and decided to expand the project. In the following years, many colleagues and institutions have contributed in big and small ways to the genesis of this book.

A sabbatical and a leave of absence from the University of Minnesota-Twin Cities took me to Hong Kong and Singapore, where I had the opportunity to sharpen and broaden my views on the spirit and practices of Chinese news media. As a visiting scholar in the then Department of Journalism and Communication at the Chinese University of Hong Kong (CUHK) in 1993–1994, I benefited greatly from the friendship and scholarship of Joseph Man Chan, Zhou He and Paul S. N. Lee through conversations, correspondence and readings of their scholarly and journalistic articles. From June 1996 to June 1997, I spent a year as a senior fellow in the School of Communication Studies at the Nanyang Technological University (NTU) in Singapore and learned considerably from the direct contact with, and exposure to the useful works of, Hao Xiaoming and Yanru Chen on the legal and technological aspects of Chinese mass media.

Yanru Chen helped collect the second set of CCTV newscasts in December 1996 and co-authored an earlier paper comparing the 1992 and 1996 data. The study was published as a book chapter in a volume of Ablex's Contemporary Studies in International Political Communication released in 2000. Most of the findings and comparisons, however, have never been reported before. The research support of the School of Communication Studies at NTU, especially the warm welcome and administrative assistance from Eddie Kuo and Ang Peng Hwa, made my stay in Singapore enjoyable and fruitful. Many of the ideas used in the book grew out of the projects completed there. Hao's contribution to some of these projects was also helpful.

Jian Wang aided in gathering the third set of CCTV newscasts in 1998, when he was on the faculty in the School of Journalism and Communication at CUHK. Wang has corroborated with me on several projects that all led to publications in the mainstream journals. Both he and Yanru Chen have produced an impressive record of publications of their own. Because their previous studies remain relevant, I invited them to write chapters for the book. Wang prepared the first drafts for Chapters 1 and 3 and Chen for Chapter 2. The three chapters have been extensively rewritten to put them in a coherent perspective and a historical context for better understanding of the remaining chapters that emerged from laborious quantitative and qualitative analyses of CCTV news as texts. Although Chen and Wang contributed to the respective chapters, I am solely responsible for the interpretations and any mistakes found in the book.

Parts of the book have been first presented at conferences and later published separately in *Journal of Broadcasting & Electronic Media* (Spring 1996 and Summer 1998), *Journal of Communication* (Summer 1994), and *The Global Dynamics of News: Studies in International News Coverage and News Agenda* (2000). Throughout the writing of the earlier report and later papers, valuable comments and suggestions from

Leonard L. Chu, Dennis K. Davis, Chin-Chuan Lee, John Jirik, Anandam P. Kavoori, Robert J. Levy, Judy Polumbaum, Yuan Xin and many anonymous readers paved the way for the project to follow a sound theoretical foundation and a vigorous analytical approach. The permission from the USIA Office of Research for the presentation and from the Broadcast Education Association, Oxford University Press, and Greenwood Publishing Group for the use, with substantial revision in whole or in part, of copyright materials is highly appreciated. Presentations of the findings and their interpretations, of course, do not represent the views of USIA or of the U.S. government.

This book would not have taken its final shape without the foresight of Barbara Bernstein of Hampton Press in seeing the need for such a book. The intellectual input and thoughtful criticism from Lee B. Becker, editor of the Hampton Mass Communication and Journalism Series, was very instrumental. His scholarship and editorship challenged the manuscript to maintain a consistent body of knowledge and a high degree of quality. The skillful editing by Robin B. Weisberg and the production assistance by Joni Choi made the flow of ideas smooth and kept the whole project to stay on course. I am grateful to their encouragement and good-natured suggestions for revisions. Although they share the fruits, I bear single responsibility for any errors that may remain in the book.

As usual, I am deeply indebted to my wife, Linn, and our two sons, James and Alex, who have supported me with their understanding and tolerance over the past 10 years when I worked on the book project in various stages. Through good times and bad times, Linn has always been patient and loving. Like other teenagers in a defensive mode, James and Alex often questioned me whether I was going to finish the project myself whenever I asked them to complete theirs. May this book be a modest dedication to their love, sacrifice and fighting spirit.

Tsan-Kuo Chang
March 4, 2002
Twin Cities

INTRODUCTION

No country in the world can boast as large a TV audience as China. In fact, the size of audience for the primetime national news on China Central Television (CCTV) would be an envy of any television network around the world. Not only does the *Xinwen Lianbo* (Network News) command a tremendous number of viewers nationwide, it also stands as the most authoritative and prestigious television news source in China because of its monopolistic status and power as the sole national network allowed to broadcast news to the Chinese people without much rivalry. Although general TV programming, especially entertainment, at the provincial level has increasingly challenged, and to some extent weakened, the domination of CCTV in China because of the cut-throat competition among the mass media in recent years across the country, the control over national news broadcast has remained firmly in the hands of CCTV-1.

As the world's most populous country with 1.2 billion people, China certainly would, by default, have the largest pool of potential TV viewers. Population alone, however, does not necessarily constitute a television audience. There must be broadcasting infrastructure, such as TV stations, relay stations and a viable industry to reach and serve the Chinese people scattered across a vast territory from the coastal to inland regions. With the hardware comes the software that must cater to the needs and tastes of the audiences. The footprint of Chinese television now covers nearly every corner of China and TV programming has become highly diversified at a pace that was unimaginable some 10 years ago. For one thing, the once ideologically charged political mission is being replaced by a commercially sponsored consumer orientation.

Amid the rapid technological and conceptual changes, CCTV has taken a leading role in broadcasting development in China. In the face of shifting global geopolitical landscape, the reporting of the changing social reality, whether domestic or foreign, on CCTV news has also evolved dramatically over the years. The metamorphosis of CCTV from a rigid class ideologue in the 1960s to a market-oriented network in the 1990s is part of the remarkable transformation of Chinese society in general and the mass media panorama in particular. This phenomenon has captured the attention and imagination of China observers in academic and journalistic circles.

Since China embarked on the path of economic reforms and opened its door to the West in the late 1970s, the structure and processes of Chinese mass communication have increasingly become the central focus of fascination and investigation in social science research. A search of the literature reveals that studies of the Chinese media systems as an object of intellectual inquiry and journalistic critic have apparently surpassed those of many other countries. Little systematic evidence and knowledge exist, however, about how Chinese mass media, particularly the national television, present the world out there in the news. Most of the existing studies and findings have looked at the mass media in China from various perspectives, ranging from the earlier Marxist mass propaganda and persuasive model (e.g., Houn, 1961; A. Liu, 1971; Schurmann, 1966; F. Yu, 1964) to the more recent political economic approaches (e.g., He, 2000; C. Lee, 2000; P. Lee, 1997; Y. Zhao, 1998).

With varying degree of conceptual sophistication and empirical richness, previous studies have provided either descriptive or insightful analysis concerning the functions, position, and evolution of Chinese mass media in society as well as their interaction with other political and social institutions in China. Among the most extensively scrutinized area is the Communist state–media relationship and the subsequent functional prerequisites of mass communication in China that result from the fundamental ideological formation and implementation. The outcome of such essential arrangement—the news—had often been taken to be "once and for all" in its propagandistic and persuasive nature, leaving little room for the reality yet to come.

Rooted in the state ownership and absolute Party leadership, the relationship between the state and the mass media in China has nevertheless undergone extensively adjustment and realignment as a result of internal reforms (four modernizations of agriculture, industry, science, and defense) and external openness (open door policy). From an epistemological point of view, it is a serious and indefensible mistake to presume that, under the Communist system, the form and content of Chinese news media would remain unchanged or unchanging when the larger environment has created new ventures and opportunities that make it difficult for the status quo, particularly the central authority, to run against the tide. China can no longer be peeked with a fixed prism. Existing knowledge and inquiries that grew out of the overarching Cold War framework, while still instructive within a historical context, need to be revisited against the evolving and unexplored terrain that has been rapidly taking shape in China.

After the Tiananmen Square crackdown on the pro-democracy student movement in Beijing in 1989 and the collapse of Communism in eastern Europe and the former Soviet Union in the late 1980s and early 1990s, China as the last Communist stronghold continues to defy conventional wisdom and common understanding in terms of its internal and external behaviors. The surprised live broadcast of the press conference between President Bill Clinton and President Jiang Zemin on CCTV during Clinton's visit to China in June 1998 epitomized the extent to which Chinese national television news has more or less forayed into the uncharted territories. President Jiang's pointed exchange with Mike Wallace regarding the Tiananmen Square incident and other sensitive issues (e.g., press freedom and human rights) in China on CBS and on CCTV with an edited version in September 2000 further underlined the Chinese leadership's savvy strategy in exploiting television's role as an effective vehicle to reach and convey preferred messages to the vast number of audiences in China and the United States (e.g., "Bejing leadership," 2000). A detailed and longitudinal exploration of China's window on the world should help unravel the complexion and complexity of news that has witnessed the unfolding Chinese revolution of a different kind since the reforms (e.g., Davis, 2000).

This book represents the first extensive examination of Chinese national television news from a long-term point of view. Unlike some small-scale research in the 1970s and 1980s, the project covers a 7-year time span, beginning with the deepening of China's economic reforms in 1992 and ending with the year when CCTV celebrated its 40th anniversary in 1998. Essentially, it is an assessment of the burgeoning Chinese TV phenomenon in the 1990s. As China enters the 21st century with an ever unyielding velocity, its recent trail holds the key to knowledge of where and how far it may be going. In addition to some historical, legal, and international standpoints that render background exposition of CCTV as an institution and its structural constraints, the theoretical framework that guides the main thrust of this book is the sociology of knowledge perspective, the essence of which—social construction of reality—underpins the analysis of CCTV news throughout the study period.

This book is written and organized in a way that each chapter can be read by itself without being interrupted by the discussion of methodological procedure used in the content analysis for data collection. The source of data and the coding scheme are included in the Appendix. The first three chapters locate Chinese television in history, the state–media relationship and international context that do not directly touch on the news, but have clear implications for the normative and journalistic approaches CCTV takes to presenting the world out there. The next five chapters analyze CCTV news from a variety of dimensions that closely document its technical professionalism, domestic coverage, survey of the foreign vista, portrayal of China's international relations and foreign policy in general, and presentation of the United States in particular over time. Together, the eight chapters depict Chinese television through a general-to-specific mode of inquiry, focusing on its way of seeing the world in the news. In summary, the last chapter pays particular attention to the social reality created on CCTV.

Chapter 1 offers an overview of how television in China has evolved from an ideological instrument in Communist propaganda to a major outlet in commercial and entertainment programming. The historical trajectory identifies a phenomenal path of the TV growth dictated by the determined pursuit of revolutionary mass education during the early two decades and by the necessity of the market logic after the reforms. Throughout the process, as China's window on the world, CCTV occupies a strategic position in technological innovation and journalistic leadership, rising from a local TV station to a formidable national network that has set its goal to become a world class broadcast center in international communication. This chapter places the development of Chinese television in a chronological order to demonstrate how its inception, expansion and mission have followed China's quest for the economic modernization and political liberalization in an up and down fashion. Against this backdrop, the world of CCTV news stands as a symbolic representation of the social reality in and out of China.

Part of the political liberalization in China lies in the transfer of power and delegation of authority in decision making between the central and provincial governments by way of economic reforms and open-door policy during the past two decades. Although the state still dominates many aspects of the Chinese everyday life and the central authority continues to wield a considerable amount of power in social control and policy considerations, both the market itself and local governments have enjoyed greater autonomy in recent years. Within the managerial perspective, chapter 2 addresses the impact of interaction between the market and the state on television regulations in terms of official rationality in China. This chapter delineates the sociopolitical and legal-rational context in which decentralization of control and depoliticization of content of the mass media take place. These dual processes ultimately delimit the outer parameters, both conceptually and practically, for CCTV news to report on the world about what is permissible and possible.

The rational division of labor of Chinese television at the organizational level can be best seen in its import of foreign TV programming before and after the economic reforms. It is the focus of chapter 3. The central thesis is that as far as functional prerequisites are concerned, television in China has become less of a class ideologue and more of a state manager. The positional shift has serious implications for the boundaries of TV operations and content management, especially when they involve programs from other countries. This chapter offers evidence regarding content diversity of Chinese TV programming at both the vertical and horizontal levels. The move from parochial—and often Communist—countries, to multinational and Capitalist markets of foreign programs indicates a fundamental structural transformation of Chinese national television through the rationalization of China's open-door policy. In a sense, the playing field is much wider for China now than before. For the CCTV news, it means a broader vista to survey the world's diverse countries and more choices to play out the scenarios.

From an organizational point of view, CCTV clearly stands out as a prominent national medium and maintains an undisputed status as the leading news center in China. As a media organization with an apparent task of nationwide news broadcasting, CCTV, like its Western counterparts, unquestionably has to operate within various constraints generated by either internal institutional logic or the larger external social structure or both. At the practical level, not much has been learned about the length, speed, format, attribution, and visual element of the news presented on Chinese television. Driven by technical rationality, these factors make up part of the defining characteristics of journalistic professionalism, especially in television news. Chapter 4 represents the first such empirical examination of CCTV news that should be indicative of the professional character of Chinese mass media in general.

Because of the developing sociopolitical structure in China since the late 1970s, Chinese mass media now enjoy relative autonomy in the consumer-oriented market that deviates greatly from the earlier command economic system, under which political calculation tended to dictate what was to be known and how it was to be done. For the most part, the rules of the game were taken for granted and did not face much challenge or resistance. Given the propensity of monotonous media content before the reforms, the transmission of certain type of news preferred by the Chinese central authority undoubtedly contributed to the prevalent Western tenet of a monolithic and propagandistic press in China.

Chapter 5 departs from the received belief by contending that news in China should be better conceived as a form of social knowledge designed to help the Chinese audiences make sense of contemporary social practices and policy commitments in their immediate environment and the remote locale.

Using the sociology of knowledge as a framework, chapter 5 first establishes the theoretical foundation for the chapters that follow. It also details, both quantitatively and qualitatively, how CCTV news orients the Chinese people about what is going on in the domestic setting, including who is to speak, what is to be seen, how much is to be heard, what the context is, and where the actions are in China. What is more important, this chapter illustrates the patterns of construction, presentation, and interpretation of Chinese social reality in the news that far exceeds the traditional profile at the national level. The juxtaposition and comparison of coverage of provinces or regions on CCTV news accentuate a form of social indicator about the range and sector of reality in China that is accessible and knowable in the symbolic world.

The interior world, at least the one that falls within familiar geographical or psychological confines, may be reachable one way or another for the Chinese people. Indeed, the economic boom and the ensuing rise of living standards in China have made social mobility less restrictive and more dynamic, if not volatile. Beyond the domestic, however, lies another world that is as foreign and disparate as the number of countries out there for most people in China. Although overseas traveling in the forms of tourism, education, and immigration is no longer prohibitive or unimaginable, there is still a great wall that erects around the edges of Chinese sociopsychological boundaries. Open as it might be in recent years, China has yet to allow a free flow of news and information across national borders. In the domain of foreign events and issues, Chinese national media, especially television, therefore function primarily as mediating agents between the world outside and the audiences inside.

Following the social construction of reality perspective, chapter 6 underscores the size and shape of that intersection as manifested in foreign news on CCTV. It explores the extent to which the world of foreign spectacles is molded by the vintage location of China as an observer, not as a participant, in the process of international and global communication. The survey of the world's landscape is bound to be affected by where China may stand, what it may perceive in it and how it brings to the attention of the intended audiences. This chapter seeks to identify the general configuration and hotspots in the world map drawn on CCTV news and to sort out how the ebb and flow of foreign events and issues as well as the nature of their composition might serve as ways of perceiving and accepting, and thus thinking and behaving, for the Chinese audiences regarding the reality that largely defies their direct observation or experience. The pictures in our heads are not simply images. They function as a sign post for direction or as a springboard for action.

Foreign policy news is distinct from *foreign* news. What sets the two categories apart conceptually in international communication research is a crucial policy dimension. When China becomes engaged in the diplomatic community of nations or is involved in bilateral or multi-lateral relationship, it obviously assumes the role of a player, not that of a bystander. A player in any given context and contest, whether political or nonpolitical, obviously has much at stake one way or another while an onlooker on the sideline can hardly determine the outcome. Because China is part of the equation in international relations, its survey of the world's landscape apparently should be expected to predicate less on geographical distance and more on psychological proximity and functional provisions. In the process of map making, CCTV news thus could not ignore the fact that China itself furnishes some of the pieces that make up the larger picture in the world of cross-national affairs. What those pieces are and where they are placed in the world map of China's foreign policy and international transactions should help further exemplify the range of vision of Chinese mass media and their logic in social construction of reality.

Chapter 7 presents an extensive investigation of CCTV news that dwells on the structure of its worldview when Chinese national interests and global aspirations become the driving force in China's external behaviors. Along the same conceptual line of thinking postulated in the previous chapters, this chapter attempts to chart the contours and elevations of reality in the foreign policy news terrain on Chinese television. The analysis is more focused than that of foreign events or issues, but is less specific than the scrutiny of China's relations with a particular country. Inclusion of both general news and reports of certain events in international communication research allows for a more systematic and powerful exploration to specify why the news is reported the way it is (e.g., Rosengren, 1970). The relationship between China and the United States provides an ideal opportunity and site to investigate the dynamics of news as a body of empirical observation and a form of social knowledge.

The breakdown of Communism in the eastern Europe and former Soviet Union leaves China as the last Communist stronghold that is unwavering in its insistence and adherence to the Marxist and Maoist ideologies in theory, if not in reality. In practice, Beijing continues to advocate its march toward building a socialist state with a Chinese characteristics. For all practical purposes, China hence supersedes the successor of Soviet Union, Russia, as the arch-rival of the United States in the post-Cold War power equation. By China's own reckoning, as the only superpower in the global political stage, the United States poses even greater threat, whether real or imagined, to the Chinese national security and international interests. Unlike the 1950s and 1960s when China branded the United States as the number one enemy, however, the post-Cold War era has witnessed the two countries moving cautiously and uneasily toward each other. China's trade status and the U.S. annual criticism of Chinese violation of human rights often set the two countries on a dangerous colliding course.

In light of either conceptual or practical significance of Sino-American relations, the United States as seen through the Chinese news media thus symbolizes China's predilection and deliberation of interplay between the two countries. Chapter 8 delves into a meticulous assessment of the United States as an issue and an actor in different settings on Chinese national television news, including President Clinton's 1998 state visit to China. From China's point of view, the United States could be couched as a distant entity that does not immediately impinge on Chinese internal and external concerns or as a close contestant who may cause instant losses if China fails to heed its moves in a competitive situation. A comparison of collective and individual representation of the United States through an array of milieu on CCTV news should be illuminating as to how China comes to construct the reality between here and there.

The last chapter wraps up major findings and addresses their importance for a better grasp of the spirit and practices of Chinese national television news. The future of Chinese television is also discussed in the context of China's continuing economic reforms and political restructuring. As China's window on the world, the primetime news on CCTV is certainly only part of the growing multiplicity of news-related programming and does not necessarily capture the full spectrum of reality from within and without the Chinese polity. It is, by any measure, the most important one that encapsulates what is to be seen in the eyes of the Chinese state and what is to be understood among the people in China.

Domestically, several noon-hour news programs and magazine-type shows on CCTV have enjoyed great success since their inception. Internationally, the long-term plan of CCTV is to develop "conglomerate operations" and to become a world class TV station. In the 21st century, whether and when CCTV will achieve such an ambitious goal remains to be seen. There are signs that it is determined to forge ahead with the creation of the world's largest Chinese TV network. Because China is increasingly emerging as a world power, the way it sees itself and other countries through its national window, however, has profound implications for a global understanding and cooperation. It can be expected that the *Xinwen Lianbo* on CCTV-1 will persist as the dominant news channel in China for years to come.

Because it deals with the Chinese conception and representation of reality at the national level, the form and content of CCTV news should not be overlooked in the intellectual inquiry, especially in mass communication research. Nor can it be easily dismissed as a mere ideological apparatus in journalistic approach. What are the ideas, tradition, standard operating procedure, regulatory device, vocabulary, and imagery that have given CCTV news a reality and a ubiquitous presence in China? How does CCTV news define, perceive, describe, produce, present, and interpret the fast changing surroundings across China and around the world? What can be known about CCTV news is, of course, what it has made to be seen. If history is any guide, part of the ontological and epistemological answers can be found in this book.

CHAPTER 1

From National Ideologue to International Player: History and Politics of Chinese Television

The year 1999 marked the 50th anniversary of the founding of the People's Republic of China (PRC) by the Chinese Communist Party. A year before, China Central Television (CCTV) celebrated its 40th anniversary of broadcasting. Since the birth of PRC in 1949 and CCTV in 1958, Chinese politics and television have become intertwined in the never-ending struggle and adjustment to define, locate, and maintain the position and identity of China in the symbolic world at home and abroad. From a historical point of view, Chinese television, like China itself, goes through phases of transformation driven by internal imperatives and external pressures. The institutionalization of television in China is a system of vision and practices framed by a whole set of political forces and activities that brought PRC into the world stage.

Under the Communist rule, China has undergone dramatic social, political and cultural changes since the defeat of the Nationalists in a long, bloody civil war, which broke out in the early 1930s between the U.S.-supported Nationalist regime headed by Generalisimo Chiang Kai-shek and the Soviet-back Chinese Communists led by Mao Tse-tung. From the mid-1930s to the early 1940s, China suffered heavy losses as a result of Japanese aggression during the World War II. Following the end of Sino-Japanese war and the failure of U.S. mediation, armed conflicts between the Nationalists and the Communists resumed. Because of political corruption, military incompetence, high inflation, and social instability, the Nationalist government eventually lost control of China and fled to Taiwan, a small island about 100 miles off the mainland coast, to continue its rivalry with the Communist regime. On October 1, 1949, Mao proclaimed victory, establishing the first Communist state in Asia.

Unlike the first two decades when a rigid revolutionary climate engulfed China, the past 30 years witnessed the country shifting away from a centralized command system to the so-called "socialist market economy" system of today. Tied to the economic development and ideological discord in the process of China's nation building, CCTV has also evolved from a local television station to a formidable national network with more than 1 billion viewers. Its aspiration is to become a world class TV network.[1] This ambition has a humble beginning and a foreign origin. It is a culmination of historical legacy, political calculation, and economic rationality in China's revolutionary orbit and evolutionary trajectory. Throughout the 40 years of Chinese television, the bumpy path has been punctuated with technological breakthrough, institutional setbacks, organizational reforms, political clash, de-politicization and commercialization of programming, and the more recent drive to internationalization.

The history of broadcasting in China can be traced to the early 20th century when radio followed the footprints of Western merchants and missionaries into the Middle Kingdom. On January 23, 1923, founded by an American E. G. Osborn, the first radio station (Radio Corporation of China) went on air in the colonial Shanghai (Huang & Yu, 1997; Y. Zhao, 1987). Unauthorized by the warlord in the region, however, the radio station lasted only a few months. In May 1924, another radio station was established by an American company and ran for the next 5 years. Many other stations owned and operated by foreigners soon emerged in the Chinese coastal colonial territories. At that time, there were about 500 radio sets in Shanghai. Since then, radio stations had sprung up in other parts of China.

As elsewhere around the world, radio broadcasting ushered in a bold new era of mass communication in China during the 1920s. Its significance in the national campaigns for control of political power was clearly recognized by various ideological camps, including the rising Chinese Communists. The ruling Nationalist government opened the Central Broadcasting Station in 1928 to promote its policies and wage

---

[1]CCTV published a special report, titled "The Glorious 40 Years," on its Web site to commemorate its 40th anniversary (www.cctv.com/specials/cctv40/guanghui). Part of this chapter is based on that special report.

rhetorical warfare against the Communist insurgence. The Chinese Communist Party was slow to start due to its lack of resources and technological know-how, but eventually broke into radio broadcasting in territories under its command. With the help of a Soviet transmitter, the Communists started the New China Radio Station on December 30, 1940 in Yanan (T. Zhang, 1992), a communication and propaganda boost to the Communist movement.

From the 1920s through the late 1940s, radio became a political instrument of ideological battle between the Nationalists and the Communists to win over the hearts and minds of the Chinese people. Limited broadcast in foreign languages—mainly in English and Japanese—was introduced by both parties to court support from overseas or to undertake propaganda against Japan's invasion, planting the seed for the outreach of foreign audiences both within and without the Chinese territories. After the founding of the PRC in 1949, the Communist regime established the Central Broadcasting Bureau as the authority in charge of broadcasting policies and operations. Under the bureau's supervision, the Yanan New China Radio Station was formally renamed the Central People's Broadcasting Station. With the wide installation of public loudspeakers, radio broadcasting was extensively used in the war-torn country for educational and political purposes (Huang & Yu, 1997; T. Zhang, 1992; Y. Zhao, 1987).

It took another 10 years before China started to explore television broadcasting. Modeled on the Soviet mode of development, the Chinese Communist Party initiated a grand, ambitious, and radical socialist experiment that would affect almost every facet of political, economic, and social life in China. Despite the widespread poverty in the aftermath of a series of wars in the first part of the 20th century, Chinese people's optimism for the newly founded republic and its prospects seemed unlimited and contagious. The mood of the nation was to catch up with the industrialized countries through discipline, honest effort, and hard work. Such idealism and enthusiasm without sophisticated technical knowledge and technological capability ultimately resulted in the misguided and disastrous Great Leap Forward movement in 1958.

It was during this early period of the Communist governance that the first television broadcasting station was born in China. Since its inception, television in China has always been bound by the pace of political necessity, economic growth, and social progress. Beginning with its introduction and throughout its nascent development, Chinese television was wrought with political symbolism and ideological purity. When China was caught in the midst of the Great Leap Forward fever, the mid- and late 1950s also saw the mounting tension and competition between the "socialist bloc" dominated by the Soviet Union and the "free world" led by the United States. Television stations started to spring up in many of the Eastern bloc countries. As a Soviet ally, China's entry into television broadcasting was a matter of time.

When the Chinese Communists learned that, with the assistance of U.S. technology and equipment, the Nationalists on Taiwan were planning to set up a television station, launching TV broadcasting before its antagonist did (Guo, 1991) carried a sense of sudden urgency in China. It would be a huge psychological and propaganda blow to the Communist Party in its continuing rhetorical campaigns against the arch-nemesis. The Soviet adviser believed that China could not possibly catch up with Taiwan's scheduled time to start TV broadcasting in October 1958. Determined to "show to Taiwan and the Soviet Union what we could do," the Chinese Communists planned and instituted China's first TV station within a surprisingly short period of time (Huang & Yu, 1997, p. 566). National pride and political resolution apparently played a major part in the birth of Chinese television.

THE BEGINNING OF CHINESE TELEVISION

Beijing Television Station (BTS) officially went on air in the capital city in May 1958, several months ahead of Taiwan's timetable. Its inaugural broadcast took place on May 1—the International Labor Day for the socialist-block countries. The occasion was obviously chosen to show-case the prowess and contribution of the Chinese workforce in the Communist revolution. Before its launch, the Central Broadcasting Bureau spelled out the three major tasks of the new TV station in China: propaganda, education, and cultural enrichment (Huang & Yu, 1997). Although there are explicit changes in methods (e.g., commercial and less ideological bent) and subtle nuances in content (e.g., occasional reports of sensitive issues), these broad tasks have remained largely an integral part of the mission of Chinese national television today. To a great extent, the first-day broadcast set the tone for a distinct political orientation, assumptions and practices that would dominate Chinese television for many years to come.

The programming on BTS began with a 10-minute report on a meeting organized to celebrate the May 1 International Labor Day. Model workers from various industries made patriotic and upbeat speeches about the proud achievements in production output at their factories. The report was followed by a documentary entitled "Go to the Countryside," which, as the title implied, described communist cadres journeying into the countryside to work with and learn from the farmers. Next came cultural programs, including dance and poetry reading.

To conclude the inaugural programming, the broadcast schedule ended appropriately with a feature on "Television" produced by the former Soviet Union (Guo, 1991). Through the entire broadcast, it is not difficult to discern that the programming, totally devoted to communicating the Party's ideology and official performance, was more instructive than entertaining.

During the initial stage, BTS programs were aired at 7 p.m. only twice a week, with each broadcast lasting between 2 and 3 hours. The programs consisted of news, documentaries, social education, arts and culture, and entertainment. After 4 months of experimentation, BTS formally launched its programs on September 2, 1958. Its programming schedule was expanded from twice a week to four times a week. On October 1, BTS broadcast the military parade and public celebration of the ninth anniversary of the founding of the PRC, thus beginning prearranged live coverage of important political, social, and cultural activities in China. Later that year, a second television station was established in China's largest and most cosmopolitan city, Shanghai. Both stations shared similar form and content in that they carried one channel, offered 2 to 3 hours of programming four times a week, and served only their local audiences. Following the lead of Beijing and Shanghai, TV stations soon appeared in a dozen provinces. Of the 29 provinces in China, 16 set up their own TV stations between 1958 and 1960. All TV programs were transmitted in black and white.

On January 1, 1960, BTS began a fixed programming schedule, at the same time increasing the number of broadcasts from six in the previous year to eight. Its reach went beyond the domestic audiences, too. During the 26th World Ping-Pong Championship held in Beijing in 1961, BTS produced a number of news films that were sent not only to foreign TV stations having exchange agreement with China, but also to TV stations in East Germany, Brazil, Australia, and other countries for sale. It was the first time that a Chinese TV station sold its own news films to foreign counterparts. Since then, foreign exchange and reporting have become a key component of television news in China. Because of the mechanism of absolute centralization and the necessity of political control, only the state television station, BTS, was authorized to import and distribute foreign programs (Hong, 1998).

Chinese television's international activities moved quickly along the ideological divide in the world's geopolitics. From 1958 to 1965, BTS obtained agreements of program exchanges with a dozen of countries in Europe, Asia, Africa, and the Americas. They were mostly China's Communist allies: Soviet Union, Romania, Hungary, Poland, East Germany, Czechoslovakia, Bulgaria, Egypt, Cuba, North Korea, Albania, and North Vietnam. As is shown in chapter 3, these countries supplied a large quantity of China's foreign imports in the 1970s. Considered to be a taboo or risk, any exchange with the Capitalist countries, particularly those from the United States, was virtually nonexistent. As the political tide changed, however, imports from Western nations eventually replaced the Communist block as the dominant sources of foreign programming after the economic reforms picked up momentum in the 1980s. A majority of these programs came from U.S. companies, such as CBS, Disney, Lorimar-Telepictures, Paramount Pictures, RCA, and 20th Century Fox (e.g., Schell, 1987, 1988).

Not only did China bring in foreign news and programs, Chinese correspondents were also sent overseas to Africa and Vietnam to cover China's foreign affairs activities and the war in Indochina. Although coverage of international news on Chinese television was limited and focused completely on the Soviet Union and other Communist countries in the early 1960s, the practice began to evolve later. In 1964, the Central Broadcasting Bureau directed BTS to "take root in Beijing, but face the world" in its programming and news broadcasting. It was both an official instruction and challenge to BTS in its commission as the nation's leading broadcasting medium. With this mandate, the predecessor of CCTV thus embarked on a long journey in its quest to become an international news center and a global media player. Throughout its path, Chinese television would encounter internal power struggles, undertake technological innovation, and go through economic rationalization that have more or less continued to this day.

The fledgling development of Chinese television was, however, interrupted by the sudden deterioration of the Sino-Soviet relations and the worsening domestic economic conditions in the early 1960s. The former Soviet Union began to withdraw its technical support and economic aid in the late 1950s. Because of the setback of agricultural productivity and economic disasters, millions of Chinese people died of the subsequent famine and starvation. Under such harsh circumstances, television became a luxury and an easy culprit of concerns over the waste of resources. By 1963, only five of the newly established stations remained in service—Beijing, Shanghai, Tianjin, Guangzhou, and Shenyang. All these television stations were located in the coastal areas where the economic infrastructures were relatively solid and the audiences more affluent than those in the inland provinces and regions. China soon faced a massive calamity in the Chinese history that would put TV development on hold for nearly 10 years and turned it into a highly charged propaganda tool and a means of social change. Compared to today's dynamic and variegated TV programming, the tragedy and absurdity of Chinese television during the Cultural Revolution are unimaginable and unfathomable.

TELEVISION AS A VICTIM AND
A TOOL OF CULTURAL REVOLUTION

The year 1966 heralded the beginning of China's Cultural Revolution unleashed by Mao Tse-tung's all-out anti-revolutionary campaigns to weed out capitalists ideas, Confucian values and artifacts, and feudalistic traditions. The entire nation was quickly embroiled in a series of far-reaching political and class struggles unprecedented in the Chinese history. The ideological campaigns commandeered human and material resources—especially the mass media—from national to the local levels in a concerted fanatic to revolutionize the country and the people. As in many other facets of the Chinese economic, political and cultural life, television broadcasting was deeply affected by the onset of the Cultural Revolution directed by Mao and executed by his militant Red Guards. Many stations ceased operation temporarily. As a matter of fact, no TV station was spared in an offensive war against the class enemies from within and without. Television as a mass medium was expected to serve no other purpose and function than a catalyst for the Communist spirit and revolutionary change.

Under the order of the Central Committee of the Communist Party, BTS switched its programming to the mandatory content of class struggles on the one hand and banned all shows produced before the Cultural Revolution on the other hand. The imperative of ideological purity reined supreme in both content and form on Chinese television. In Shanghai, the epicenter of the Cultural Revolution, television like other forms of modern mass media was employed primarily as an indispensable apparatus of propaganda to broadcast political meetings and teachings. Sanctioned by the Central Cultural Revolution Unit in January 1967, BTS suspended its programming momentarily. The rampant and intensified anarchist campaigns apparently made it difficult for television to stay above the fray. It resumed broadcasting a month later. Its schedule increased gradually from once a week to once everyday. The revolutionary fervor also took its toll on Chinese television elsewhere. Only two TV stations in Shanghai and Guangzhou remained in operation irregularly. They had not much to do on the air, either.

During this period, all domestic programs, such as news, drama, music, and movies, shared one common theme: the struggles of the proletariat against the bourgeoisie, especially those guided by Mao Tse-tung thought. On television, rarely a day went by without Mao's words or ideas not being glorified here or there to organize and mobilize the people. The world on TV was reduced to a one-dimensional reality, with only one voice and a single view. Internationally, the Cultural Revolution ended almost all foreign exchange programs in 1967, including the British Visnews services. Late that year, to show its allegiance and commitment to the greater revolutionary cause, a military unit took over control of the BTS. From 1967 to 1973, the military's propaganda unit of Mao Tse-tung thought and the Beijing workers' propaganda unit both set up offices in the station and steered its propagandistic operation. It was the epitome of politics in charge and a direct outcome of the mass media as part of the national resource and political weaponry in a totalitarian system.

Under such adverse circumstances, BTS managed to broadcast some major stories about agricultural production, industrial and transportation construction, scientific, and technological achievements. Its reporters and editors also surveyed the backward countryside to produce many documentaries that captured the faces and impulses of remote communities amid the revolutionary social change. In the early 1970s, some specialized and informational programs about international affairs and children's education were resumed, but the overall programming quantity was no where near what it was before the Cultural Revolution. The setback would take years to rebuild. The signs of recovery emerged after the economic reforms in the late 1970s.

On the international front, BTS renewed in 1971 its contact with foreign television stations. With the resumption of news exchange with the British Visnews, the station began irregular broadcast of international news. Its scope and tone were reserved and selective. At the same time, it started mailing its news programs to other countries. The number of countries and regions receiving the Chinese TV news programs increased from 22 in 1971 to 83 in 1975, a year before the end of the Cultural Revolution. The resuscitation of Chinese TV was a slow process of a tug of war, however. Only when the state decided to loosen up its grips over the market in the 1978 did television breath a collective relief and exhibit momentum of full resurgence.

THE ECONOMIC REFORM AND TV REVIVAL

The political and social disruptions during the Cultural Revolution seriously curtailed the development of Chinese television. Although the content of television was under the watchful eyes for any departure from the official line, the form of television, however, kept pace with the technological advancement and the logic of economic necessity. The restoration of television to normal programming finally began in the late 1960s. Many existing TV stations were allowed to recommence broadcasting and new ones established after 1969 because of political calculation by the Communist Party. Through its symbolic presentation and amid the public's fascination, television served the state interest and purpose well when revolutionary ideas, images, exemplars, and announcements could be conveyed visually, creating an illusion of immediacy and potency.

With improvements in technology, resources, and much needed technical staff training, live broadcasting became possible for many provincial stations. Although China began to explore color broadcast transmissions as early as the 1960s, it was not until 1973 that color was introduced to TV stations in Beijing, Shanghai, and Tianjin. In September 1970, with the support of the central authority, BTS formulated a 5-year plan to develop color television, with two channels in color and one in black and white. By the early 1980s, all television stations were equipped to broadcast in color on the phase alternation line (PAL) system (X. Li, 1991), which was formally approved by the State Council.

The installation of microwave trunk lines in the early 1970s was a major technological and technical breakthrough that at long last enabled BTS to cater to a national mass audience, making it a powerful presence in mass communication. With 32 television stations around the country, its footprint covered 20 provinces, municipalities, and autonomous regions. When the Cultural Revolution ended in 1976, 25 provinces, municipalities, and autonomous regions could receive BTS signals. Because of this quasi-network linkage, the provincial stations agreed in July 1976 to broadcast BTS network news—the forerunner of CCTV's *Xinwen Lianbo*—on a trial basis. The BTS' news at 7 p.m. thus was carried by all TV stations from around the country every evening, paving the way for BTS to become a national TV network in China.

Following the end of the Cultural Revolution and the death of Mao Tse-tung in 1976, the post-Mao era saw China taking a significant conceptual and practical departure from Mao's unyielding class struggles and ideological indoctrination. With Deng Xiaoping at the helm, China started to reshape its Soviet party–state monolithic system by opening up opportunities for foreign trade and investment on the one hand and by restructuring the domestic economic infrastructure for the transition to the so-called "socialist market economy" on the other hand. The dual approach of open–door policy and the market orientation called for a fundamental shift in Chinese media regulation and operation, the essence of which was the institutional reorganization. In May 1978, with the blessing of the central authority of the Communist Party, BTS was officially renamed China Central Television (CCTV), becoming the country's most authoritative television network and delivering for the first time a truly national broadcast service. CCTV not only produced many shows itself, but also repackaged programs contributed by regional stations. Its status and prestige as the sole national TV network were enhanced by its close ties to the powers that be. The unquestionable "Central" marker, like the "People's" sticker, carries an unspoken and imposing superiority in China.

Beginning in 1982, major stories about the Communist Party and the government were often announced through CCTV Network News, thus establishing its important voice and commanding standing. The number of CCTV news programs also expanded in 1984. It has since launched a series of news programs, such as "News at Noon," "News at Ten," "English News," "Economic News," "Sports News," and "Morning News." CCTV's emphasis on news can be seen in the increasing number of news stories it broadcasts every year. In the early 1980s, CCTV transmitted about 4,000 news items every year. By the end of 1980s, the news volume had reached more than 20,000 items. The number subsequently increased to about 40,000 news items, including international news, in the 1990s. In the 21st century, television news in China has come of age, representing a substantial channel for the Chinese people to see and know both domestic and foreign affairs.

Although BTS (and later CCTV) bore the brunt of strategic broadcasting during the ups and downs of China's march to modernization, the development of Chinese television in general limped along for almost two decades. It was not until the 1980s that, as a result of the drastic social and political changes at home and abroad as well as rapid technological advances, Chinese television began to develop into what has now become an essential part of Chinese people's everyday life.[2] The turning point occurred in the mid-1980s when decentralization made possible for the rapid expansion of television in China. In 1983, the Communist Party issued "On the Programme of Radio and Television" decree, allowing TV stations to be established at the county, city, provincial, and national levels, further solidifying the television infrastructure.

TV BROADCASTING INFRASTRUCTURE

Chinese television enjoyed tremendous growth in the 1980s. In 1965, the year before the Cultural Revolution, there were only 12 television stations nationwide. Ten years later, 32 stations were in operation around the country. As China entered the 1980s, the number of television stations increased considerably. In 1985, the number of television stations reached 202, a significant increase from 52 stations only 2 years before. This was the outgrowth of a new policy that aimed at setting up a four-

---

[2]For a detailed description of the early history of Chinese television, see Guo (1991).

level television broadcasting system to replace a centralized mechanism. Before advertising became the primary means of revenues, television from the national to the county levels in China was heavily subsidized by the state. There was no incentive for market competition, nor was there any organizational need to do so.

The Chinese administrative division consists of four levels: the central government at the top, followed by the provinces (30), cities (about 450), and counties (about 1,900). Until the mid-1980s, the Chinese government had exercised a total financial and administrative control over television stations by decreeing that only the central authority could establish and operate a television station. This monopoly guaranteed CCTV's domination in the broadcasting industry. But with the new policy, if a county or local city could raise enough money, it was allowed to own a TV station. Supported by the local authorities, many TV stations were consequently set up at the county and city levels. Decentralization obviously breeds competition in the media industry. China is no exception.

As can be seen in Table 1.1, the number of television stations continued to grow over the years, reaching 509 by the end of 1990 and surging to nearly 1,000 in 2000. A significant jumped occurred in the late 1970s, when China launched its economic reform and decided to open up the market to the outside world. Apparently, the infusion of foreign capital, goods, and services has contributed to the transformation of Chinese society from a top–down political system to a market-oriented structure. As part of the social system, Chinese television not only captured the transition, but also was shaped by the sociotechnological process.

Table 1.1: The Growth of Chinese Television

	1965	1975	1985	1989	1997	2000*
Television stations	12	32	202	469	923	980
Relay stations	—	—	12,159	22,139	41,205	42,830+

Source: *China Broadcasting Yearbook* (various years)

* The number of TV stations is based on an unofficial count reported in the Chinese newspapers. The number of relay stations is taken from the 1999 official statistics. In the broadcasting yearbook, the number of TV stations dropped to 347 in 1998 and 352 in 1999. One reason is the merger of radio and TV stations at the county and city levels.

The rapid growth of television centers coincided with the establishment and proliferation of broadcast relay stations across the country (Table 1.1). In the early 1980s, approximately 400 relay stations helped transmit television signals from the 52 existing TV stations. By the end of 1980s, there were more than 22,000 relay stations in China, transporting TV signals around the country. In the mid-1990s, the number of relay stations nearly doubled at more than 40,000 nationwide. The trend continues into the 21st century. It is difficult, if not impossible, to pinpoint the exact number of TV and relay stations because of the booming demand at the local and regional levels. One thing for sure is that this complex network allows CCTV news and other programs to penetrate almost every corner of the vast Chinese territories.

Another notable milestone in the TV development is the introduction of cable and satellite. Cable wiring technology was developed to ensure better program reception in remote and mountainous areas. It first began in China in the 1960s and the 1970s. Cable systems were set up at large state factories and apartment complexes on a limited scale (X. Yu & Sears, 1996). This condition changed dramatically when municipalities started to wire many smaller, surrounding communities on a large scale in the late 1980s. To help solve the reception problems, China launched and rented several communication satellites in the mid-1980s, including the Intelsat. These closed-circuit systems were no longer used solely for improving the quality of over-the-air programming. Instead a new development took place as cable stations initiated to broadcast their own programs.

By 1997, there were about 2,000 stations (above the county level) around the country, providing news and entertainment programming. A typical television audience can normally access 10 to 20 channels with a cable system. Illegal or unauthorized cable systems aside, the explosion of channels has presented significant challenges to the Chinese government concerning how best to manage the stations and to ensure that they offer quality programming and stay within acceptable boundaries. Within the four-tiered decentralized system, control over television is essentially exercised at two levels: central state supervision of CCTV and provincial stations and local management at the grass-roots level.

The role of television and its significance in China's national development could be seen in the government's economic policies and political goals as well as the constant attention TV received at various national conferences. In October 1980, China held the 10th national broadcasting and television conference to review the TV progress during the previous 30 years and to chart its new course and mission in the future. In 1981, the Chinese Communist Party Central Committee decided to include the construction of a color TV center as part of the sixth 5-year major economic and industrial projects. A year later, the National

People's Congress disbanded the Central Broadcasting Bureau and authorized the formation of the Ministry of Broadcasting and Television to oversee the fast booming broadcasting and television industries. As is discussed in Chapter 2, since the mid-1980s the Ministry of Broadcasting and Television has issued numerous decrees, regulations, and laws governing every aspect of TV and cable production, dissemination, and consumption as well as foreign imports and services.

With the rapid growth of stations, television programming further expanded in both quantity and quality. Several TV stations added 24-hour channels (e.g., CCTV-4) and CCTV itself spawned no fewer than 11 distinct channels. On the technological side, CCTV introduced digital television on October 1, 1999 to telecast the National Day parades. The broadcast was received by 25 terrestrial stations in Beijing. In addition to CCTV, Shanghai Satellite TV has established 24-hour channels to broadcast news, business, sports, movies, social education and youth programs, and other variety shows around the clock (Shanghai Satellite TV, 1998). It also provides its programs to more than 600 cable stations in other cities from coastal to inland regions (Xiao, 1999). This phenomenon signifies the intensification of television competition in China as more provincial and local cable TV systems entered the market in the 1990s, aggressively vying for a share of the huge Chinese audience pie and potential advertising profits.

Before the early 1990s, CCTV stood as the dominant player in the Chinese television industry. By virtue of its national status and historical legacy, CCTV had the blessing of the central authority to be monopolistic in broadcasting. As far as programs were concerned, the Chinese viewers around the nation could only pick up either CCTV or local TV programs, but not regional or provincial programs. The situation changed in 1993 when satellites were used by regional TV stations to transmit signals. Other than carrying programs from CCTV, most of the provincial stations also developed extra channels for additional programming. At the end of 1998, 28 provincial stations transmitted their programs via satellite, hence greatly increasing audience's choice of channels and content. On the average, almost 60,000 hours of programs are broadcast nationwide on a weekly basis. Through a number of channels, each station broadcasts about 600 hours per week (*China Broadcasting Yearbook*, 1998). The shape and size of the world's largest television network, not to mention the massive market, make it necessary and rational for CCTV to turn to the wants and needs of the people. To some extent, the market is the message even in a Communist society.

In the midst of the technical improvement and infrastructure expansion of TV stations across China, CCTV used its national position, dedicated personnel and resources to broaden its spectrum of programs and its reach to various segments of the general population. One of the focuses was to survey the Chinese economic landscape and relate its changes to the public's everyday life. In 1985, CCTV opened a 30-minute show, *Economic Life*, on Channel 2 to report current economic projects and address public issues and citizen concerns in the business arena. The program was first shown on fewer than 100 TV stations, but can now be seen in more than 1,430 cities and towns. Following the success of the economic-oriented program, a wide variety of shows dealing with domestic and foreign customs, cultures, animals, and people were, among others, introduced in the recent years. The diversity and influx of TV programming mean that the Chinese audiences have been exposed to a full array of content.

The advent and progress of economic reforms not only opened the door to lively programming, but also brought back noneditorial content—advertising—to television in China. Since the Communists took over power in 1949 and until the reform movement in the late 1970s, advertising had often been considered a form of decadence and a means of capitalist exploitation. It was initially discouraged and later totally banned in any media content. Because television was entirely funded by the state budget before the reform and decentralization, no station had any financial need and incentive to generate its own revenues. When the market was allowed to function properly according to its logic, the restoration of the missing link between manufacturers and consumers became inevitable. Advertising first appeared on CCTV in October 1979, a year after China embarked on the economic reforms. Since then, commercials have been formally endorsed as the necessary resource for the financial viability and stability of television, hence becoming a permanent fixture of TV stations around the country.

The advertising sales on Chinese television exploded quickly, increasing from 3.25 million yuan in 1979 to 2,050 million yuan in 1992 (Huang, 1994). In 1998, the commercial revenue for the TV industry was 13.6 billion yuan, nearly one third of which went to CCTV. Although CCTV does not air any commercial during its prime-time 7 p.m. newscast, it charges a hefty fee for the prestigious 5-second slot immediately after the broadcast. In the first quarter of 1999, for example, that 5-second spot cost a total of $4.5 million (U.S.) for a nightly commercial. CCTV's dominance in the advertising market has, however, declined as a result of heavy competition from more regional TV stations that have emerged with satellite-transmitted programs across regions in the early 1990s. Some regional TV networks were established as early as the 1980s, such as the "Yangzi River Delta TV Co-Op Network" initiated by the Shanghai TV Station and consisted of TV stations from six other provinces in eastern China.

The introduction of commercials on the Chinese national television sion opened a window on the world of consumerism and commercialism that was unimaginable before the reform and openness. Social taboos are bound to be broken sooner or later. In 1987, CCTV broadcast public service commercials during its prime-time slot, a move that clearly demonstrated the network's efforts to inform and educate the nationwide audiences about China's national commitment and social practices. On November 28, 1999, CCTV Channel 1 carried a 42-second commercial about sexual behavior, pregnancy, and AIDS prevention (CCTV broadcast, 1999). It was the very first time that such a theme and the use of condoms went on air on national television. This public service commercial was hailed as a breakthrough in the Chinese television history. Three days later, however, the commercial was removed because of the alleged violation of the advertising law (CCTV public service, 1999). As is shown in chapter 2, there are a variety of laws, regulations, and executive orders that govern the spirit and practices of television in China.

In addition to content diversity, the form of television begins to respond to the logic of the market and the demand of the audiences. Under the old economic command system, the division of labor among media organizations means that competition between similar outlets was virtually nonexistent. With economic reform deeply entrenched, another important development in Chinese television was the initiation of competing stations within a single city. Shanghai was selected as the testing ground. In January 1993, Shanghai East TV was officially launched to compete head on with Shanghai Television Station. Its programming has enjoyed wide success almost from the start.

Although other major cities in China have yet to introduce new TV stations in the same market area, the precedent in Shanghai has apparently been set for a more competitive television environment to emerge throughout the provinces around the country. It may, however, take China years to have widespread competitive television stations at local levels because of the unequal distribution of resources and varying pace of progress between the coastal and inland provinces. The recent campaigns to push economic construction and social progress further into the western and remote regions in China indicate that there still is room for television to grow.

Despite its humble beginning, Chinese television has in the last two decades made great strides in building its technological infrastructure and programming sophistication. The development of Chinese television on these two tracks has laid the foundation for the creation of the world's largest television audience. As is shown in chapter 2, this enormous audience becomes more or less captive because of the legal regulation and content control as well as the restrictive access to foreign media.

Chapter 5 demonstrates how the state speaks through the government and the Party to such audiences on the Chinese national television in an unrivaled manner. China's window on the world is built on a colossal base of audiences who have often been considered as "the masses" in the process of mass communication (Y. Zhang, 2000).

THE WORLD'S LARGEST TV AUDIENCE

When Chinese television first broadcast on the air in 1958, there were only about 30 television sets in use in all of Beijing. They belonged to high-ranking party officials. For the better part of the first 20 years of Chinese television, television viewing was extremely limited and was mostly a collective activity at work units. Although the number of TV sets might have been small in the early years, the size of audiences that TV reached could be substantial as a result of public viewing. Except in very rare cases, private ownership of television sets was unheard of. In an economic and political sense, having a television set at home was therefore a symbol of status and authority. It was not until the boom of reforms and the rise of living standards in the 1990s that television became a common household commodity.

In 1976, at the dawn of the reform movement, there were about half a million TV sets in China, and broadcasting signals reached only one third of the population. With a population of 800 million at that time, about 1,600 people shared per TV set (Z. Guo, 1991). It was clearly a manifestation of the paucity of resources and accessibility of TV in the Chinese society. Part of the plight certainly could be attributed to the destructive impact of the 10-year Cultural Revolution on the production of consumer commodities and the construction of television infrastructure. Afterward, economic reform and the subsequent increase in family income apparently made TV ownership affordable for many people. Besides, in addition to the CCTV network news, there were more programs to see on a regular basis. Mostly gone were the monotonous and ideologically laden shows produced during the Cultural Revolution.

By 1986, about half of Chinese households owned TV sets, resulting in 600 million TV viewers in the country. This represented an incredible increase in both TV ownership and viewership within a 10-year span. Chinese households now own at least 380 million TV sets (W. Wang, 2001). If the Chinese population of 1.2 billion is factored in, one in every three Chinese owns a television set. The penetration rate, especially for color TV, however, is much higher in the urban households (105%) than the rural countryside (33%) (*China Statistical Yearbook*, 2000; H. Li, 1999). Content aside, the world of Chinese TV indicates an uneven flow of income, consumer goods, and services in China. As the country forges forward in its economic modernization, more and more Chinese people will see their lives changed accordingly and profoundly.

With the proliferation of broadcasting centers and relay stations as well as the growth of ownership, the size of the Chinese television audience has increased dramatically since the 1970s. In 1975, the 32 Chinese television stations served 18 million viewers. Five years later, more than 200 million viewers were able to watch programs transmitted from 52 stations. In 1985, the audience doubled that of 1980. Television now reaches more than 90% of the Chinese population, a remarkable increase from 45% in 1978 when the reform policy was first outlined and implemented. The dramatic expansion of TV audience and market can be partly explained by the sales of satellite dishes and the penetration of overseas programs from nearby TV centers in Hong Kong and Taiwan (Huang, Hao, & Zhang, 1997). Launched in 1991, for example, Star TV (Satellite Television Asia Region), a Hong Kong-based media conglomerate, has since been watched by more than 40 million viewers in China, most of them in the coastal regions. As China has increasingly being drawn into the global economic system, the competition of TV market from within and without is unavoidable.

The Chinese television audience can sometimes be as big as 1 billion, truly the largest television audience on the face of the earth. The third national TV audience survey conducted by CCTV and some local TV stations in 1997 found that at the end of June the TV population reached 1.094 billion. On average, viewers in rural areas had access to 8 channels and urban viewers 15. The Chinese government is implementing a program to ensure that every village in the country has access to television and radio broadcasting in the early 21st century (TV and radio, 1999). When television eventually saturates the entire market, the world of Chinese television should provide a site of great political and economic opportunities and challenges for the government and business alike in and out of China. The question becomes: How will the Chinese authority strike a balance between the many directions that television may be pulled or pushed by the various political, economic, and social forces?

FROM POLITICAL INDOCTRINATION
TO INFORMATION AND ENTERTAINMENT

Historically, television was born into a politico-economic command system in China, but has gradually become a market-oriented commercial vehicle. Like in other countries, any communication medium in China is a function of the social, political, and cultural arrangements. As a mass medium, television in China was regarded in much the same way and accorded the same mission as other major media, such as newspaper, news agency, magazine, and radio. They were all molded to be mouthpieces for the Chinese Communist Party and the government, with positive propaganda and ideological education as their political and social tasks. The Chinese Constitution unequivocally indicates that above anything else, the state itself takes charge of the cultural industries, including print and broadcasting media, in order to serve the people and socialism (Wong, 1990). As is seen in chapter 2, the number of regulations, directives, and laws issued by various governmental agencies also stands as a clear and constant reminder as to what is expected and permitted of the mass media in the Chinese setting.

Television is no exception. Because of its increasing ubiquity and the sophistication of new communication technology, it is subject to even higher pressure and control to stay within the parameters defined and delimited by the interests of the state. This is particularly true when television was tied to the structure and process of China's national development and ideological purification since its inception in the late 1950s. Throughout the 1960s and early 1970s, the opening of its window on the world was largely hinged on the direction of the political wind and the degree of autonomy television might enjoy as a result of shifting national priorities.

Before the 1980s, Chinese television programming was limited not only in quantity but also in variety and quality, serving merely as an instrument for political indoctrination and social education. The entire cultural climate in China was highly politicized and ideologically infused. Television, as a piece of modern communication technology and a cultural institution, only transmitted the dominant ideology of class struggle at the time and cultivated the official knowledge sanctioned by the central authority. Even seemingly entertainment programs (e.g., comedies, dramas, and movies) were imparted with political ideology or preferred perspective. Government control was total and effective. The commonly accepted information and entertainment role of television was absent in Chinese television during those years.

It is precisely due to such domination of official knowledge on television dictated by the functional prerequisites of the state that led Western observers to believe that the Chinese mass media were essentially designed for propaganda and indoctrination purposes. As such, the received knowledge among the academic community is that any research on Chinese mass communication system has to trace its ideological root and factor in the inherent propagandistic nature of its practices (e.g., Pye, 1978), as exemplified during the first 30 years of the

Communist rule. But this view was reductionistic and did not allow enough room for consideration of the social realities that emerged after China shifted gear and altered the course of its economic trajectory. It is difficult to imagine that when the object of observation has moved from one location to another, a fixed lens would continue to see the same thing in an identical landscape. As Galtung (1990) argued, "A good theory should never leave us with the idea that the world is made once and for all" (p. 102). The change in both quantity and quality in Chinese television during the past two decades has clearly defied the conventional wisdom and background belief of a monolithic and monotonous propaganda machine in China, which has been found to be inadequate in explaining the reality (e.g., Chang, Chen, & Zhang, 1993).

When China embarked on the economic reform and adopted open-door policies in the late 1970s and early 1980s, television started to enter Chinese households in earnest. At the same time, the disposition of television programming began to transform. Although the Chinese government did not, and has no intention to, relinquish its state ownership and firm control over the mass media, the form and content of the media in general and television in particular became more diversified. Aside from serving as the mouthpiece of the Chinese government and the Communist Party, television took on other roles as well, becoming a viable source of information and criticism, a mass entertainer, a mass educator, and an advertising vehicle (J. Yu, 1990). Many TV stations have offered business news and consumer information programs since the reforms, which were generally void of a distinct communist ideology or political indoctrination.

Through a well-developed network of 1,000 educational stations (X. Zhang, 1996), Chinese television's task as a mass educator is far reaching. The educational channels schedule courses on a wide array of subjects to correspondence students through television universities. Degrees are conferred when students have successfully completed all the courses. The first Chinese television university—Beijing Television University—was co-founded by the BTS and the Bureau of Education of the Beijing City in the late 1960. In 1997, China Educational Television broadcast more than 15,000 hours of programs, 30% of which were for China Central Television University courses (*China Broadcasting Yearbook*, 1998).

One of the fundamental changes in Chinese television programming is the increase of purely diversion programs, such as variety shows. Major stations also produce original television series and television dramas. As is shown in chapter 3, the entertainment function of television has been further enhanced as imported television programs from Japan, the United States, and Hong Kong graced the Chinese TV screen and became hugely successful with the Chinese audience. If these programs espouse any ideology, it will be the ideology of hedonism. After the hyper-politicization years during the Cultural Revolution, the Chinese people seem to have rediscovered pleasure and entertainment. No medium can compete with television as a source for diversion and social escapism. It did not take long before the Chinese people began to spend more and more of their leisure time in front of the TV box.

With the maturation and rapid penetration of the TV market in China comes American A. C. Nielsen Media Research. The Nielsen Co. decided to set up its ratings services in 10 major cities in1999, covering 60% of the Chinese domestic TV market (AC Nielson, 2000). In addition to the independent ratings services, CCTV has relied on its own audience survey and feedbacks to allocate primetime slots for various news and social programs. Those shows that do not score a high rating are degraded to other slots or risk to be cancelled (H. Jin, 2000). Television in China now has an audience to attract and a market to compete. Like its counterparts in other countries, television has increasingly positioned itself as the primary source for news, information and entertainment in China.

A 1995 Gallup survey shows, for example, that television was the most popular medium among the four major mass media—TV, radio, newspaper, and magazine (C. Li, 1998). The centrality of television in the everyday life of Chinese people applies not only to city dwellers but also to rural population. According to a survey conducted in one of the major agricultural provinces Henan, television was found to be the most frequently used medium in 1992. Five years, later, despite a decline in the number of people who watched television every day due to the increasing variety of entertainment choices, television continued to be the dominant medium. The vast majority of the people (92.8%) watched TV at home (*China Broadcasting Yearbook*, 1998). Furthermore, the Chinese are more likely to choose television watching as their primary activity in their leisure time than other activities such as doing domestic chores and reading newspapers and magazines. This pattern has been confirmed by other surveys on the Chinese people's leisure activities (see Pan & Chan, 1998).

One of the key factors that have contributed to the entertainment turn of Chinese television is the growing importance of advertising. Shanghai TV made history in January 1979 when it aired China's first television commercial (a 90-second ad for a Chinese medicinal wine). The re-introduction of advertising into the Chinese media in the late 1970s signaled a fundamental configuration in the structure of media management. While maintaining its firm control on the political orientation of the media, the Chinese government now espouses the policy of managing media outlets as business units, keeping financial support and subsidy for media operations to a minimum. Commercialization of the Chinese media and for that matter television is well underway. There has been dramatic growth of advertising revenue in television (See Table 1.2). In short, for Chinese television stations, propaganda and profit are equally important, without one or the other they won't be able to survive.

Amid all the flurry and flux in the Chinese television industry and among the variety of shows on the screen, news and other related shows remain the most watched programs in China. In 1995, all TV stations in China produced 2,739 news programs with a total of 80,799 hours, representing a tenfold increase from 7,444 hours in 1985 (*China Statistical Yearbook*, 1996). The significance of news programs on Chinese television lies in the fact that their total hours (140,529) far outnumbered those of educational programs (23,048 hours) by a 6 to 1 ratio in 1999. Among all TV programs, they are also ranked the highest by Chinese viewers. For example, news programs on CCTV are watched the most by 73% of the viewers, with the prime-time news topping the list at 91.2% (Bo, 2000).

Being the only national network, CCTV stands as the most authoritative station in news and investigative reporting in China. From 1993 to 1997, CCTV launched extensive reforms in its news programs, increasing news broadcasts from 4 times a day to 12 times daily. All major news stories were carried on various programs throughout the day. And the amount of newscasts rose from 65 minutes to 150 minutes per day. As a result, some major events, especially those pre-arranged or scheduled, were broadcast live and most stories were delivered more timely. The timeliness or immediacy of news delivery in both domestic and foreign news on CCTV continues throughout the 1990s (see chapter 4).

Table 1.2: Development of Advertising Revenue in the Chinese Media (million yuan)

Media	1983	1990	1993	1995	1998
Television	16	561	2,944	6,486	13,564
Newspaper	73	677	3,771	6,468	10,435
Radio	18	86	349	738	1,330
Magazine	11	87	185	382	713

Source: *China Advertising Yearbook* (various years)

Since its beginning, CCTV's *Xinwen Lianbo* (network news) has established itself as a premium source of important government policy announcements and major Communist Party activities. It is most watched by the general public. By its own account, this network news on CCTV enjoys a viewership of more than 45 %, with an audience of more than 500 million nationwide. The *Jiaodian Fangtan* (Focus Interview) program—a news magazine modeled on the CBS Show, *60 Minutes,* known for exposing corruption and social injustice through hard-hitting investigative reporting—commanded a daily viewership of about 300 million, including the Chinese Premier Zhu Rongji (Undercover reporting, 1999).

In June 1998, CCTV surprised the Chinese and Western observers by carrying a live broadcast of the news conference between President Jiang and President Clinton during the latter's visit to China, in which the two leaders exchanged strong statements and pointed views concerning human rights issues, Tibet and the controversial 1989 Tiananmen Square incident. For the first time in China, television viewers, if they watched at all because the live broadcast was never listed or announced in advance, were witness to an unedited, freely aired discussion of sensitive issues by a Chinese leader, not to mention a high-level international debate between leaders of the world's superpower and its most populous nation. This rarity on Chinese television in the home setting is even more striking when compared to the coverage of Jiang's visit to the United States a year before. According to *The New York Times* (1998), all events of Jiang's U.S. visit and difficult discussions, including his joint conference with Clinton in Washington, were "taped, edited and shown later."

Probably encouraged by the positive response to the unprecedented move, within 2 weeks CCTV beamed a live coverage of a court trial in Beijing nationwide, creating some openness to China's tightly shielded legal system (see chapter 2 for details). Although the case itself—copyrights infringement—was neither new nor sensational, its direct broadcast was hailed from within and without as a major breakthrough in both Chinese court proceedings and journalistic practices (Central TV, 1998). Chinese radio did not lag far behind. In February 1999, the music channel of the Beijing People's Radio Station broadcast live the 41st Grammy Awards from Los Angeles, becoming the first Chinese radio station to do so. The presence of a Chinese team from Beijing stirred some excitement among their counterparts at the Grammy Awards (First live, 1999). There should be little surprise that CCTV news programs can now be seen occasionally on C-SPAN in the United States. It is an indication of how far Chinese television has evolved in its programming and vision.

In 1980, C. Lee observed that "Chinese television stands in the threshold of a great change, unmistakably towards the pragmatic use of television in the future" (p. 229). Twenty years later, China has turned into the largest television viewing country in the world and hence the world's biggest audiovisual market. "Amidst the domestic changes and global challenges of the 1980s and 1990s," Polumbaum (1994) pointed out, "Chinese newspapers, magazines, radio, television and other media have increased in number, expanded in scope and ambition, and become ever more variegated in character and content" (p. 1). With low television penetration prior to the 1980s and an extremely limited amount of programs, the social significance of television could hardly be noted in China. Today, however, watching television has been part of everyday life. For many Chinese people, television viewing is their dominant evening activity.

China has entered a new TV era, with sights and sounds from all over the world on the screen right in the living rooms. From the coastal to inland regions, television has truly opened a window on the world for the Chinese people. According to one TV viewer, "When we first got color TV, it was just like going to a foreign country" (Lull, 1991, p. 171). Perhaps it is. As Lull aptly observed, "[t]he introduction of television into the homes of Chinese families may be the single most important cultural and political development in the People's Republic since the end of the Cultural Revolution" (p. 59). This development has yet to reach its full potential. As the embodiment of Chinese television, CCTV has set its eye on an even higher ground—the international marketplace on the world stage.

CCTV'S INTERNATIONAL VISION AND AMBITION

As of 2001, CCTV had 11 channels, covering a wide range of programs around the clock. CCTV-1 is the flagship channel of the national TV network, with its emphasis on news and current affairs. These programs include the prime-time *Xinwen Lianbo, Focus Interview, Oriental Time and Space, Evening News, To Tell the Truth, News Investigation, World Reports, Sports News,* and *News 30 Minutes*. Its footprint now reaches more than 84% of the population, with the size of regular viewers exceeding 900 million. Most of these news shows enjoy high ratings and are revered among officials at various levels because of their expose and investigative journalism.

The other CCTV channels are set up according to specific content and targeted audiences: CCTV-2—economic topics; CCTV-3—music and variety shows; CCTV-5—sports; CCTV-6—movies; CCTV-7—children, agriculture, military, and science; CCTV-8—TV dramas. Also known as CCTV International, CCTV-4 produces news and other programs in several languages for overseas viewers. Opened in September 2000, CCTV-9 is a 24-hour English channel that broadcasts news, cultural and arts programs to domestic and foreign English-speaking audiences. Debuting in July 2001, CCTV-10 is devoted to science and educational programs. The newest addition, CCTV-11 is a specialized channel designed to promote interests and knowledge among young people about operas, folk music, and culture. All of these channels use nationwide microwave network and satellite transmission systems to reach audiences in China and abroad.

The long-term plan of CCTV is "to develop conglomerate operations" and to become "a first class international TV station by 2000" (Deng, 1997, p. 1). As indicated on its Web site, this international orientation has two basic objectives: "to become a bridge for contacts and exchanges between China and the rest of the world" and "to serve as a window, through which the world gets a better understanding of China."[3] As a bridge, CCTV has used a number of international satellites to transmit news and sports programs to and from overseas. With the first English channel in China, for example, CCTV-9's footprint covers 98% of the lands in Asia, Africa, Americas, Europe, Western Pacific, and the Middle East. Its objective is "to provide a window for the English speaking audiences to know China" (L. Jin, 2000, p. c6). This is a remarkable milestone in Chinese television history.

In 1972, when President Nixon first visited China, CCTV rented U.S. color television facilities to assist the three U.S. networks to broadcast Nixon's trip. It was the first time that China sent television programs abroad via satellite. Six years later, CCTV broadcast via satellite the 11th World Cup Soccer Game from Argentina to the Chinese audience, breaking new ground for such sports activities. On the 35th anniversary of the founding of PRC in 1984, CCTV inaugurated a live broadcast of the military parade and celebration at the Tiananmen Square to both the domestic and foreign audiences.

The Chinese television's international effort can be best seen in the handover of Hong Kong from the British rule to China's sovereignty on June 30, 1997. CCTV dispatched 339 journalists (289 in Hong Kong and 50 in major international cities) to provide live coverage of the ceremony. This was the first time in CCTV's history for a single event to involve so many reporters, not to mention 500 to 600 hundred more staff members in Beijing (Deng, 1997). The Hong Kong case, of course, is

---

[3]On its Web site (www.cctv.com/english/profile/cctvgk.html, November 11, 1999), CCTV has a short profile about its history, programming, and mission. Part of the information in this chapter is based on this profile.

unique and represents a combination of national pride, political calculation and international communication showmanship. It is, however, consistent with CCTV's determination to become a world-class broadcaster.

To assist in this effort, CCTV has expanded the size of its staff. When the economic reform started around 1979, CCTV had about 700 staff. In 1992, the number increased to more than 2,000. In 2001, its employees stood at about 4,000 who worked in various departments and units. Another sign is CCTV's investment interests in well-established TV companies, such as Television Broadcasting Ltd. (TVB) in Hong Kong. Although this tie-up might be designed to prevent the Pacific Century CyberWork to launch its cable Internet business in China, it obviously has implications for the reach and scope of CCTV services because the Chinese government oversees the operation of CCTV and controls access to the national satellite and cable networks. For one thing, it underscores China's determination to harness the dynamics of TV's internationalization process.

In 1964, the Central Broadcasting Bureau directed BTS to "take root in Beijing, but face the world" in its program planning and development. Thirty years later in 1993, under the leadership of the Ministry of Broadcasting, Television and Film, CCTV reaffirmed its developmental strategy and programming design to position itself among the world's best TV stations. This time it was to "take root in China, but face the world." For CCTV and for that matter the Chinese television, to face the world is to be a global player. A strong indication of that attempt is the number of foreign bureaus that CCTV has already set up or is planning to establish in the following places: Bangkok, Brasilia, Brussels, Cairo, Delhi, Hong Kong, London, Macao, Moscow, New York, Sydney, Tokyo, and Washington, DC (John Jirik, CCTV consultant, personal communication, December 18, 1999). Courting western media giants, such as AOL Time Warner and News Corp., for the huge TV market in China on the condition that they ensure U.S. access for CCTV's English language channel, CCTV-9, is another official effort to step up the global presence of Chinese television footprint (Associated Press, 2001). On the Chinese window on the world, it means not only to take China to the world out there, but also to bring the world back home. The formation of China's largest media group—China Broadcasting, Film and TV Group—in December 2001, which consists of CCTV and five other central broadcasting and electronic media organizations, is the latest strategy to beef up CCTV's competitveness in the international marketplace.

CHAPTER 2

THE STATE, MARKET, AND TV REGULATION IN CHINA: DECENTRALIZATION, DEPOLITICIZATION AND LEGAL RATIONALITY

In a news broadcast of Chinese President Jiang Zemin's visit to the newsroom of the *People's Daily*—the mouthpiece of the Communist Party in China—on September 26, 1996, CCTV, the only national television network, quoted Jiang as saying that as part of the life of the Communist Party, journalism was tied closely to the destiny of both the nation and the party (Kwang, 1996). Indicating that the authority over the news media lay in the hands of the party and the people, Jiang urged Chinese journalists to obey the party's leadership and seek the truth. CCTV devoted 10 minutes of its 30-minute news program to Jiang's visit and his speech, signifying the importance of the presidential words and deeds. Notwithstanding the content, this lengthy report clearly underscored the hierarchical relationship between the state and television in China.

The purpose of this chapter is to examine, within the managerial perspective (Alford & Friedland, 1985; Mosco, 1988), the interplay between the state and the market in Chinese TV regulation against the backdrop of the fast changing Chinese social structure and processes. This perspective suggests that, as the structure of Chinese society and state becomes more complex, the imperative of efficient and effective management calls for greater specific knowledge, bureaucratic capacity, and managerial skills that mostly depend on a rational division of labor at the organizational level. In the realm of mass communication, decentralization has thus created a structural change in the traditional rigid command system, leading to the fragmentation of the central authority or the emergence of multiple centers (e.g., J. Wang & Chang, 1996). As such, state regulation and control over the form and content of mass media require a more formal legal-rational mechanism to oversee their general practices, particularly television because of its access to the vast population and increasing influences in the Chinese society.

As noted in chapter 1, the advent of television in China started in 1958, when some trial broadcasts became available in parts of the country. Historically rooted in radio broadcasting, Chinese television is therefore subject to state regulations and control inherited from its predecessor. Before the Communist Party came to power in 1949, a variety of regulations and laws regarding radio broadcasting were issued by the Nationalist government. One purpose was to promote the Nationalist ideological campaigns against the Communists. Those regulations and measures apparently laid the rational and legal foundation for the Communist authority to follow after it controlled the country.

As early as the 1950, the Central Press Bureau under the new Chinese Communist regime issued "The Decision on Establishment of Radio Receiving Network," stipulating that radio receiving stations be set up at state institutions, military units, organizations, factories, and schools throughout China (T. Zhang, 1992). Consequently, establishing a radio receiving network became a top national priority. By 1952, more than 20,000 radio receiving stations emerged around the country. To solve the subsequent problems of low frequency and poor programming quality, the Central Broadcasting Bureau held in December 1952 the first national broadcasting conference and adopted a 5-year plan to develop a central national radio station. It was a state broadcasting system by design.

Three years later in 1955, the bureau convened a national seminar on broadcasting work in villages, requiring that wired broadcasting networks be established within 2 years at the village level in selected provinces and regions. At the same time, the State Council issued "Regulations on Management of Local People's Radio Stations" (Gan, 1993), which was the first key regulation on radio broadcasting. Since then and until the reforms, no major broadcasting regulations or rules were adopted and released. Shortly after television was introduced, China soon was driven into a series of ideological campaigns and class struggle movements during the next two decades that eventually culminated in the devastating Cultural Revolution.

Before it reached the fledgling stage of development, the expansion of TV in China was frequently disrupted by countless political tribulation and social turmoil, including the disastrous Cultural Revolution from 1966 through 1976. The 10-year calamitous destruction of human spirit and social infrastructure all but paralyzed the entire national economy and rendered the sphere of media culture and mass entertainment pale, sterile, and impoverished. Under such circumstances, the state exercised, either in the name of the government or the party, a brute tight grip over every aspect of the social life and its presentation as well as interpretation in the mass media. In the planned economic system with a distrust of any hint of capitalism, there was no media market to speak of. It was a state-dominated landscape, with little room for the market to take shape. The revival of China's market economy and its openness to the outside world since 1978 have triggered a major increase and fast expansion in the number of Chinese media industries, especially television (e.g., Hong, 1998).

By the mid-1980s, Chinese television was relatively ubiquitous and institutionalized, with a noticeable degree of penetration into the population (Jiang, 1995; J. Yu, 1990). As a result of the remarkable transformation during the past two decades, the tripartite relationship among the state, market, and mass media has gone through uncharted processes of negotiation, adjustment, and repositioning in China's pursuit of economic modernization and political stabilization, particularly after the collapse of Communism in the former Soviet Union and eastern Europe around the late 1980s. One official strategy is to free the state from the heavy economic burden that had plagued and led to the demise of China's former Communist allies by cutting off the financial umbilical cord to the bulky state industries, including the mass media industry. Financially, the market is allowed to take charge.

Except for a few national organizations, such as the *People's Daily*, Xinhua News Agency, and CCTV, the state has terminated its financial subsidy to the mass media, leaving them to scramble on their own for survival. To stay in the business, from the coastal to inland regions, mass media in China therefore have to face the logic of the market in order to attract the audiences. What counts most is advertising revenues and commercial opportunities. To help secure the market and to forge vertical and horizontal alliance in the media industries, more than 14 newspaper groups have been formed nationwide (Jiang, 2000; Subscription papers, 1998a, 1998b), creating a quasi-competitive environment where the bottom line is often at odds with the party line (e.g., Zhao, 1998). It forges an unavoidable tension between the state and the market.

The market competition, no matter how imperfect in China, brings challenges to the established order and threatens to change the existing mass media landscape. The Chinese official response is to loosen its grips over the form and content of the media in various settings. As discussed in chapter 1, for example, within a short time span in mid-1998, CCTV not only carried a live news conference between President Jiang Zemin and President Clinton, but also transmitted a first live courtroom hearing in Beijing to the national audience. The trial took place at the Beijing No. 1 Intermediate People's Court. The 5-hour hearing involved violation of copyrights and was watched by hundreds of millions of Chinese TV viewers nationwide. The 4.5% of audience rating was higher than that of CCTV's news program at noon (Shao, 1998). Although these cases are the exception, not the norm, in Chinese media practices, the boundary of television and radio content structure is undoubtedly being pushed further. The responses to such rarity in Chinese journalism were generally positive from both inside and outside of China.

The first live coverage of court proceedings at the local level was at the Nanjing City Television Station in April 1994. But it did not catch fire or the imagination among local TV stations until the CCTV tried it in an experimental fashion at the national level. The demonstration effect trickles down. Among the huge number of TV stations at the provincial, municipal, and local levels, decentralization, and depoliticization mean a higher degree of freedom for content variation and more room for direct appeal to the audience needs. For example, the Fuzhou TV station and Fuzhou People's Intermediate Court in the southern Fujian province decided in March 1999 to start a weekly live broadcast of the court's proceedings so that the court's activities could be placed "under people's surveillance" (Fuzhou broadcast, 1999). In fact, the Supreme People's Court has urged various lower courts to open up their proceedings to journalists, including foreign correspondents, for reporting, recording and live broadcasting (High court requires, 1999). More than 40 TV stations across the country have now aired court trials. From the national to local levels, these live broadcasts were hailed by political and judicial officials as a breakthrough in promoting judicial reforms and legal education in China.

In the face of a quantitative increase in content and a qualitative change in form in the world of Chinese television since the reforms in the late 1970s, state regulation of TV has therefore increasingly become a compelling and complex task. No longer could the central authority rely, by default, on the strict and absolute command structure under the highly centralized social and economic system during Mao Tse-tung's rule to harness TV. After all, when the ideology of supreme

Communism gave way to the market mechanism of Capitalism, even in the disguise of socialist market economy, the Chinese social structure cannot remain unchanged or unchanging. In the climate of guarded openness and amid the emergence of embryonic civil society, China has begun to build a legal system that gradually moves toward a rule of law to codify the relationship among institutions, citizens, and the state.

In the post-Mao era, the booming and blossomed TV industry, with all its technical and economic rationality, has produced a huge insatiable market driven not only by its internal logic, but also by external forces unleashed through political pragmatism and realistic appraisal of the Chinese socioeconomic conditions (e.g., J. Wang & Chang, 1996). It is a phenomenon that unequivocally demands a systematic legal-rational supervision. If history is any guide, the state will control the evolving media market in China with laws, regulations, rules, and provisions as it sees fit or when the situation calls for. The legal rationality seems inevitable when the market forces have broken old structure and rules, set loose existing control mechanism, and created new social relations and power centers in the process of state–media interaction.

Not until the early 1980s, however, did formal and legal regulations of Chinese television appear in response to the rising conflicts between the state purpose and the market interests (J. Yu, 1990). When it seemed that nominal political allegiance could not continue to extract collective acquiescence in the TV industry, the state turned to regulatory measures that would be legally binding and systematically enforceable. While allowing managerial leeways, the state has insisted on curtailing press freedom and freedom of expression (Beijing heightens, 1999, p. A1; Journalism and publishing, 1999). The cautious approach and the uneasy reluctance can be detected from the changing official conceptualization of television in China.

EVOLUTION OF THE OFFICIAL CONCEPTION OF TV IN CHINA

As a result of the economic reforms and external openness since 1978, television in China has become a vibrant industry with its various programs viewed as commodities by domestic and foreign business interests. Like its counterparts in other countries, Chinese TV ranks ahead of newspapers and radio among the advertising vehicles. Because of the growing market demand, the advertising rate has continued to soar over the years. In 1993, for example, both TV and other major media charged their advertising fees by a significant increase. In the case of CCTV, the rate rose a whopping 127%. Compared to foreign TV imports, the domestic production is much more expensive. It costs 50,000 to 60,000 yuan to produce one episode of Chinese TV dramas, while one episode of foreign imports can be bought for only 2,000 yuan (e.g., Guo, 1994; Zheng, 1998).

Thanks to the evolving conception of television and the disparity of cost between domestic and foreign TV production, growing concerns have been raised among official, academic, and media circles regarding the proper role and functions of TV in the Chinese society. At a changing time when multiple value clashes are present and manifest, it is argued (e.g., J. Liu, 1998), TV in China has yet to examine its cultural role and adjust its position in mediating between conflicting values and realities. Considering the state ownership of all forms of mass media, such adjustment, of course, implies some kind of arrangement at the managerial level within media organizations without altering the fundamental sociopolitical configuration at the national level. It requires administrative and procedural solutions by the technocrats and managers to make sure Chinese TV does not veer beyond the boundaries of official parameters.

Unlike Western conceptualization, regulations of television in China are essentially rooted in political and ideological determinations—functional prerequisites of party propaganda and public mobilization in social movements (e.g., T. Zhang, 1992), not necessarily in technical necessity and resource considerations, such as scarcity of spectrums. As part of the mass media system, control of TV in terms of state ownership and party leadership is clearly stipulated in the Chinese constitution (e.g., Wong, 1990). The supremacy of the party-state domination and the official guidance over the mass media is not to be questioned or challenged (e.g., Plafker, 1999).

Under the encompassing constitutional umbrella that determines the overall control structure and conceptual framework, however, the past two decades have witnessed China taking more legal-rational procedures to regulate the media industry in general and television in particular. It represents an epistemological move from doctrinal authority to pragmatic rationality. Since the end of the anarchical and chaotic Cultural Revolution and as China embarked on the new reform movement, various executive, legislative and practical attempts have sought to bring the spirit and practices of Chinese television more in line with China's contemporary economic commitment and open-door policy.

Although no legal framework has been established that would essentially shift the hierarchical structure of media–state relationship to a check and balance equation, there have been changes that appear to result from philosophical reorientation and practical consideration. The most notable example is certainly the live broadcast on CCTV of the Clinton–Jiang joint press conference mentioned earlier. Whether this particular case serves as a harbinger of things to come for a more spontaneous and less inaccessible TV remains to be seen. The extent to which TV regulations in China may be loosened still depends on the rules that are defined and delimited by the powers that be. Although the Chinese mass media have enjoyed a higher degree of autonomy, there is little sign that press freedom in the Western sense is likely to emerge soon.

Media regulation in China is often justified on the basis of official conception that historically has underscored the potential power of the media to influence the public. As a medium that has reached more than 90% of China's population, television obviously occupies a significant part in the Chinese sociopolitical structure. How the Chinese authority positions TV as an institution in relation to the state and the market through various control and regulations should serve as a useful indication of its social location. In the West, the broadcasting media have been looked at from a variety of perspectives, with television being conceptualized as a commodity, an instrument, or a public service (Merrill, 1983). For different reasons, China places its television on somewhat similar dimensions, but varies its emphasis according to the specific historical context and the prevalence of current philosophical conception and managerial needs.

Traditionally, the Chinese media were bound by the authoritarian, if not totalitarian, Communist ideological prerequisites with little regard to the market conditions. In recent years of economic reform, with cautious gradation, China has come to define itself as a developing nation. The sociological conception of the Chinese media system now largely follows that of a development model (Y. Chen, 1998). Technologically, TV as a fast developing medium has outpaced the change and adaptation of conservative official conceptions of the mass media. Following the changes in political and economic spheres in China, the conventional view of a propaganda and persuasion model of the Chinese mass media should thus be re-examined, if not abandoned (e.g., Chang et al., 1993), although in large national campaigns and at times of crisis, it is still discernible in the operation of the Chinese mass media, which would, under the leadership of the Party and the government, organize all their persuasive channels to promote the state's point of view.

J. Yu (1989) argued that the advanced technology has led to the rapid expansion and penetration of TV in China in the 1980s, to some extent exceeding the boundaries set for other media. As such, legal and nonlegal state regulations of TV may fall behind the economic, technical, and professional advancement of the medium. Chinese TV's participation in the 1989 Tiananmen Square movement, at least its practitioners' involvement, was a case in point (e.g., C. Lee, 1990b). The transformation of form and content of mass media in China might have created a public space where the state and market forces would have to negotiate and re-articulate the processes and structure of television in the Chinese society (e.g., X. Zhang, 1993; Zhao, 1998). Legal justification and regulative mechanism over television provide the authority the necessary means to do so. Both can be traced to the traditional conceptions of China's media system.

It has been well documented that China's ideological structure and media organizations were historically intertwined (e.g., Gan, 1993; A. Liu, 1971; F. Yu, 1963). A classic view about China's pre-TV decades is that the structure of the media was integrated with the configuration of the state's governance, and that the media content tended to be products of state dictation (e.g., A. Liu, 1971). As an instrument of the Party and the government, the paramount tasks of the media were to propagate state policies, educate the masses, and mobilize them for national development (Bishop, 1989; Hong, 1998). Although students of Chinese politics still see the media as an integral part of the state apparatus (Jiang, 1995), some nuances have been found in the state–media relationship that deviate from the past when the Party was concurrently the owner, the manager, and the practitioner (e.g., L. Chu, 1994). Although unwilling to relinquish the state ownership, the Chinese central authority has allowed media practitioners some managerial freedom to run the daily operations so long as they do not challenge its leadership and policies.

The inception of reform after the resolution by the Party's Central Committee in late 1978 to shift the focus of national energy from the class struggle to economic construction stimulated the growth of the media market and a rising expectation among the audiences. The structural differentiation and subsequent progress inevitably resulted in a parallel outlook on the relationship among the state, the media, and the burgeoning market. Hao and Huang (1996) indicated that, instead of the traditional model of media operation solely at the dictate of the Party, the Chinese broadcast media now wield greater autonomy, but are caught between two masters in the process of commercialization: the Party command and the mass audience desire. A commonsensical understanding is that the command from the top echelon of leadership rarely, if ever, coincides with the demands of the audiences at the grassroots level. At the heart of the issue is the official conceptualization and social trajectory of TV in China.

The growth of TV in China differs largely from that in the developed countries. For example, the United States offered an affluent and leisurely ground for the growth of TV in its formative as well as mature decades. In China, TV as a medium apparently prospered in parallel to the nation's economic development. This path suggests that since its maturing years in the past two decades (1978–1998), Chinese TV has been partly an instrument of socioeconomic progress. China as a nation in reform bestowed on the new medium a special public interest and official character (e.g., C. Lee, 1994).

As television continues to reach wider and farther in the Chinese society in terms of both its form and content, how to curb its potential power and influences within the larger political landscape naturally becomes a central concern at the national level. Ideological and historical reasons aside, the technological sophistication and commercial orientation of television requires systematic management from within and without the industry itself. A thorough search through related and relevant materials and documents suggests that most, if not all, of the rules and regulations of TV in China were cognizant responses from the government to the medium's fast development and vast expansion.

At a higher and more abstract level, these rules and regulations, mostly issued by the Ministry of Radio, Film and TV (MRFT) before mid-1998, reflected not only the changing philosophy and conception of the medium, but also the government's desire and effort to formalize and legalize its jurisdiction over the procedural and substantive matters involving the production, distribution, and consumption of Chinese television programming. With its root in the Central Broadcasting Bureau, MRFT was established in 1982 to oversee the broadcasting operations in the country. In June 1998, its status was changed to the National Bureau of Radio, Film and TV (NBRFT). From 1984 through 1999, more than 140 major laws, regulations, measures, notifications, and rules were issued by MRFT/NBRFT and other agencies to regulate TV (e.g., *China Broadcasting Yearbook*, 1996, 1997, 1998, 1999, 2000). Of them, 90% appeared in the 1990s (see Table 2.1).

Historically, conceptions of the nature, attributes, and perceived possible influences the media content might have on the public have been monopolized by the central government (e.g., X. Zhang, 1993). The increasing economic independence of the media, especially China Central TV (Jiang, 1995), however, does not necessarily presuppose the media's editorial independence. In the words of the vice head of NBRFT, TV as a modern mass medium is capable of strong subtle influence on the culture and value of the nation and people, to the extent of affecting the stability of the society (Ji, 2001). Accordingly, regarding the administrative sanction on operation by stations at the grassroots level, MRFT often emphasized TV programs' possible threats to the public morality and proposed that strict standards be followed in the production and distribution of contents.

Table 2.1: Number of Major Regulations Issued by the Ministry of Radio, Film, and TV and Other Agencies

Year	Number	Agency
1984	1	Ministry of Radio, Film and TV (MRFT)
1985	1	Communist Party Central Office and State Council
1986	3	MRFT (2) and State Council General Office (1)
1987	2	State Council (1) and MRFT-Ministry of Public Security (1)
1988	4	MRFT (2), MRFT-National Management Bureau of Industry and Commerce (1), and MRFT-Ministry of Law Enforcement (1)
1989	4	MRFT (2), State Education Commission (1), and MRFT-National Secrecy Bureau (1)
1990	7	MRFT (6) and MRFT-Ministry of Public Security and Ministry of State Security (1)
1991	4	MRFT (3) and MRFT-Ministry of State Security and Ministry of Public Security (1)
1992	7	MRFT
1993	9	MRFT (7), Ministry of Domestic Trade (1), and Central Propaganda Department of the Party (1)
1994	7	MRFT (6) and MRFT-National Archives Bureau (1)
1995	15	MRFT (14) and MRFT-National Management Bureau of Industry and Commerce (1)
1996	22	MRFT (18), MRFT-State Education Commission (1), MRFT-Ministry of Culture (1), 1MRFT-Central Propaganda Department (1), and State Council Taiwan Affairs Office (1)
1997	20	State Council (1), MRFT (19)
1998	13	MRFT/National Bureau of Radio, Film and Television (NBRFT)
1999	24	NBRFT (20), State Council (1), NBRFT-Ministry of Information Industry (1), NBRFT-Ministry of National Security (1), and NBRFT-Central Propaganda Department of the Party (1)

Source: *China Broadcasting Yearbook* (various years)

Since its founding in 1949, the Chinese government has long believed in the strong power of the mass media in general and TV in particular. Although the leadership realizes TV can have a negative impact, it also recognizes TV's potential in linking the government and the people by way of transmitting and propagating state policies, educating and mobilizing the masses, in addition to serving the mass need for entertainment. The classic conception of the media's positive function in terms of "informing, educating, and entertaining," although not systematically pronounced by the authority, has manifested itself as a working philosophy in the daily conduct of China's national media. In the wake of TV's penetration and expansion in society, however, certain problems follow, such as the lack of regulation on content and/or programming. In 1986, MRFT set up a general framework to guide the processes of research, drafting, release, and implementation of TV regulations.

From the beginning, the role of TV as defined by the government and perceived by the public carried inherent conflicting ends. TV is often conceptualized concurrently as a technology, a state instrument of propaganda, a commodity, a mass entertainer, or a mass educator. Under the influences of regulations, these overlapping and sometimes conflicting roles become established in both official and popular perceptions and conceptions at different points in time in China's history. After all, any regulation of a medium is essentially a process of coordinating between the potentially clashing functional roles of a medium and current social practices and policy commitments. China is no exception. Given the revolutionary origin and its insistence on the "people's democratic dictatorship," China's legal-rational system allows, in theory, a centralized media control although in practice it has become more decentralized and depoliticized as a result of continuing economic reforms and social transparency (e.g., Kwang, 1997).

LEGISLATION AND BUREAUCRACY OF TV REGULATION

The legislative branch of the Chinese government is the National People's Congress. It convenes annually to deliberate on the laws, rules, and regulations drafted and submitted by various departments and agencies of the government. After approval by the delegates, the legislative outcomes are submitted to the State Council, the executive branch in charge of national affairs, for the final approval and promulgation. As the highest authority in the broadcasting sector, MRFT/NBRFT is required to go through the legal and administrative procedures before a law/regulation takes effect. It follows its own internal procedures in overseeing the broadcasting industry within its jurisdiction. An examination of the process and its products should help shed light on how the rules and regulations of television are produced and executed in China. As shown in Table 2.1, the regulatory work began in the mid-1980s.

On April 15, 1986, MRFT issued the *Trial Guiding Orders for Regulatory Work* that covered radio, film, and TV. The *Orders* stipulated the functional procedures and personnel in research, drafting, and approval of the rules and regulations concerning the operations of the electronic media, including TV. A special leadership team was established to take charge of the examination of both long-term and annual legislative plans. The team was also to deliberate on the regulations prepared by MRFT and to submit them for approval by the minister. As for the rules and regulations submitted to the National People's Congress and in turn the State Council for promulgation, they should pass the team's scrutiny before being submitted to the minister for the final approval.

Based on the scope of responsibility and function, the levels of legislative authority in TV regulation were specified in the following bureaucratic order: the ministerial leadership team, overseeing the drafting of laws and regulations; the policy study section, in charge of actual research and drafting; and provincial and municipal units, initiating their own rules and regulations and submitting them to the policy study section, with the latter's due participation in decision making. With such a hierarchical structure, the legal process could be time consuming and wide reaching. The combination of bureaucratic guidance and overlapping organizational mechanism is a form of political and managerial control in China that is set up to guarantee the central government's overall grasp of policy determination and implementation.

Since TV's inception, an extensive variety of laws, rules, provisions, and regulations have been issued by the various sections of MRFT/NBRFT and other governmental and party agencies, such as the State Council, Ministry of Public Security, State Administration for Industry and Commerce, Ministry of Justice, State Education Commission, National Secrecy Bureau, Ministry of State Security, Ministry of Domestic Trade, Central Propaganda Department of the Communist Party, National Archives Bureau, and State Press and Publications Administration. The involvement of security, commerce, education, and law agencies in TV regulation clearly demonstrates the state's intent, attempt and authority to lay out the parameters within which television and its practitioners are to practice their trade in China. It is also obvious that, although information security and propaganda are of concern, the focus of TV regulations is less political and ideological, but more managerial and technical.

As indicated in Table 2.1, these regulations cover almost every aspect of TV production, dissemination, reception, and consumption in China. They vary from technical to substantive areas, covering such matters as drama production, security of facilities, advertising, technological innovation, management, foreign satellite TV, imports of foreign programs, ethics and integrity, personnel, community antenna, internal auditing, ground reception devices, network, relay programs, staff training, licenses, secrecy, educational TV, overseas Chinese TV productions, and local TV in foreign relations. Many were laws submitted to the State Council for approval and the Standing Committee of the National People's Congress for examination, while others were administrative statutes submitted to the State Council for promulgation, protocols and regulations issued by MRFT/NBRFT, and laws and regulations jointly issued by MRFT/NBRFT and other ministries and/or commissions under the central government.

Regardless of the types, the general principles underlying these processes of regulations are defined and delimited by the greater policy demands of the central government. More specifically, the rules and regulations by MRFT/NBRTF are in accord with the nation's constitution and other statutory laws. Whether explicitly or implicitly, they also uphold the Communist Party and the central government as the ultimate authority in TV regulation. That notwithstanding, the regulatory rationale and extensive coverage are apparently driven by the conditions of economic reforms and the general direction of the market in China.

It is evident that the experiences of the economic reforms and the subsequent TV practices tend to be incorporated into the regulation to serve as references for future work. The fact that the number of regulatory measures increased over time suggests that the continuing market growth and the proliferation of content, both domestic and foreign (e.g., Hong, 1998), as well as the development of technology, have created a dynamic and competitive TV environment that needs to be policed with a set of ground rules. One essential state stipulation is that the market reality is to function as the pragmatic guide for regulation and no rules are made just for their own sake, hence disregarding the actual needs and demands of the industry. At the managerial level, holistic planning and prioritization in TV regulation are internally observed by the MRFT/NBRFT planners. Externally, they pay close attention to opinions and ideas from the audiences, experts, and foreign sources for guidance and consideration.

After a few years of trial enforcement, in March 1989, the temporary regulations became crystallized and formalized as executive orders by MRFT, showing an integrated pattern between the internal structure of the TV industry and their corresponding levels of administration in the government. A division of labor set up the procedural pecking order and the realm of administrative and legislative duty. Laws governing the overall operation of the industry, if any, were to be prepared and promulgated by the National People's Congress Standing Committee; administrative orders regulating one aspect of the industry, by the State Council; regulations and rules governing specific aspects of TV, by MRFT or provincial or local government. MRFT was in charge of 5-year regulatory plans to be submitted to the State Council for approval.

According to the refined stipulations in 1989, the legal procedures in law making took the following format: resolutions by the National People's Congress, decisions by the State Council, and recommendations set forth by MRFT and approved by the State Council. As for rules and regulations, they were determined by a series of consideration: state policies guiding the broadcasting industry; state stipulations for laws and regulations; decisions made by the ministerial meetings; and the need for institutionalization of general management within the industry. In the whole process, the National People's Congress Standing Committee retains the authority of interpretation of laws, while the policy study section of MRFT/NBRFT is in charge of interpretation of rules and regulations.

Administratively speaking, work meetings and conferences are convened at all levels from the local to the national periodically for the higher authority to spell out the guidelines of television regulation. In January 1998, the conference convening municipal broadcasting authorities and higher saw the reassertion of broadcasting as an opinion guide/leaders in China's new phase of market economy era, with a strong emphasis on strengthening the news programs. With regard to entertainment, a new strategy was recommended to vastly improve the quality of programs such as TV dramas. It was suggested that above and beyond regular regulations of TV and other broadcast media, administrative policies could be given to highlight certain themes to adapt to the larger needs of propaganda. For example, Sun Jiazheng, the then minister of radio, film and television, called for renewed and concentrated efforts at propagating the policies promulgated at the Communist Party's 15th National Congress (J. Sun, 1998). At the beginning of each year, the Party's Central Committee would gather propaganda heads from all over the country for a meeting to receive new directives from the Party regarding propaganda work.

In anticipation of China's resuming sovereignty over Macao and the celebration of the nation's 50th anniversary in 1999, for example, Ding Guangen, head of the CCP's Central Propaganda Department, directed the news media to maximize their efforts in promoting "praise of the nation, praise of socialism, and praise of the reform era" (Speech to, 1999). In January 2000, another such national meeting was convened, at which Hu Jintao, the Party's virtual second-in-command, called upon the media to "sound the key note of socialism, patriotism, and collectivism." He emphasized that the Party must insist upon its leadership over all propaganda work to ensure the nation's stability (Speech to, 2000). The extent to which such call for propaganda of Communist policies has been followed by the broadcasting industry remains to be determined. It can be safely assumed, however, that in the process of implementation such policies and directives are bound to be compromised one way or another.

Over the past years, TV regulation in China has proceeded on several conceptual and technical dimensions. Conceptually, the regulations dwell mostly on what television may do with its informational and entertainment content. The underlying assumption is that media messages are powerful, especially when they reach a huge number of audiences like TV viewers. As such, television content must be carefully scrutinized and produced. Technically, new communication technologies have made it possible for media practitioners to experiment novel ways of production, reception, dissemination, and presentation of all sorts of content that may not fall within the confines of tolerable standards. At a time when social transformation in the reform era is triggering many unstable factors in China, such as unequal distribution of resources and income, the presumption is that technology should serve the best interests of society.

REGULATING TV AS A MASS ENTERTAINER

Despite the state's conception of TV's role as an instrument of propaganda, the audiences embraced the medium as a mass entertainer. TV dramas have been one of the most popular types of content in China. Until the mid-1980s, the Chinese TV screen was almost "dominated" by imported TV dramas from Japan and Western countries (e.g., J. Wang & Chang, 1996). For example, *Garrison's Guerrilla* attracted a large number of audiences, especially children and youngsters (Jiang, 1995). The influence of imported programming alerted the official censors and regulators, who appealed to the domestic program producers to "occupy" the primetime slots with TV dramas of China's own making. In 1986, national annual TV drama production totaled more than 1,500 episodes. The number grew to more than 15,800 by 1999. In 2000, there were on average 25 new drama episodes shown on Chinese television per day (G. Zhu, 2001). It is estimated that the production of TV dramas in 2001 would grow by nearly 44% from a year before. As domestic TV drama production has grown at a rapid rate since the mid-1980s, official concern with the production of such TV dramas increased at the same time.

The current state of TV drama production in China has been criticized as showing life styles way ahead of the nation's average living standards (e.g., X. Zhang, 1995). The content of TV dramas has also been accused of providing an erroneous sense of spiritual perplexity of the people in excessive material prosperity. According to some accounts (e.g., Shi, 1998), the reasons are twofold: first, the nature of the production of TV dramas as a commodity has subtly turned an original artistic pursuit into a commercial process and second, high-brow artists and men of letters hesitate to commit their efforts to TV dramas, which are regarded as part of the popular (and hence vulgar) culture.

Because the economic reform and opening policies have improved the living conditions of the Chinese people and hence stimulated their demand for pleasure, programs such as dramas have gradually accentuated the entertainment side of television. Since the government would not relinquish its hold on TV as a far-reaching medium for educational and propagandistic purpose, official and formal regulations of TV drama production became a must in the eyes of the authority in order to confine non-news programming within permissible and acceptable limits. TV content has to be monitored through prior license and censorship.

On June 1, 1986, the *Temporary Regulation of TV Drama Production Permit* issued by MRFT went into effect. Three years later, the Regulation was finalized as official administrative orders by MRFT. According to the stipulations, institutional applicants aspiring to produce TV dramas must first obtain official permit issued by MRFT or, in cases where the applicant operated at the local level, provincial radio, film, and TV bureaus were given the authority to grant such permits. Under this regulation, TV drama permits were divided into two categories: long-term permits for 5 years (in 1989, the provision was later changed to 3 years) subject to review and assessment by the granting authority, and short-term drama-specific shooting permits. The determination and issuance of permits follow a set of comprehensive rules.

The main qualifications for such permits depend on technical, financial, and human resources, including a shooting team equipped with sufficient funding and competent facility. Individuals may not apply for such a permit. The more subtle yet also powerful way of control was stipulated for the airing stage: All TV stations are to show only those dramas that had been produced by permit-holders, and previewing and censoring must precede airing wherever necessary. Financial sponsors from other sectors of the society are forbidden from exerting any influence on the content of the programs. As for possible cooperation between domestic and foreign stations/drama producers, the authority of approval resides with MRFT/NBRFT.

Starting in 1987, even the content of TV programs to be shown exclusively to foreign tourists at major hotels has been subjugated to official control and censorship. The economic reform and opening policies have brought many foreign businessmen and tourists to China. To cater to the rising needs and interests of foreigners for information and entertainment, major tourist hotels operate closed-circuit television. According to the regulatory measures issued by the General Office of the State Council on the management of such TV programs, the task is not merely a service to foreign guests or overseas Chinese visitors. Rather, the closed-circuit TV is regarded as a Chinese window on the world and an effective means of propaganda and is taken seriously as a way to promote China's international image. To be more specific, the central government considers the operation of closed-circuit television as a major "political task," with a strong calculation on how China should be presented to foreigners and overseas Chinese from Taiwan, Hong Kong, and Singapore.

For the closed-circuit television, program suppliers must be video producers licensed by the national government, such as motion picture companies and national news agency targeted at foreign audiences. Programs must be previewed by designated officials to prevent possible inappropriate contents. Additional program supply should come from taping CCTV programs relevant to the themes of promoting China's land, people, and culture. The management of closed-circuit television in tourist hotels is subject to the authority of the National Tourism Bureau. Application for permit to operate such services in hotels must be approved by the Bureau. To keep the screen "clean," other relatively "minor" rules and regulations on TV programs include a notification in 1988 against the airing of performances by criminals serving their jail terms. This regulation stands as a reminder that TV is foremost looked at as the mouthpiece of the Party and the government or an instrument of propaganda. In China, dissidents, deviants or anyone who violates social norms, laws or state policies are often removed from any media content unless they happen to be useful to teach others a lesson.

As Chinese television experiences a rapid growth, imported TV dramas from various countries start to flood the domestic market on a large scale because the number of stations around the nation has increased and China has further opened its door to the outside world. For example, China imported 1,306 episodes of foreign TV drama in 2000, accounting for 14.3% of the total dramas shown that year (G. Zhu, 2001). The presence of foreign TV dramas poses potential problems for content discipline. In 1990, MRFT placed explicit constraints on the airing of imported programs on the grounds that they might threaten or erode national values or indigenous culture. Six types of contents were endorsed and encouraged: programs with serious, positive themes featuring progressive thoughts; entertainment contributing positively to culture and morals; programs aimed at spreading knowledge about science and technology; accurate rendition of history revealing laws of progress; programs edifying to the youth and constructive to their growth; and programs with relatively higher aesthetic values. Such general and abstract vocabulary certainly leaves room for different interpretation and potential disagreement among TV stations, making it possible for the market to navigate through a wide array of choices sanctioned by the state.

Like those in many other countries, programs with any hints at pornography or overt violence were prohibited on Chinese television, although after some editing these programs could still be broadcast. Several other categories of programs were strictly banned altogether. These include TV dramas with themes advocating Western political, religious, and cultural values to the extent of threatening the value integrity of the People's Republic or socialism, romanticizing colonialism, and parodying the seamy side of Third World countries, glorifying sex and violence and hence potentially harmful to youthful hearts and minds, or any other drama content that might undermine the racial and ethnic harmony or national sovereignty. These categories are undoubtedly vague and broad, thus allowing the central authority greater opportunity and power to censor imported programs whenever it is convenient or desirable to do so.

Most noteworthy is the 1990 order from MRFT that indicated that the airing of TV dramas must adapt to the larger purpose of Chinese diplomacy and international disputes. For example, even if a particular foreign TV drama carried with it all the acceptable contents, it could be banished from airing if it might do a disservice or was counterproductive to the main goal of the nation's diplomacy or the preferred state of international relations. Given the timing of this regulation, whether or not it was a response to the 1989 Tiananmen incident in which China's heavy-handed crackdown on the student democratic movement was severely criticized by foreign media worldwide is open to debate. This measure nevertheless demonstrated the connection between non-news TV programs and the images China hopes to project to the domestic audiences as well as its use of TV as a tool in foreign relations.

Other types of TV programs that could be imported fell under the constraints set by MRFT in February 1994 in its *Rules for Management of Imported Programs.* Acknowledging such programs as necessary to the nation's spiritual civilization and cultural exchange, the rules allowed the exchange and purchase of TV programs between Chinese domestic stations and TV stations in Taiwan, Hong Kong, and Macao. Collaboration in shooting and airing was also permitted, provided that the permit number assigned by MRFT be shown with the program, which should be aired only within the geographical scope allowed by MRFT; it must be aired only locally or regionally. Perhaps the most noticeable stipulation is the quota system: imported programs must not exceed 25% of the total airtime allotted to TV dramas. No more than 15% of the prime-time slots (6 p.m.–10 p.m.) should be given to foreign or overseas programs. In doing so, MRFT and lower levels of governments attained to an overall control of the program makeup of each station and the proportion between domestic and foreign programs. It also demonstrated China's determination to avoid the pitfalls of international communication in that dependency has become a problem for many developing and underdeveloped countries.

TV REGULATION AND THE
POWER OF NEW TECHNOLOGY

Cable TV and satellite TV are among the most recent new technologies in the Chinese broadcasting industry. In today's medium-size cities with 300,000 population or more, access to two dozen or more TV channels is common, including local, provincial, and national channels. Such availability and accessibility are made possible only through cable and satellite technologies. How does the central government harness their power of rapid expansion and diffusion—not only as technologies but also as a powerful source of impact on the population's social and cultural life? According to X. Wu (1997), Chinese cable TV entered its phase of substantial development and penetration only in the 1990s. Until then, it had been widely used in various work units, but little or no regulation had been issued to put a check on the scope it should cover. As it was, the development of cable TV was relatively spontaneous.

In November 1990, MRFT issued the *Temporary Management Measures of Cable TV*, approved by the State Council. By its definition, cable television included stations receiving and transmitting TV programs from conventional TV stations and airing programs of its own making, as well as public antenna receiving and transmitting programs from conventional TV stations. The measures allowed MRFT the authority to make overall plans for the development and coverage of cable TV around the country. To establish and operate a cable TV station, each institutional applicant must meet seven criteria. Again, individuals are not allowed to apply. First and foremost, the station must fit into the existing plan for TV coverage in the local area where the applicant seeks permit for operation.

Other criteria include sufficient specialized talent for the production and management of a station, adequate funding, technologically competent facility, a reasonably equipped production/shooting base for programs, transmission facilities recognized by provincial or higher levels of technical authority, and a specialized geographical area targeted for airing. If an applicant meets all these criteria, the application must first pass scrutiny by the relevant sections of provincial government in charge of radio, TV, and film activities, which in turn submits it to

MRFT. Ministerial approval must precede the granting of license to the station. The same Measures also stipulated that the technical quality of facilities built into a cable TV station and the programs broadcast by the station are subject to review and recognition by relevant higher authority, usually the local government. A special stipulation is leveled against any program that is anti-state, anti-social, or pornographic, with a perceived negative impact on the audience.

In April 1991, MRFT followed up on the *Temporary Measures* with reified detailed stipulations, further establishing the pivotal principle that the central government is in general charge of the development of cable TV, even though cable TV is subject to supervision by the provincial and local governments. Additionally, operation and maintenance fees were to be collected from users. But again, the most notable regulations concerned actual programs. What was prohibited of imported TV dramas also applied to cable TV programs. Each station was required to set aside a special channel for relaying CCTV programs. News programs produced by the station itself should be no less than 30 minutes per week. To air videos already released, a special permit must be obtained from the provincial level of broadcast administration. Several regulations are within the jurisdiction of the provincial leaders in broadcasting who are to preview and approve programs. Videos to be aired must bear provincial permit and program suppliers must be those designated and recognized by the central government. Moreover, programs from foreign sources including Hong Kong and Taiwan must not take up more than one third of the total amount of TV dramas, films, and videos broadcast on cable TV (e.g., Y. Liu, 1994). The quota system is again designed to ward off foreign competition.

Similar constraints were placed on satellite TV programs from foreign countries, the reception of which tended to be limited to the professional needs of institutional recipients in China. In 1990, in the wake of the aftermath of the June 4 incident, MRFT, the Ministry of Public Security, and the Ministry of State Security jointly issued an executive order in this area. According to this order, if satellite TV programs were "pure" in content, covering education, science, international news, finance, economy and trade—knowledge that is necessary to domestic development and progress, they would be looked on with approval. However, the right to receive foreign programs via satellite must be granted by the provincial government, which should scrutinize the technical, managerial, and financial capacity of the applicant, as well as the soundness in its justification for accessing such programs.

In October 1993, Premier Li Peng endorsed the finalized *Regulatory Orders on the Management of Facilities Receiving Satellite TV Programs*. Essentially, the orders stipulated that the licensing power of the state be exercised on the production, importing, sales, installment, and usage of such facilities, all to be produced and sold by enterprises designated by MRFT. No individual was allowed to install facilities for receiving satellite television. As for institutions, the orders indicated that the scope of program coverage must be specified, with the state-recognized facility, specialized managerial staff, and a complete management system. Once approved by municipal or local governments, the operation must not exceed the geographical scope granted by the permit. The orders prevented the showing of foreign TV programs at public locales such as bus and train stations, harbors, airports, shopping centers, cinemas, and theaters. In other words, foreign TV programs are restricted within predetermined areas.

By the end of 1995, cable TV stations directly approved by MRFT numbered 1,200, with an estimate of more than 30 million users (X. Wu, 1997). That figure grew to 80 million by the end of 1997 (Cable TV network, 2000). What was more, there were 980 conventional TV stations around the country, covering more than 90% of the population. In the presence of such growth of TV, MRFT established in 1996 a set of procedures for setting up new radio and TV stations, with authority of approval firmly in the hands of the central government. These stations refer to those established by county-level governments or above. As the procedures indicated, each application aspiring to set up new stations must be considered in the broader context and fit into the general plan of distribution, so that around the nation there could be a well-coordinated development of TV. The central, provincial, municipal, and county governments were the four levels of planners, each with its own administrative duties in the chain of command. Provincial governments are the highest authority in charge of verifying each application, while the national government grants final approval and issues license.

REGULATING THE PROSPERING TV AND ITS MULTIPLE ROLES

In the midst of television expansion, a national network of TV stations covering various levels and scopes throughout China was formed. But the center–periphery relationship between stations is still clearly charted. Collaboration between domestic and foreign stations is cautiously termed and scrutinized on a case-by-case basis. However, a more important rule is that no domestic applicant is permitted to collaborate with foreign stations in setting up new stations in China. Local stations are not allowed to jointly set up stations across provincial boundaries. With justification of need and actual capacity, however, local stations are free to branch out into specialized stations and add to existing channels or transmit programs via satellites. One recent example is the Shanghai Satellite TV station mentioned earlier. Nevertheless, the structure of application procedures remains rigid and tightly controlled by the central authority.

In 1994, the Communist Party's Central Propaganda Department, together with MRFT, issued a regulation on the programming relationship between CCTV and local TV stations. The emphasis was clear and forceful in that the foremost priority of local stations was to relay a complete set of programs aired through CCTV Channel One. CCTV, of course, is posited as the most important propaganda vehicle for the nation, especially its Channel One. Partnership between local and central stations in producing other programs were encouraged, and the priority for local network formation and expansion was ranked high, for a distinctly pronounced reason—to broaden CCTV coverage of the population through local TV networks. This requirement makes CCTV newscast the most authoritative source of news in the nation.

The staffing of grassroots TV stations is also a legislative concern of MRFT/NBRFT. According to the MRFT regulation in 1990, each radio and TV station in the rural areas was jointly controlled by local village leaders and relevant sections of local or county-level governments, although the station might be staffed with as few as two to three persons mainly to relay the programs from higher level stations such as CCTV. It follows without surprise, then, that in its ruling in 1990 MRFT retained within its authority the establishment of specific technical criteria for the grassroots-level broadcast leaders to examine and endorse major construction projects, such as a new cable TV station, and so on. This particular regulation unquestionably extends the state's regulatory control from the national all the way down to the local level. The state's power in TV regulation recognizes no boundaries of the market. On the contrary, the market shape of the Chinese TV industry is mostly drawn by the state in its own chosen configuration.

REGULATING TV'S GEOPOLITICAL BOUNDARIES

In addition to the prohibition preventing joint endeavor in setting up new stations across national boundaries, the scope of possible influence of foreign stations in China is also limited. With the development of the domestic TV industry and the larger policy of opening up the country to the outside world, TV stations from Hong Kong, Macao, and Taiwan often opt for program production in China due to the latter's relatively low cost and greater access to natural and studio settings. In response to this production demand, MRFT ruled in 1996 and 1998 that such undertaking must be first approved by the Ministry. No TV station is allowed to allot air time to overseas stations or individuals to show their programs directly. In 2001, the Chinese authority reiterated its determination to keep foreign capital and interests from entering into TV operation, programming and news broadcasting (Authority still, 2001).

Previous analysis of Chinese television often regards the year 1989 as a watershed, thanks in large part to the intensive involvement and performance of CCTV and other national media during the world-shocking June 4 incident (e.g., Jiang, 1995). According to Jiang, for a few days the national media seemed opened up to the events with candid views, but again in a short period, control from the top was tightened, and China was reverted to a state more conservative and constrained than before the incident (Polumbaum, 1990). Considering the extraordinary social and political contexts surrounding the media performance at that time, however, this part of history in TV regulation can only be looked on as a reaction to an unplanned event that became so dominant in the media as to amount to a special situation of the nation. The behavior of the media, once politicized to the extent of taking sides on issues, could be labeled as aprofessional, if not less than professional.

Apart from the juncture in 1989, as early as December 1989, possibly out of security concerns, MRFT and the National Secrecy Bureau jointly issued a decree spelling out the boundaries of what information should be withheld from the broadcast media. Major categories of information with a secret tag included new high technologies in the electronic media, Chinese external propaganda policies, technologies, and resources imported through secret channels, state secrets yet to be disclosed in due course, and China's jamming and monitoring of foreign TV and radio stations. If the flow of information through the broadcast media needs to be carefully monitored against the backdrop of national security and secrecy, then those who use the media can be expected to display some professional awareness of their functional prerequisites.

TV REGULATIONS AND PROFESSIONALISM

As stations multiplied and programs abounded, MRFT increased and tightened its indirect discipline of stations and screening of contents— not imposing such control, but rather, relying on the professionalization of the TV industry. Now that television in China has been prospering in a burgeoning economy as a mass informer and entertainer and a new technology, another attribute of TV—programs as a commodity— becomes increasingly salient in the midst of market competition and begins to challenge a yet more fundamental dimension of TV as a profession. Since the market reform took shape and the mass media were required to sustain their existence through their own means, there have been numerous reports of questionable journalistic practices and media organizational wrongdoings over the years (e.g., Zhao, 1998), prompting the central authority to take measures against the tide. As noted earlier, the definition of the functional roles of the media often constituted the conceptual basis for TV regulation.

Although Chinese television is a vehicle for advertising in the market economy, it is at the same time a news medium. In the eyes of MRFT, the boundary between these two roles must not be blurred. In November 1990, MRFT issued administrative orders reaffirming and regulating the electronic media as the mouthpiece of the Party and the government. A variety of rules aimed at rooting out corruption and unethical practices in the media industries were released. Paid news was to be banned; journalists should in no way accept gift from the news sources; no financial sponsor was allowed to interfere with the content of news; and no journalist could solicit ads under the pretext of news reporting. Media advertising was designated as a task to a specialized department and personnel. These rules were in part a response to the general trend with the news media, which had often run virtual advertisements masqueraded as news.

As noted earlier, making profits and informing the public are two ends that sometimes conflict with each other in the Chinese media industry. When the state and the market collide in China, professionalism is supposed to enter as a wedge. The rapid expansion of TV in China coincided with the growth of the nation's advertising industry. As a result, various problems emerged at all levels, such as advertisements disguised as news, illegal sponsorship from the commercial sector for media events in order to gain free or cheap air time, TV reporters soliciting ads in exchange for journalistic interviews, and local stations cutting out CCTV ads and replacing them with local ads when relaying CCTV programs.

Facing such rampant disorder and chaotic phenomenon, MRFT and the State Administration for Industry and Commerce issued a joint regulation in June 1988 to put a forceful ban on the alarming practices threatening the professional morale and ethics of the industry. The undisciplined TV competition and unhealthy market orientation turned out to be part of a larger mass media mayhem that appeared to be running out of control. In 1993, the Propaganda Department of the Communist Party and the State Press and Publications Administration issued a similar joint circular, prohibiting all forms of paid journalism in the print media (Zhao, 1998).

Television is a relatively new medium in China. The various conceptions of television, as mentioned earlier, have yet to find mutual compatibility between the state's ideal type and the market prototype. One key step taken by policymakers is to increase the competence of the professionals. Echoing the nation's second 5-year plan to teach the masses with understanding of the law, in 1991 all the cadres and staff in the broadcast industry were mobilized to be educated and to educate themselves with knowledge about the legal system, especially certain laws crucial to the TV trade, such as the law to protect and preserve national secrets and the rules and sanctions governing the protection of broadcast facilities. Cable TV management and the receiving of satellite TV were subjugated to administrative regulations.

To facilitate the transition from the totalitarian command system to a more legal and judicial order, propagandists were trained to implement such education at the grassroots levels. In fact, at every level a leader was designated to fully attend to this education campaign and a final examination was required to assess the outcome. The highly promoted speeches by the late Chinese leader Deng Xiaoping on furthering the reforms in 1992 intensified the systemwide education campaign. But after a short time it seemed to gradually trail off and vanish from the media discourse. Replaced is a slow awakening among the population of a sense of civil society in which citizens seek legal remedies ignored by the state through increasing lawsuits, including those against the mass media (First court, 1999).

Within the Chinese TV industry, new progress in science and technology has been increasing rapidly over the years, especially since the late 1980s (Jiang, 1995). Technology breeds new ideas and innovative ways of doing things on television. In 1992, MRFT issued rules governing the assessment of such progress. Awards were offered to technological breakthroughs. All regulations, of course, have to be carried out ultimately by the professionals. Whether regulating content, structure, or technology, they all add up to controlling one way or another the professional mind and behavior. The training of the mind included not only ideological orientation, but also technical sophistication. A watershed year for the entire country came in 1992, which was highlighted by Deng's speeches calling for deepening reform and improving productivity. As a direct response, a new and full round of on-the-job training in the broadcast industry started in early 1993 across the country.

During the 5 years between 1993 and 1997, all the staff members from high-level managerial and other professional positions down to grassroots workers were to have a full grasp of Deng's theory of building socialism with Chinese characteristics, as well as the professional knowledge of broadcasting required of their positions. Station heads were trained by MRFT directly, whereas other people at lower levels were trained by broadcasting institutes, departments, and teachers at their corresponding levels (national, provincial, or local). Beyond 1997, the emphasis of scrutiny should shift to controlling the entry level of knowledge and skills of those aspiring a position in the industry.

The individual training programs were followed by the regulation of institutional behaviors of the TV industry, on a relatively macro-level. In 1994, when the larger cultural climate was being regulated under the Party and the State Council, as a general segment of the cultural market, TV products were no exception. Rules for regulation of TV were to be drawn by MRFT, under the greater auspices of the Party and the State Council, to scrutinize, censor, and control the content of programs right from the stage of written script before shooting. Joint production of TV programs with foreign institutions or individuals, along with movies targeted at major international awards, must be approved by MRFT first. Programs aired by cable TV stations must be stamped with the permit issued by provincial broadcasting authorities.

Each year in the 1990s witnessed a greater growth in TV coverage of the population in China. The last step before airing—the final scrutiny and censoring of programs within each station—became crucial. In 1996, MRFT issued a systemwide notification calling on radio, TV, and cable TV stations to watch this last step of responsibility in particular. At a delicate stage of social transformation when the gap of social inequality was on the rise, themes of broadcast programs were required to be in line with this general reality of the nation, as well as cater to mass interests with due consideration to possible impact on the youth. Programs exuding lowly tastes were barred. Pirated programs were to be banned from the screen as well. Local stations were prohibited from airing news programs received from foreign satellites.

Implementation of rules and regulations requires frequent review and assessment. Such a reviewing system had been long awaited for 10 years since the institutionalization of rules and regulations on broadcasting in mid-1986s. In July 1996, MRFT issued a set of guidelines on the annual review of TV station performance. Although ideology was no longer the top priority in television operation, the first item on the review check list was as follows: "Did the station make any political mistake in broadcasting during the past year?" What that political mistake was, of course, depended on the political wind that might be blowing at the time. Whether real or imagined, it appears that politics still keeps an invisible hand behind television broadcasting.

Other main items of the 1996 list asked questions about transmission of CCTV Channel One program, channels of acquisition of programs, imported programs, illegal use of satellite programs, broadcast of educational programs, rental of frequency, channel or time slots, satisfaction of MRFT standards, and violation of laws, rules, and regulations. If the results are satisfactory, a certificate is granted after the annual review. If not, sanctions ranged from minor ones such as "renewal of certificate pending improvement in performance" to suspending broadcasting to total shutdown of the station. The formation of the review mechanism, coupled with other regulations, put the state firmly in charge of the form and content of TV broadcasting process from the beginning to the very end.

The Sixth Plenum of the 14th Party Congress passed the "Resolution on Building Socialist Spiritual Civilization" in October 1996. The document smacked of a tightening of control on the broadcast media. Each station was required to preview programs at three internal levels: specific program manager, department, and station. Most important programs with a bearing on the government must be inspected by the broadcast officials in the local government. Live broadcasts must pass the station head's pre-examination. This stipulation makes the unprecedented live broadcast of the press conference between President Clinton and President Jiang more remarkable as it signified the approval of the central authority for it to take place at the national level. Foreign programs, including those received via satellites, must be previewed. Major accidents in broadcasting must be reported to the provincial level broadcast administration within 48 hours. Within 3 days, the provincial authority must submit reports to MRFT on the actions taken. This oversight system obviously favor the state power over the market logic.

STATE VERSUS MARKET POWER IN TV REGULATION

The year 1992 stands as the turning point for China in the reform era. Deng Xiaoping set forth the criteria for evaluating media and propaganda work, based on whether the Chinese people were satisfied, liked it, or agreed with it. These practical standards have since triggered much reform effort on the part of television stations, especially in the areas of news programs. As noted before, new shows such as the *Focus Interview* on CCTV have received endorsement and praise from both former Premier Li Peng and current Premier Zhu Rongji. For instance, Zhu publicly commended the *Focus Interview* for its opinion surveillance function (Gu & Zhang, 1998). Such official recognition and encouragement of the need for open monitor on social practices and public services underline the potential contradiction and conflict between the state's resolution to hold on the control of propaganda apparatus and the market's momentum to unravel the intertwined structural dependence in the media–government connection.

To examine the relationship among the state, the market, and TV regulation in China, several new factors confronting Chinese television must be taken into account. At a critical juncture of reforms and openness, the Communist Party's demand on the smooth and accurate transmission of its policies to the public is ever greater, whereas the public's desire for access to the government is also higher. Chinese national television has to strike a balance between the two competing forces on a seemingly colliding course. It cannot favor one without snubbing the other. The problem is complicated by the increasingly fierce competition between CCTV and more than 20 provincial stations that are now broadcasting to other parts of the country through satellites. Furthermore, the rise of press conglomerates poses another threat to TV, especially when major newspapers have made their presence felt nationwide through the Internet.

There is little doubt that economic reform has brought about many changes in the relationship between television and the central government in China. Although television is gradually maturing into an industry and the world of advertisers and consumers, because of the imperfect competition in the Chinese media market the state still wields a considerable amount of power and control over TV regulation. As discussed earlier, since 1986, a significant number of laws and regulations have been issued to monitor the form and content of television at all aspects, ranging from mundane empirical practices to more ideological issues of its existence. This, however, does not necessarily mean that the rules and regulations are all duly observed.

On the contrary, like many other laws and regulations concerning other industries in China, there is no guarantee of full implementation at the grassroots level. This can be observed in the emphatic repetition of certain regulations over the years. Such frustration does not nullify the central government's regulatory efforts, which are mostly reactions to the changing situations in the market. In recent years, new communication technologies, such as satellites and the Internet, have further pushed the envelope of production, dissemination and consumption of Chinese television products. It is difficult, if not impossible, to fully comprehend the complexity and propensity of TV regulations in China. The analysis presented here leads to several conclusions.

First, economic independence has surely empowered most TV stations to transgress certain bounds such as the ban on pornography and violence that are seen most often on cable TV. Decentralization and depoliticization in state regulations have generally been found in the media market. TV is no exception. When the entire nation has become a market, TV has come to be conceptualized at once as a mass entertainer and new technology, in addition to being an instrument. The institution-alization of commercial Chinese television and the outburst of a market-oriented mentality among its practitioners grow, to some extent, out of the official mold and the state's desire to move forward in its economic structuring.

The irony lies in this: The nature of TV technology itself has enabled it to expand and span across such vast space in two decades, moving beyond the state's control and into the market of audiences. Yet with the financial autonomy allowed by the state, Chinese television is willingly subjecting itself to more subtle control by the state just to gain greater freedom in programming and other industrial operations. This points out the structural dilemma facing the entire media system in China today: Until the state transfers the ownership to the media them-selves by relinquishing its control and privatizing the mass media, at least some of them in a mixed public and private system, media practi-tioners will continue to function as state managers and employees in a struggle to strike a balance between the pull of market logic and the push of state ideology.

To change the well-entrenched state–media hierarchy, however, is to reconfigure the foundation of the legitimacy of Communist Party and to abandon its strong hold on the absolute power in China. There is little indication, if any, that this is going to happen anytime soon. The embryonic civil society that is emerging in China, of which the gradual opening of the news media is a part, does not necessarily resemble the one in the Western sense. A growing sign is that the state will insist on exercising its legal and administrative power to place television in check on the one hand, while loosening its control over areas of content that do not challenge or threatens its authority on the other hand.

Second, a large number of rules and regulation are devoted to the macro-operation of television as a new media technology. When the new technology is eagerly embraced and the market begins to outgrow its initial boundaries, from the state's point of view, effective means of management and control must be put in place. A division of labor and a chain of command are rationally set in motion. Administratively, although the authority of licensing/granting permits resides mostly with the central government, local and provincial governments often serve as gatekeepers in the application/approval procedure. It is reveal-ing that in terms of defining the role and functions of TV as well as other media, state leaders often have the final say. Their guidelines may con-tribute greatly to the making of rules and regulations. It is a manifesta-tion of the centrality of the market concerns that can only be best observed at the point closer to reality.

Third, the state sees television as an instrument of propaganda and education in China, at the same time acknowledging its being a commodity and technology. This dual conception creates an uneasy tension between TV as a national resource by the state's virtual monopoly of media ownership and TV as an informational and advertising tool in the vibrant market economy. Television program producers may see it primarily as a commodity catering to the public as a mass entertainer, facing an increasingly picky and demanding audiences and more crucially, confronting the challenges from other new, multimedia technologies. The eyes of the audiences are fixed on the content of the programs, as well as the types of information and entertainment they could get. In any market system, whether socialist (as China claims it is) or capitalist, the laws of demand and supply tend to dictate what comes out of the process, especially when the market outpaces the state. The growing legal system in China is a rational response to the market logic.

Fourth, television regulations in China operate between disparate state perceptions and market conceptions of TV's functional roles. Such disparity is reflected in the implementation of the rules and regulations. One thing most certain is this general observation: State policy and new technology allow TV stations to prosper financially in a market economy; in exchange, the state retains the authority to define the boundaries of TV's territory of freedom in the market. Notwithstanding, it remains a regulatory problem (e.g., Zi, 1998) to be solved: Following the current system of management of television in China, the authority on personnel, finance, and logistics all resides with the local and provincial governments, rendering the central government very limited in forceful regulation of regional and local TV stations. If the overall economic reform movement stays on course, at the end, the state may continue to keep control of the ownership while the market gradually chips away the ability and power of the central authority to run the media show in its own design on a grand scale. The 21st century may see a better balanced, albeit more delicate, relationship among the state, TV, and the market in China.

CHAPTER 3

TV PROGRAMMING AND FOREIGN IMPORTS: FROM PAROCHIAL UNITY TO MULTINATIONAL DIVERSITY

Since the adoption of Deng Xiaoping's reform policy in 1978, China has transformed itself in economic, political, social, and cultural respects. In the realm of mass media, a noticeable metamorphosis has altered the fundamental structure and processes of Chinese public communication. A major change, as C. Lee (1980) pointed out, is toward more pragmatic use of the mass media, especially television. This pragmatism has shifted the role and function of television in China from one of a class ideologue to that of a state manager (e.g., J. Wang & Chang, 1996). Against the backdrop of the managerial perspective (Alford & Friedland, 1985; Mosco, 1988), this chapter examines the impact of China's changing socioeconomic landscape on its foreign TV programming and its implications for the spirit and practices of the contemporary Chinese media system. It also provides some empirical evidence to support the decentralization and depoliticization of TV regulation in China, as discussed in chapter 2.

As a major stock of social knowledge (e.g., Chang, Wang, & Chen, 1994) and because of the large illiterate population in China, television has become an important part of everyday life for hundreds of millions of Chinese people. The popularity of television as the chief source of information and entertainment follows its rapid technological sophistication and market penetration into Chinese society in recent years. Since the end of the Cultural Revolution in 1976, this phenomenon in both cultural and political sense may have been the single most important social change in China (e.g., Lull, 1991). As noted in chapter 1, the fact that China boasts the world's largest TV audiences testifies to the extraordinary effort of the government to open up the country from the coastal to the inland regions. The "television revolution" described in Chinoy's (1999) *China Live* is, to some extent, applicable to the Chinese situation.

Since the reform movement in the late 1970s, the relaxation of the central command system has created a less rigid environment for the liberalization of the mass media. One such indicator is the emerging internationalization of Chinese television in its production and presentation (e.g., Chan, 1994; Hong, 1993, 1998). The process of TV's internationalization takes two basic forms: import and export of television programming. Both involve movement of capital and exchanges of programs and services. In the case of CCTV, the only Chinese national network, the flow of TV programs, including news, across national borders has long been its organizational goal. As shown in chapter 1, to be a world-class TV station is to become an international player on the global stage. It is a two-way street.

Whether import or export, media internationalization has swept countries around the world, particularly in Asia where nations from Australia to Taiwan have increasingly been subject to the impact of globalization even though many of them have resisted for years (e.g., Hong, 1998). Given its internal economic reforms and external open-door policy, China has gradually been drawn into the global economic process partly by design (see chapter 1) and partly by default through the logic of the international marketplace. As a major component of the total media system and because of its ubiquity in China, television has attracted both professional and scholarly interests as to what it may mean when it goes international. Except for a few recent studies (e.g., Hong, 1998), little is known in this area from a longitudinal point of view, particularly when the Chinese media environment has been fast changing.

MAKING SENSE OF CHINESE MEDIA

Previous studies have provided useful information and knowledge in describing the specific role and general functions of Chinese television (e.g., J. Chu, 1978; Hong, 1993, 1998; C. Lee, 1980; X. Li, 1991; Warren, 1988; X. Yu, 1990). Especially informative and analytical are those studies in the 1980s and 1990s that have factored in sociopolitical changes in the larger landscape. However, some major questions remain unanswered: How did the TV content change from the revolutionary era to the recent reform stage? What were the relationships between the changing social and economic structures and the organizational patterns of TV programming? Did domestic conflicts such as the 1989 Tiananmen Square incident have any impact on the flow of foreign programs into China? Some of the answers were discussed briefly in the previous chapters. This chapter seeks to further address the empirical and the conceptual questions.

Underpinning these questions is an epistemological consideration that calls for a broader theoretical approach to the study of Chinese television before and after the implementation of economic reform policies. The key question to ask is: What perspective could better explain the evolving Chinese media system over time? In the case of Chinese television, the diversity of domestic content and the process of internationalization have cast doubt on the conventional knowledge in the West that the political character and mission of Chinese mass media have mostly stayed monolithically ideological over the years simply because of the inherent structural constraints on the media ownership and organizational management.

Earlier studies have tended to focus on the propagandistic and persuasive aspects of mass communication in China (for a review, see Chang et al., 1993). Within this perspective, mass communication channels were characterized as limited outlets with a centralized hierarchical command structure, a unified circulation system, an ideologically charged worldview, and a monotonous content. With little variation in command and practices, the mass media as part of the superstructure in China thus became class ideologues, defining and reproducing the central knowledge dictated by the state's political and ideological calculations. Such a once-and-for-all conceptual approach often obfuscates rather than illuminates the reality (e.g., Galtung, 1990). If the landscape is changing or has changed, to look at it with a fixed view is to ignore the obvious. There is no denying that the Chinese media in their outlook and performance today are not what they used to be before the reforms.

This chapter departs from previous conceptualization about Chinese mass communication research. The general thesis is that the economic pragmatism initiated by the late Chinese leader Deng Xiaoping has resulted in both vertical fragmentation (e.g., decentralization of state authority) and horizontal fragmentation (e.g., division of power across organizations) of the mass media in China. As far as their functional prerequisites are concerned, the Chinese mass media have become less of a class ideologue and more of a state manager. This transformation of the Chinese society from a rigid totalitarian rule to a soft authoritarian system has been keenly observed in the U.S. media and elsewhere (e.g., CNN).[1]

Such a perspective does not imply that the Chinese state authority has willingly relinquished its power grip over the mass media and their political guidance; nor does it necessarily condone the government's suppression of press freedom in China. Notwithstanding the reforms and openness, on both counts, the media–state relations in China still leave much to be desired. What is clear is that when the larger sociopolitical setting changes, the picture one takes, even a snapshot of it, cannot remain unchanged or unchanging. The same is true for media and society relations. As clearly demonstrated in the previous chapters, the Chinese mass media are still firmly situated in a subordinated position of the Communist hierarchical structure. Yet, the form and content of their practices have often shown signs of relative organizational autonomy and bold management initiatives to compete in the Chinese media market. The practice of paid journalism and its consequences are a case in point (Zhao, 1998). Although the central authority has banned journalists from receiving money or material benefits in exchange for publishing news or features, this form of journalism corruption is difficult to stamp out, especially when the market competition drives the mass media toward profits for survival.

TELEVISION AS STATE MANAGER IN CHINA

Using the managerial perspective as a framework (Alford & Friedland, 1985; Mosco, 1988), chapter 2 discussed the process of decentralization, depoliticization, and legal rationality of television regulations in China. Following the same logic, this chapter argues that, as the structure of Chinese society and state becomes more complex, the procedure for effective decisions requires greater technical and economic rationality. The necessity of efficient management hence calls for expert knowledge, bureaucratic competence, and managerial proficiency that could be effectively realized through a lucid division of labor at the organizational levels. This is particularly true when China's economic reforms and openness since the late 1970s have more or less integrated the country into the global economic system and the community of nations.

In the arena of mass communication, decentralization has altered the structural relations among national, regional, and local components of the command system, thus resulting in the emergence of multiple centers or fragmentation of the central authority. The four-

[1]See CNN In-Depth Specials—Vision of China on its Web site at http://cnn.com/SPECIALS/1999/china.50/red.giant/human.rights.dalpino/.

tiered broadcasting system, as reported in chapter 1, is a good example. Huang (1994) even went as far to suggest that "the old centralized broadcasting system is being replaced by the new *federation-style* one which, in the long term, can favour building a democratic media system in the process of communist state transformation" (p. 226, italics added). Given its nationwide reach and the increasing competitiveness, Chinese television has positioned itself either internally or externally to move beyond, as will be seen later, the narrow boundaries delimited by earlier political considerations to a wider international playground.

For television programming in China, like that in any other country, technological complexity and the division of labor in the TV subsystem inevitably lead to a quantitative increase in content and a qualitative change in form. Both have apparently veered the control of program selection and presentation from the central unit of the state to regional and local organizations. Because of the cumulative wealth and resources and the newly acquired power that comes with economic success in various provinces and regions, unlike the old, unyielding top–down vertical command system, the new arrangement appears to be horizontal, loose and bottom–up. It creates a contentious environment across the country (e.g., Ding, 1998).

The emerging configuration of the Chinese political and economic landscape is most visible in the coastal regions, from Guangdong province in the south to Liaoning province in the north, with the inland provinces somewhat lagging behind. As is shown in chapter 5, the differences in coverage between the coastal and inland provinces on CCTV network news are striking. There is indication of regional differentiation in the news. According to the managerial perspective, increasing autonomy creates a fundamental need for effective and efficient decision making that tends to undermine the power of the central authority. This transformation can be best seen in the changing Chinese socioeconomic environment that dictates administrative solutions by managerial elites to monitor the state affairs at various levels on the one hand and to supersede class interests on the other.

From 1949 to 1976, China under Mao Tse-tung developed a highly centralized economic, political and cultural system. Modeled on the Soviet Leninist–Stalinist rule, both the Chinese Communist Party and the central government exercised unchecked coercive power to attain an absolute control and domination in every aspect of society. The dominant ideology held that China should rely on the "wisdom of the masses" to seek economic development rather than attract foreign investment and pursue international trade (Joint Economic Committee, 1978). The latter was considered to be the source of capitalist imperialism and exploitation that had contributed to the social ills, economic injustice, and political corruption for years in China before the Communist revolution. The belief is clearly rooted in the Marxist perspective that attempts to explain the contradictions between planned production and private appropriation through class struggle and state intervention. Such revolutionary fanaticism inevitably resulted in a catastrophic outcome as witnessed by the 10-year Cultural Revolution from 1966 to 1976.

In contrast, the end of the Cultural Revolution and the arrest of Maoist zealots shifted the national focus from revolutionary ideological campaigns to more pragmatic matters, such as education, economic prosperity and improvement of living standards. The previous decades of class struggle had greatly undercut the vitality of public productivity, destroyed national resources, and created suspicion or distrust among the population, not to mention isolating China from contact with most countries around the world. The new philosophy stemmed from Deng Xiaoping's pragmatic calculations over China's influence in the world affairs and put economic modernization as the top priority in China's nation building.

The post-Mao Chinese leadership realized that its legitimacy and political success hinged on its ability to rejuvenate the economy in general and to raise people's living standards in particular (Joint Economic Committee, 1991). It was a tall task and demanded immediate attention and action. Deng's pragmatism advocated a dramatic change in China's economic structure and practices, essentially reversing the tight state control policies under Mao. Putting aside the politics-in-charge ideological principle, the content and scope of economic reforms included, among other things, decentralization of the decision-making power of state enterprises (Ellman, 1986). Economic and administrative elites are increasingly entrusted to manage the state and the economy, not merely to respond to the ups and downs of current situations.

For Chinese television, this means more degrees of technical freedom to depart from the requirement of uniform program scheduling, as was the case when little variation existed in the earlier years of domestic programs and foreign imports. In fact, during the decades when BTS (and later its successor CCTV) was the only TV station authorized to import foreign programs, not much TV programming came from abroad. From 1962 to 1980, less than 2% of BTS (and CCTV) programming was foreign imports (Hong, 1998; C. Lee, 1980). Shortly after the economic reforms and openness went into effect, the proportion increased significantly to eight percent in 1982 (Wildman & Siwek, 1988). By the end of 2000, imports of foreign TV dramas grew to about 15% of the dramas shown on Chinese television. It is evident that the loosening of control has opened up China's window on the world.

DECENTRALIZATION, FOREIGN TRADE, AND TV PROGRAM IMPORT

Within the managerial perspective, this chapter highlights two crucial aspects of the reform campaign in China and its impact on Chinese foreign TV programming: decentralization and external economic relations. Through decentralization, the state and the economy have become more organizationally or bureaucratically oriented and the central government has relegated reform power to provincial governments (e.g., Oksenberg & Tong, 1991). By way of international trade and foreign investment, Deng's reform movement exemplifies the growing complexity of China's open-door policy and its corresponding sophistication of technical decision making. Both have serious implications for the parameters of media operations and content management, especially when they involve TV programs from other countries.

The centralized social structure during Mao's rule placed heavy constraints on mass media form and content. There was virtually no room for deviation. Mass communication channels were highly controlled in terms of media outlets, organizational hierarchy, functional distribution of products, and standardized messages. Political imperative and ideological necessity basically rendered the Chinese mass media an indispensable component of the giant state apparatus that permeated all layers of social fabrics from top to bottom. Following the realization of decentralization in post-Mao China, provincial and local governments have achieved greater autonomy in managing media-related affairs. J. Yu (1990), for example, showed that between 1979 and 1989 local television stations had become more autonomous through advertising and sponsorship and less dependent on the central station for programs and support.

In the post-Mao era, foreign trade and capital investment in China further transcend the conventional Marxist dictation of class struggle on the international scene. No longer was ideological affiliation or loyalty the guiding light in China's search for overseas cooperation or joint partnership. The door was ajar and all visitors were welcome so long as they played according to the Chinese rules of the game. This new policy and the relative liberalization of thought have brought about a continuing development of economic relations with countries of diverse ideologies. From the Communist allies to the former capitalist enemies, China aggressively courted foreign companies to invest in the vast Chinese domestic market that was untouched by capitalism for nearly three decades.

One significant consequence of China's international trade connections was an increasing influx of information and news into the country. If the tangible in the forms of capital, people, products or services becomes available in international communication, the intangible would soon follow. As both Hester (1973) and Rosengren (1974) postulated, economic relationships tended to generate more flow of information, ideas, or values across national borders. In the information age, knowledge is indeed power. It gives the recipients some leverage to overcome the unknown and to see for themselves what lies beyond the horizon. The closed environment during the heydays of the Cultural Revolution when little from the outside world could slip through the bamboo curtain unless otherwise permitted is one key factor that paved the way for total control in China.

As can be expected within the managerial perspective, the growing traffic of foreign programs into China provides an instrumental rationality, making procedural freedom possible by allowing local and regional TV stations to resist and delimit the intervention from the central unit in their programming selection and presentation. When there is little or no choice, a forced consensus becomes predictable, but really does not tell much about the essence of decision. Only in a setting where the range of options is relatively unrestricted can the interplay between the commanding unit and the subordinate turn into a site of contention. In the case of foreign TV imports in China, the variance of foreign TV programming between national and provincial stations suggests to some extent a vertical fragmentation in decision making.

Closely related to the decentralization of TV programming was China's development strategy and priority that had favored foreign capital and investment in the coastal regions (Cannon, 1990). Part of the reasons is historical because many major coastal cities were beachheads of Western incursion into China in the late 19th and early 20th centuries. Throughout the Chinese Republican years and until the Communist revolution in the late 1940s, the coastal areas developed into financial, business, and trade centers. Although the Communist power grew out of the countryside with a vast base of hundreds of millions of peasants and workers, its victory brought the party onto the stage of modern China with a huge number of bureaucracies, institutions, businesses, and industries left behind by the retreating Nationalists. The rapid development of a complex radio broadcast network in the early 1950s was partly built on the existing radio stations taken over from the Nationalists around the country (T. Zhang, 1992).

As the whole country was encircled in the revolutionary dogmatism, the destructive 1960s and early 1970s did not necessarily cause a widening financial gap among regions. From the coastal to the inland regions, it was a matter of relative deprivation. Most areas were poor and underdeveloped. Since the late 1970s, the economic reforms have greatly benefited some regions more than others. Those regions started to demand greater autonomy and more financial initiatives in local affairs and policies. As early as 1980, according to Huang (1994), many local authorities in the newly-rich coastal areas began to "challenge the existing centralized regulations regarding broadcasting development" (p. 221). The central government eventually complied.

It is a task that clearly would rely on efficient managerial planning at the local organizational levels. The regional Chinese TV stations and relay centers are structurally tied to the provincial governments. Because of divergent degrees of progress and financial strength, when external economic activities vary, the quantity and quality of television programming could be expected to differ from region to region. Against the backdrop of the managerial perspective, the logic of efficiency and the necessity of managerial flexibility should make it desirable for the regions to go their own ways in localized decision making. The variance of foreign TV programs between the coastal and interior regions therefore serves as an index of the horizontal fragmentation that contributes to content regionalization and programming diversity.

From Mao's class struggle and ideological indoctrination to Deng's social pragmatism and economic rationality, the decentralizing process appears to transform the functional prerequisite of Chinese television from one of class ideologue to that of state manager, the essence of which is greater technical management with a less ideological bent. This metamorphosis certainly has been affected in one way or another by the tempo and pulse of the larger social structure and contemporary commitment, especially political openness and economic reforms. The internationalization of TV programming in China is exemplary and offers an excellent opportunity to determine the extent to which that process transpires.

After its inception in 1958, the internationalization of Chinese television, at least in the form of foreign imports, can be roughly divided into four distinctive periods: 1958–1966, the nascent years; 1966–1978, the Cultural Revolution and recovery; 1978–1989, the reform years and the Tiananmen Square incident; and 1989 to present, the maturing years. As should be obvious, imports of foreign programs were naturally disrupted by the catastrophic Cultural Revolution and the path had not always been smooth. Since the reforms in the late 1970s, according to Hong (1998), foreign imports of television programs during the past two decades have increased substantially. It appears that once the reform engine was set in motion, destructive forces such as the Tiananmen Square massacre did not necessarily derail it. What follows is a detailed cross-section analysis of foreign TV imports from the national to local levels on the one hand and from the coastal to inland regions on the other hand.

For comparison purpose, foreign programming patterns of three TV stations—CCTV, Gansu Television (GTV), and Shanghai Television
(STV)—between 1970 and 1995 were examined. As noted in chapter 1,
CCTV, China's only national network, stands as the flagship of the central television authority. Because it was the only authorized TV station
to import foreign programs for many years, its inclusion made sure that
the data covered a wide range of imported programming on the Chinese
TV menu. The situation changed in the mid-1980s when decentralization
permitted major provincial and large city TV stations to import foreign
programs on their own.

GTV and STV are local stations, catering to their respective audiences in Gansu province and Shanghai municipality. Shanghai is the
most cosmopolitan city on the prosperous east coast, whereas Gansu is a
less developed inland province in northwestern China. STV has often
been considered as the "most liberal television" station in China in that
foreign programs rejected by CCTV as "inappropriate" on national TV
often ended up on the Shanghai station and distributed nationwide
(Hong, 1998). The two local stations are by no means representative of
the more than 2,000 TV stations around the country. Given their location
and the degree of economic development of the respective areas
involved, they do provide some useful indication for determining decentralization and managerial autonomy in Chinese TV programming.

Whether national or regional, Chinese television stations, as
noted by Hong (1998), either did not maintain their programming data,
including foreign imports, systematically or simply treated those data as
"state secrets." To overcome the inaccessibility of long-term programming records, this study used newspaper listings of TV schedules as the
source for data collection.[2] Unfortunately, not all channels of the three TV

---

[2]Because no video library of Chinese TV programs existed, a detailed content
analysis based on actual broadcast was impractical from a longitudinal point of
view. Given the limitations on data collection, the best sources available for TV
programming information in China were the daily listings in newspapers and
television program guides. These published TV schedules were found to be reli-
able and TV stations rarely changed their programs without any advance notice
in the newspapers. The TV schedules were compiled from the following sources:
Wenhui Daily (STV), *Gansu Daily* (GTV), *Beijing Daily* (CCTV), and *Television
Broadcast Weekly*. The unit of analysis was the individual program listed, excluding nightly news and purely educational programs. The coding procedure identified program sources, types of program, and country involved according to the
classification developed by Katz and Wedell (1977) and Lau (1991). The average
intercoder reliability coefficient between two independent coders was .96, ranging from .89 to .99.

For each TV station, a 4-week period of programming in each year was randomly chosen. Because GTV started in October 1970, only 1 week of program-

stations were listed in the newspapers in 1995, making it harder to determine exactly how many programs were foreign imports. Also, many of the special features such as "World Sports" were foreign imports, but repackaged at the stations. Their origin was not necessarily identified. It is apparently difficult, if not impossible, to compile complete and up-to-date data for a comprehensive analysis of TV programming in China. The data for 1995 in Table 3.1 were therefore weighted, based on the available information from newspaper listings of each station.

THE QUANTITATIVE CHANGE IN CHINESE FOREIGN TV MENU

Notwithstanding the limitations, the pattern reported in Table 3.1 was comparable to that of Hong's (1998) study from a longitudinal perspective. Strictly speaking, however, because of the use of different measure (program hours vs. program items) the data in Hong's study were not directly compatible with the current set. The similarity in the distribution of proportion of foreign imports over time and other related aspects nevertheless increases the validity of data and confidence in the interpretation of the findings presented in this chapter. Unlike Hong's research, this study goes beyond the quantity of foreign imports by examining the types and origin of foreign TV programming on Chinese television.

Although the 25-year study period covered only about two thirds of the 40-year history of Chinese television, it included several important phases of the time span. Considering that there was virtually no foreign TV imports in the 1960s, the chosen period from 1970 onward is both conceptually and practically sound. Conceptually, it allowed for a closer look at the relationship between the socioeconomic structure and external TV programs from several historical vantage points: 1970 (mid-way of the cultural revolution), 1975 (a year before the end of cultural revolution and Mao's death), 1980 (beginning of the economic reforms), 1985 (acceleration of the reforms), 1990 (post-Tiananmen Square incident), and 1995 (new momentum for the reforms). Practically, given the inaccessibility of systematic data, especially those concerning local TV stations over time, the data are manageable and should still capture the trend, if any, of patterns in Chinese foreign TV imports because of their longitudinal nature.

---

ming was analyzed for that year. In the 1990s, all three channels have spawned new channels. Because of the expansion of TV channels, the amount of TV programming also increased substantially. Two days were missing in the 1990 sample for STV and the 1995 sample of GTV, and a composite month of TV programming was constructed.

Table 3.1: Types of Foreign Programs and Imports on CCTV, GTV and STV, 1970–1995

TV Programs	1970	1975	1980	1985	1990	1995[a]
Movies	100%	100%	20%	33.3%	18.8%	11.3%
Documentary	–	–	30	6.7	3	4.1
TV series	–	–	20	40	54	45.4
Variety shows	–	–	10	3.3	3	1
Children	–	–	10	6.7	10.4	23.7
Information	–	–	5	3.3	–	–
Theater	–	–	5	–	–	–
TV drama	–	–	–	3.3	1.5	–
Sports	–	–	–	3.3	5.9	14.4
Others	–	–	–	–	3.5	–
$n =$	6	3	21	30	202	388
% of total programming	10.5%	1.6%	9.5%	11.8%	29.7%	13.0%
Foreign Imports (billion US$)	2.2	7.4	21.2	42.4	53.3	113.6

[a]The entries are weighted data, based on available newspaper listings for the three TV stations during a 4-week period.

Sources: *Chinese Economy Post Mao* (vol. 1), Joint Economic Committee, Congress of the United States, U.S. Government Printing Office, 1978; China's Economic Dilemmas in the 1990s: *The Problems of Reforms, Modernization, and Interdependence* (vol. 1), Joint Economic Committee, Congress of the United States, U.S. Government Printing Office, 1991; *Statistical Yearbook of China*, China Statistics Publishing House, 1991; *The People's Daily*, December 27, 1995, p. 1.

As shown in Table 3.1, the growing complexity of imports of foreign TV programming in China before and after the reform is obvious. For all three Chinese TV stations, before the reforms in the late 1970s the number of foreign programs was minuscule (six in 1970 and three in 1975) and accounted for a small share of total TV programming. Two explanations are plausible. Politically, the period from 1970 to 1975 witnessed the Cultural Revolution at its peak and coming to an end. The preoccupation with this unprecedented ideological revolution with its internal political, social, and cultural consequences apparently did not enable Chinese television to turn outward. When the bourgeoisies, Soviet revisionists and their sympathizers were under attack nation-wide, it was obviously unwise for Chinese television, even for the central TV station, to carry much of any foreign import. It would be a sure indication of reactionary practice and was bound to invite external criticism and assault.

Economically, because all TV stations were engaged in revolutionary activities either through their programming or staff participation, as mentioned in the previous chapters, there should be little room on the airwaves or much incentive to schedule programs from overseas. If not a single TV drama or series was ever produced for TV during the Cultural Revolution from 1966 to 1976 and only "revolutionary model operas" were allowed to be shown on Chinese television as entertainment programs (Huang & Yu, 1997), it is logical that foreign imports would be kept at the minimum. Indeed, by the time the Cultural Revolution had nearly run its course in 1975, the proportion of foreign imports accounted for only less than two percent of the TV total programming reported in Table 3.1, a figure remarkably similar to Hong's (1998) study.

The growth of foreign TV programming took off shortly after the reforms started. Two years after the economic restructuring, the number of foreign imports increased seven times from 3 in 1975 to 21 in 1980. It rose steadily through 1985 (30) and reached more than 200 in 1990. Within the first decade of reforms, the proportion of imported TV programs jumped significantly from less than 2% in 1975 to 9.5% in 1980 and 11.8 % in 1985, eventually reaching 29.7% in 1990. The number grew almost 10 times. Again, the trend corresponds to that in Hong's study, even though he used program hours as a measure of foreign TV imports. An impressive increase in foreign imports on Chinese television occurred between 1985 and 1990, when the Chinese society became more dynamic and volatile. It was an impelling and explosive time that ultimately culminated in the June 1989 Tiananmen Square democratic movement and its subsequent crackdown by the heavy-handed Chinese government. The brutal suppression of the spontaneous student demonstration on television shocked the whole world and raised serious concern that the hard-liners in China might suspend or even terminate its international contact. If the large number of foreign imports on the three TV stations in 1990 was any indication, the Tiananmen Square incident appeared to have no discernible impact on Chinese television. Nearly one in three TV programs (29.7%) shown on CCTV, GTV, and STV was a foreign import a year after the tragedy.

Five years later in 1995, although the number of foreign imports continued to rise, the proportion of foreign programs (13%) for the three channels was lower than that in 1990. This is most likely the result of two possible factors. One is the introduction of multiple channels for each of the three stations. CCTV now has 11 channels, offering a wide variety of programs, whereas STV and GTV have two channels each. As the number of channels increases, so does the total amount of programming. Foreign programs, mostly entertainment-oriented programs, were also presented on other channels of the same station, thus reducing its overall proportion. The other explanation is China's increasing production capability and viewers' propensity for more local entertainment programming. When the number of domestic programs increased on any channel, what had to give were foreign imports since the broadcasting time was fixed. As noted in chapter 2, a percentage cap has been imposed on the number of foreign TV programming to be shown on Chinese television.

THE QUALITATIVE SHIFT OF CHINESE FOREIGN TV PROGRAMS

The changing complexity of foreign TV programming on Chinese television over time appeared not only in quantity, but also in quality. In the first half of the 1970s, when China was still going through the heydays of the Cultural Revolution, imported programs were limited in content variety. Movies from the Communist bloc appeared as the only foreign staple on Chinese television. Under the centralized control of ideas and behaviors, China's internal engrossment of the Cultural Revolution obviously played a key role in confining the Chinese foreign exposure to a monotonous aspect of fiction that had little to do with reality. To some extent, imported movies were functional in that they helped fill the time slots on television because local production of dramas was halted from 1966 to 1976. This arrangement changed when the number of domestic dramas increased significantly in recent years. As a result, foreign TV programming has accounted for a small proportion of the programs in China.

In the early 1970s, by its virtual status as the state TV station, BTS, the predecessor of CCTV, stood at that time as the only broadcasting institution specifically authorized by the central authority to import foreign programming. Such centralization of foreign TV imports in both size and shape inevitably reduced competing forms or alternatives throughout the internal broadcasting system. It was no coincidence that Mao's dominant concept of reality—class struggle—had prevailed in society during the pre-reform years. When the state commanded tremendous resources and power to demand attention and action through either persuasion or coercion, a forced consensus nationwide was bound to emerge. There was simply little or no room for variation or deviation. If the entire domestic TV production of certain programs could be shut down for political purpose, restriction of foreign imports to a particular type should not be difficult to do technically.

Decentralization in media control, however, breeds diversity in form and content. As China progressed through the 1980s with intensified economic reforms and external openness, more foreign TV programs and a wide array of categories, such as documentary/features, drama series, variety shows, information programs, theater, children's shows, and sports filled the Chinese television line-up. The change was gradual, of course, as the total number foreign imports was still relatively small. Eventually, all sorts of foreign programs were allowed to "pass through the bamboo curtain" (Hong, 1998, p. 69). In the early 1990s, not only did the volume of foreign TV imports increase many fold from the 1980s, a full slate of programs also became available, with drama series, movies, children's programs, and cartoons most visible. In 1995, children's programming and sports saw great increase in imports. The range of options was undoubtedly wider and greater than it was in the 1970s. TV organizations could not sit idly when there were time slots to consider and programs to schedule.

According to the managerial perspective, when the socioeconomic structure becomes intricate, the process of rationalization ultimately leads to the division of labor in order to handle the increasing differentiation of social relations and the accompanying specialized type and volume of work. In the case of foreign TV imports in China, the multiplying traffic of various programs over time represents a rearrangement of bureaucratic capacity and institutional interaction from the national to the local level. As is shown later, the economic reforms expanded the parameters of foreign TV content, making the organizational choice more variegated than before and creating greater opportunity for deviation from the prevalent way of doing things.

An indication of the impact of structural change on Chinese TV programming can be inferred from the positive correlation between the flow of foreign TV programs and Chinese external economic relations. Also shown in Table 3.1 is the volume of foreign imports (e.g., goods and services) into China from 1970 to 1995. From the long-term point of view, the amount of Chinese foreign imports showed an unmistakable upward trend, growing more than 50 times from $2.2 billion before the reforms and openness went into effect in the late 1970s to nearly $114 billion in the mid-1990s. As far as the number was concerned, the import of foreign TV programs during the same period displayed a corresponding pattern. The data indicate an apparent effect of economic reform and openness on China's window on the world.

But the number per se does not often reveal the political significance of the story behind the influx of overseas programs on Chinese television. The increased content categories aside, it should be more telling to look at where the foreign TV programs might come from if China's open-door policy indeed moved beyond the ideological divide. One of the underlying assumptions behind the reform and openness is that any country that would assist China's quest for modernization with mutual benefits should be the target of Chinese international contact regardless of its ideology or political affiliation in the global arena. If the TV imports followed such an approach, it would certainly signal a departure from the previous practice. It should also exemplify how wide open or receptive China's window on the world might be to the external landscape out there and to the views, ideas and ways of life that might flow through it.

THE COMMUNIST VERSUS CAPITALIST
DIVIDE ON CHINESE TELEVISION

As indicated in Table 3.2, foreign TV programs during the Mao's era all originated from a few parochial Communist allies. This was in line with the Communist dogmatism that China's socialist revolution and reconstruction could not and should not depend on the ideas, technology, or resources from the capitalist countries. Absolute centralization and complete compliance in media content, including importation of foreign programs were the order of the day before the Cultural Revolution (e.g., Gan, 1994). Against this context, the notion of capitalist entertainment would be unthinkable, if not blasphemous. At a time when ideological purity was supreme, the totality of Communist loyalty took precedence. In the early 1970s, when China was halfway through the campaigns of the Cultural Revolution, Albania, the former Soviet Union, and North Korea constituted the exclusive sources of foreign programs on Chinese TV. These were among the few countries with which China still maintained formal diplomatic relations. The eyes of the whole country focused mostly on internal affairs, rather than external matters. During this trying period, political, social, and cultural allegiance to the Communist ideology in the domestic sphere was essentially a prerequisite for individual or collective survival in the sea of class struggle. Media organizations from the national to the local levels, especially the

Table 3.2: Origin of Imported Programs on CCTV, GTV and STV, 1970–1995[a]

1970 (6)[b]	1975 (3)	1980 (21)	1985 (29)	1990 (174)	1995[c] (200)
USSR	N. Korea	Japan	Japan	U.S.	U.S.
Albania	USSR	U.S.	U.S.	U.K.	Hong Kong
		Argentina	Italy	Japan	Japan
		Australia	Brazil	Brazil	Singapore
		Finland	Romania	USSR	U.K.
		W. Germany	U.K.	Taiwan	France
		Hong Kong	Egypt	Australia	Russia
		India	E. Germany	W. Germany	
		Pakistan	Hong Kong	Poland	
		U.K.	N. Korea	France	
		Yugoslavia	Tanzania	Singapore	
			USSR	Italy	
				Thailand	
				Argentina	
				Czechoslovakia	
				Algeria	
				Cuba	
				Hong Kong	
				Hungary	
				India	
				Macao	
				Turkey	
				Latvia	

[a]In descending order of program frequencies.

[b]Number of programs, excluding those of unknown origin.

[c]Weighted data, based on information available in the newspaper listings for the three stations.

broadcasting media, had to answer the call for the revolutionary war against the class enemies, both real and imagined, had they not ceased operation as discussed in chapter 1.

Under such circumstances, being charged to mobilize and organize the masses in China, no television station had either the authority or the resources to schedule foreign imports that would deviate from the anti-feudalism, anti-imperialism, or anti-capitalism party line. A safe and politically correct mode was to carry programs, whenever and whatever available, from the officially sanctioned sources. The default equation obviously did not allow much room for country negotiation and content variation, thus leading to a forced convergence on China's window on the world. At best, it was a small world, with a limited hue and shape. At worst, it was a skewed one, tilted toward a chosen sector that was viewed from a preferred angle. Not until the revolutionary flame was put out did the country recover to see that the world was much bigger than it was shown on Chinese television.

When the reforms started in the early 1980s, TV programs from such capitalist countries as Japan, the United States, Australia, Finland, West Germany, and the United Kingdom began to emerge, along with some developing, non-Communist countries like Argentina, India, and Pakistan. Although TV imports from countries in the Communist block—Romania, North Korea, Soviet Union, and Yugoslavia—were still visible, they were clearly outnumbered by the multinational markets in the capitalist camp. The wider opening of the TV window was made possible because of the relaxation of ideological intrusion and the realization of the necessity of international communication and understanding between China and other countries (Howkins, 1982). It means that, while not necessarily discouraged, the totalistic mindset and political devotion to China's own kind in the community of nations no longer prevailed.

After the reform movement gained momentum in 1985, Japan and the United States continued to lead in the number of foreign programs on Chinese television, with Italy, Brazil, Egypt, and Hong Kong joining the group. Compared to 1975, albeit the number of imports (29) and countries (12) were still relatively small, the survey of the world's TV programs in the mid-1980s covered countries from the capitalist to the communist on the political spectrum and from the developed to the developing on the economic scale. The galaxy of countries and entities extended further in 1990 to include Taiwan, France, Singapore, Thailand, Algeria, Cuba, Hungary, Macao, Turkey, and Latvia. They displayed a mixture of new states, friends, and foes from near and afar.

The TV import from Taiwan was significant in one particular aspect: Chinese tolerance of ideological diversity and competing cultural genres (e.g., C. Lee, 1990b). Since its debacle in the Chinese civil war in 1949, the Nationalist Party had set up a contending government on Taiwan, vowing to recover the mainland for four decades until the late 1980s. Both within and without the Chinese geopolitical sphere, it had challenged the legitimacy and legality of the Communist rule over China and in the world arena. China has always kept a watchful eye and a vigilant attitude toward the potential threat from across the Taiwan Strait. Its acceptance of TV programs from Taiwan represented an unspoken acknowledgement that not everything from its arch-rival, and for that matter Western capitalist countries, is bad or even poisonous.

With more than 170 selections from 23 countries available in 1990, the scope of scheduling and hence organizational management presented opportunities for TV stations to choose programs that best met the needs of their regional or local markets. In addition to a long variety of TV programs (Table 3.1), the expanded list of countries added more flavors of choice as different countries with varying political, social, and cultural backgrounds were bound to produce shows with idiosyncratic themes and communication appeals. As is shown later, the pluralistic menu provided two useful practical solutions in television broadcasting: First, it gave TV managers a certain degree of freedom to select and present programs as they saw fit without necessarily considering the need for national conformity. Second, it allowed TV stations to field a broad range of international programs that would attract diverse segments of audiences.

The quantitative change in foreign imports naturally leads to a qualitative reconfiguration of the composition of countries involved. The number of foreign countries as represented by programs on Chinese television swelled from a very few states to more than 20 nation-states in 1990, covering a varied political landscape across several continents. Before the collapse of communism in eastern Europe in 1989 and the former Soviet Union in 1991, the Cold War tension created two major camps of political alliance and military allegiance. The Communist and Capitalist division among countries served some useful conceptual purposes from the 1970s through the early 1980s. For one thing, the submission to the thesis of Communism superiority over the Capitalism decadence had been the supreme guidance of China's external behaviors. By default, it stood as a threshold for domestic institutions, including the mass media, to guard against deviating from the national ideology.

In 1995, the range of foreign TV program sources seems to begin to narrow as the Chinese domestic market became more mature and sophisticated. Only fewer than a handful of the major foreign TV producers were represented on the three TV stations: the United States, Hong Kong, Japan, Singapore, United Kingdom, France, and Russia. Unlike the early years, this concentration of country origins is likely not to be a functional necessity of ideological allegiance or political affiliation, but rather the result of the increasing market orientation and competition among TV stations. It is difficult to imagine that TV programs from such countries as Turkey or Cuba (both appeared in 1990) would continue to attract any viewership when more selections were readily available. Because the Chinese people had various channels (as many as 20 to 30 in some regions and cities) to choose from, without a broad base of viewership, TV stations would not be able to sell advertising, hence affecting the revenues and their own livelihood. The initial excitement over international programs was long gone. Given the market response and financial incentive, it makes sense that foreign TV programming has started to concentrate on a few countries that produce programs most likely to appeal to the Chinese audiences.

A comparison of foreign TV programs along the ideological divide showed that since 1980, capitalist countries have dominated Chinese television, whereas in the pre-reform era communist countries predominated (Table 3.3). The absence of foreign TV imports from any capitalist country between 1970 and 1975 was remarkable for two reasons. First, although the size of Communist countries was relatively small compared to that of Capitalist or non-Communist countries, the number of Communist countries capable of exporting TV programs was even much smaller, of which the former Soviet Union, Albania, and North Korea were key players (see Table 3.2). They did not offer a full plate of genre selection and political-cultural diversification.

Second, outside the Communist block, countries like the United States, Japan, India, and some other major western European nations have long been known for producing and distributing internationally acclaimed and successful commercial films and TV programs around the world. Take the United States for example. Its cultural and media products, particularly movies and TV programs, have penetrated nearly every corner of the potential global market since the 1950s, including the Asian media market. The overwhelming U.S. domination and its threat

Table 3.3: Comparison of Imported Programs Between Capitalist and Communist Countries on CCTV, GTV and STV, 1970–1990

	1970	1975	1980	1985	1990	1995[a]
Communist	100%	100%	4.8%	17.2%	13.2%	–
Capitalist	–	–	76.2	69.0	73.6	–
Others	–	–	19.0	13.8	13.2	–
n =	6	3	21	29	174	–

[a]Because of the collapse of Communism in eastern Europe in 1989 and the former Soviet Union in 1991, the classification of Communist versus Capitalist countries was no longer conceptually useful in 1995. For comparison purpose, most of the foreign imports came from the Capitalist countries or others.

to the indigenous cultures among the developing and underdeveloped countries have obviously upset the world communication order, raising concerns over intrusion of national sovereignty and erosion of cultural identity under the broad rubric of cultural or media imperialism. For China, it represents a means of American hegemony.

The Third World resistance and the movement of non-aligned nations in the 1970s, of which China was a part, prompted the call for a new world information and communication order (e.g., Masmoudi, 1979). Its self-reliance policy aside, throughout the Cold War period, China obviously was aware of the conflicts and confrontation between the dissemination of Western capitalistic cultural or media products and the haphazard one-way reception of such products (e.g., television programs) among countries in Africa, Asia, and Latin America (Varis, 1984). From 1975 to 1980, why did China shift gear in its foreign imports from the communist to the capitalist countries? As far as ideology was concerned, the outside world remained largely unchanged in its political contour. Such a striking changeover on Chinese television could well be attributed to the economic reforms that by design facilitated the structural alteration in the preference of foreign TV content selection and presentation. Hong (1998) made a sound argument that internal factors of decentralization, depoliticization, and marketization were the decisive reasons for the singular changes in the process of Chinese TV's internationalization.

As Chinese TV audiences became more sophisticated and television stations grew increasingly responsive to their tastes and interests in the early 1990s, the sources of foreign TV programs appeared to consolidate in the hands of a few countries, suggesting a tendency of common appeal as a result of market competition. By 1995, imported TV programs from only a handful of countries and entities such as the United States, Hong Kong, Japan, Singapore, the United Kingdom, and France were presented. The successor of the former Soviet Union, Russia, was visible, but failed to enjoy the leading role as its predecessor did during the height of the Cold War. This convergence of program sources seemed to be a natural outcome of the fact that movies and TV series from the three major producers—the United States, Hong Kong, and Japan—had been the most popular among audiences in Asia due to their innovative techniques, advanced technology, powerful distribution network, and strong financial base. The logic of international marketplace in television programming has simply pushed aside other foreign suppliers that are less savvy and competitive in attracting Chinese domestic audiences.

REGIONAL DIFFERENTIATION AS A FUNCTION OF DECENTRALIZATION

As noted earlier, decentralization and depoliticization of the socioeconomic structure in China would lead to a greater variation in foreign TV programming between national and local stations. In the Chinese command media system before the economic reforms and external openness, the central authority often decided what to buy, where to import and how to select foreign programs. Regional and local stations were expected to follow this hierarchical scheme and made do with what was possible and permissible in broadcasting. Hong (1993, 1998), for example, provided an informative description of the national screening mechanism and import criteria for foreign TV programming before and after the reforms.

Although the central status and authority of CCTV have remained unquestioned and unchallenged, in addition to imported programs through the national channel, major provincial and metropolitan city TV stations were given permission in the mid-1980s to seek their own foreign imports. Either way, the sheer increase in the quantity of TV programs and the quality of content variety since the reforms leaves enough room for organizational flexibility and reduction of scheduling uncertainty in the managing process. To better illustrate the divergence in programming across different types of stations, prime time (8 p.m.–10 p.m.) foreign programs on CCTV, STV and GTV were specifically examined in Table 3.4.

As is evident, the first half of the 1970s saw a high degree of centralization in foreign programming on Chinese television. Among the three stations, the imported programs invariably came from one of the three communist block countries: Albania, North Korea, and the Soviet Union. The provincial station, GTV, and the metropolitan station, STV, obviously had little choice but to take the cue from the central station, CCTV. Whether willing or not, a forced consensus among the three stations was predictable and unavoidable. When the reforms were set in motion in 1980, however, the picture quickly changed, with each station having its own slate of foreign programs from a variety of countries that showed little resemblance. Except for Japanese programs that appeared on both CCTV and STV, the origin of foreign programming varied significantly from the national to the local: the United States, Pakistan and the United Kingdom on CCTV; Australia, Hong Kong and Yugoslavia on STV; and India on GTV. The disparity between STV and GTV, moreover, demonstrated the impact of uneven economic development between the coastal and inland regions on the broadcasting of foreign programs.

Table 3.4: Foreign Programs on Prime Time CCTV, GTV and STV, 1970–1995[a]

Stations	1970	1975	1980	1985	1990	1995
CCTV	Albania USSR		U.S. Japan Pakistan U.K.	U.S. E. Germany Japan N. Korea U.K.	Taiwan Japan Thailand U.K. France	U.S.
Percent[b]	5.7%		15.5%	11.2%	17.3%	4.9%
STV	Albania	USSR	Australia Hong Kong Japan Yugoslavia	Japan Brazil Italy Romania	U.S. Poland U.K. Brazil W. Germany Algeria Taiwan USSR	U.S. HK Japan
Percent	13.3%	1.5%	4%	11.8%	42.6%	12.1%
GTV	Albania USSR	N. Korea	India	Japan U.K.	U.K. Japan USSR	U.S.
Percent	28.6%	7.4%	5.6%	11.8%	15.6%	8.3%

[a]In descending order of countries represented on prime time (8 p.m.–10 p.m.); excluding programs of unidentifiable origin.

[b]Percent of total programming.

This differentiation of the origins of foreign TV programs persisted in 1985. Japan, as a major producer of TV programming, was apparently favored by all three TV stations. Britain came in second and was preferred by CCTV and GTV. Beyond Japan and Britain, no similarity in the origins of foreign TV programs could be found from the national to the local stations. Programs from the United States topped the CCTV lineup, followed by those of East Germany and North Korea. STV carried TV programs from Japan, Brazil, Italy, and Romania, in that order while GTV had Japanese and British programs only. Again, the discrepancy

between the coastal TV station (STV) and inland station (GTV) was manifest. And unlike the pre-reform years, the laxity of ideological uniformity
across TV stations was unmistakable, too. The two communist countries
represented on the CCTV's foreign programs, East Germany and North
Korea, were nowhere to be found on either STV or GTV. Also noteworthy is that from 1980 to 1985, U.S. TV programs capped the CCTV foreign
menu, but were invisible on the other two stations.

The divergence between CCTV and the two local TV stations
was most apparent in 1990, the year after the 1989 Tiananmen Square
crackdown. Except for the fact that TV programs from Britain were
shown on all three stations, little likeness in the origins of foreign programming existed among them. In fact, no consistent pattern could be
identified from the national to the local levels. Although CCTV did not
show any programs from the Soviet Union, STV and GTV did. Programs
from Taiwan appeared on CCTV and STV, but not on GTV. STV carried
foreign programs from the greatest number of countries (eight), with
CCTV a distant second (five) and GTV the least (three). What was presented on CCTV in foreign programs (Thailand and France) did not
show up elsewhere. The same was true for STV (the United States,
Poland, Brazil, West Germany, and Algeria). Compared to the pre-reform
period, this content diversification served to indicate a clear structural
difference in program management across Chinese TV stations.

In the context of Chinese political calculation, the absence of
U.S. programs on CCTV, the only national television network, in 1990
was neither accidental, nor trivial. Although the 1989 Tiananmen Square
incident did not seem to stop China from pursuing its open–door policy,
following the world's indignation and retaliation against Beijing, its
impact and ramifications lingered. In its aftermath, the Chinese government accused the United States of instigating the student movement and
meddling with China's internal affairs. In 1980 and 1985, TV programs
from the United States stood out among all foreign programming on
CCTV. The sudden disappearance of U.S. programs on CCTV in 1990
served an explicit and subservient function. By singling out the United
States, it expressed the displeasure of Chinese central authority on the
one hand and constituted a symbolic suspension of cultural relationship
between the two countries on the other hand. Other countries such as
Japan and Britain were not affected.

If the Chinese TV system was as centralized as it used to be in
the 1960s or 1970s, the removal of U.S. programs from CCTV's lineup
should have some demonstration effects on the primetime programs of
regional and local stations. This did not appear to be the case. Because
GTV had never carried anything from the United States throughout the
previous years, it was not surprising that U.S.programs were still miss-

ing in 1990. On the other hand, STV gave U.S. TV programming an impressive share (39%) that year even though it did not pick up any program from the United States in 1980 and 1985. Furthermore, it slated programs from other countries that departed from the foreign TV lineup on the national station. GTV did not follow the complete script of the central TV station, either. The variation between the national and two local stations, especially between CCTV and STV, underscored the regional or local autonomy in broadcast decision making and vertical fragmentation at the organizational levels.

As indicated earlier, within the managerial perspective and amid the unequal distribution and flow of foreign investment and products across China, greater regional difference or horizontal fragmentation in foreign TV programming could be expected. Being part of the economic activities, this inequity of cultural products came out in the number of foreign TV programming on both STV and GTV (Table 3.4). In 1970 when the number of foreign imports was limited, GTV (28.6%) had a higher proportion of foreign programming than that of STV (13.3%), suggesting a lack of local production and a higher degree of dependency on the central supplier CCTV to fill the program hours. When the Cultural Revolution reached its last leg in 1975, both TV stations had a small proportion of foreign programs, indicating the predominance of domestic programming as a consequence of China's suspension of foreign imports. Those TV programs from a select few communist countries still showing on Chinese television, according to Hong (1998), were largely imported in the past years.

Shortly after the reforms started in the early 1980s, the difference in the proportion of imported programs between STV and GTV was minimal. Other than the origins of countries, the proportion of foreign programs actually accounted for a similar share of the total programming on the two stations. When the reform movement accelerated after 1985 and regional and major city TV stations were authorized to import foreign programs, the unequal access to the outside world of information and entertainment became wider. STV notably increased its number of foreign programs, but GTV remained relatively unchanged, with the former running 10 times as many foreign programs as the latter.

This inconsistency in the flow of foreign programs from region to region could be seen in the share of total TV programming over time. Although TV stations in China all reaped the fruits of economic reform and openness, the stride and momentum of each television station were clearly not created equal. As shown in Table 3.4, the proportion of imported programs on STV went up from 4% in 1980 to about 43% during prime time in 1990. In a 10-year time span, the rate of increase was unparalleled at either the national level or regional level. During the

same period, GTV moved from 5.6% to about 16.0%, lagging significantly behind STV. The trend lasted in 1995 when foreign programs on STV
and GTV constituted 12.1% and 8.5% of the total programming, respectively. For CCTV, its proportion of foreign programs remained moderate
and stable. The decrease in the proportion of foreign TV programs on all
three stations during prime time (8 p.m.–10 p.m.) in 1995 largely resulted from the increasing domestic production.

Because the economic environment had improved generally for
the production and dissemination of TV programs around the country
after the reforms jump-started the sluggish conditions in the early 1980s,
the widening gap between STV and GTV could no longer be attributed
to a shortage of domestic programs. Rather, a more plausible explanation is that a larger market base and greater financial reward through
advertising led STV to show more foreign TV programs than did GTV.
After all, foreign companies were allowed to advertise in the Chinese
mass media around the mid-1980s. Television stations in the coastal and
major cities, such as Shanghai, Guangzhou, and Tianjin, naturally
became the prime targets of foreign advertisers because of their wider
reach of audiences with stronger purchasing power. Within this context,
the variance in foreign TV programming serves to indicate the relative
autonomy and degree of freedom different stations now enjoy as to
what to present to their viewers.

FROM PAROCHIAL UNITY TO MULTINATIONAL
DIVERSITY ON CHINESE TV

The discussion here centered around the impact of China's changing
socioeconomic structure on its foreign TV programming over time and
across space. From the national to the local levels, the managerial perspective predicted that the structural pluralism in the Chinese television
broadcasting system would result in a higher capacity of programming
options and greater organizational decision making, hence leading to
the diversity of content and multinational sources. This chapter also presents some unmistakable evidence concerning the effect of decentralization and depoliticization in China's march to economic modernization
on its window on the world, especially the foreign imports on Chinese
television at different levels.

The findings indicated that before the inception of economic
reforms, foreign programs on Chinese television were extremely limited
in quantity and quality, originating essentially from a few Communist
countries. The parochial unity in foreign TV programming demonstrated the centrality and single-dimensionality of the Chinese media system

under the Maoist unyielding rule in terms of the tolerance of competing ideologies and reception of cultural genres. Television became an integrated constituent of a colossal state apparatus bent on molding the deed and thought of the general populace through a calculated selection and presentation of preferred text and context. In foreign programming, Chinese television simply could not represent what was out there without a pre-existing stock of approved images of reality.

The excessive rigidity smeared the Chinese opening to the outside world and stifled the intake of fresh air into China. The pernicious 10-year Cultural Revolution motivated the pragmatic Chinese leadership to reverse the detrimental course by abandoning Mao's utopian blindness and his class struggle that had inflicted on the entire society. Before the outside world could be utilized to help China recover from the near total disaster, it needed to be seen and imagined. The distance between the real and the symbolic must be shortened to prepare the Chinese for the daunting task of rebuilding the nation. A venue had to be found to inject a sense of empathy in the Chinese society. The twofold strategy of economic reforms and open-door policy in the late 1970s and early 1980s was not only empirical, but also theoretically inevitable.

For a vast country like China, closing off the window to pretend the world beyond the Communist polity did not exist was no longer a viable option. The Chinese inability to modernize under Mao's internal self-reliance policy called for an immediate action to resume contact with the external world. As part of the total imports, the flow of foreign TV programming into China represented an opportunity to map the cultural range of vision of the world on the one hand and to survey the sectors of political reality on the other hand. It is not surprising that after the reforms and openness took off, not only did the number of foreign programs flourish dramatically on Chinese television, the assortment of content variety also increased greatly, with capitalist countries becoming the dominant suppliers. The logic of international marketplace apparently outlasted the dogma of communist solidarity.

These phenomena defy the persisted background belief among the Western scholars and researchers that Chinese television, and for that matter all other mass media, have been fundamentally hardwired as a class ideologue since the Communist Party came to power in 1949. The massive and prolonged campaigns of anti-imperialism, anti-feudalism, and anti-capitalism displayed during the fanatic and anarchic Cultural Revolution mayhem appear to further reinforce the received knowledge. The distance between such canonic certainty and the reality in China, however, is too great to illuminate the contemporary Chinese society. It obfuscates clear-sightedness and invites illusion. The findings in this chapter raise serious doubt about the validity of the mass propaganda and persuasion model as a social science inquiry in explaining the commitment and practices of Chinese mass media since the economic reforms and openness.

The central thesis of this chapter is that in the context of managerial perspective, the changing Chinese socioeconomic structure would result in the reconfiguration of perceptions and political orientation about the larger world landscape out there. In the case of TV programming from other countries, it means diversity of content and sources on Chinese television at both the vertical and horizontal levels. From 1970 to 1995, while the origins of programs cut across the ideological spectrum, the former Communist bloc constituted a small and dwindling portion throughout the period whereas the capitalist countries nearly saturated the foreign TV menu, especially after the reforms. This transformation unquestionably results from the rationalization of external open-door policy and internal economic restructuring in China. As illustrated in the comparison between the coastal, affluent station (STV) and the inland, relatively poor station (GTV), the domestic flow of foreign TV programming appears to follow the reason of market priority and viability. Its root could be traced to the differential treatment and redistribution of economic resources across the vast Chinese regions during the reform era.

Because many local, municipal, and provincial stations in China often do not produce their own programming, the rational responses to the changing environment deserve closer attention. They are indicative of content decentralization that shifted away from the uniform circulation of media products throughout the country under the mass propaganda mechanism (e.g., Robinson, 1981). It means organizational TV managers no longer had to choose among a narrow range of programs from a few select communist countries or to come after the central line. Although not necessarily independent of the state ownership or free of political intervention or devoid of Party guidance, there is evidence to believe that Chinese television has become more autonomous and less ideological in its foreign TV programming. Along with the lively and dynamic domestic entertainment programming, Chinese television as a whole has cast away the dry and dreadful stereotypical images as typecast before and during the Cultural Revolution.

The findings in this chapter also provide some evidence regarding the impact of social conflict and disorder like the 1989 Tiananmen Square crackdown on foreign TV programming. As the 10-year reform campaign was picking up momentum in China, the student-led democratic movement in Beijing came to a shocking and tragic end in June 1989. Many scholars and researchers believed that China under the hard-liner's rule would return to the dialectic mode of Maoist practices by using orthodox Communist ideologies in total organizational and social control. For example, J. Yu (1990) noted that "the change in the political climate has affected, and will continue to affect, television development. As the Party heightened ideological control, television content—whether in newscasts or entertainment—had to toe the Party line" (p. 87). Remarks by both Jiang Zemin, secretary general of the Communist Party, and Li Ruihuan, a senior member of the Political Bureau, indicated in late 1989 that the party would tighten the control over the mass media in China (X. Li, 1991). Rhetoric nevertheless appeared to give way to reality.

After the Tiananmen Square incident, China repeatedly stated that its door would remain open to the world outside and economic reforms unchanged. On both counts, China keeps its words and follows through with its deeds. As an indication of that commitment, the flow of foreign TV programming into China has continued unabatedly ever since. The momentum is in favor of the market, not the state. Although the Chinese authority has attempted to place the mass media under more strict control or has to remind them that they are still the organs of the Communist Party (Officials still, 2000), the process of decentralization that has been set in motion and the relative autonomy that many regions have enjoyed make it difficult for the state to successfully turn back the forces of the market.

CHAPTER 4

FORM AND STRUCTURE OF NEWS ON CCTV: PROFESSIONALISM THROUGH TECHNICAL RATIONALITY

Any mass medium, whether Chinese or Western, is an organization itself and part of the broader social system. It is subject to the organizational constraints delimited by internal institutional logic (e.g. Epstein, 1973) or imposed by external social structure (e.g., Ball-Rokeach & Cantor, 1986). Its state ownership aside, CCTV is no exception. Although CCTV's organizational character and concerns may be different from those of Western television stations because of its submissive position under the larger political configuration, there should be little doubt that the Chinese national television network, for all its purposes and functions, must work within the parameters of available resources, access to sources, routines, and time limits in its programming. Among others, these factors mediate between the reality out there and the one constructed in the news media.

Either by design or by default, the mediating factors entail order and tempo on the standard operating procedures of media organizations in the processes of production, dissemination, and consumption. For the most part, the news on television faces more acute technical challenges, such as speed and use of visual images, than other types of media products. If "the medium is the message," as McLuhan (1964) argued, then the form of news is relatively autonomous, carrying its own story that is not necessarily part of the content (e.g., Griffin, 1992). As far as the mode is concerned, television in China is predicated very much on the same working principle. Mostly free of ideological influences, the technical rationality of CCTV news, if any, underscores the extent to which Chinese television strives to be professional in its delivery and presentation.

The 7 p.m. *Xinwen Lianbo* (network news) on CCTV is a prime-time evening news program that comprises of a domestic segment, including foreign policy and international relations stories, and a foreign segment at the end of the newscast. It is presented by a pair of anchorpersons: one female and the other male. Unlike their Western counterparts, they usually open the broadcast with a brief greeting, followed by an outline of major stories and ending with a recap of the day's top stories. During the study period, even the wording of the introduction changed, demonstrating ostensibly the transformation of the conception of audiences.

. In 1992, the anchorperson on CCTV would begin by saying "viewers and comrades" before introducing the highlights. In the Chinese vocabulary, a comrade is someone who shares a common interest in or devotion to a political ideology. The inclusion of the word *comrades* in reference to the vast viewers who were usually unknown signifies the explicit politicization of TV viewing. Along with the use of comrades in the news stories, such terminology certainly could be traced to a time when the Communist ideas and practices dominated the everyday life in China. It was later changed in 1998 to "viewers and friends," a phrase clearly devoid of ideological or political connotation. The more neutralized identification to some extent removes the politically sensitive designation and experience for television viewers in China.

On the *Xinwen Lianbo,* no commercial is allowed during the newscast. The actual amount of time for foreign news varies according to the length of domestic segment. The CCTV network news program is usually preceded or followed by a 15- or 30-minute local newscast on a different channel at the provincial or local levels. Important national news may be carried on the local channel before CCTV's network news goes on the air. Notwithstanding, as noted in chapter 1, CCTV's network news has been the most authoritative source of news and announcements. The foreign news segment was introduced in 1976, with footage provided by international news agencies. In April 1980, with agreements with the British Visnews and U.S. UPITN, CCTV began broadcasting foreign news on a daily basis. Since then, the division of the two main segments has remained unchanged. A brief CCTV logo separates the two segments. Sports stories are often presented at the end of domestic news.

During the study period from 1992 to 1998, as shown in Table 4.1, the number of stories per newscast showed a decreasing trend. On the average, CCTV carried about 32 stories per newscast in 1992. It was higher than the 28 stories in 1985 (Warren, 1988). The number dropped slightly 4 years later to 30 stories in 1996. It had a dramatic cut in 1998 with about 22 stories per newscast. This decrease in the number of stories per newscast occurred in both the domestic and foreign segments. In the former, the number of stories per newscast changed from about 23 stories in 1992 to about 16 stories in 1998. In the latter, it decreased from about 10 stories per newscast in 1992 to 6 stories in 1998. Given the small number of stories per newscast in the foreign segment, the proportion of its drop was more significant than that in the domestic portion. The shrinking foreign news has raised some concerns among TV critics over the amount of attention given to the outside world (Pei, 2000). The following sections examine the technical aspects of CCTV news.[1]

TYPES OF NEWS ON CCTV

Like that of any other TV stations, the type of news on CCTV can be classified into three categories: domestic news, foreign news, and for-

Table 4.1: Number of Stories per Newscast on CCTV News, 1992–1998

Segment of News	1992	1996	1998
Domestic segment[a]	22.8	21.4	15.6
Foreign segment[b]	9.5	8.8	6.0
Total newscast	32.3	30.2	21.6
Number of stories	840	754	582
Number of days	26	25	27

[a]Domestic segment includes domestic news and foreign policy news. It also includes "foreign news at home" and "home news abroad." For definitions of domestic news, foreign news and foreign policy news, see notes in Table 4.2.

[b]Foreign segment is separated from the domestic segment by a brief CCTV logo. It may be preceded by a sport story. Stories about international relations involving China from a foreign country's point of view are often included in this segment.

[1]For the CCTV news data and the coding scheme used in the content analysis, see the appendix.

eign policy news. Domestic news refers to stories about the activities of domestic individuals, groups, or other entities in China that do not involve any foreign country or Chinese diplomacy. It includes "home news abroad," which describes mainly the activities of domestic individuals, groups, or other entities in a foreign country (e.g., Chinese sports activities overseas), but does not clearly engage China's diplomatic activities or international relations with the host country. As shown in chapters 6 and 7, the distinction between foreign news and foreign policy news is important because they underline two different dimensions—foreign image versus government policy. Different concepts evidently have varying domains with differing indicators.

By definition, foreign policy involves discrete governmental actions "intended by the decision makers to influence the behavior of international actors external to their own polity" (Hermann, 1972, p. 72). It specifies a deliberate effort of countries in the international context. The reporting of foreign policy hence deals with the news about a country's foreign policy, whether in words or in action, toward another nation (e.g., President Clinton's visit to China in 1998 or Chinese President Jiang's trip to the United States in 1997), whereas the reporting of foreign news concerns events or issues occurring in country that has nothing to do with the country whose news media are under study. In the Chinese mass media, for example, the story about school shootings in the United States is foreign news.

Foreign policy news, therefore, is "distinct from general foreign news" and "involves the relationships among nations and their efforts to make their way in the world and manage the problems this presents" (Trattner, 1982, pp. 103-111). Furthermore, not all foreign news is relevant to foreign policy questions of government interests (Davison, Shannon, & Yu, 1980). As Cohen (1963) indicated, "a large part of what is properly called 'foreign news' is not, strictly speaking, foreign policy news—i.e., it does not deal with foreign policy or international affairs" (p. 10). Simply put, foreign news lacks a key ingredient in foreign policy news: domestic implications or cross-national ramifications. In other words, involvement or relevance to the host country's interests sets the two categories of news apart.

The differences between foreign news and foreign policy news cannot be underestimated. Conceptually, foreign news constitutes the world landscape as seen by China without its being part of the picture. It is the world "out there" that China sees "from here." Foreign policy news clearly dwells on China's position in the world in relation to that of other countries. It is the world that is viewed according to the degree of Chinese participation in international matters. Between these two settings, the ranges of vision and the sectors of total reality (e.g., Mannheim,

1936) that can be observed are certainly different. "To deny there is no difference in the journalistic views between here and there," as Chang (1999) argued, "is to accept the conceptual implausibility that our perspective of the world does not change according to where we may stand and what we perceive in it" (p. 35). In news reporting, one of the consequences of such structural differentiation is the amount of attention given to each worldview that is prearranged in accordance to some technical rules, organizational philosophy, or scheduling considerations.

Except for some specific programs (e.g., *CNN World Report*) that gear toward a worldwide audience, no television station in any country would ever devote less time or space to domestic news than to foreign stories. Given that relevance or proximity, both social and psychological, is part of the elements of newsworthiness, ethnocentrism or regionalism in foreign news reporting (e.g., Wilke, 1987) is thus a matter of degree, not kind. Countries undoubtedly would report more about themselves first or what is happening within their own geopolitical sphere. They would then go beyond the national boundaries to include the news in remote settings as they see fit. Oftentimes, as is true in most countries, when there are more domestic stories to report, their presence tends to cut into the time slots or space reserved for foreign news. This is particularly true in the Soviet style media system where the zero-sum environment generally gives the state an upper hand in the monopoly and distribution of news content in society (e.g., Mickiewicz, 1999).

Although the economic reforms have transformed the Chinese mass media from a rigid command system to one with a market orientation, the media environment is still guided by the principles of zero-sum game. The limitations of time and space mean that the production, organization, and distribution of television news must conform to the ground rules delimited by the economic and technical rationality (e.g., Gruneau & Hackett, 1990), if it is to be effectively and efficiently processed in the "news factory" (Bantz, McCorkle, & Baade, 1981). Technically, the division of news on CCTV follows very much the same journalistic rules: Domestic news and foreign policy news take a lion's share of the 30-minute newscast, with the rest for foreign news at a smaller proportion.

During the study period, excluding news highlights at the beginning and the recaps at the end of newscast, CCTV's network news had between 28 minutes and 29 minutes of air time for presentation of news on the prime-time evening broadcast. As reported in Table 4.2, it devoted an overall average of 17.1 minutes to domestic news, 5.7 minutes to foreign news, and 5.6 minutes to foreign policy news. With the highlights, recaps, and promotions for other news-related shows appearing in the later years, the length of broadcast per newscast on CCTV has declined

Table 4.2: Minutes of Broadcast per Newscast on CCTV, 1992–1998

Type of News	1992	1996	1998	Total
Domestic News[a]	14.6	19.6	17.2	17.1
Foreign News[b]	7.8	5.1	4.1	5.7
Foreign Policy News[c]	6.8	3.6	6.4	5.6
Total	29.2	28.3	27.7	

[a]Domestic news refers to stories about the activities of domestic individuals, groups or other entities in China that do not involve any foreign country. It includes "home news abroad" that describes mainly the activities of domestic individuals, groups or other entities in a foreign country, but does not clearly involve any diplomatic activities or international relations with the host country. A negligible percentage of stories falls into this category. They deal with Chinese sport activities overseas.

[b]Foreign news refers to stories about the activities of foreign individuals, groups or other entities in any other country that do not involve China. It includes "foreign news at home" that describes the activities of foreign individuals, groups or other entities in China, but does not clearly involve any diplomatic activities or international relations with China. A negligible percentage of stories falls into this category. They deal with foreign tourists in China.

[c]Foreign policy news includes stories about both foreign policy and international relations. Foreign policy refers to discrete governmental actions intended by the decision makers to influence the behavior of international actors external to the Chinese polity. International relations concerns foreign relationships, such as joint ventures, trade and cultural exchanges between China and at least one other country. It does not necessarily involve governmental activities.

steadily. The shortened newscast apparently cut into the amount of time given to foreign news. In 1985, foreign news on CCTV averaged 7.4 minutes per newscast (Warren, 1988). This amount remained very much the same at 7.8 minutes in 1992. It dropped by more than 2 minutes in 1996 and was reduced further by 1 more minute in 1998 (Table 4.2). Since then, the amount of time allotted to foreign news on CCTV has remained below 5 minutes at about 4 minutes (Pei, 2000).

The fact that less time was devoted to foreign news does not necessarily mean, however, a smaller proportion of any newscast accounted for by foreign news on CCTV. According to Warren (1988), the foreign portion took up 26.4% of the average newscast on CCTV in 1985. This proportion increased slightly throughout the study period. As shown in

Table 4.3, from 1992 to 1998, domestic news accounted for more than 50% of the stories carried on the CCTV network news, followed by foreign news at about 29% and foreign policy news at 17%. Although there were variations in the number of stories among the three types of news, the ups and downs obviously took place between domestic news and foreign policy news. In other words, if more foreign policy stories were covered, they were done at the expense of domestic news and vice versa. The proportion of foreign stories tends to be stable over the years, even though the amount of time has given way to other two categories.

From a long-term point of view, the division of news types on CCTV turns out to be highly similar during the study period, with a ratio of 71% of domestic/foreign policy news and 29% of foreign news. Because the data sets in 1992 and 1998 were taken from the same time span (from June 15 to July 15), the remarkable consistency in the form of news suggests the institutionalization of a window on the outside world. Although the opening time of that window on foreign news has been shortened considerably from 1985 to 1998, its size stays unaltered. This news radar should allow Chinese viewers an opportunity to take a glimpse of the world out there. What that world is, as discussed in chapter 6, depends on the interplay of two separate and discrete processes: what really exists and how Chinese television chooses to report it. As is true in any TV broadcast, the length of its reporting confers a status of prominence of the events or issues involved.

LENGTH OF NEWS ON CCTV

The frequency of a particular type of news on television, and for that matter in all other news media, tells something about its salience in both

Table 4.3: Type of News on CCTV, 1992–1998

Type of News[a]	1992	1996	1998	Total
Domestic news	50.5%	60.3%	50.3%	53.9%
Foreign news	29.4	29.2	27.7	28.9
Foreign policy news	20.1	10.5	22.0	17.3
Total	840	754	582	2,176

$X^2 = 41.0$, $df = 4$, $p < .01$

[a]For description of type of news, see notes in Table 4.2.

the organizational and journalistic sense. Organizationally, the location of correspondents and the availability of resources (e.g., camera crews) may determine how often stories of specific nature or origin get covered (e.g., Graber, 1993). Journalistically, the notion of a news net (e.g., Tuchman, 1978) necessitates the inclusion of certain kinds of stories from the local to international levels. Frequency is only part of the story, however. The length of news goes beyond the threshold of what to cover by adding depth to the story. In countries around the world, it is not what, but how much, a story is reported on television that gives it a flavor of significance, at least in the eyes of those who produce it. On the Chinese television, the length of news is unquestionably an indication of its importance and, by implication, its subtle invitation for public attention to the person or issue under observation.

The decrease in the number of stories per newscast on CCTV (Table 4.1) obviously results in the increase in the length of the news (Table 4.4). During the study period, the average length of a news story on the Chinese national television network was expanded from 54 sec-

Table 4.4: Length of News on CCTV, 1992–1998[a]

Type of News[b]	1992[c]	1996[d]	1998[e]	Total
Foreign policy news[f]	62.6 (57.0)	67.6 (50.8)	80.5 (64.2)	69.8 (58.8)
Domestic news[g]	53.8 (58.5)	64.7 (70.4)	95.1 (79.1)	68.3 (70.6)
Foreign news[h]	49.5 (17.7)	34.5 (23.5)	41.7 (29.6)	42.3 (24.1)
Total	54.3 (49.9)	56.2 (60.1)	77.1 (69.3)	

[a]Entries are average length in seconds. Figures in parentheses are the standard deviation. A low standard deviation means the lengths of news stories are tightly clustered around the mean. A high standard deviation indicates that the news stories are widely dispersed.

[b]For description of type of news, see notes in Table 4.2.

[c]$F = 3.52, p < .05$

[d]$F = 21.37, p < .01$

[e]$F = 34.65, p < .01$

[f]$F = 3.49, p < .05$

[g]$F = 32.35, p < .01$

[h]$F = 24.38, p < .01$

onds in 1992 to 77 seconds in 1998. This expansion took place in both foreign policy news and domestic news, but not necessarily in foreign news. In fact, although foreign news on CCTV maintained a steady proportion of all news stories (Table 4.3), its length shrunk in the face of other stretching stories. It is apparent that the limited amount of time (between 4 and 8 minutes) did not leave much room for longer stories from abroad that might affect the breadth of China's survey of foreign landscape.

Compared to the earlier data (Warren, 1988),[2] the length of domestic news on CCTV increased from 64.3 seconds in 1985 to 95.1 seconds in 1998, whereas the length of foreign news decreased from 49.8 seconds to 41.7 seconds during the same time span. When the news about both China's internal and external behaviors was combined, its average length exceeded 2 minutes (138.1 seconds), more than three times of the length of foreign news (42.3 seconds). Of the three types of news, foreign policy news tended to be the longest. Although fewer than one in five stories on CCTV's network news from 1992 to 1998 was about China's foreign policy or international relations (Table 4.3), this type of news was usually longer than either domestic or foreign news. It speaks of the significance accorded to China's diplomatic activities and international relations in its window on the world for the Chinese viewers to see. What they might find, as shown in chapter 7, is a world that was projected from the vantage point of view of official China as an active member in the community of nations.

Several things are worth noting in Table 4.4. First, the larger standard deviations for both foreign policy news and domestic news on CCTV indicate that they were more widely dispersed than foreign news, suggesting that their lengths varied greatly from newscast to newscast or from year to year. The length of foreign news stories, however, tended to be tightly clustered around the mean, implying that they did not deviate significantly from the average story. In other words, foreign stories seemed to be given a consistent amount of time. Second, at any

---

[2]Strictly speaking, the 1985 data were not directly comparable because Warren's study did not distinguish between foreign news and foreign policy news. His data of domestic and foreign news on CCTV in 1985 included stories of international relations. According to Warren (1988), domestic stories on international relations pictured the Chinese government as "significant on the world scene" whereas "many of the 'foreign' stories dealt with Chinese diplomatic activities in other countries" (p. 222). It is obvious that these stories concerned China's foreign policy and international relations. As such, Warren's data might have inflated the length of both domestic and foreign news stories because of his failure to separate foreign policy news from either category. Still, with 20 newscasts in 1985, his data provide some useful baseline for comparison from a historical point of view.

given point in time during the study period, foreign news had the short-est length, averaging from about 35 seconds to less than 50 seconds. Foreign policy news often outplayed the other two types of news, with its stories taking an average of more than 1 minute to broadcast throughout the newscasts. Its length trailed only to that of domestic news in 1998. The lengthy domestic stories, particularly those regarding meetings, were one reason that prompted former head of CCTV, Yang Weikuan, to lament the small share of news that really concerned the interest of the people (B. Li, 2000).

Third, there is a tendency for the lengths of foreign policy news and domestic news to increase consistently over time. The opposite appears to be true for foreign news. Fourth, the data show the conceptu-al importance of classifying the news into three distinctive categories because of the apparent amount of time placed on different types of news and their implications. As shown in later chapters, the world CCTV presents to the Chinese viewers through either foreign policy news or foreign news represents divergent worldviews.

Individually, the average duration indicates the relative amount of time or attention a typical story may command in comparison to the other types of news in a given newscast. Collectively, the proportion of stories having the same length demonstrates the extent to which certain type of stories has the power to saturate the available air time. It is also an indication of the overall importance that the Chinese national televi-sion might have placed on different types of news. Because the amount of television news time is fixed, for every minute devoted to a given type of news, another minute is lost to other kinds of stories. One appar-ent consequence of such zero-sum equation in the newscast is that the higher the proportion of a particular type of news appearing, for exam-ple, in longer stories, the lower the percentage of other types of news to be in a similar length. This structural constraint makes differential treat-ment of news more profound.

In Table 4.5, more than 8 out of 10 foreign news stories, but only 6 out of 10 stories in domestic and foreign policy news, on CCTV had a run time of less than 1 minute. From 1992 to 1998, no more than 20% of the foreign news stories under study in each year enjoyed an air time of greater than 1 minute. For domestic and foreign policy news, the pro-portion of stories taking up more than a minute expanded from 20% in 1992 to more than 50% in 1998. Although most of the stories in foreign news were short, more stories in domestic and foreign policy news became longer as time went by. Rarely did foreign news stories (1.8%) get reported in more than 2 minutes even though the amount had been increasing from less than 1% in 1992 to 4.3% in 1998. Moreover, no story in foreign news was ever longer than 3 minutes, compared to at least 5%

Table 4.5: Variation of Story Length on CCTV, 1992–1998

	1992	1996	1998	Subtotal
Domestic News				
Less than 1 minute	76.2%	63.5%	39.2%	62.0%
1 minute to 2 minutes	17.5	22.0	35.2	23.6
2 minutes to 3 minutes	4.0	9.2	15.4	8.9
More than 3 minutes	2.4	5.3	10.2	5.5
Subtotal	424	455	293	1,172
Foreign News				
Less than 1 minute	79.4%	90.5%	81.4%	83.8%
1 minute to 2 minutes	20.2	8.2	14.3	14.5
2 minutes to 3 minutes	0.4	1.4	4.3	1.8
More than 3 minutes	—	—	—	—
Subtotal	247	220	161	628
Foreign Policy News				
Less than 1 minute	69.8%	51.9%	49.2%	59.0%
1 minute to 2 minutes	20.7	40.5	35.2	29.8
2 minutes to 3 minutes	5.3	2.5	9.4	6.1
More than 3 minutes	4.1	5.1	6.3	5.1
Subtotal	169	79	128	376
Total	840	754	582	2,176

[a]Two minutes and 1 second to 3 minutes

of the stories in either domestic or foreign policy news. This means that domestic and foreign policy news stories were more likely to be covered in greater depth on CCTV, especially when they were at least 3 minutes long, than was foreign news that lasted mostly less than 1 minute.

TIMELINESS OF NEWS ON CCTV

The amount of time allocated to each type of news and the proportion of stories reported in a certain length of time are measures of emphasis in news reporting. Time has another dimension that is a vital component of professionalism: timeliness. Without a timely report, the news would be less competitive in the marketplace of ideas and therefore would not be appealing to the audiences as a key source of information. For television in the information age, timeliness becomes imperative, whether in China or elsewhere. According to the most authoritative Chinese journalism dictionary (Gan, 1993), "timeliness is constrained by the tempo of social life and the technology of information communication. The pursuit of timeliness is one of the goals of modern journalism industry" (p. 14). Content aside, the presentation of news on television, therefore, has a time value in that its report of events or issues often loses newsworthiness after the lapse of certain hours or days.

Following the economic reforms in the early 1980s, part of the Chinese journalism reform is the requirement that the news be fast, short, and good (e.g., X. Sun, 1994). To be fast in news reporting means to be timely. In this study, timeliness refers to the time lag between the occurrences of events or issues and its reporting on CCTV's network news. It was analyzed in six different categories: today, unidentified, recently/this week, yesterday, last week/last month, and future. Improvement of this technical journalistic standard is most discernible on CCTV news, particularly in domestic and foreign policy arenas, during the study period.

Table 4.6 reveals that more than 70% of the domestic stories reported on CCTV news in 1992 either took place recently or this week (30%) or had an unidentified time of occurrence (41.5%). All these stories tended to feature agricultural progress, economic development, and business practices in coastal and inland areas. With only 23.6% of the domestic stories occurring either today or yesterday, timeliness apparently was not a major concern for CCTV news. What matters obviously is the stories themselves. This phenomenon changed in 1996 when the proportion of domestic stories taking place today increased substantially to 33.4% and that of stories with time unidentified or occurring recently/this week dropped considerably. The trend continued in 1998 as about 55% of the domestic stories was reported on the same day (46.4%) or within a day of their occurrence (8.5%). This was the most noticeable speed-up in timeliness of CCTV news. It certainly indicates a journalistic devotion to move the stories faster on the pipeline of national television.

The timing of foreign policy news was significantly better than that of domestic news on CCTV. As indicated in Table 4.6, more than two thirds of the foreign policy stories (70.4%) were reported on the day (today, 34.9%) or within a day (yesterday, 35.5%) it happened in 1992. The proportion reached around 85% in 1996 and 1998. This increase was accompanied by the decrease in foreign policy stories with unknown

Table 4.6: Timeliness of News on CCTV, 1992–1998

	1992	1996	1998	Subtotal
Domestic News				
Today	17.0%	33.4%	46.4%	30.7%
Unidentified	41.5	27.0	20.1	30.5
Recently/this week	30.0	27.9	21.8	27.1
Yesterday	6.6	9.5	8.5	8.2
Last week/last month	3.1	1.1	1.0	1.8
Future	1.9	1.1	2.0	1.6
Subtotal	424	455	293	1,172
Foreign News				
Yesterday	70.0%	69.1%	72.0%	70.2%
Recently/this week	18.6	18.2	9.9	16.2
Today	4.5	8.2	14.9	8.4
Unidentified	6.1	4.1	2.5	4.5
Last week/last month	0.8	–	–	0.4
Future	–	0.5	0.6	0.3
Subtotal	247	220	161	628
Foreign Policy News				
Today	34.9%	64.6%	57.0%	48.7%
Yesterday	35.5	20.3	28.1	29.8
Unidentified	14.2	11.4	6.3	10.9
Recently/this week	13.0	1.3	5.5	8.0
Future	0.6	2.5	2.3	1.6
Last week/last month	1.8	–	0.8	1.1
Subtotal	169	79	128	376
Total	840	754	582	2,176

time occurrence from 14.2% in 1992 to 6.3% in 1998. The number of foreign policy stories that were several days old (recently or this week) also declined significantly during the study period. Undoubtedly, CCTV has been increasingly capable of bringing foreign policy news to the viewers in a more timely fashion. When the content overrides the necessity of timeliness on CCTV, however, stories that would be considered old in the Western sense of newsworthiness might see the light of the day.

Although the number was small, both the domestic news and foreign policy news on CCTV occasionally reported stories that happened last week or even last month. This was particularly true in 1992. Again, for these stories, timeliness was evidently irrelevant. What transpired is the content that mostly highlighted different aspects of national construction, social order, and technological progress in China, such as economic reform, industrial and agricultural production, transportation development and capacity, and anti-drug campaigns. A few were obituaries about prominent Communist party members. As seen in chapter 5, obituaries about major governmental or Communist party figures, whether brief eulogies or detailed accounts, are a unique part of Chinese national television news that generally finds no counterparts in many other countries. It is often an obligatory tribute to those who have made contributions to the party or the country through their individual work or position in the sociopolitical structure.

Due to the time difference between China and many other countries, foreign news on CCTV could not, for the most part, be reported on the day it happened. Nevertheless, a clear trend emerges in Table 4.6, showing that a growing number of foreign news stories were reported "today." In 1992, CCTV carried about 5% of foreign news stories on the same day of their occurrence. Seven years later, in 1998, the number nearly tripled to about 15%. Considering the different time zones involved, the high proportion of foreign news (70%) reported as "yesterday" from 1992 to 1998 on CCTV was as timely as it could be. Throughout the years, the number of foreign news stories with an unknown time occurrence also decreased from 6.1% in 1992 to 2.5% in 1998. This decreasing pattern is similar to that in both domestic and foreign policy news, suggesting a common inclination of CCTV to identify the time element in its news reporting.

If timeliness is any indication of professionalism, the data in Table 4.6 unquestionably demonstrate that CCTV has increasingly become more immediate in its news reporting. From 1992 to 1998, the most conspicuous turnaround in speedy coverage could be found in the domestic news. As far as timeliness of news is concerned, however, there is still room for improvement in the domestic area on CCTV news as more than one quarter of stories during the entire study period was reported several days after they happened. Other than those events that are prearranged or pre-rehearsed, the absence of immediacy in the news reporting on Chinese television, it is argued (X. Li, 1999), makes TV no better than films. The Chinese national network news seldom carried any spontaneous broadcast.

FORMATS OF NEWS ON CCTV

For television news, timeliness is one of the descriptive characteristics at the story level that include length, formats and use of visual images. According to Larson (1984), each of the major formats—anchor report, domestic video report, and foreign video report—"has important implications concerning the newsgathering and selection process of the network news division" (p. 37).

As a state-sponsored and controlled media institution, CCTV differs significantly from any of the U.S. commercial networks in terms of its relationship with the powers that be and its function and role in the marketplace of ideas. Being a television organization, however, CCTV needs, by default, as much video image as any other TV stations around the world. As observed by Warren in 1985 (1988), "Chinese television news has an enormous appetite for images" (p. 223). This visual imperative can only be determined by looking at the use of video. Unfortunately, Warren did not analyze how CCTV news used the videos or where they might come from. This chapter represents the first systematic analysis of news formats on CCTV.

Four kinds of news formats were examined: domestic video report, foreign video report, anchor report with no video, and commentary. The use or the absence of video suggests the way pictures may be used by CCTV to shape the view of the world presented in the news. It also shows the extent to which CCTV news gathers or selects the images to go with the various types of stories. This is a function for the visual elements to lend "confirmation and authority" to the verbal reports (Griffin, 1992). As an old Chinese saying points out, "seeing once is better than listening 100 times." The visual information brings an impeccable quality to television news.

Table 4.7 presents an overall distribution of news formats on CCTV, regardless of the type of news involved. Unlike the U.S. commercial television networks, the Chinese national network news never had a single live coverage during the entire study period. In fact, sources familiar with the operation of CCTV news indicated that the 7 p.m. network news was pretaped and edited before it was aired. This apparently is a function of political consideration. According to John Jirik (CCTV consultant, personal communication, January 5, 2000), the Xinwen Lianbo on CCTV "has had live presenters since 1997, but none of the reports are live. The reason is it is not possible to censor the news properly if the reports are live." Like other types of programs, the taped broadcast is considered to be the biggest problem on the Chinese television today (X. Li, 1999).

One thing stands out from the data in Table 4.7: CCTV hardly presented any commentary in its newscast during the study period. In

Table 4.7: Format of News on CCTV, 1992–1998

Format of News	1992	1996	1998	Total
Domestic video report[a]	64.3%	62.7%	57.7%	62.0%
Foreign video report[b]	22.7	29.6	32.0	27.6
Anchor report/no video	12.9	7.7	9.8	10.2
Commentary	0.1	–	0.5	0.2
Total	840	754	582	2,176

$X^2 = 30.32$, $df = 6$, $p < .01$

[a]Domestic video report includes "foreign news at home."

[b]Foreign video report includes "home news abroad" and foreign policy/international relations concerning China reported in a foreign country.

1992 and 1998, a few commentaries were added at the end of some feature stories as "editorial epilogues." These rare editorial epilogues dealt with the best counties in China, police–citizen relationship of a local township, workers' welfare at a motor company, and competitive services of public transportation. The tone of these editorial epilogues was inspirational or even approving of what was reported in the news.

Given that domestic news dominated the CCTV prime-time evening broadcast (see Table 4.3), it is natural that domestic video reports accounted for more than 60% of visual images during the 1992–1998 period. What is telling is that the proportion of domestic video reports gradually declined from 64.3% in 1992 to 57.7% in 1998. So did the anchor reports with no video. The decrease in domestic video reports and anchor reports with no video obviously translated into the increase in foreign video reports. The proportion of foreign video reports shifted from less than one quarter of stories (22.7% in 1992) to nearly one third of stories (32.0% in 1998). A logical question to ask is: What contributes to the expanding use of foreign video? Table 4.8 details the breakdown of video uses on CCTV news.

It is evident that there is a close relationship between the types of news and the source of videos used on CCTV. During the study period, nearly 9 out of 10 domestic stories carried video reports supplied by the Chinese sources, whereas 1 in 10 had no video at all. From 1992 to

Table 4.8: Comparison of Format of News on CCTV, 1992–1998[a]

	1992	1996	1998	Subtotal
Domestic News[b]				
Domestic video report	89.6%	91.2%	84.3%	88.9%
Anchor report/no video	10.1	7.7	14.7	10.3
Foreign video report	–	1.1	–	0.4
Commentary	0.1	–	0.3	0.3
Subtotal	424	455	293	1,172
Foreign News[c]				
Foreign video report	75.5%	92.3%	95.7%	86.6%
Anchor report/no video	15.8	5.5	0.6	8.3
Domestic video report	8.5	2.3	3.7	5.1
Subtotal	247	220	161	628
Foreign Policy News[d]				
Domestic video report	82.2%	67.1%	64.8%	73.1%
Foreign video report	2.4	19.0	25.0	13.6
Anchor report/no video	15.4	13.9	10.2	13.3
Subtotal	169	79	128	376
Total	840	754	582	2,176

[a]For description of domestic video report and foreign video report, see notes in Table 4.7.

[b]$X^2 = 23.01$, $df = 6$, $p < .01$

[c] $X^2 = 45.73$, $df = 4$, $p < .01$

[d]$X^2 = 34.72$, $df = 4$, $p < .01$

1998, there was a slight increase in the use of anchor report with no video. These stories covered a wide variety of topics, with the majority focusing on economic policies, political activities, announcement of laws and measures against crime and corruption, and obituaries. Such reports apparently were part of the practices aimed at publicizing official commitments or acknowledgment of individual contributions to China. The visual was, therefore, less significant than the audio.

In foreign news, a reversed pattern existed between the use of foreign video reports and anchor reports with no video. As the proportion of foreign video reports climbed steadily from about 76% in 1992 to about 96% in 1998, the proportion of anchor reports with no video dropped significantly from about 16% to less than 1%. The changing pattern indicates that foreign news stories on CCTV have mostly reported with visual images in the background. As is shown later, the essence of these images sketches changing views of the internal and external world over time. One thing that CCTV tried to do is "to rewrite the stories based on the original video, based on the original scripts" in order "to add Chinese perspective with foreign news agency video" (Jiang, cited in Jirik, 2001, p. 25).

In contrast to domestic and foreign news, a different pattern of video use can be seen in foreign policy news on CCTV. Without the conceptual separation between foreign news and foreign policy news, this distinctive configuration and its implications would be lost because the use of foreign video reports in foreign policy news could be subsumed by its inclusion as part of either domestic or foreign news, as was the case in Warren's (1988) study. As noted earlier, mixing foreign news and foreign policy news as a single concept would obfuscate, not illuminate the subtle nuance that might help explain how television selects and presents the news. Given the longer time devoted to China's foreign policy news, it is conceptually essential to treat the two categories separately.

The data in Table 4.8 reveal some important aspects about the way the Chinese national television network used video in its newsgathering process. For one thing, most of the Chinese foreign policy stories were reported within domestic parameters during the study period (73.1%). A closer examination of these stories show that the visual images were often taken inside the official government compound or the People's Hall in Beijing, hence projecting an unequivocal image of the world coming to China. From 1992 to 1998, however, there was a tendency of decreasing use of domestic video reports. The proportion of foreign policy news stories with domestic video reports saw a sharp decline from 82% in 1992 to about 65% in 1998.

At the same time, the proportion of foreign video reports involving China's foreign policy or international relations rose from a mere 2% in 1992 to 25% of all stories in 1998 on CCTV. A detailed look at these stories with foreign video reports indicates that they depicted China from foreign locations at two standpoints of observation. On the one hand, China was cast as a powerful member of the community of nations in an international setting, such as the United Nations, by its presence in the world organizations. On the other hand, it was identified as a key factor in other countries' foreign policy design, especially that of the United States, either through the initiative of other nations or China's own diplomatic activities abroad. An unmistakable image was China going to the world and playing a major role or becoming an influential actor in international affairs. The galaxy of images of diplomats and dignitaries gracing the Chinese national television in both domestic and foreign context is indicative of where China places itself on the global geopolitical stage.

CCTV's emphasis on the use of video reports is also reflected in the extended length of formats of news. From 1992 to 1998, the average length of anchor reports with no video showed no statistical difference over time, as indicated in Table 4.9. In 1992, the average length of stories with video reports or no video at all did not display any difference among the three major types of formats, either. Since then, however, domestic video reports increased from less than 60 seconds in 1992 to a little more than 90 seconds in 1998. In both 1996 and 1998, domestic video reports were apparently much longer than that of the other two formats. For the foreign video reports, the average length dropped slightly from about 53 seconds in 1992 to 47 seconds in 1998.

Across the three types of news (Table 4.10), the length of domestic video reports all became longer, with domestic news the longest (102

Table 4.9: Length of Format of News on CCTV, 1992–1998[a]

Format of News	1992[b]	1996[c]	1998[d]	Total
Domestic Video Report[e]	54.9 (47.2)	67.2 (67.5)	97.5 (76.8)	69.8 (65.1)
Anchor report/no video[f]	54.3 (87.6)	40.7 (59.7)	57.7 (55.0)	51.6 (73.6)
Foreign video report[g]	52.7 (18.5)	36.8 (31.1)	47.1 (40.8)	45.0 (32.1)
Commentary	35 (0)	–	30.3 (9.8)	31.5 (8.4)
Total	54.3 (49.9)	56.2 (60.1)	77.1 (69.3)	

[a]Entries are average length in seconds. Figures in parentheses are the standard deviation. A low standard deviation means the lengths of news stories are tightly clustered around the mean. A high standard deviation indicates that the news stories are widely dispersed.

[b]$F = .143, p =$ n.g.

[c]$F = 22.69, p < .01$

[d]$F = 26.36, p < .01$

[e]$F = 48.09, p < .01$

[f]$F = .90, p =$ n.g.

[g]$F = 13.76, p < .01$

Table 4.10: Comparison of Length of Format on CCTV, 1992–1998[a]

	1992	1996	1998	Total
Domestic News				
Domestic video report	51.3 (41.9)	66.3 (70.3)	101.9 (80.8)	69.3 (67.2)
Anchor report/no video	76.5 (134.6)	45.7 (75.1)	60.8 (58.7)	62.0 (96.4)
Foreign video report	–	60.0 (13.6)	–	60.0 (13.6)
Commentary	35.0 (0)	–	30.3 (9.8)	31.5 (8.4)
Total	53.8 (58.5)	64.7 (70.4)	95.1 (79.1)	
Foreign News				
Domestic video report	46.4 (12.7)	89.4 (50.8)	93.2 (34.8)	61.9 (33.3)
Foreign video report	52.5 (17.9)	33.7 (21.5)	39.9 (27.7)	41.9 (23.7)
Anchor report/no video	37.1 (13.0)	24.3 (6.1)	24.0 (0)	33.9 (12.9)
Total	49.5 (17.7)	34.5 (23.5)	41.7 (29.6)	
Foreign Policy News				
Foreign video report	64.3 (40.1)	70.5 (84.2)	81.9 (68.3)	77.1 (70.8)
Domestic video report	66.2 (60.9)	71.9 (40.9)	84.7 (64.6)	72.9 (59.1)
Anchor report/no video	43.2 (27.2)	42.6 (26.1)	49.9 (43.2)	44.8 (31.4)
Total	62.6 (57.0)	67.6 (50.8)	80.5 (64.2)	

[a]For description of domestic video report and foreign video report, see notes in Table 4.7.

seconds) in 1998, followed by foreign news (93 seconds), and foreign policy news (85 seconds), respectively. In foreign news, although infrequent (see Table 4.8), the domestic video reports were relatively longer than foreign video reports. They involved "foreign news at home," dealing with stories about foreign residents or visitors to China that had nothing to do with diplomatic or governmental activities. During the entire study period, the fact that domestic video reports concerning foreign news in China (61.9 seconds) were longer than foreign video reports involving other countries (41.9 seconds) is telling. In a sense, they echoed the projected image of China as a world center that attracted foreign attention. Indeed, through visual images and words of Westerners on CCTV, these stories showcased how China was positively perceived in the eyes of foreigners. It was a social self of China as seen through the prism of others.

In some respects, the use of foreign video reports on CCTV is important because of its implications in international communication and foreign affairs. By nature, video reports are visual, requiring commitment of journalistic resources and technological linkage in the process of newsgathering across national borders. In foreign policy news on CCTV, not only did the proportion of foreign video reports rise over time (see Table 4.8), the average length of such reports also became longer at the same time. From 1992 to 1998, foreign policy stories with foreign video reports consistently were almost as long as domestic video reports, averaging more than 1 minute throughout the study period. The data suggest that, whether in domestic or foreign settings, when China was involved in international affairs one way or another, CCTV tended to cast the country in video formats of growing length. Although live coverage is absent, the Chinese national television news has increasingly presented China in the world of international affairs from a foreign location or within a remote context.

ATTRIBUTION OF NEWS ON CCTV

The presence of video reports on CCTV clearly indicates the newsgathering effort either directly or indirectly by the Chinese national television network in the process of news production and presentation. It does not specify how the stories might be generated or where they might come from. This information lies in the attribution of news, if any, when the source of the story is identified in the beginning or at the end of presentation. In the case of CCTV news, these sources could be placed into one of the following categories: CCTV own correspondent and staff, Xinhua News Agency, other domestic medium, foreign medium, or other/unidentified. Table 4.11 presents the results of attribution of stories in each of the three types of news on CCTV.

During the study period, there is little question that CCTV increasingly relied on its own correspondents and staff to gather the news from both internal and external locations. Throughout the years, more than three-fourths of domestic news stories (76.9%) were reported by CCTV's own correspondents and staff. Less than 20 percent of the stories was supplied by other domestic TV stations. A visible pattern is that from 1992 to 1998, CCTV used more of its own correspondent and staff to do the reports around the country and at the same time reduced news reports prepared by other provincial and local TV stations. This phenomenon testifies to the reforms of news programs initiated during 1993 and 1997 that saw the expansion and reach of CCTV news services (see chapter 1).

Table 4.11: Attribution of News on CCTV, 1992–1998

	1992	1996	1998	Subtotal
Domestic News				
CCTV correspondent or staff[a]	57.5%	87.9%	87.7%	76.9%
Other domestic medium	30.0	10.3	9.6	17.2
Other/unidentified	11.3	0.4	1.7	4.7
Xinhua News Agency	1.2	1.3	1.0	1.2
Subtotal	424	455	293	1,172
Foreign News				
Other/unidentified[b]	80.2%	88.6%	81.4%	83.4%
CCTV correspondent or staff	1.6	10.0	18.0	8.8
Xinhua News Agency	11.7	1.4	0.6	5.3
Foreign medium	3.2	–	–	1.3
Other domestic medium	3.2	–	–	1.3
Subtotal	247	220	161	628
Foreign Policy News				
CCTV correspondent or staff	76.3%	96.2%	84.4%	83.2%
Other/unidentified	7.7	–	10.2	6.9
Other domestic medium	12.4	1.3	0.8	6.1
Xinhua News Agency	3.6	2.5	4.7	3.7
Subtotal	169	79	128	376
Total	840	754	582	2,176

[a]CCTV correspondent or staff includes stories jointly reported by CCTV and other TV stations. CCTV was identified first.

[b]Other/unidentified includes foreign stories "edited and reported by" CCTV. The origin of those stories, however, was unknown.

Another noticeable finding is that the Chinese national news agency, Xinhua, was more likely to be a source in foreign policy news on CCTV than in domestic or foreign news. As a news source on CCTV, Xinhua news agency appeared in a negligible proportion (1.2%) of domestic news and had a dramatic decrease in foreign news from 11.7% in 1992 to less than 1% in 1998. Although the number was relatively small, the Xinhua news agency apparently maintained a steady proportion of stories in foreign policy news on CCTV. Almost all of these stories were anchor reports with no video, covering such topics as diplomatic or governmental activities and military as well as defense matters. The authority of Xinhua to deliver the official information and knowledge in China is unmistakably affirmed in this form of journalistic ritual.

A third obvious pattern is the high proportion of unidentified sources (83.4%) in foreign news on CCTV from 1992 to 1998. Often, many of these stories were reported with no reference to or identification of their sources. Sometimes, they were simply presented as "edited and reported" by CCTV without any acknowledgment of the origin. At first glance, this might leave an impression that the video reports in foreign news on CCTV came from its own correspondents doing the shooting in foreign locations. But the grouping of foreign news stories in one single segment and the apparent lack of CCTV's own correspondents in the background gives away the fact that these foreign news stories were clearly provided by some foreign news services, not CCTV or even the Xinhua news agency.

In April 1980, CCTV subscribed to the British Visnews and U.S. UPITN for international news services and started broadcasting international news on a daily basis. Reuters later bought Visnews and turned it into Reuters TV News (RTN) services. Other foreign television services are later added to the CCTV exchange agreements, such as CNN in 1987 and Associate Press Television News (APTN) in 1994. According to sources familiar with CCTV operation (John Jirik, CCTV consultant, personal communication, December 18, 1999), it is a standard deal between APTN and RTN and its clients to pay for foreign news services without acknowledging the sources, thus making it appear that the client TV station has produced the video reports itself. Apparently, CCTV follows such a practice in its foreign news segment. In fact, as noted earlier, CCTV added a Chinese point of view by rewriting the stories according to the original script.

Nonetheless, Table 4.11 shows that foreign news on CCTV was increasingly reported by its correspondents stationed in foreign locations. In 1992, only less than 2% of foreign news stories was transmitted by CCTV own correspondents. By 1996, that proportion jumped to 10% and two years later to 18%. These stories were mostly reported from Hong Kong, Moscow, New York, and Washington, DC. As reported in chapter 1, these cities were among CCTV foreign bureaus that have been already set up or in preparation. The increased foreign representation would surely allow CCTV news to present China's position in the world of international affairs within a Chinese perspective. In the words of Sheng Yilai, deputy director of CCTV International, "although we depend on the agencies for supplying us with international coverage, we find that their news values are sometimes different to ours. So we need our own reporters to look at stories from our own viewpoint" (cited in Jirik, 2001, p. 24). In addition to frequency, timeliness, and format, the visual elements of television news represent an important aspect of a particular way of constructing the reality of everyday events.

FOCUS OF VISUAL IMAGE ON CCTV NEWS

As Griffin (1992) argued, instead of serving any informational function, the visual elements of TV news "most often serve to promote and legitimize the newscast itself by reinforcing the dramatic structure and attractiveness of the program and by lending confirmation and authority to verbal reports" (p. 139). One aspect of the dramatic structure of television programs, whether news or otherwise, is the sort of visual images that may situate the viewers "in a particular position or location in relation to that object or event," hence creating a preferred meaning (Gruneau & Hackett, 1990, p. 283). For example, the predominance of coups and earthquakes in international news reporting (e.g., Rosenblum, 1979) has been accused by critics of building negative images about the Third World countries among audiences in the West.

The news pictures or videos involving acts or deeds that may lead to a real or potential damage to properties and human life are capable of priming TV viewers to see the reality in a given way. Such pictures or videos are often violent in nature. On television news, visual images are usually dichotomous: either they contain violent elements or they are not. In the process of news reporting, the presence of violent images in the stories signifies the interplay between two discrete things: "what really happens" and the report about it through selection and presentation. The former is part of reality and the latter a conscious journalistic judgment. Table 4.12 reports the focus of visual images in the three types of news on CCTV.

It is apparent that in foreign policy news CCTV did not carry violent visual images throughout the study period, except for one single story in 1998 that depicted diplomatic efforts to resolve the military conflicts in Burundi in Africa. The same can be said of domestic news. From 1992 to 1998, more than 95% of the domestic stories used visual images that were nonviolent in nature. This is consistent with the Communist Party's long-term principle of "positive propaganda." For example, in the mid-1980s, the Chinese news media were instructed to report "about 80%" of positive stories and "about 20%" to negative stories (Hu, 1985, p. 18). Positive stories like economic progress, scientific achievements,

Table 4.12: Focus of Visual Image on CCTV News, 1992–1998

	1992	1996	1998	Subtotal
Domestic News[a]				
Violence[b]	0.3%	0.2%	4.5%	1.2%
Non-violence[c]	99.7	99.8	95.5	98.8
Subtotal	380	420	247	1,047
Foreign News[d]				
Violence	19.3%	11.7%	11.3%	14.3%
Nonviolence	80.7	88.3	88.8	85.7
Subtotal	207	206	160	573
Foreign Policy News[e]				
Violence	–	–	0.9%	0.3%
Non-violence	100.0	100.0	99.1	99.7
Subtotal	143	68	115	326
Total	730	694	522	1,946

[a]$X^2 = 27.2$, $df = 2$, $p < .01$

[b]Violence: The news pictures/TV films involve acts or deeds that lead to real or potential damage to properties and human life. Excluded were stories with no video or films.

[c]Nonviolence: The news pictures/TV films do not involve acts or deeds that lead to real or potential damage to properties and human life.

[d]$X^2 = 6.65$, $df = 2$, $p < .05$

[e]$X^2 = 1.84$, $df = 2$, $p = $ n.g.

and civilized behaviors in television news, of course, would not have any violent visual image.

Although still very small, the proportion of violent visual images on CCTV nevertheless increased from less than .5% in 1992 to about 5% in 1998. A majority of these stories were related to disasters/accidents, such as damages to properties caused by flooding, and a miniscule number about crime/law (e.g., personal harm to policeman inflicted by criminals). The significance of these stories goes beyond their violent nature. Unlike the earlier years when the news was upbeat in general and free of negative implications in particular, there is an unspoken sense of relaxation concerning how far the national television may venture in bringing the social ills and natural woes into the Chinese people's living rooms. To some extent, it is a sign of confidence and an indication of the diversity of journalistic practices that CCTV and other mass media have increasingly enjoyed regarding the form and structure of news selection and presentation since the economic reforms in the late 1970s (e.g., Huang, 1994).

The use of violent visual images on CCTV news characterized two different maps of the world when domestic and foreign news stories were juxtaposed during the study period. As shown in Table 4.12, although more than 80% of the foreign news stories from 1992 through 1998 did not have any violent visual elements, on a year-to-year basis, the proportion of foreign news with violent images was significantly higher than that of domestic news. These stories focused on terrorist attacks and killings, natural and human-made disasters or accidents, wars and destruction in various countries around the world. By comparison, viewers of CCTV news should have little difficulty observing that the world outside China was a much more violent place, at least by the way it was presented on television. In a nutshell, on Chinese national television, China is a peaceful, safe country as opposed to other countries out there. This worldview is present in CCTV's English news service, too (Jirik, 2001).

TECHNICAL RATIONALITY AS PROFESSIONALISM ON CCTV NEWS

What does the preceding analysis of the form and structure of CCTV news mean in terms of the changing patterns of frequency, length, timeliness, and visual images in domestic, foreign and foreign policy news over time? This question is both conceptually and practically important, because the newscast stands as the basic unit or package in which CCTV news is delivered to the Chinese viewers nationwide. Although there have been sporadic studies about television news in China (e.g., X. Li, 1991; Warren, 1988), no empirical research exists to delineate the technical aspects of Chinese television news broadcast. This chapter represents the first of its kind from a longitudinal point of view.

The findings show that the technical structure of CCTV news has undergone significant changes from 1992 to 1998. As far as delivery and presentation are concerned, the Chinese national television news has become highly rationalized, and consequently more professional, over time. Several conclusions are worth noting.

First, as far as timeliness is concerned, over the time span under examination (1992–1998) and compared to some previous study (L. Chu, 1978), the Chinese national TV news has shown a pattern of more speedy transmission in international and foreign policy news and less delay in domestic news. It indicates a technical triumph of the journalistic reform that required news be reported on a timely basis. The shift to more timely reports of news inside and outside China could be expected to lead to a faster "knowledge about" the world out there.

To some extent, it underscores China's commitment to enlightening the Chinese society, not only in theory (e.g., Greenberg & Lau, 1990), but also in practice, in its quest for modernization. Amid the changing media market, if "the Chinese society keeps on differentiating and pluralizing, the demands for *timely*, *objective* and *diversified* political information will grow" (Chan, 1993, p. 25.16, italics added). In news reporting, it means that television will have to fulfill the public needs for quicker understanding and sharing of the aspects of everyday life, the essence of which constitutes social knowledge. Like any other country, China needs certain type and amount of social knowledge to circulate in the society so that the system will function properly at the collective level.

Second, technically speaking, the worlds of domestic, foreign, and foreign policy news on CCTV are presented to the Chinese national viewers at different pace and in different length. Although all three types of news have become more immediate, it is domestic and foreign policy news, the two categories of news most relevant and directly related to China's contemporary social practices and political commitments, that see remarkable transformation during the study period. Evidently, the successful economic reforms since 1978 and the decentralization in media control since 1984 (e.g., Huang, 1994) have resulted in technological innovation and improvement of journalistic standards in the media environment that allow television news to experiment and implement more efficient and effective ways of newsgathering in and out of China.

Although the amount of time for foreign news is getting smaller and the stories shorter as a result of the expansion of both domestic and foreign policy news on CCTV, the Chinese national television network has maintained a stable proportion of foreign news over time. As shown in chapter 6, its window on the outside world continues to take snapshots of a wide variety of geopolitical landscape out there, which generally serves as a point of reference for the domestic scene.

Third, CCTV news has used video reports increasingly, particularly foreign video reports in the areas of foreign news and foreign policy news. In foreign news, it indicates CCTV's institutional agreements with foreign news services to bring visual images from outside the country to the Chinese viewers nationwide. The lack of attribution of the origin of foreign videos and the editing of text, however, make it difficult for the TV viewers to determine the context under which foreign news is brought to China. In foreign policy news, the presence of foreign video reports signals CCTV's professional efforts to report on China's international relations and diplomatic activities from a foreign setting, but within a Chinese perspective.

Fourth, the conditions of the world as mapped by the visual images on CCTV news show distinctive patterns over time. The visual images in both domestic and foreign news generally carry nonviolent elements during the study period. When it comes down to violent images, there is a different configuration between the two types of news, however. The visual world in foreign news appears to be more violent than that in the domestic arena. Given that foreign videos on CCTV news are not given, but chosen for presentation, it suggests a conscious selective process that prefers a certain kind of visual images from the external reality, thus a body of knowledge of observation and understanding.

In summary, throughout the years from 1992 to 1998, CCTV news has largely expanded the depth, speed, and scope of images of news inside and outside of China during its prime-time newscast. The technical rationality has been in line with CCTV's determination to become an international news player. If the trend remains on track, the Xinwen Lianbo on CCTV will not only cover the world much faster in quantity, but also better in quality.

A CHANGING WORLD OF DOMESTIC NEWS ON CCTV: TALES OF ECONOMIC SUCCESS, SOCIAL PROGRESS AND MORE

On a particular day in 1970, a visiting British broadcaster did a little content analysis of how the evening newscast on BTS covered domestic news in China. He reported that 18 minutes of the entire 26-minute broadcast were nothing but "rolling captions" of quotations of Mao Tsetung's thoughts against the background music of "The East Is Red" (Howkins, 1982; see also, Chang, 1989). BTS was not alone. Other Chinese TV stations took cues from BTS's glorification of the Chairman Mao. In the same year, a U.S. news team from NBC in Hong Kong observed a similar ritual on the Guangdong Provincial TV Station. Mao's portrait and the sound of "The East Is Red" started the TV broadcast, followed by newscasts of mostly paternal leaders, heroes, and intrepid activities (J. Chu, 1978).

The year 1970 marked the mid-point of the Cultural Revolution during which Mao was anointed as the Great Helmsman. It was a trying time for the Chinese people and society when reason gave way to intuition, truth to falsehood, and inquiry to dogma. In the domain of mass media, the news turned fiction into facts, report into adulation, and the world into personal incarnation, especially Mao himself, by those of his cronies. Given the act of faith that seeing is believing, television news became the consummate tool in shaping how the world was to be seen and heard by the viewers because the mass media in China were considered the eyes and ears of the people. They still are today. It is, however, inconceivable that since the end of Maoist fanaticism Chinese television would remain as propagandistic as it was before. As shown in previous chapters, decentralization of the state power and depoliticization of content in broadcasting have somehow released China's window on the world from latching at the same time or opening to the same sight. Other than nostalgia, the days of "The East Is Red" were long gone.

The thesis of this chapter departs from past research on mass communication in China by arguing that the Chinese news media are the major stock of social knowledge, serving as ways of seeing and thinking for the general public on the one hand and allowing people to make sense of the changing environment both within and without the Chinese polity on the other hand. Unlike earlier studies that focused on news as ideology, this chapter first discusses how, within the sociology of knowledge perspective, news in China can be understood as a form of knowledge. Looking at the news presented on CCTV from 1992 to 1998,[1] it examines the form and content through which the news orients the Chinese people about what is going on in their domestic world. This orientation includes who is to speak, what is to be seen, how much is to be heard, what the context is, and where the actions are in China. The choice of these elements of news is not random, but depends on what Sigal (1973, p. 66) called "the standardized exceptional" in that the news tends to go beyond the daily mundane and produces recurrent patterns.

Previous studies of media sociology have often considered the news as a commodity, in the sense that the product itself (e.g., a newspaper story or a television broadcast) has distinctive characteristics and is thus recognizable in the marketplace of ideas (Glasser, 1992). Like other consumer goods, the mass-produced news is assumed to have a tangible, if not material, base that makes it movable from here to there in society, much like the physical movement of commercial products from producers to consumers. This view of news as a thing is perhaps best illustrated by the conception of media organizations as a "news factory" (Bantz et al., 1981) in which news is what comes out of the assembly line operated by a team of skilled professional workers according to a set of standard operating procedures and specific organizational objectives.

Within the general framework of the state–media relationship in China, although the Chinese journalists have become more professional in terms of formal academic training and technical expertise (e.g., J. Chu & Fang, 1972; Greenberg & Lau, 1990; Hao & Xu, 1997; Kenny, 1987), what they do is not simply journalistic practices, but to some extent the

---

[1]For the data and the coding procedure of content analysis used in this chapter, see the appendix.

work of the party and the state, too. Since the economic reforms, while the bottom line of financial interests and the standard operating procedures of the Chinese news media organizations might function as much as those of the Western counterparts, there is an added social dimension of news in China that could not be fully explained by the conception of news as a commodity.

Because no private media ownership is allowed in China, Chinese journalists are, in a strict sense, state employees and many of them are likely to be members of the Communist Party if they work for the Party controlled media. They wear different hats and operate under competing or even conflicting sets of ideals and guidelines. As Porter (1992) keenly observed, the journalist in China "is faced with the dilemma that he must both report accurately on all aspects of life and single-mindedly propagate the policies and perceptions of the party" (p. 5). The policies of the Communist Party are unequivocally supreme and outcome-based, demanding due attention and action among the news media. The Party's perceptions of the reality, whether internal or external, however, are symbolically ambiguous and flimsy, often requiring cautious journalistic response.

Unlike that in many other countries, the news in China cannot be freely peddled in the marketplace of ideas, even the new information technology makes it possible and desirable to do so. The fact that 23 major news media organizations with online services on the Internet passed a covenant on April 16, 1999 to oppose the dissemination or reproduction of news from their reports on commercial Web sites indicates an unspoken expectation that the news is a sanctioned entity in China and must be generated according to the rules of the game approved by the central authority. In fact, the State Council issued, in March 1997, certain guidelines to regulate online news services in China. One specific rule was that Chinese news media must apply and receive permission before they could go online and the news content must be posted through the centralized platform for external publicity (L. Guo, 1999).

Along the same lines of news as a commodity, media economics as a field of inquiry has attracted increasing attention in mass communication research. Various economic terms are used to examine media performance and market interplay (e.g., Gomery, 1989). To a large extent, media content is being reified as something that the producer can put a price on and sell in the open market (e.g., McManus, 1992). In a capitalistic, commercial system, the application of economic concepts and ideas to the investigation of mass media content is appealing and appears to make sense. Although not necessarily couched in the traditional Marxist-based superstructure distinction (Dant, 1991; Merton, 1973), this perspective nevertheless implies that media behavior and other journalistic patterns are causally determined by media economic conditions. Within a comparative framework, however, this approach leaves a great deal to be desired, both theoretically and empirically (e.g., Merton, 1973).

Theoretically, the origin of media content, particularly the enduring news values or journalistic paradigms, cannot be entirely explained by the economy or reduced to a material basis. It has often been linked to a host of noneconomic factors like shared culture, political philosophy, and institutional autonomy (e.g., Berger, 1991; Chan & Lee, 1991; Gans, 1979; Shoemaker, 1987; Tuchman, 1978). Little concrete evidence exists to indicate that cultural, political, and social influences on media content fundamentally grow out of the basic economic structure at the system level within which media organizations situate themselves and practice their trade. Even in China, where the country was founded in part on the firm belief in the control of the means of production, the economic reductionism in news reporting is deficient. Examining the external news service (Duiwaibu) of Xinhua News Agency, for example, Porter (1992, p. 1) indicated that, in addition to the role of politics and the party, "other non-political dimensions, including the skills and attitudes of journalists, and various structural factors" all had an impact on what Chinese journalists might write about and how well they might do it. A study of CCTV's English news service further confirmed the influences of technical and organizational rationality on the production of television news (Jirik, 2001).

Comparatively speaking, in a noncapitalistic, command system such as that in China, the analysis of media content within a media economics perspective is unsatisfactory. For one thing, the assumptions (e.g., free-market competition) do not hold true in the Chinese system, which continues to subscribe to the Marxist and Maoist thoughts and where the Communist party shows no intention of relinquishing its grip over the mass media. Although media commercialization and internationalization have been emerging in China in recent years (Chan, 1993; Hong, 1998; Zhao, 1998), the mass media as a whole have yet to demonstrate their independence as a genuine social and market force. The state, not the market, still reigns unchallenged in the control of media ownership and its boundary of operation in China. A strong Chinese state naturally weakens the civil society or the market.

As such, it is empirically difficult to establish a goodness of fit between key economic concepts and real-world indicators when the *causal process* that produces the indicators of abstract variables (e.g., media structure) remains mostly political, not necessarily economic. Given the different processes, it is an epistemological question to specify the conditions under which the concepts used in one social unit can be effectively applied to another (e.g., Blumler et al., 1992; Smelser, 1976). By taking into account the notion that news is a mode of inquiry about social reality, a sociological approach provides a useful point of departure. Within the cultural, social, and political context of any given macro human relations, the news is sensible as far as it is serviceable.

NEWS, KNOWLEDGE, AND EVERYDAY LIFE

Using the sociology of knowledge as a framework (e.g., Berger & Luckmann, 1966; Mannheim, 1952; Merton, 1973; Tuchman, 1978), this chapter contends that news should be conceptualized as a form of social knowledge (Park, 1955), not as an economic product. The latter is tangible and has a material base, whereas the former is intangible, referring to a journalistic way of looking at, and thus constructing, the world of everyday life. With its ephemeral nature, news is not really a thing, but a form of socially distributed knowledge that appears to be a thing. Its significance lies not in any sense of a physical being, but in the symbolic social reality it creates. This perspective recognizes that the object of interest must exist out there in the reality before it can be socially perceived and processed. It also acknowledges, as Williams (1996) aptly put it, "societies and cultures vary in their ability to 'read' reality" (p. 10).

For the purpose of this chapter and those that follow, several premises can be derived from the perspective of sociology of knowledge. First, the sociology of knowledge approach rejects the Marxist assertion that knowledge is determined by the control of economic means. It argues that sociological, not economic, forces are more powerful in determining how and what type of knowledge is cultivated in society at a given point in time (Mannheim, 1952). In the domain of news, it suggests that newsgathering and presentation are collaborative social activities performed by many journalists working together (e.g., A. Cohen, Adoni, & Bantz, 1990), not a corollary of media control by either the capitalists or the state. As discussed in the previous chapters, the increasing decentralization, depoliticization, and diversification of the spirit and practices of Chinese mass media since the early 1980s is a case in point. It is evident that the state in China can no longer effectively decree the pace and pulse of media operations that are increasingly subject to the logic of the market.

Second, whether Capitalist, Communist, or any type in between, a society must have effective means of communication to function efficiently and properly. Social communication requires a shared culture or common national identity, which in turn depends on the continued cultivation and transmission of specific knowledge to members of the community (e.g., Hirsch, 1987; Wentworth, 1980). By reason of its communicable nature, the news thus provides a kind of knowledge that is "culturally bound and socially constructed," helping to hold society together and stay intact (e.g., Glasser, 1992; Park, 1955; Shoemaker & Reese, 1991).

Much like scientific knowledge (e.g., Longino, 1990), the news as a form of knowledge is social both in its creation for mass consumption and in its public functions. If it is to provide social knowledge or "common knowledge" (Neuman, Just, & Crigler, 1992), it must be rooted in macro-practices developed through socialization (e.g., social understanding and integration) rather than in micro preferences dictated by individual orientation (e.g., Party leadership or Capitalist publisher). This is one reason why China in the post-Mao reform era could not afford to maintain a totalistic system built on the ultra-left orthodox ideology commandeered by individual charisma. As CNN noted, "economic reforms of the past two decades have created new distance between state and society and have transformed some key institutions."[2] One of the key institutions that have been changed or are fast changing is the news media in China.

Third, a society's stock of knowledge is often organized by a functional system of relevances or familiarity (e.g., Bernstein, 1976). This means a society takes and counts as social knowledge certain features in the immediate and remote environment, taking some to be relevant and others to be irrelevant. It suggests a process of conscientious judgment and deliberate selection. When the internal and external settings change, so do the definition of situations and the system of practices (Berger & Luckmann, 1966; Bernstein, 1976; Tuchman, 1978). In news reporting, the question is: What aspect or sector of the social reality gets to count as knowledge that should be recorded? Within the sociology of knowledge perspective, the choice and presentation of news should be based not so much on its attributes as on its place or location in the larger social structure. The ultimate criterion for relevance is the ability for the news to provide the public with "knowledge about" themselves and others through some systematic means (Park, 1955). More than anything else, the news undeniably constitutes the most visible resource.

Fourth, a society's fundamental worldview is reproduced in its social transcript (Boulding, 1956)—the news. The news describes a series of social matters and current involvements based on the kind of knowledge that is needed collectively or deemed important by the society (e.g., A. Cohen et al., 1990). Through its selective description, the news also stands as a sign post and points out direction. In essence, it is a device of knowing. "Ways of seeing," according to Dahlgren and Chakrapani

---

[2]See CNN In-Depth Specials—Vision of China on its Web site at http://cnn.com/SPECIALS/1999/china.50/red.giant/human.rights.dalpino/.

(1982), "are a reflection of existing social practices and commitments, and they serve as a force for the promotion of those commitments" (p. 46). The news media, as part of the knowledge-extending institutions, therefore tend to choose their reporting areas and problems in accordance with the needs and desires of their society to make sense of the dynamics of their own world and beyond. Whether in China or elsewhere, there should be little variation in this regard.

Although the conception of social construction of reality is fundamentally rooted in socio-psychological processes, it can be extended from the personal to the institutional on the one hand and from the obtrusive to the unobtrusive on the other hand. According to Wirth (cited in Mannheim, 1936), "by virtue of its concern with the role of knowledge and ideas in the maintenance or change of the social order," the perspective of social influences on knowledge of reality "is bound to devote considerable attention to the agencies or devices through which ideas are diffused and the degree of freedom of inquiry and expression that prevails" (p. xxix). Wirth considered "the functions of the press, of the popularization of knowledge and of propaganda" to be one of these agencies or devices (p. xxix). "An adequate understanding of such phenomena as these," as he put it, "will contribute to a more precise conception of the role of ideas in political and social movements and of the value of knowledge as an instrument in controlling social reality" (p. xxix). In a broader sense, this line of reasoning echoes Weber's (1949) methodological viewpoint that "only a part of concrete reality is interesting and *significant* to us, because only it is related to the *cultural values* with which we approach reality" (p. 78). For the vast world out there that is often beyond direct observation or experience, the mass media usually stand as a given or available starting point.

MASS MEDIA AND
SOCIAL CONSTRUCTION OF REALITY

The structural perspective—social construction of reality—has in recent years attracted growing attention in mass communication research and other related fields (e.g., Adoni & Mane, 1984; Benavot, Cha, Kamens, Meyer, & Wong, 1991; Chang, Wang, & Chen, 1994; Cohen et al., 1990; Gamson, Croteau, Hoynes, & Sasson, 1992; Neuman et al., 1992). Previous studies have focused on news content as a form through which the mass media view an event or issue, what they perceive in it, and how they construe it in their production and presentation process. Using content analysis as a method, they seek to analyze the concepts, categories, and thought models the mass media employ to formulate problems (e.g., what constitutes news) and their expression (e.g., how it is to be reported). Although content analysis can be used to study how social reality is constructed (e.g., Gamson et al., 1992), it should be emphasized that it examines the static reality as it is manifest in the news. In the process of mass communication, this mediated traffic of news flow takes some aspects of the reality to be relevant and others to be irrelevant to the context involved.

What constitutes the reality of a society, especially in a remote setting, is never given and generally comes from the news media (Lippmann, 1922). Social reality is a product of the interaction between the objective reality and a society's own pragmatic and social needs (A. Cohen et al., 1990). The end result—verbal rituals and other crude forms of record in primitive societies and news in modern societies—is preserved in a collective memory. Within the boundaries and operational logic of the recording medium, it takes note of events, issues, values, ideas, images, personalities, institutions, and experiences in and about a society, the totality of which becomes social knowledge that is relevant and useful to its members (e.g., Bernstein, 1976). In other words, the content and validity of social knowledge are ultimately tied to the general interests and common experience in society. The organization and circulation of social knowledge help to shape "the individual and collective consciousness" of a society about its everyday life and the more remote context of their lives (McQuail, 1972, p. 13). To paraphrase Barnes (1988), how a society acts, whether nationally or internationally, depends on what it knows before it makes a move. What the society can know, of course, is what it has made.

Although Berger and Luckmann (1966) did not discuss how the news may become part of the foundations of knowledge in everyday life, the essence of their treatise—the social construction of reality—can be applied, both theoretically and methodologically, to the field of journalism (e.g., Tuchman, 1978). As Hallin (1994) said, "it is naive to imagine that journalists are free of social location" (p. 7). Journalists' social location certainly is part of "the complex relationships that can exist among the political, cultural, and economic contexts in which [media] content is produced and distributed" (Ball-Rokeach & Cantor, 1986, p. 10). At the risk of oversimplification, the social construction of reality conceptualizes knowledge in everyday life on three dimensions: function (e.g., understanding and interpretation of subjective reality and sharing), formation (e.g., routinization, classification or typification, and relevance), and distribution (e.g., social dissemination and access to information). A careful analysis of "the interplay between social structure and communications" (Merton, 1968, p. 493) is in order.

SOCIAL STRUCTURE AND THE NEWS IN CHINA

As far as the mass media system and social structure are concerned, a large body of literature has, since the 1950s, examined the structural position of the mass media with other social systems to determine how that relationship may affect the way media content, particularly the news, is produced. From earlier studies (Breed, 1958; Gans, 1979; Gitlin, 1980; Tichenor, Donohue, & Olien, 1980) to more recent research (Hallin, 1994), sociologists and mass communication researchers have provided consistent evidence indicating that media content is often shaped by the dominant conditions of the system, such as the power structure and social alignments. Roshco (1975) was succinct, arguing "social structure is the major influence on the content of the press" (p. 5). Ball-Rokeach and Cantor (1986) summarized this line of research best when they wrote, "before the content is even created, there are political, economic, and social realities that set the stage for the nature of media content" (p. 14).

As bound by these political, economic, and social realities, the news tends to be generated, according to Gans (1979), in a way that concentrates on nation and society about "their persistence, cohesion, and the conflicts and divisions threatening their cohesion" (p. 19). In other words,

> news stories and news commentaries can be understood as a continuous processing of raw information that makes the experience of a society comprehensible in terms of more general categories. These categories represent both previously articulated normative guidelines and more general value assumptions about *what to expect from social life*. (Alexander, 1981, p. 20, italics added)

It is part of the devices or modes of thinking that, within the perspective of social construction of reality, individuals or groups use to "accumulate, preserve, reformulate, and disseminate" their intellectual heritage in society and their connection to the social conditions in which they occur (Wirth, cited in Mannheim, 1936, p. xxix).

As noted earlier, a key premise of this chapter is that a society's stock of knowledge, including its fundamental worldview or image of itself and others, is selectively constructed by a functional system of relevant or familiar practices (e.g., Bernstein, 1976) and is mass reproduced in the news. This extends Roshco's (1975) argument that the publication or rejection of specific news stories is "based upon a social frame of reference derived from the social structure within which the press functions" (p. 113). The end of the Cold War provides an excellent opportunity to determine how television in China reproduces views of the social world amid the structural change of its larger landscape.

Although not necessarily couched in the social construction of reality perspective, the linkage between social structure and the production of news has been explicitly or implicitly addressed in studies on mass media in China. The effect of sociopolitical structure on the spirit and practices of mass media prior to the Chinese reform movement taking shape in the late 1970s has been well documented (e.g., Houn, 1961; A. Liu, 1971; Schurmann, 1966; F. Yu, 1964). A common agreement indicates that news in China often results from the strategic position of the mass media embedded in the broader political system and their attachment to the powers that be as part of the ideological state apparatus. Chinese news tends to be predicated on how it might best serve the interests of the state's structural needs in political and social control, not necessarily on enlightening or alerting the public.

This is the essence of the mass propaganda and persuasion model that became the received perspective on mass communication in China throughout the first three decades after 1950. In this model, mass media were characterized as "limited outlets, a centralized hierarchical organizational structure, a unified circulation system, and an invariable content" (J. Wang & Chang, 1996, p. 197). As class ideologues, the media defined and reproduced the central knowledge dictated by the state's political and ideological deliberations. Following China's economic reform and open-door policy in the late 1970s, although the central authority has loosened its rigid control over the scope of content, the specific role, and general functions of the mass media (e.g., Chan, 1993; Hong, 1998; C. Lee, 1990b; Starck & Yu, 1988; X. Zhang, 1993), the structural submission or subjugation of the mass media to the state in the form of party or governmental ownership and editorial guidance remains fundamentally unchanged.

Notwithstanding, as a result of vertical fragmentation (e.g., decentralization of the state authority) and horizontal fragmentation (e.g., division of labor across media organizations) in the mass media (J. Wang & Chang, 1996), instead of acting solely as an ideological mouthpiece under the old command system, the mass media now have a market to serve and an audience to attract, creating a public space in which the media are expected to perform dual roles. There is evidence that media content in China, especially TV programming, has been closely tied to the changing socioeconomic structure both within and without Chinese geopolitics (e.g., Hong, 1993; Wang & Chang, 1994, 1996). As is shown later, the news is no exception.

RETHINKING NEWS IN POST-MAO CHINA

The discussion just presented provides a general framework for examining the relationship between the news and social structure in China. The central idea in this chapter is that the news in China is necessarily a form of socially constructed knowledge for public consumption and understanding, not purely a politically cultivated ideology for mass indoctrination or persuasion. The sociology of knowledge approach could be used as a conceptual "range of vision" (Blau, 1975) to analyze news in China under both Mao's ideological dominance and the post-Mao market orientation. To the extent that the state, whether in the Marxist or capitalist system, has complete control of information and its dissemination, the public has few, if any, other sources for acquiring and transmitting its shared culture at the collective level. The controlled news thus becomes the dominant stock of knowledge from which to construct a commonly experienced social reality in any given society and culture.

The preconception of news as ideology in China by the Western journalists and scholars, at least before the economic reforms in the late 1970s, has created a misconstrued image of China unmatched by the reality. The neglect of the real in China has one serious consequence: China is either underreported in its badness or overreported in its goodness. More often than not, the news in China is generally dismissed as nothing but an official propaganda designed to manipulate or indoctrinate the Chinese public mind. Such "ideological conditioning" in the Western journalistic and academic communities gravitates the observers to see China "only as a repository of the weird and wonderful" (Becker, 1992, p. 72). In between, there is much more than meets the eyes in the dynamic Chinese society.

Since the Chinese reforms, the accepted background belief has evidently become empirically untenable, calling into question the underlying assumptions as to how the news is brought into being in China. The questioning is predicated on identifying the approach an insider takes to the problem at hand vis-à-vis that of an outsider. As Becker (1992) argued: "It was easy to condemn domestic reporting in China by Chinese journalists as entirely the product of the ideological imperatives of the communist party. It was something else to realize that Western reporters were guilty of the same sin, albeit in a more subtle way" (p. 65). To criticize the conventional ways of looking at the news in China does not by any means imply condoning the state intervention in media operations and the abrogation of Chinese press freedom. The former is a legitimate academic enterprise whereas the latter verges on political evaluation and interpretation. To some extent, fear of expression in various forms still prevails in China (e.g., Tefft, 1993).

Although many previous studies had focused on ideology—a highly politicized, exclusive worldview—in the Chinese news media (e.g., Cheek, 1989; Edelstein & Liu, 1963; A. Liu, 1971; Oliphant, 1964; K. Wang & Starck, 1972; Yao, 1963; F. Yu, 1953), they more or less implied a narrow sense of the sociology of knowledge perspective: a distinct way of looking at social reality. Reality, however, "is subject to endless change" (Williams, 1996, p. 11). As a representation of reality, the news cannot but comply with the boundaries of what is available and allowable. In Park's (1955) view, the news as a form of social knowledge is "knowledge about" fact that "has been checked, tagged, regimented, and finally ranged in this and that perspective, according to the purpose and point of view of the investigator" (p. 74). Because journalists in China must carry out investigation and research (e.g., Porter, 1992), this conception was as true in Mao's years as it is in the post-Mao era.

Since China started its reform movement in the late 1970s, serving the people and socialism, especially the former, has become the prominent role and function of the Chinese media (Y. Sun, 1993). Although the state still owns the mass media, the news in China has been found to be less as monolithic as previous studies had assumed (e.g., Chang et al., 1993). In fact, it has been driven more by the bottom line than the party line (e.g., Zhao, 1998). The erosion of ideology such as Marxism and Maoist Thought in domestic stories and the greater diversity of foreign content (e.g., J. Wang, 1993; Warren, 1988) are further indications of the evolving nature of the Chinese mass media. Conceptually it is necessary to go beyond the earlier mass propaganda and persuasion model in explaining the spirit and practices of the emerging commercial media in China (e.g., Chan, 1993; X. Yu, 1993; Zhao, 1998) and their inevitable integration and opening to foreign influences (e.g., Chinoy, 1999; Fukuyama, 1992).

As noted in previous chapters, following the pragmatism initiated by China's paramount leader Deng Xiaoping in the late 1970s, Chinese national priorities have been shifted from class struggle and ideological campaigns to economic reforms and social reconstruction. The transformation from a command economy to a so-called "socialist" market economy, accompanied by decentralization, relative local autonomy, and less political control of rigid lifestyle, creates a loosening situation that was unthinkable, if not impossible, during the Mao era. For the Chinese people who have survived the suppression and suffering of the Cultural Revolution, the post-Mao China thus emerges as a changing social world. Collectively, they need to know what it is like and why it is happening.

Since the collapse of Communism in eastern Europe and the former Soviet Union, China, as the last Communist stronghold and as a rising economic power, faces growing international challenges and pressures to change. Because of the government's public commitment to, and continued practices of, internal reforms and external opening, it also becomes socially desirable and economically beneficial for the Chinese people to reassess China's position relative to others in the world political landscape. To know the shifting reality, either domestic or foreign, is to seek to develop a picture of the world. Both fiction (e.g., movies and pop music) and nonfiction (e.g., news and documentaries) in the domestic mass media (e.g., L. Chu, 1993; Lull, 1991) as well as foreign media help contribute to the Chinese people's knowledge about the world. From the real to the imagined, they differ in varying degree of substance and superficiality.

The major stock of formal knowledge in China, however, lies in the news. By the symbolic representation of news, things become knowable and publicly known. As noted in chapter 1, at the national level, the most important and widely watched news is the *Xinwen Lianbo* (network news) on CCTV, which sets the official news agenda for other media to follow. With other national media such as the *People's Daily*, CCTV preforms and performs a kind of social knowledge that allows hundreds of millions of Chinese people to keep pace with the current social development and cultural reorientation. If the news content of this ubiquitous national television, under the watchful eye of the state, shows significant changes following the reforms, it stands to reason that other regional and local TV stations might have undergone an even greater shift in their worldviews.

The following sections detail coverage of actors, their placement in news, length of stories, topics, origin or location of stories, and stories devoted to various provinces on CCTV domestic news from 1992 to 1998. Because of the difficulty in data collection, little previous empirical research exists that has charted a longitudinal pattern of these aspects of Chinese domestic news over time. Given China's vast territories, nothing is also known about how the network news on CCTV is devoted to individual Chinese provinces. As a news organization, CCTV cannot afford to assign as many teams of reporters and cameras as possible across the country. In fact, as mentioned previously, division of labor in the Chinese broadcasting industry has led CCTV to rely on provincial and local stations to cover the news in places where its own news staff and equipment could not reach.

Although CCTV has increasingly used its own correspondents and staff to report the domestic news in recent years, about 22% of stories still came from other provincial and local TV stations (see chap. 4 for details). Whether these regional or major city TV stations were selected with an intention of equal coverage of all parts of the country or of diverse settings on CCTV is difficult to determine. Through their selection, however, the prominence of 27 provinces and 4 municipalities on Chinese television, and for that matter in China, can be gauged. Because CCTV is the only national news network, its coverage of events and issues in the provinces and cities represents, to a large extent, how different sectors of the country were to be seen and in what context.

WHO SPEAKS ON CCTV NEWS?

The identification of actors in the news helps determine the various players involved in the process of mass communication. Actors may be individual, plural, or institutional. Given the limited space or time in the news, it is obvious that, for every actor included in the news by design, another is excluded by default. The visibility of actors, therefore, implies some kind of status of legitimacy and authority in news making. On the negative side, it denotes a standing of notoriety and impropriety in the events or issues covered. Within the Chinese context, the presentation or the absence of certain actors on CCTV news further projects an atmosphere of who gets to speak to or be seen by the national audience.

In a country where open deliberations are uncommon in both the chamber of legislature and the court of public opinion, the opportunity to appear on national television news often carries a sense of prominence and relevance. During the study period, CCTV presented prevailing national thoughts and social priorities in its news coverage. The "knowns" or familiar names or people with well-known positions (Gans, 1979) dominated one way or another the national news landscape on the air. These knowns included the Chinese president, premier, various ministerial officials, and political and party officials, whose share in the news limelight was greatly enhanced by their location or status in the power structure. Table 5.1 reports the main actors that were portrayed on CCTV domestic news from 1992 to 1998.

Unlike previous studies (e.g., Warren, 1988), the domestic news in this chapter does not include foreign policy or international relations stories that usually deal with activities between governments or across countries. By focusing on news that had nothing to do with other state or political entity, the data in Table 5.1 delineate what position each of the main actors might hold and how they might play their role in the Chinese social structure as seen through the news on CCTV. Unfortunately, no comparable data existed in the 1980s to offer a benchmark for the distribution of actors on Chinese television news during China's first decade of reforms and openness. The longitudinal pattern shown in Table 5.1 thus adds new knowledge and insight into the composition of who the important actors in the domestic news settings were.

Table 5.1: Main Actors in Domestic News on CCTV, 1992–1998

Main Actor[a]	1992	1996	1998	Total
Interest groups[b]	31.8%	16.2%	11.1%	20.6%
Ministries/cabinet members	12.9	29.2	19.2	20.5
Public/public opinion[c]	11.9	12.3	15.8	13.1
Political/party officials	8.8	12.7	15.8	12.1
Military/public security	17.3	7.5	6.4	10.8
Heads of state/government[d]	2.5	8.1	13.2	7.4
Local governments	6.3	4.5	8.5	6.3
Congress	2.5	4.2	6.0	4.1
Provincial governments	5.3	3.6	2.1	3.8
Courts	.6	1.6	1.7	1.3
Total	318	308	234	860

$X^2 = 114.0$, $df = 18$, $p < .01$

[a]Main actors refer to primary individuals, groups or other entities that do things or are affected by events in a way that is essential to the story. Actors may be individual, plural, or institutional. Some individual actors held concurrent government positions and were coded in terms of either their highest positions or the position most relevant to the story. Other or unidentifiable actors were excluded.

[b]Interest groups include business, labor unions, companies, and mass organizations.

[c]Public/public opinion mainly refers to nonofficial individuals. For instance, if peasants or citizens were interviewed about the market or harvest, they would be considered as the main actor and coded as public/public opinion.

[d]Heads of state/government include vice head of state and government.

From 1992 to 1998, the most visible actors in the domestic news on CCTV were interest groups (20.6%) and ministries/cabinet members (20.5%). They each appeared in 2 out of 10 stories. Other actors did not come close to that kind of coverage during the study period. Individuals and the general public (13.1%) slightly led political and party officials (12.1%) on CCTV domestic news, followed by members from the military and public security sector (10.8%) and head of state/government (7.4%) and local governments (6.3%) at a distance. The People's Congress (4.1%), provincial governments (3.8%) and courts (1.3%) were barely discernible on CCTV news. The overall pattern indicates a preference for news concerning special organizational interests and administrative functions at the ministerial level.

Because activities of organized negotiation and lobbying rarely occur in China, interest groups were broadly defined to include entities of factories, companies, mass organizations, or labor unions whose activities were officially recognized and whose interests catered to particular segments of the Chinese social structure. Further analysis shows that CCTV carried many reports of achievements by factories and companies in their productivity or technological innovations in various areas. This demonstrated the special position held by the collective interests such as factory workers in the Communist society. It also explicitly underscored the success of reform policy in transforming Chinese commercial and manufacturing sectors from a rigid command system to a socialist market system. As is shown later, stories about economic, trade, and business activities outnumbered other categories of news.

Over time, however, the data display a shifting and interesting configuration of emphasis on the various actors reported on CCTV news. Some actors gained ground at the expense of others. In 1998, interests groups (11.1%) no longer commanded as much national attention in the news as they did in 1992 (31.8%). This signals that 20 years after the economic reforms, the successful stories of business and companies did not appear to be as prominent as they used to be, especially when the whole country has experienced a tremendous growth over the last decade. To some extent, it means the institutionalization of economic reforms as part of life in Chinese society has evidently diminished the news appeal of those actors who had led the country in economic, trade, and business activities.

The decline was also true for military and public security actors, with their presence on CCTV news decreasing from 17.3% to 6.4% during the study period. In 1992, for example, CCTV ran on average almost two stories per day (41 stories in 26 days) about the People's Liberation Army (PLA), ranging from military performance and personal sacrifice to its contribution to economic progress, social construction, and nation building. Six years later, however, CCTV showed only five PLA related stories in 27 days, reporting the commencement of military academies, meeting of the defense minister with foreign counterparts, fighting against flooding, and political study of Deng Xiaoping thought. Because the study period (June 15 to July 15) was nearly identical between 1992 and 1998, the dramatic reduction of the PLA-related news on CCTV could not be attributed to the opportune factors, but rather due to a shift in national priorities. It suggests a less pervasive role of the military and security forces in Chinese society when the country has moved from a command structure to a market-oriented system.

The PLA is controlled by the Central Military Committee of the Chinese Communist Party. Although the PLA's involvement in reform movement stories might be considered a logical outcome of China's process of modernization, its significance lies in the fact that the military constitutes one major pillar in buttressing the success of Communist authoritarian rule (e.g., the 1989 crackdown on the pro-democracy movement at the Tiananmen Square in Beijing). The recurring positive images of the military in the Chinese scene, albeit in a reduced proportion on CCTV news, apparently are functional in that they serves as a force to promote the maintenance and continued transmission of certain social knowledge. After all, the appearance of PLA news on CCTV, a state-owned party apparatus, clearly underscored the state, military, and media complex in the legitimacy of state power in China.

Although ministerial actors remained salient throughout the study period, heads of state/government saw their presence in domestic affairs news increased significantly from 2.5% in 1992 to 13.2% in 1998. Other than its dominant role in foreign policy news (see chapter 7), the notable rise of heads of state/government in domestic news could be traced to the protocol and ritualistic activities of the two highest offices in China. Both Chinese President Jiang Zemin and Premier Zhu Rongji were relatively high profile in 1998, touring the country, holding meetings, and talking to people. On the increase in exposure also were nonofficial individuals, the general public, and public opinion as well as high-ranking political and party officials. Except for some minor criticism of local officials, when public opinion was presented on CCTV news, it came often from the views of those who supported the party line or government policy, entailing a sense of status among actors on CCTV news.

THE HIERARCHY OF ACTORS ON CCTV NEWS

The hierarchy of actors on CCTV news can be best seen in their placement on the lineup of newscast.[3] Table 5.2 shows the results. A detailed examination of the story location on CCTV news clearly distinguishes the ranking of actors on Chinese national television. Some actors always appeared before others on the CCTV broadcast regardless of how often they might show up in the news. This phenomenon was true from 1992 to 1998. Throughout the study period, the placement of actors on CCTV news appears to mirror the pecking order of Chinese sociopolitical structure. It prioritizes who should speak first on Chinese national television.

[3]The placement refers to the average location of all stories for a given actor during the study period in the CCTV newscast lineup. The lower the number, the higher the story was placed in the broadcast and vice versa.

Table 5.2: Placement of Main Actors in Domestic News on CCTV, 1992–1998[a]

Main Actor	1992	1996	1998	Total
Heads of state/government	5.0	4.2	4.2	4.3
Congress	5.9	7.9	3.9	5.8
Political/party officials	8.0	10.2	7.0	8.5
Provincial governments	10.6	7.5	5.2	8.7
Ministries/cabinet members	10.6	11.9	8.6	10.7
Local governments	13.0	10.4	9.3	10.9
Courts	13.0	13.6	10.0	12.2
Public/public opinion	16.1	12.0	10.6	12.9
Interest groups	15.6	13.7	8.8	14.1
Military/public security	15.6	14.2	8.6	14.1
Range	30	33	18	33

[a]Entries are the average location of all stories for a given actor in the CCTV newscast lineup. The lower the number, the higher the story was placed in the lineup and vice versa.

In the domestic news, heads of state/government did not appear as frequently as those of interest groups on CCTV news; neither did the Chinese Congress. They nevertheless were among the first to be introduced in the news, whereas interest groups tended to be buried at the bottom of newscast. The latter might have enjoyed greater coverage, but was not necessarily given better treatment in the news. The salience of other actors had little to do with the frequencies of their occurrence on CCTV news, either. Political and party officials came in third in the placement of stories, followed by provincial governments, ministries/cabinet members, local governments, courts, individual/public/public opinion, interests groups, and military/public security, in that order. The consistent placement of public opinion near the end of domestic CCTV newscast from 1992 to 1998 speaks of its insignificant role in public deliberations in China. As a matter of fact, public opinion as a voice on the national television news often appeared to endorse the official social practices or policy commitment.

As noted in the previous chapters, decentralization in the command system in China has resulted in the expansion of power and administrative role of regional and local governments in domestic affairs. The placement of actors on CCTV news shows to some extent the effect of decentralization at both the provincial and local government level. Although the provincial governments did not attract as much news attention as other actors on CCTV news, when they turned out in the news they were usually placed ahead of actors at the ministerial levels. Like the provincial governments, local governments had insignificant proportion of exposure on the national television network, but its average location in the news trailed only behind that of the ministerial actors from 1992 to 1998. The story length for the main actors paints a slight different picture on the domestic news of CCTV.

STORY LENGTH FOR MAIN ACTORS ON CCTV NEWS

Chapter 4 indicated that the length of domestic news on CCTV increased from 1992 to 1998. The expanded story length, however, did not necessarily translate into a general rise for all sorts of actors. As reported in Table 5.3, the average story length shows that the amount of time devoted to the actors on CCTV news varied significantly over time for some players, but not for others. On the average, the Chinese heads of state/government commanded more than 2.5 minutes on CCTV news per newscast, followed immediately by congressional members at a little more than 2 minutes. Both types of actors were accorded a growing amount of time on CCTV news.

A detailed look at coverage of heads of state/government, and for that matter other top Chinese leaders, reveals that these stories often took place in meetings where the TV camera would move in a pendulum manner between left and right and zoom in and out while the anchorperson read a lengthy text over the visual image. The voice of the Chinese President Jiang Zemin or the Premier Zhu Rongji (or his predecessor Li Peng before 1998) was seldom heard directly in the news report. It is obvious that in settings like meetings or conferences, the visual image was not as important or relevant as the textual element. Often, the same visual images were repeated to accommodate the reading of policy statements or political and military announcements. The back and forth movement of TV camera usually showed participants seriously taking notes while the leaders spoke. At the end of meetings or conferences, a common practice was to present a relatively long and ordered list of names that read like a who's who in China. It is an overt announcement of who is to watch and be reckoned with in politics. In the Chinese world of political symbolism, no news is bad news, especially when one could not be seen or heard on the national TV network.

Although other actors saw slight extension of news time (between 30 and 40 seconds), the average story length for the courts stayed largely unchanged at a few seconds over 1 minute. The only actor that had news time reduced was political and party officials, whose

Table 5.3: Story Length for Main Actors in Domestic News on CCTV, 1992-1998[a]

Main Actor	1992	1996	1998	Total
Heads of state/government	69.6 (51.5)	166.2 (140.7)	168.6 (143.1)	155.3 (136.6)
Congress	111.6 (89.7)	78.5 (66.8)	179.3 (114.1)	126.4 (101.4)
Political/party officials	134.2 (165.8)	84.9 (65.6)	82.9 (51.8)	97.4 (101.2)
Local governments	67.6 (44.3)	106.6 (67.5)	106.4 (47.3)	92.1 (54.6)
Public/public opinion	51.1 (45.6)	83.7 (89.9)	91.9 (58.7)	75.4 (69.1)
Military/public security	60.2 (41.8)	71.4 (43.4)	93.3 (51.7)	68.3 (45.0)
Courts	65.5 (6.4)	68.0 (43.3)	67.0 (35.0)	67.2 (33.5)
Ministries/cabinet members	49.2 (19.0)	61.4 (51.9)	86.2 (63.3)	64.9 (51.4)
Interest groups	41.2 (27.2)	73.2 (68.9)	76.2 (62.7)	55.4 (50.7)
Provincial governments	43.9 (18.0)	64.6 (34.8)	69.6 (26.6)	54.7 (27.6)
Total	59.3 (65.1)	81.3 (77.0)	103.5 (84.0)	

[a]Entries are average length in seconds. Figures in parentheses are the standard deviation. A low standard deviation means the lengths of news stories are tightly clustered around the mean. A high standard deviation indicates that the news stories are widely dispersed.

average story length was cut from more than 2 minutes and 10 seconds in 1992 to less than 90 seconds in 1998 even though they still enjoyed an overall coverage of 97 seconds during the study period. The loss of time for political and party officials resulted in the gain for other actors. In addition to placement, the conspicuous attention given to local governments is reflected in the story length. In 1992, the stories about local governments ran just over 1 minute on CCTV, but were extended to more than 1 minute and 40 seconds in 1998.

A further qualitative analysis shows that the longer stories mean one thing: When they did appear on national television, local affairs received lengthened coverage through the activities of governmental officials at the grassroots levels. These were often stories that showcased how local officials carried out their duties in serving peasants, workers, and other ordinary citizens or what county and township governments were doing to help modernize the countryside and raise the general living standards in their areas since the economic reforms in the late 1970s. These stories appeared to carry an imprint of glorifying the virtues of state policies that might be reminiscent to the era under Mao. To dismiss such stories as an official propaganda, however, is to fall into the trap of the canonic belief that the entire mass communication system in China is a giant propaganda machine. Although these stories were apparently selected for their upbeat content, they were as real as the success of the Chinese economic reforms and openness, the trickle-down effect of which would eventually spread from the national to the local.

A WORLD OF ECONOMIC SUCCESS AND SOCIAL PROGRESS ON CCTV NEWS

From 1992 to 1998, the domestic news on CCTV tended to be ritualistic, progressive, and "puritanical" in that events and issues often revolved around current national efforts and governmental activities or achievements in moving the country forward, including collective concern and action against such natural disasters as flood and drought. For example, in 1992 an anti-drug campaign aired one day after the opening of the National People's Congress and the Political Consultative meeting and the conference on the study of Deng Xiaoping's speech, with 11 stories running over four consecutive days. Similar cases abound in 1996 and 1998, with frequent coverage of activities against social ills like smuggling and illegal copying of computer softwares, pornographic materials, and film and music CDs that were brought out by the success of economic reforms. Table 5.4 shows how CCTV news covers the various topics.

As far as the topical content was concerned, two related studies conducted in the 1970s (L. Chu, 1978) and the 1980s (Warren, 1988) provided some useful baseline for comparison of the domestic worldview on CCTV news throughout the process of China's pursuit of domestic economic liberalization and open-door policy. Whether one likes it or not, the fact that China has transformed itself in many aspects since the 1970s is undeniable. According to Chan (1993), as a result of the changing media market and if "the Chinese society keeps on differentiating and pluralizing, the demands for *timely, objective* and *diversified* political information will grow" (p. 25.16, italics added). News reporting in China means that the mass media would have to fulfill in a rational manner the public's needs for understanding and sharing of the everyday life, the essence of which constitutes social knowledge. The timeliness of CCTV news is clearly documented in the previous chapter. This section looks at how CCTV diversifies the scope of its news coverage.

Table 5.4: Topics of Domestic News on CCTV, 1992–1998[a]

Topic	1992	1996	1998	Total
Economic/trade/business	35.8%	18.3%	21.9%	25.7%
Transportation/travel/tourism	9.4	13.1	7.4	10.3
Law/crime	5.8	10.5	13.3	9.4
Education/arts/culture	7.3	11.4	6.3	8.6
Technology/science	7.7	11.9	4.8	8.6
Politics	4.4	5.9	17.8	8.2
Agriculture/forest	4.8	9.7	3.3	6.3
Social service/health	7.3	5.9	2.6	5.6
Disasters/accidents	3.4	0.5	8.9	3.6
Entertainment	2.2	3.1	5.6	3.4
Military/defense	4.8	2.6	0.7	3.0
Human interest/lifestyle	0.5	3.8	3.7	2.5
Sports	2.9	1.2	–	1.5
Ecology/environment	1.7	1.0	2.2	1.5
Obituary	1.9	1.2	1.1	1.4
Religion	–	–	0.4	0.1
Total	413	421	270	1,104

[a]The focus is on the main topic—what the story is mainly about. Excluded were other or unidentifiable stories.

The diversification of domestic news, and thus the expansion of knowledge, on the Chinese national television apparently grew with passage of the reform years. In 1977, a year before the reforms, for example, L. Chu (1978) found no coverage of crimes and disasters, either domestic or foreign, on BTS. By 1985, CCTV reported a small proportion of accidents and disasters (0.3%) and crime and justice (1.4%) in its domestic newscast (Warren, 1988).[4] Throughout the 1990s, crime and disaster-related stories appeared on CCTV on a regular basis, with both categories showing an upward trend (Table 5.4). This phenomenon is a substantial deviation from the early years.

[4]Because of the combination of domestic and foreign policy news, the proportion of topical content in Warren's study might be affected. Still, the proportional distribution of various topics in 1985 offered some point of reference.

It could be argued that the apparent lack of coverage of crime and disasters on the Chinese television in the late 1970s might be due to the small sample size in Chu's 1977 study. But, it was difficult to imagine that no crime or disaster occurred in China or around the world during the 1-week period. Common sense would suggest otherwise. Thus, the sample size did not seem to explain the absence of coverage. Because the news is essentially a matter of choice and presentation, an event or issue has to go through some control mechanism before it appears on the air or in the print page. A review of Chinese publications on the functions of news media in China (X. Sun, 1992) supports the observation that the absence of crime or disaster news was due to something else other than a sample selection.

A more plausible explanation for the absence of such news on the Chinese television then, at least in the domestic realm, is that crime and disaster stories, because of their negative nature, could undercut the Chinese authority's claim of a clean and superior Communist society. Because two thirds of the international news stories in Chu's study dealt with China's "good relationship" with Third World countries and events in Communist nations, avoiding coverage of crimes, disasters, or accidents from those countries and inside China would certainly imply that China was in an "ideal" company, hence serving some useful political purpose.

In fact, it was a standard practice before the reforms for the Chinese officials to cover up disasters caused by nature or human errors. For example, the devastation of an earthquake in January 1970 that killed more than 15,000 people in southwestern China was not publicly acknowledged by the Chinese government for three decades until relatives of the victims gathered in January 2000 for a memorial service (Associated Press, 2000). Unlike the situation in the 1970s, the presence of crime and disaster news on CCTV in the 1980s and throughout the 1990s represented a reasonable presentation of the real world in China. The economic reforms and openness have obviously made changes in what news is considered relevant to the formation of knowledge about the objective reality in Chinese society.

According the Associated Press, the Chinese government in recent years "has reported more openly about earthquakes and other disasters and accepted foreign assistance, although access by foreign journalists to rescue operations is still severely restricted" (Associated Press, 2000, p. A7). This openness in news reporting of domestic disasters and accidents is shown in the data in Table 5.4. Twenty years after the reforms, the proportion of disasters- and accident-related stories on CCTV reached a high point (8.9%) in 1998 when they ranked among the top four topics carried on the national television network. It is an indication that, given the rapid changes in communication technologies (e.g., the Internet) and competition in news reporting in China, disasters and accidents could not be effectively suppressed at the national level for political reasons. As harsh as it might be, the reality must be reported in some way.

For the most part, however, the news on CCTV is far from gloom and doom. On the contrary, it recurrently shows the country on the move and the people making headway in their daily lives. From 1977 to 1998, economic stories remained the main stock in domestic news on CCTV, indicating China's persistent concern over the economic progress and national development. In 1977, L. Chu (1978) found that 36.4% of news on BTS was related to "economic and social issues." By Warren's measures (1988), stories about "economics and industry" were the single most covered topic on CCTV (35.1%) in 1985. Although these two previous studies were not exactly comparable because of wording and coding, they nevertheless shared one thing in common: The economic aspect and other related areas were the staple of news on Chinese national television in the 1970s and 1980s.

In the 1990s, stories about economy, trade, and business still dominated the CCTV newscasts. The trend, however, is clearly moving toward diversification of the news content on CCTV. The proportions of CCTV domestic news coverage were remarkably similar between Warren's 1985 and the 1992 data in this study. Much like that in Warren's study, Table 5.4 shows that economic stories alone accounted for 36% of the total newscast on CCTV in 1992, with no other categories receiving coverage of double-digit proportion. In 1996 and 1998, although stories related to economy, trade, and business continued to outshine other types of news in the Chinese society, there were fluctuations of national concerns and social interests over time. What is certain is that disasters and accidents (3.6%), entertainment (3.4%), military and defense (3.0%), human interest and lifestyle (2.5%), sports (1.5%), ecology and environment (1.5%), obituaries (1.4%), and religion (0.1%) appeared only sporadically on CCTV news. Little has changed in the overall coverage of these types of news since the 1980s.

From 1992 to 1998, an interesting pattern to note is that entertainment stories saw a small, but steady increase (from 2.2% to 5.6%) on CCTV news over time, whereas the reverse was true for news about the military and defense, which dropped from 4.8% in 1992 to less than 1% in 1998. Considering that stories about the military occupied 4.6% on CCTV news in 1985 (Warren, 1988), the decline in the proportion of military news from a persistent level of about 5% to less than 1% suggests a visible shift to promote the soft side of the Chinese society, thus softening its image as a rigid, military country. The fact that entertainment stories clearly outnumbered the military and defense news (5.6% vs. 0.7%)

in 1998 probably indicates CCTV's subtle response to the market competition from provincial and major local TV stations that usually lean toward entertainment programs to attract viewers (X. Li, 1999).

Although the proportions of news coverage varied from year to year on CCTV, an indisputable fact is that economic news easily stood out as the dominating focus in the 1970s, 1980s, or the 1990s. Reform in China is essentially economic in nature. The Chinese government's commitment to reform was well captured in CCTV's prominent coverage of economic and other related issues. The dominant coverage of economic news, coupled with the paucity of environment stories (less than 2%), on CCTV partly supported Heuvel's (1993) observation that "issues that took a back seat to the Cold War—the environment or economic development—now receive more media attention" in the post-Cold War period (p. 13).

Unwavering quantity does not project an enduring worldview, however. A qualitative examination of the content then and now indicates that the substance of economic stories has transformed over time in China. In the late 1970s, the tone was general and abstract, in that the Chinese people were encouraged to work hard and forgo personal well-beings for the ultimate construction of the socialist motherland, whereas in the 1990s the pitch was more specific and concrete, dealing with joint ventures, investment opportunities and regulations, the success and failures of companies and businesses, and banking services. It is obvious that these kinds of knowledge perform different functions. In the 1970s, they served the needs of internal integration; in the 1990s, those of external interaction. The juxtaposition shows evidence of a differentiation of objectivation of news events or issues on CCTV that corresponds to the situational change in Chinese society.

Such emphasis on CCTV news about economic activities reflects existing social practices and policy commitments in China. Within the framework of sociology of knowledge, the circulation of economic news in the Chinese society suggests that its members are able to understand and thus participate in China's economic reforms and social reconstruction. Luo (1993), for instance, reported that the economic and trade news in the mass media increased communication and sharing of knowledge between mainland China and Taiwan. This kind of knowledge eventually helps orient the public mind and, by implication, the collective activity in China's march toward modernization. The news as a form of knowledge, in Park's (1985) view, has an interest that is "pragmatic rather than appreciative" (p. 82).

Pragmatic news in China does not lie in economic, trade and business stories only. As shown in Table 5.4, stories about transportation, travel, and tourism also ranked high on the overall CCTV newscast

(10.3%). Indeed, they were the second most covered category on CCTV news. Although no comparable data existed in the 1970s and 1980s, since the early 1990s, stories about transportation, particularly the completion of vital infrastructure such as highways, railroads, airports, and seaports, have been a constant feature on CCTV news. These stories usually were part of brief domestic reports, obviously grouped together to "show off" the leap and bound of national construction and social progress on a large scale in China. They were factual and free of ideological connotations, therefore conveying a panorama of a vibrant country in the news. The same can be said of stories about education, arts and culture (8.6%) as well as technological development and scientific advances (8.6%).

Like that of the actors, the placement of various topics on CCTV news discloses a subtle nuance in how the news is to be perceived in its significance in the world of Chinese television (see Table 5.5). Although the number of stories about crimes and disasters was small compared to other types of news, the openness and more receptiveness to present such kind of news on the national television network were reaffirmed by their lineup in the CCTV newscast. Stories related to crime and law issues as well as disasters and accidents generally were arranged before other categories of stories that did not pose any potential threat to the stability of social order or protection of properties and lives. A qualitative analysis presents different formation of news.

In crime and law stories, the high placement on CCTV news imparts a national priority to curb the rising tide of criminal and illegal activities on the one hand and to maintain social harmony and stability within an emerging legal and judicial order on the other. A typical crime story would be trials of criminals in court or police raids against smuggling or bulldozers crushing illegal CDs and softwares. A law-related story would be about meetings and conferences to draft, pass, or promulgate legal rules and their enforcement. As for news about disasters and accidents, the higher location in the CCTV news lineup established an official solicitude to safeguard people's lives and their properties. It is presented in the context of soldiers of the PLA fighting a flood or top national leaders surveying the disastrous areas and inquiring about the damages. Undoubtedly, both types of news promote an aura of official concern and authority to undertake serious domestic matters that require urgent attention and action.

Despite their moderate coverage on CCTV news (see Table 5.4), stories about politics and agricultural development in China generally topped other kinds of news (Table 5.5). In China, political stories usually involved activities of the Chinese Communist Party and other so-called democratic parties and occasionally concerned the legislative function of

Table 5.5: Placement of Topics in Domestic News on CCTV, 1992–1998[a]

Topic	1992	1996	1998	Total
Politics	8.9	10.0	5.8	7.6
Agriculture/forest	13.1	7.8	7.1	9.2
Law/crime	11.3	11.6	7.9	10.3
Economic/trade/business	11.5	11.7	7.4	10.7
Disasters/accidents	14.3	8.5	9.4	11.1
Obituary	8.5	15.8	13.0	11.6
Human interest/lifestyle	20.0	14.1	11.0	13.4
Military/defense	18.1	6.2	6.5	13.4
Technology/science	14.5	14.7	8.3	13.8
Ecology/environment	17.0	15.8	9.3	14.0
Transportation/travel/tourism	12.7	16.1	10.6	14.0
Education/arts/culture	18.6	14.2	9.7	14.8
Social service/health	17.6	14.6	11.3	15.7
Sports	14.8	20.2	–	16.4
Entertainment	20.9	17.8	13.9	17.0
Range	31	33	19	33

[a]Entries are average location of stories in the CCTV newscast lineup. The lower the number, the higher the story was placed in the lineup and vice versa. Because of the small number, religion was excluded.

the Chinese People's Congress. To a great extent, the activities of the Communist Party, of course, denote certain governmental operations because high ranking Chinese officials usually hold positions in both the government and party bureaucracies. For example, Chinese President Jiang Zemin is also the general secretary of the Communist Party. Likewise, other central governmental officials below him might assume corresponding positions in the Party hierarchy. As such, it is auspicious that stories about Communist Party officials, even though their governmental post might be omitted in the news due to the nature of settings (e.g., meetings of the Central Committee of the Communist Party), would usually appear first on the CCTV news lineup. It is an explicit reminder of the linkage politics in the media–state relationship in China.

The fact that stories about agriculture outdistanced many other types of news in the placement of CCTV news lineup should come as no surprise, either. Although the economic reforms since the late 1970s have unquestionably reshaped the Chinese sociopolitical foundation for national development, China remains fundamentally an agriculturally oriented nation. The agricultural sectors and the vast number of peasants across the country constitute the backbone of the Communist Party's power base. They might be farther removed from the power center in Beijing, but retain an indelible mark on the national psyche by their sheer number. Increases in agricultural productivity, construction of infrastructures in villages and the improvement of farmers' living conditions and standards on the CCTV news therefore signify China's conscientiousness over the general populace in the countryside. This observation is further affirmed by the amount of time devoted to each type of stories.

As is clear in Table 5.6, stories about entertainment, human interest and lifestyle, social service and health, sports, technology and science, ecology and environment, and transportation, travel, and tourism all averaged less than 1 minute on CCTV news during the entire study period, even though some of them (e.g., entertainment, social service and health, technology and science, and transportation and other related stories) ran more than 1 minute in 1998. Relatively speaking, these stories were not as noticeable as obituaries, politics, law/crime, economy/trade/business, agriculture/forest, disasters/accidents, education/arts/culture, and military/defense that on the average took more than 1 minute to report on CCTV news. Although obituaries were infrequent, their length was unusually long, averaging more than 2 minutes from 1992 to 1998. Length is certainly tied to the rank and achievements of the individuals involved. A closer examination of the obituaries shows that the news on CCTV was often used as a vehicle and platform to pay the last official tribute to those who have made significant contribution to either the Communist Party or the government or both.

As mentioned in chapter 4, the length of news on CCTV expanded over time, varying from less than 1 minute in 1992 to more than 1 minute in 1996 and 1.5 minutes in 1998. It represents a shift from more stories, but shorter reports to fewer stories, yet longer accounts on the Chinese national television network. In 1992, except for politics and obituaries, no other stories averaged more than 1 minute. Four years later in 1996, 10 out of the 15 news categories in Table 5.6 ranged, on the average, from 1 minute to more than 2 minutes. Although there were only two disaster- and accident-related stories—one about the snow storms in Neimonggol and the other about flooding in Hebei and Shandong—in 1996, CCTV news spent more than 3 minutes and 26 seconds showing the disaster and the efforts to control the damages. Although disasters were readily admitted in the news, they were constructed in a way that demonstrated the will of the government to overcome natural adversity.

Table 5.6: Length of Topics in Domestic News on CCTV, 1992-1998[a]

Topic	1992	1996	1998	Total
Obituary	196.1 (281.6)	49.4 (42.5)	80.7 (44.2)	128.6 (206.7)
Politics	79.7 (72.7)	75.2 (55.6)	114.1 (117.0)	96.6 (96.5)
Law/crime	50.7 (22.2)	83.8 (71.1)	115.5 (91.7)	87.1 (75.3)
Economic/trade/business	57.3 (25.8)	77.5 (94.7)	106.3 (83.4)	73.0 (75.2)
Agriculture/forest	39.0 (19.0)	74.3 (42.3)	122.6 (66.9)	70.4 (48.0)
Disasters/accidents	44.0 (23.6)	125.0 (114.6)	74.9 (43.6)	66.6 (45.4)
Education/arts/culture	46.0 (37.4)	70.5 (83.7)	91.6 (53.1)	66.5 (68.3)
Military/defense	53.1 (25.8)	67.4 (28.7)	115.5 (99.7)	61.6 (34.6)
Entertainment	32.0 (8.7)	73.7 (94.2)	64.1 (30.5)	59.7 (60.0)
Human interest/lifestyle	47.5 (38.9)	63.1 (45.5)	50.2 (44.1)	57.4 (43.6)
Social service/health	42.4 (23.6)	60.4 (66.0)	73.1 (37.7)	53.1 (47.4)
Sports	48.5 (40.8)	54.4 (9.5)	–	50.2 (34.3)
Technology/science	45.5 (21.9)	38.5 (41.8)	96.8 (75.4)	48.8 (46.6)
Ecology/environment	31.3 (11.2)	54.3 (38.4)	53.5 (22.5)	44.5 (24.8)
Transportation/travel/ tourism	39.0 (23.7)	24.7 (34.3)	77.5 (63.2)	38.9 (42.2)

[a]Entries are average length in seconds. Figures in parentheses are the standard deviation. A low standard deviation means the lengths of news stories are tightly clustered around the mean. A high standard deviation indicates that the news stories are widely dispersed. Because of the small number, religion was excluded.

By 1998, other than human interest/lifestyle and ecology/environment news, most stories on CCTV received longer treatment in the newscast, with stories about politics, law/crime, economy/trade/business, agriculture/forest, and military/defense running about 2 minutes in length. The most significant extension of length could be found in stories about agriculture and other related issues. Their average length jumped dramatically from around 30 seconds in 1992 to more than 2 minutes in 1998. The remaining types of news also doubled their amount of time, suggesting a more extensive coverage of stories on CCTV news. The lengthening of time for some stories, coupled with more frequent coverage of other types of news, leaves little doubt that CCTV news content has been more diversified in the late 1990s than it was earlier. Against the backdrop of social construction of reality, this phenomenon points out a growing tendency of CCTV to cast its "news net" (Tuchman, 1978) wider to capture more story elements in China.

Since the network news on CCTV is the only national news broadcast of its kind in China and every provincial and regional TV stations are required to carry it, the 7 p.m. prime-time newscast stands as a virtual monopoly of what part of the country and how much of it can been seen simultaneously by the national viewers. As the sole conveyor of news and information to the vast Chinese territory from the coastal to the inland areas, CCTV is situated in an unrivaled position to determine the kind of social knowledge that is deemed necessary and consequential to be shared across the nation. Given its physical limitations (e.g., amount of time) and other constraints (e.g., distance between locations), it is apparently impractical and unattainable for CCTV to survey and bestow every region as much exposure on national television as it might hope for. It must choose and its choice has implications. For one thing, the production of a particular kind of news, information, or knowledge cannot disclaim CCTV's involvement as a state apparatus in the Chinese circumstance.

UNEVEN COVERAGE OF PROVINCES ON CCTV

The administrative structure in China covers 27 provinces and autonomous regions, 4 municipalities, and 2 special administrative regions (Hong Kong in 1997 and Macao in 1999). They vary in population size, historical significance, natural resources, and degree of social and economic development. Geographically, the municipalities and provinces spread from the coastal regions to the inland areas that border with North Korea, Russia, Mongolia, some former Soviet Republics, India, Nepal, Pakistan, and Indochina in the northern, western, and southern territories. The extent to which provinces and municipalities appear on CCTV news transmits to the national audiences an explicit measure of their social and political significance in the eyes of the central TV network. In the Chinese context, the Middle Kingdom, as China is called sometimes, has a center of its own.

Beijing is the heart and mind of China. All government branches and agencies are located there, including the Zhongnanhai compound where the Chinese leadership works and the People's Great Hall where important meetings and receptions take place. By its mere location, Beijing naturally would garner more news attention than any other municipalities and provinces. To avoid an undue "inflation" in news exposure, unless Beijing as a municipality was clearly mentioned on CCTV news, stories about the central government's activities were excluded in the analysis. This conservative procedure gave, at least in theory, all other municipalities and provinces an equal, if not higher, chance to be identified on CCTV news.

Little systematic and longitudinal analysis of news coverage of China's vast territories has been documented before. Albeit insufficient, Warren's 1985 study of CCTV news nevertheless offered a glimpse into the configuration of Chinese domestic landscape. In the mid-1980s, "[t]wenty seven of China's provinces, autonomous regions, and national-level cities received one or more stories. Beijing, the capital, received the greatest coverage (179 stories). Hubie (sic), in central China, was second (12 stories)" (Warren, 1998, p. 220). This brief observation left too much to be desired, however. It did not capture the full range of Chinese landscape in the symbolic world of news. Table 5.7 reports how various provinces and municipalities in China were covered on CCTV news from 1992 to 1998.

Without any doubt, coverage of the individual provinces and municipalities in China was extremely unequal. From 1992 to 1998, Beijing as the power center of China was firmly affirmed on CCTV news. During the study period, nearly one third of news on CCTV occurred in Beijing. It is indicative of Beijing's ability to generate newsworthy events and issues, the spectacle of which deserved to be observed nationwide. Except for Hong Kong in 1998, no other municipalities or provinces received more than 10% of news coverage on CCTV. Next to Beijing and Hong Kong on CCTV news were Shanghai municipality and Guangdong and Heilongjiang provinces, each with more than 3% of coverage. As a matter of fact, in the same year, of the 32 provinces, municipalities, and special region, 24 were covered in less than 2%, or none at all, of the total stories carried on CCTV: Liaoning, Jiangsu, Shandong, Tianjin, Hebei, Hubei, Anhui, Jiangxi, Neimonggol, Sichuan, Xinjiang, Fujian, Xizang, Shanxi, Yunnan, Henan, Hunan, Zhejiang, Guizhou, Gansu, Hainan, Qinghai, Ningxia, and Chongqing. Such meager coverage denied the problems of these provinces and municipalities a national attention and perhaps national solutions.

Before 1997, Hong Kong was still under the British rule. Its relative high visibility on CCTV news in 1996 indisputably underlined China's eagerness about the resumption of sovereignty over the island ceded to Britain for more than 150 years. The prominent attention devoted to Hong Kong on CCTV news in 1998 centered around stories about its continuous prosperity and stability under the Chinese rule that had defied Western expectation and prediction. CCTV news also touted the success of its "one country, two systems" policy that was said to have made Hong Kong's transition from the British to the Chinese control smooth and democratic. In 1992, Hong Kong as a British colony did not enjoy as much coverage on CCTV news as it did before and after the 1997 handover. This particular case offers a concrete piece of evidence supporting the central thesis of news as a form of social knowledge that builds around prevalent national priority and policy involvement.

Table 5.7: Coverage of Province/Municipality on CCTV News, 1992–1998

Province/Municipality[a]	1992	1996	1998	Total
Beijing Municipality	26.8%	34.8%	38.9%	32.5%
Hong Kong[b]	3.8	7.3	15.6	7.9
Shanghai Municipality	5.7	4.8	4.7	5.2
Guangdong	3.6	7.3	3.8	4.9
Liaoning	6.0	2.6	1.4	3.7
Heilongjiang	4.9	2.2	3.3	3.6
Jiangsu	4.6	2.9	1.4	3.3
Shandong	5.5	1.6	0.5	2.9
Tianjin Municipality	3.3	3.8	0.9	2.9
Hebei	3.0	3.2	0.9	2.6
Shaanxi	2.5	2.2	2.4	2.4
Hubei	3.6	0.6	1.9	2.1
Anhui	2.7	1.9	0.9	2.0
Jiangxi	2.2	1.9	1.9	2.0
Jilin	2.5	1.0	2.8	2.0
Neimonggol	2.7	1.9	0.9	2.0
Sichuan	1.6	2.6	1.9	2.0
Xinjiang	1.4	2.2	1.9	1.8
Fujian	1.4	1.9	1.4	1.6
Xizang	1.1	1.9	1.9	1.6
Guangxi	1.1	1.0	2.8	1.5
Shanxi	1.1	1.9	1.4	1.5
Yunnan	1.6	1.3	1.4	1.5
Henan	0.5	2.6	0.9	1.3
Hunan	1.4	1.0	1.9	1.3
Zhejiang	2.5	1.0	–	1.3
Guizhou	0.5	1.0	0.5	0.7
Gansu	0.8	0.6	–	0.6
Hainan	0.5	0.3	0.9	0.6
Qinghai	1.1	0.3	–	0.6
Ningxia	–	0.3	–	0.1
Chongqing Municipality	–	–	0.5	0.1
Total	366	313	211	890

[a]Unless the municipality of Beijing was clearly mentioned, stories about the central government's activities were not considered. Excluded also were foreign stories and those domestic stories with unclear or multiple locations.

[b]Hong Kong was considered foreign when it was ruled by Britain before 1997. It was included for comparison purpose.

Not only did CCTV news coverage favor certain provinces and municipalities, it also followed some geographical divide. As shown in Table 5.8, from 1992 to 1998, CCTV displayed no variation over time in its coverage of coastal and inland regions. Almost two thirds of CCTV stories during the study period were given to coastal regions that included less than half of the 32 provinces, municipalities, and regions: Beijing, Hebei, Hong Kong, Fujian, Guangdong, Guangxi, Hainan, Jiangsu, Liaoning, Shandong, Shanghai, Tianjin, and Zhejiang. The remaining 19 provinces and municipalities represented only about one third of CCTV news coverage. This discrepancy could largely be attributed to the fact that CCTV own correspondents had more direct access to the coastal regions than the inland areas while stories about inland provinces tended to be supplied by regional and local TV stations (see Table 5.9). Much like the Western practice, it is an organizational imperative that dictates television news to be reported in a cost-effective rationality (e.g., Epstein, 1973). But, of course, CCTV news would cover events or issues in any remote area in China when important people were involved or special occasions called for.

A comparison of coverage between coastal and inland provinces on CCTV exposes some differential treatment of varying regions in China regarding how fast they come to be presented in the news, what brings them to the attention of the nation, and who makes news in the respective settings. Taken together, these aspects put forward some clues as to where, when and why national priorities might be placed the way they do on CCTV news. To a large extent, they also reflect the effects of production constraints, social development and political clout on the news content in China. In this sense, regional stories on CCTV news become indicators of technological efficiency of communication, inherent dynamic of secular evolution, and strength of power base across geographical areas in China.

Table 5.8: Geographical Coverage of Provinces on CCTV News, 1992–1998

Geographical Location	1992	1996	1998	Total
Coastal regions[a]	62.3%	68.3%	69.0%	66.2%
Inland regions	37.7	31.7	31.0	33.8
Total	284	281	168	733

$X^2 = 3.08$, $df = 2$, $p = $ n.g.

[a]Coastal regions include the following provinces and municipalities: Beijing, Hebei, Hong Kong, Fujian, Guangdong, Hainan, Jiangsu, Liaoning, Shandong, Shanghai, Tianjin, and Zhejiang. The rest are inland regions.

Table 5.9: Attribution of News by Provinces on CCTV, 1992–1998

Attribution of News	Coastal Provinces[a]	Inland Provinces	Total
CCTV own correspondents	79.4%	50.8%	69.7%
Other domestic medium	17.1	43.1	25.9
Unidentified	3.1	5.6	4.0
Xinhua	0.4	0.4	0.4
Total	485	248	733

$X^2 = 64.82$, $df = 3$, $p < .01$

[a]Coastal provinces include the following provinces and municipalities: Beijing, Hebei, Hong Kong, Fujian, Guangdong, Hainan, Jiangsu, Liaoning, Shandong, Shanghai, Tianjin, and Zhejiang. The rest are inland provinces.

According to the data in Table 5.10, stories about coastal provinces were more likely to be reported in a timely fashion than those from the inland provinces. For example, during the entire study period from 1992 to 1998, about 40% of stories concerning coastal provinces went on the air on CCTV "today," but only about 9% of stories from inland provinces did so. In a technical and journalistic fashion, the transmission of stories from local or regional TV stations in inland provinces to CCTV in Beijing apparently was slower than their counterparts in coastal provinces. By the time the stories appeared on CCTV, they were mostly old news. Nearly 50% of stories reported on CCTV about inland provinces took place either "yesterday" (10.2%) or "recently/this week" (39.0%), compared to 8% and 23%, respectively, of stories from coastal regions. Such shortage of timely delivery seems to create an air of less urgency at the national level for news events and issues happening in more remote areas of China. The fact that they were reported at all means the content itself was more meaningful than the requirement of timing. Table 5.11 supports this observation.

Stories about economy, trade, and business evidently did not distinguish CCTV coverage of news between coastal provinces (26.8%) and inland regions (23.7%) even though there was a slim difference in favor of the former. After more than 20 years of economic reforms, this general category of news has outstripped all other types of stories irrespective of their geographical location. What set coastal and inland provinces apart on CCTV news rests mainly in stories regarding transportation, education/arts/culture, politics, agriculture/forest, and disasters and accidents. They indicate territorial interests, national priority or natural vulnerability faced by individual provinces.

Table 5.10: Timeliness of News by Provinces on CCTV, 1992–1998

Timeliness of News	Coastal Provinces[a]	Inland Provinces	Total
Unidentified	26.6%	39.9%	31.1%
Today	40.0	8.5	29.3
Recently/this week	22.9	39.1	28.4
Yesterday	8.0	10.1	8.7
Last week/last month	2.0	2.4	2.2
Future	0.4	0.3	
Total	485	248	733

$X^2 = 83.23$, $df = 6$, $p < .01$

[a]Coastal provinces include the following provinces and municipalities: Beijing, Hebei, Hong Kong, Fujian, Guangdong, Hainan, Jiangsu, Liaoning, Shandong, Shanghai, Tianjin, and Zhejiang. The rest are inland provinces.

Table 5.11: Coverage of Topics by Provinces on CCTV News, 1992–1998

Topic	Coastal Provinces	Inland Provinces	Total[a]
Economic/trade/business	26.7%	24.2%	25.8%
Law/crime	9.8	11.5	10.4
Transportation/travel/tourism	7.6	15.2	10.2
Technology/science	8.9	11.5	9.8
Education/arts/culture	10.2	5.7	8.6
Politics	9.3	2.5	6.9
Agriculture/forest	4.0	10.2	6.2
Social service/heath	6.2	4.5	5.6
Disasters/accidents	1.8	7.0	3.6
Entertainment	4.7	1.2	3.5
Human interest/lifestyle	3.8	3.3	3.6
Obituary	2.4	1.2	2.0
Ecology/environment	2.0	1.6	1.9
Sports	1.8	–	1.2
Military/defense	0.9	0.4	0.7
Total	450	244	694

$X^2 = 59.58$, $df = 14$, $p < .01$

[a]The data differ slightly from those in Table 5.4 because stories about activities of the central government were excluded unless Beijing was clearly identified.

Throughout the study period, the completion of highways and extension of railroad routes as part of China's infrastructure construction showed up more frequently in stories about inland provinces (14.7%) than they did in coastal regions (8%). On the educational and cultural side, coastal provinces (10%) outpaced inland regions (6%) on CCTV news. The same was true for stories about politics (9.1% vs. 2.6%). For the inland provinces (10.8%), stories about agricultural development and productivity generally outnumbered those from coastal regions (3.9%). So did the stories about disasters and accidents (6.9% vs. 1.9%).

If the CCTV news was any guide, because the inland provinces might be more prone to natural and man-made disasters and accidents, their geographical inaccessibility probably made it easier for the Chinese authority to conceal such stories. As mentioned previously, the Chinese government not only covered up a magnitude-7.7 earthquake that killed more than 15,000 people in the inland Yunnan province during the chaotic Cultural Revolution from 1966 to 1976, but also kept silent for three decades (Associated Press, 2000). Official attention or inattention, particularly that from the Chinese national leadership, clearly plays a role in what and how news is to be diffused in China. Table 5.12 shows how various actors play out on CCTV news under different geographical context. Again, a clear-cut inconsistency can be observed.

As far as newsmaking was concerned, there existed on CCTV newscast a division of power that dictated who was more newsworthy in a given environment. In other words, the combination of sites and actors on CCTV news points out where the action is and what the concerns are. When CCTV reported about news from coastal provinces, the actors were more likely to be interest groups (24.1%), ministries and their members (18.7%), political and party officials (13.5%), and heads of state/government (8.3%). By contrast, stories from inland provinces on the whole featured more frequently nonofficial individuals or public opinion (23.7%), local and provincial governments (27.3%), and military and public security (10.8%) as actors. Such discriminant portrayal of actors captures an orientation of Chinese newsmakers and an unspoken journalistic gravitation to frame them in a preferred mode of symbolic presentation.

Although it does not have to be a zero-sum game, the higher visibility of national leadership in coastal provinces accompanied by their reduced presence in inland regions where local officials and nonofficials—in most cases peasants and workers—became more discernible fosters an astute contrast of the connection between the capability of actors and their position in the larger social structure to forge news attention in China. Basically, those who occupied a lower status or were posted in a peripheral surrounding played a supporting cast to the leading roles of major actors in administration, politics, and business arenas. Coastal provinces tended to make news as a result of their strategic loca-

Table 5.12: Main Actors in News by Provinces on CCTV, 1992–1998

Main Actor	Coastal Provinces	Inland Provinces	Total[a]
Interest groups	24.3	19.7	23.0%
Public/public opinion	13.5	23.8	16.4
Ministries/cabinet members	18.8	8.2	15.8
Political/party officials	13.8	4.1	11.0
Local governments	7.7	12.2	9.0
Military/public security	5.0	10.9	6.7
Heads of state/government	8.5	2.0	6.7
Provincial governments	2.4	15.0	5.9
Congress	4.2	2.7	3.8
Courts	1.9	1.4	1.7
Total	378	147	525

$X^2 = 68.02$, $df = 9$, $p < .01$

[a]The data differ slightly from those in Table 5.1 because stories about activities of the central government were excluded unless Beijing was clearly identified.

tions, historical significance, and economic might to attract the powers that be on the national television radar.

A CHANGING WORLD AND SHIFTING WORLDVIEW ON NATIONAL TELEVISION

This chapter began with a premise that as a form of social knowledge, the news in any given society goes beyond simply a reflection of reality by engaging in a cognizant construction of the real that is conducive for its members to make sense of their immediate environment and the distant landscape. As is well known, the world in China has been changing since the reforms and openness in the late 1970s. Being part of the total environment that has undergone conceptual reexamination and structural reconfiguration, the Chinese news media cannot but help entangle in the web and pace of the rapid social change. Notwithstanding their subjugation to the state ownership, they are a knowledge-producing institution subject to the influences of social forces and market logic. It is inconceivable that when China has transformed itself in ways that defy expectation, the news media would remain indifferent to the secularization and rationalization of the public sector.

The findings presented here show that the Chinese national television promoted current social design and prevalent undertakings in its news coverage. Both economic reform and social progress-related stories, such as transportation infrastructure, technological, and scientific achievements, and agricultural development, significantly outnumbered all other types of news in domestic coverage on CCTV. Although socialism as a thematic element in stories still appeared relevant in the 1990s, thanks mostly to a functional need for legitimacy, it was not as prominent as it was in 1977 (L. Chu, 1978). For those who follow only China's domestic activities, the leading picture would be its concerted drive toward market-oriented economy and modernization efforts since the late 1970s. The continued transmission of information or knowledge about the direction the country is heading therefore creates for the Chinese people a sense of familiarity and routinization in their everyday life. At least, it supplies a body of theory and practice through which a set of beliefs, social positions, and national orientation are made available to members of Chinese society.

Although far from dominating the airwaves, the increasing tendency for CCTV to cover stories about disasters and accidents in China departs from the past official standard practice that normally swept anything detrimental to the nation's image and authority under the rug and pretended that it never happened. This certainly can be tied to the difficulty in the information age to strictly tighten the control of information and news flow in China. It most likely represents a realization on the part of the Chinese authority that events or issues, when they are molded in certain ways into news, do not necessarily undermine its power and integrity. Instead, the dissemination of bad news about disasters and accidents, albeit in a limited amount, within the context of official efforts to resolve the problems gives the news a human touch that may help unite the country to tackle the common woes and social setbacks.

Contrary to the Cultural Revolution image, as a window on the Chinese society, CCTV did not always highlight the leadership of the Communist Party or the government or both as being omnipresent in the domestic life of the Chinese people during the last decade of China's reforms and openness. Nor did it parade the military or the security forces as frequently as it was before. In fact, there has been evidence in recent years indicating a growing inclination to include sources from not only organized groups, but also private individuals. Although the voice and views of those from the civic sectors usually do not challenge or question the policies of the state, the changing picture of who is to speak and how and what to say on national television paints a rational response to the process of decentralization and depoliticization in newsmaking.

Nevertheless, in a country where the tension between the central and the local power equation remains volatile and the economic development and social progress highly uneven (Ding, 1998), there is an unequivocal imbalance of news coverage from the coastal to the inland provinces on CCTV. Moreover, Beijing as the heart of China commands a great deal of spotlight on the country's only national television network. The unequal coverage between sectors of reality and a preferred focus on a particular site in China points out a conscious journalistic routine that gravitates toward the sector commonly deemed salient. For the most part, the integration of CCTV into the state's central control mechanism predetermines how the national TV news may perform.

Although the nature of TV networks between China and the United States is not directly comparable, the overwhelming preference given to the Chinese capital on CCTV news is similar to the U.S. network coverage of state news, in which 50% of all news stories were generated from Washington, DC (Graber, 1993). Apparently, ownership of a television network (e.g., state-owned vs. privately controlled) or organizational character (e.g., commercially oriented vs. ideologically charged) cannot satisfactorily explain why diverse networks cover the power center of their respective country in very much the same way.

The explanation lies elsewhere. Within the sociology of knowledge perspective, it means that the presentation of news in the Chinese media is determined not so much on the properties of the event or issue itself, but rather on its place in the broader social structure in China. As noted earlier, the social location of journalists more or less confines them to see the reality within a limited number of points of departure or problematic. The shifting worldview, as sketched on CCTV and circulated by it amid the changing Chinese world, represents the kind of knowledge that results from the interaction between objective reality and China's own practical calculations and social commitments.

Since the beginning of the reform movement in the late 1970s, the news as a form of knowledge in China has performed a dual function to orient the people and the society toward aspects of the social world that are most relevant and familiar to the Chinese experience. It is not only quantitatively dictated by the technical logic that requires speedy circulation and broader distribution of information and knowledge among the population, but also qualitatively designed to put the social reality into perspective within the Chinese context. Compared to foreign news coverage (see chapter 6), the domestic news stresses the government's current commitment to and practices of economic reform and social restructuring. In essence, the news in China provides the Chinese society and people with the basic knowledge and a baseline needed for the building of a forced consensus, the basis of Communist rule and legitimacy.

CCTV NEWS AND THE WORLD OUT THERE: SOCIAL CONSTRUCTION OF FOREIGN SPECTACLES FROM A DISTANCE

In an interview with the press in September 1998, Zhao Qizheng, director of News Office of the State Council, indicated that because of historical reasons, cultural differences between the East and the West, and the international barriers created by the Cold War mentality, not only did foreign countries not understand China adequately, some Western news media were also often biased in their coverage of China. Under such circumstances, he said, the best way to let the world know about China timely and truthfully is to strengthen the accuracy, transparency, and timeliness of Chinese news reporting. He specifically cited the two live broadcasts of President Clinton's visit to Beijing in June 1998 as an example of how Chinese news media might do to provide better communication and help improve foreign understanding between China and the rest of the world.[1]

Since China's reforms and openness in the late 1970s, the Chinese news media have unquestionably made significant improvement in their reporting about China and the world. Take the Chinese

---

[1]The interview was reported by the Chinese newspaper *Singtao Daily* on its Internet edition retrieved April 9, 1998 from the World Wide Web: http://www.singtao.com/news/04/0904eo03.html.

national television. As shown in chapters 4 and 5, CCTV's network news indeed became more timely and transparent in its coverage of domestic news from 1992 to 1998. Because of a lack of an external yardstick, however, whether CCTV reported the news accurately remains to be further answered. One way of determining how CCTV news covers the world, both domestic and foreign, is to compare the form and content of these two types of news during the same time span. The purpose of this chapter is to explore the approach foreign news is shown on CCTV and how it contrasts with domestic news on some common dimensions over time. The longitudinal analysis and the comparison with coverage of domestic news should help identify the fundamental pattern of the Chinese worldview on the national television news and delineate the perceptions of the world's nations in China that might still be framed by the residual Cold War mindset or lingering nervousness, as demonstrated in Zhao's remark.

    Foreign news, as defined in this study, refers to stories involving the world landscape outside the Chinese geopolitical sphere without China being part of the picture. The conceptual differentiation between foreign news and foreign policy news (see chapter 4 for more discussion) means that each type of story has different implications for the way Chinese news media cover the world. For one thing, previous studies (e.g., Chang et al., 1993) clearly documented "that the world as presented in foreign news is less likely to be affected by the Chinese responses to changes in the international environment through its assessment and redefinition of relationship to other countries in the world, than the one created in foreign policy news" (p. 179). In addition to the effect of range of vision on how sectors of the world may be perceived, involvement is also a critical factor. Any news medium that writes about the reality must locate itself vis-à-vis the object of interest and observation. This social location includes the perspective the medium adopts, the national structure it faces, and the kind of international circumstances that arise.

    One of the circumstances the Chinese news media encounter is China's gradual integration into the global system. The 20-year economic reforms and social openness have transformed the country beyond recognition. China is no longer an international pariah in the community of nations. According to Shambaugh (1991), "China has qualitatively changed during the 1980s" and is now "heavily dependent on the outside world" (p. 49). The international dependence means that China as a member of the world community cannot afford to ignore the actions that other countries may take or the reactions they have toward Chinese behaviors, as it used to in years of isolation before and during the Cultural Revolution. Any changes in the Chinese worldview are therefore likely to appear in the realm of China's interaction with other countries than in the arena of its own survey of the world's political vista. That interplay involves China's foreign policy or international relations and is addressed in chapter 7. Coverage of foreign policy news on CCTV represents an insider's point of view that is apparently different from that of foreign news.

In foreign news reporting, China stands as an outsider, detached from the events or issues involved. Observing the world from a distance, the Chinese news media should be more removed from the reality and feel less constrained by any official calculation, as opposed to an internal setting. The raison d'être is simple. Whether negative or positive, any event or issue about other countries does not necessarily implicate China one way or another, as might foreign policy news or domestic news. Because China is not part of the picture, the reporting of a foreign scene could not be effectively used as a tool for domestic damage control even though, by comparison, it might make China look good. To paraphrase Liebling (1964, p. 165), in the area of foreign news, the news media "are less trammeled" by the state's mass phobias than they might be in the arena of domestic news. There has been some observation that the Chinese news media do indeed subscribe to two sets of journalistic practices with different implications.

For example, Mark Brayne, a BBC World Service diplomatic correspondent posted in Beijing from 1984 to 1987, indicated that although Xinhua News Agency's reporting on domestic affairs was "inadequate, often inaccurate and always idiosyncratic," "its foreign coverage, where this did not impinge on direct Chinese interests, was at that time refreshingly unbiased, and was incomparably more readable, informative and comprehensive" (Brayne, 1992, p. 54). As the state-owned national news agency, Xinhua has the authority and resources to control the flow of news in and out of China. Its reporting of foreign news could be taken as an indication of how other Chinese news media might do. If the 1980s saw better reporting of foreign news among the Chinese news media, what would it be like in the 1990s when the world was no longer characterized by the U.S.–Soviet confrontation? How did the end of Cold War situate the mass media in China to decode the geopolitical reality, whose elements comprise of the familiar and the uncertain, the difference of which has toppled Communism in eastern Europe and ushered in a new wave of democratization worldwide?

CHINA AND THE WORLD
AFTER THE END OF COLD WAR

A central premise in this study is that when the world at large is changing, China cannot remain unchanged or unchanging, particularly when
the momentum of Chinese glasnost and perestroika has set the country
in rapid motion for more than 20 years. It will be hard for China and its
various institutions, including the mass media, not to search for a more
open and less ideological approach to probing and describing the world
reality. In the structure and processes of mass communication, to overlook the reality-defining or mediated role of Chinese news media in the
generation of imagery, vocabulary, narrative, and ideas with which to
say something about the world over time and across space is to ignore
the interplay between disinterested observation and subjective experience. Since the end of Cold War in the early 1990s, China has faced a
complex world that requires its news media to provide an adequate
empirical and interpretive window to reassess the world's nations and
their problems. The Chinese mass media need to supply the people with
a mentality or a set of beliefs that allow them to deal with or see the
shifting world as a regular phenomenon embracing some knowable
characteristics.

As noted in the previous chapters, for the first three decades
since 1949, the mass media system in China had been looked at within
the propaganda and persuasion model against the backdrop of the
East–West conflict. Internally, the Chinese social control and political
arrangement helped contribute to the scholarly and journalistic views
from outside. During the Cultural Revolution, the Chinese mass media
were structurally situated and ideologically charged to promote the official worldview and the state power dictated by the imperative of class
struggle and revolutionary necessity in a totalitarian system. Given the
rigid centralized command system, the accepted knowledge is that the
Chinese mass media essentially served as the mouthpiece of the state in
general and the Communist Party in particular. This longstanding belief
permeates the literature that subscribes to and prescribes the perma-
nence of a total state domination and mass indoctrination mechanism in
China. The reality, however, defies traditional fixation.

As the last Communist stronghold and the rising superpower
with the world's largest population after the demise of Communism in
the eastern Europe and the former Soviet Union, China represents an
intriguing country of political, economic, social, and cultural intricacy
and complexity. How it acts and reacts to the ebb and flow of world
events or issues often contradicts the conventional wisdom and common
understanding in both academic and journalistic communities beyond

its own geopolitical sphere. The reconfiguration of the global structure undoubtedly has shifted the power balance in international relations and the subsequent coverage of the key players in foreign and domestic news around the world (e.g., Matlock, 1993). In international communication, the versatile reality therefore compels the mass media to rethink how the world is to be approached, recorded, and presented in the journalistic sense.

In news reporting, the pressing task is to find those aspects of the world that are germane to the interests and concerns of the host countries involved. As the editors of a 1993 issue on "Global News after the Cold War" in the *Media Studies Journal* succinctly put it, "for the media, the goal is to catch up with the world's changes and to develop a new overarching structure for covering news after the Cold War" (Dennis & Pease, 1993, p. xii). Among other things, the need for an "overarching structure" drives the media to make sense of a "brave and scary new world" (Heuvel, 1993), to seek "new opportunity for broadened coverage" (Graham-Yooll, 1993), to question "assumptions about coverage" (Gwertzman, 1993), and to call for "new ways of reporting" the post-Cold War world reality (Boccardi, 1993). A similar conceptual approach was also evident in the 1999 special issue on "Covering China" in the same journal. The reporting of the world and China is largely regarded as a method of regularized news writing, journalistic vision and investigation that is dominated by perspectives, imperatives and ideological preference.

Considering the internal and external transformation that has taken place in and out of China, how the Chinese window on the world reports the foreign spectacle over time therefore merits closer scrutiny. "Journalists' portraits of another country," in the views of the editors in the 1999 *Media Studies Journal*, "are usually influenced by the questions, concerns and conceptions they bring from their own land" (p. xiii). There should be little doubt that the Chinese news media have their own "questions, concerns and conceptions" about the rest of the world. These facets become more acute because of the submission of the mass media to the state authority and official guidance in China. Although the economic liberalization has the unintended effect of pushing for structural changes inside the Chinese media system, the state never fails to remind the mass media that journalism is intrinsically tied to the destiny of the nation and the Party (Beijing heightens, 1999, p. A1; Kwang, 1996).

Although there were some sporadic studies in the past (e.g., Warren, 1988), none has systematically and longitudinally analyzed the way CCT news surveyed the world that might help shape what Lippmann (1922) called "the pictures" in the heads of Chinese viewers about the remote reality. Little is also known about the hot spots and blind sites on Chinese national television. Such news geography entails a hierarchy of nations and a form of concentration of national attention or indifference in the international news flow and coverage (e.g., Harris, 1974). If all countries are not created equal to be news (e.g., Chang, 1998), the selection and presentation of other nations in the news underlie a percipient choice on the part of the perceiver. It is a system of reproduction framed by a wide variety of factors that are themselves a product of certain political forces and social activities.

This should be particularly true in China because of the state's apprehension over the mass media as means of bringing the world closer to home for most people. After all, the stream of foreign events or issues produced by the world's countries on any given day is infinite and unceasing. From this constant flow, like their counterparts in other countries, the Chinese news media, through their selective and editing processes, create a map of the world or representation of external reality for the domestic audiences. Again, the point of theoretical departure in this chapter is the sociology of knowledge perspective (Berger & Luckmann, 1966), the essence of which—social construction of reality—can be extended from the domestic to the foreign domain of news. Because of distance and ethnocentric bias, the news in China is bound to depict foreign spectacles in ways different from those of the domestic reality. The disparity of coverage between the two worlds produces not only a news discourse, but a body of social knowledge.

Earlier studies on Chinese mass communication had considered the mass media in China as the quintessential part of the ideological state apparatus firmly controlled by the central authority (e.g., Houn, 1961; A. Liu, 1971; Schurmann, 1966; F. Yu, 1964). A quick glance of the titles of these previous works, except for Houn's study, clearly indicates a common thread underpinning their ideological focus on the country—the identification of China as "Communist," a practice of condensational symbolism that was consistent with that in the news and official policy thinking before Sino-American normalization in the early 1970s (e.g., Chang, 1993). The use of this symbol was more than rhetorical. Conceptually, it endorsed the claims of Western policy makers that the social reality in China was to be qualified by an ideological propinquity. It was frequently informed by the standardized and political stereotyping of China as an idea and a reality.

Notwithstanding the symbolic undertone, at a time in the late 1970s when China was about to embark on its ambitious economic reform and open-door policy movement, such a strong background belief led Pye (1978) to argue that "any study of the spirit and practice of governance in China today *must* still take into account the *fundamental* findings" of earlier studies "on how the Chinese use the radio and the press to *propagandize* their goals and *change* the attitudes of their people" (p. 221, italics added). This line of thinking, although consonant with the behavior of a militant and revolutionary China within the Cold War framework, failed to leave room for the reality that has yet to come, particularly the emergence of China's "four modernizations" campaigns that set the economic reform in motion, leading eventually to a journalistic reform (e.g., Polumbaum, 1990). The latter has not been institutionalized as it has in the economic sphere, however.

Although skepticism abound (for a discussion, see Huang, 1995), a growing body of empirical evidence and knowledge has in recent years documented the fluctuating structure and increasing potential in China's mass media development. These changes include, but are not necessarily limited to, the following phenomena: professionalism in the Chinese journalism and mass communication education and staff training (e.g., Greenberg & Lau, 1990; Hao & Xu, 1997), decentralization in organization control and production (e.g., White, 1990; Yu, 1990), content variation in both print and broadcast media (e.g., Chang et al., 1993; J. Wang & Chang, 1996), depoliticization of messages (e.g., C. Lee, 1994), internationalization of media relations and cultural practices (e.g., Chan, 1994; Hong, 1993, 1997), and market and audience orientation (e.g., G. Chu & Ju, 1992; He, 2000; Lull, 1991; X. Zhang, 1993). All of these structural and procedural changes mostly took place in the 1990s and continues in the early 21st century.

In short, China's economic restructuring and policy reconfiguration have inevitably generated a media reform in almost every aspect of the industry at a pace that was unthinkable during or before the Cultural Revolution (e.g., L. Chu, 1994). To look at the changing phenomena in China in mid-2001, "through a narrow theoretical telescope designed years ago," as Chang and his associates (1993) indicated, "is to miss the opportunity for a better understanding of the larger picture or 'the widest range of opportunities for theory building'" (p. 192). Echoing their call for broader conceptual and methodological approaches to the study of Chinese mass media, Huang (1995) argued that as far as China's prospects were concerned, "the current wide gap between conventional wisdom and hard evidence" demanded "a more balanced and level-headed view" (p. 68). This is not simply a matter of academic debate.

In news reporting, the "old constructs" about China have been deemed inadequate in that the unpredictable society needs "a flexible and sophisticated journalistic perspective" (Tefft, 1993, p. 62). Such narrow intellectual and professional range of vision of the Chinese society has long been considered to be "rooted not in China but in the United States" (Harding, 1984, p. 307). "The very first step" toward a better conceptualization, as Huang (1995) argued, "should be to throw out much of our conventional wisdom." (p. 68). Although the evidence may still be sketchy, studies of sociology of news and knowledge have provided challenging and penetrating insights into the interplay among social communication, public knowledge, and everyday life. The presentation of foreign spectacles in news reporting is one particular aspect that specifically deals with the reality lying beyond the national frontier and habitual personal acquaintance. It is not merely imaginative, but rather a style of perspective based on an ontological and epistemological distinction made between here and there.

THE NEWS AND SOCIAL CONSTRUCTION OF FOREIGN SPECTACLES

The perspective of social construction of reality views the news as essentially a form of knowledge that is necessary for any given society, whether democratic or authoritarian, to operate efficiently and effectively. In his seminal work, Park (1955) argued that the function of news "is to orient man and society in an actual world" (p. 86). More recently, Edelman (1992) suggested that "there can be no world of events distinct from the interpretations of observers" (p. 24). Consequently, "news reports divert attention from immediate experience and help focus it upon a constructed reality" (Edelman, 1988, p. 101). If the immediate reality about the nation and society is largely delimited by a set of enduring values in the domestic news, as Gans (1979) documented, it should be more so in foreign and international news when the setting is remote and undoubtedly beyond direct observation or experience for most people. The possibilities of stories present in the news media are never unlimited. The outcome of journalistic decision making generally is a function of consensus building through which certain events, issues, and aspects of the reality are deemed newsworthy.

In many situations, events or issues that occur outside a country's territorial boundaries often come to the public not as events or issues per se, but as news stories of those events or issues reported in the mass media, especially on television. From the event itself to the report of the event in the news (e.g., Rosengren, 1970), the process moves from the reality out there to the mediated reality in the mass media through a number of gatekeeping mechanisms, producing an end result that is mostly determined by the interaction between the "objective" reality and a society's own pragmatic needs and social concerns (e.g., A. Cohen et al., 1990). Numerous studies have shown how various factors at both the micro- and macro-levels help contribute to the selection and presentation of news in the mass media. One common agreement is that news is culturally bound and socially constructed for public consumption and social integration (e.g., Shoemaker & Reese, 1991).

It is culturally bound because, like other forms of knowledge (e.g., Bernstein, 1976), the news tends to be organized by an ethnocentric system of values, such as relevance, familiarity, or psychological proximity. It is socially constructed because, as a way of seeing and charting about the social world (e.g., Gitlin, 1980), the news cannot be detached from the confines of the larger social structure in which the mass media locate themselves and practice their trade in accordance with the operational logic of their position and organizational boundaries (e.g., Ball-Rokeach & Cantor, 1986; Roshco, 1975). At the collective level, a society's fundamental worldview therefore is best captured and reproduced in the news. For Edelman (1988), news reporting is a way of "world making" (p. 4). As such, "it is not what can be seen that shapes political action and support, but what must be supposed, assumed, or constructed" (p. 105). The news can never be the way it is; it is chosen to be as stories or narratives because the reality outside must be "explored, reported and imagined" (Lippmann, 1922).

Given their "world-making" capacity in the international arena, the mass media allow members of a society to understand their national position in relation to that of other countries and to act accordingly based on what and how the news constructs the reality beyond its immediate horizon in the first place. The pictures in our head, either individually or collectively, often represent a source of private perception and imagination and may evoke public identification and expectation about the object involved. To recapitulate Edelman (1988), it is not facts or observations, but the construction of foreign spectacle in the news, that is critical in defining and constituting the political world for the audiences. In the one-party society, the Chinese news media play a key role in that process.

According to Roshco (1975), a major premise "underlying the sociology of knowledge is that all cultural artifacts"—including the news—"produced in a society are influenced significantly by the ways in which the society is organized" (p. 6). As a major stock of social knowledge in China (e.g., Chang et al., 1994), the Chinese news media would undoubtedly envision the world as foreign spectacles, providing internal interpretation to orient the people and society toward the external reality at large. The key questions to be further addressed are: What sector of the external reality (e.g., countries) did China's national television news consider to be salient in its survey of the world's geopolitical landscape? How did the construction of foreign spectacles change over time?

If history is any guide, the only thing predictable about China's internal and external behaviors is its unpredictability. Given the dynamic and volatility of the market in economic reforms and the state's avowed political interest in news control (e.g., X. Zhang, 1993), it is difficult to predict the form and content of Chinese national television news in the short run, let alone its long-term property and prospect. It becomes more esoteric to do so when China's TV news net is cast across foreign waters. For one thing, it represents an international effort to bring home the distant spectacles for a domestic audience whose appetite might have been whetted by the gradual opening of the Chinese window on the outside world. Moreover, the influx and diversity of national events or issues worldwide add to the difficulty of identifying the persistent pattern of television news that forms the contours and elevations of the world map.

Although the three sets of data from CCTV news were not randomly chosen and the time frame different, each study period was longer than that in any previous studies of Chinese national television news. For a temporal comparison between "then and now," the roughly equivalent sample size (26 days in 1992, 25 days in 1996, and 27 days in 1998) provides extensive snapshots of the news that might serve as a longitudinal indicator of the contemporary worldview of television in China.[2] Through an analytical adjustment, the history (e.g., time) and the idiosyncrasy of countries covered in the news at a given point in time was controlled as contributing factors to reveal the underlying mold of how CCTV news constructed foreign spectacles with respect to the world outside.

The identical time frame (from June 15 to July 15) between 1992 and 1998 was designed to ascertain whether "seasonable" factors (e.g., cyclical natural disasters or social or political rituals) might explicate the appearance and arrangement of countries, events or issues on CCTV news. As is true in domestic news (see chap. 5), the data in this chapter did not exhibit any similarity between the 1992 and 1998 sets of sample. It is reasonable to believe that the findings of this study were genuine occurrences of "what really happened," which were filtered through journalistic practices, not a function of opportune elements. When common coverage in the three years was taken into consideration, the results chart a regular and fixed pattern of countries and entities whose features might be counted more relevant in the eyes of Chinese national television. It was the world condensed by CCTV news to be conveyed to its viewers. For most Chinese people whose direct contact with the world abroad is restricted, the news is the starting point for social descriptions

---

[2]For details of the coding procedure, see the appendix.

and political accounts regarding the alien nations and their circumstances of life.

THE WORLD OF CHINA'S WINDOW ON THE WORLD

One major investigation of this study is to detect what sectors of the world and which countries tended to be portrayed on China's national news from 1992 to 1998. Table 6.1 reports the long-term results that eliminated the time factor and country difference as potential variables that might explain coverage of certain countries in any period of the three years chosen for analysis. In other words, the data capture one way or another those countries that were deemed newsworthy by CCTV to be included in its newscast over a time span of 7 years. To a great extent, these countries more or less represent the hot spots that appear on China's national news network. Because they are frequently reported in the TV news, within the sociology of knowledge perspective, they are likely to become objects of exploration, projection, and imagination among the viewers.

During the entire study period, 53% of the world's countries appeared on CCTV news at one point in time. Although the proportion of foreign news on CCTV remained fairly stable (see chap. 4), the number of countries and entities it carried declined over time. In 1992 and 1996, about 33% of the UN's 166 member countries was covered by CCTV news. The number decreased to 22% in 1998, suggesting a shrinking world landscape beyond the Chinese territorial horizon. Accompanied by the diminishing number of foreign news stories from 1992 to 1998, the world of China's window on the world became not only smaller, but also more focused.

Of the numerous countries reported on CCTV news, only 19 received a varying degree of consistent coverage throughout the study period: United States, Russia, United Nations, Yugoslavia, Japan, Israel, Palestine Liberation Organization (PLO), United Kingdom, France, Germany, India, Iran, Iraq, Turkey, Australia, Colombia, Italy, South Korea, and the Philippines, in that order. Excluding the UN itself, these countries and entities comprised about 11% of the world's nations. They nevertheless accounted for at least 60% of the foreign news stories carried on CCTV from 1992 to 1998. Like television in any other country, CCTV news obviously could not realistically produce a world map that matches the reality of countries out there with all their shape and size. Its "basic distortions in any given mode of projection," as Epstein (1973, p. 273) argued in a study of U.S. network television news, "can be clarified," however.

Table 6.1: Countries/Entities in Foreign News on CCTV, 1992–1998[a]

Country	1992	1996	1998	Total
United States	13.3%	7.3%	15.7%	11.7%
Russia	8.0	6.3	18.7	9.9
United Nations	6.2	10.2	8.2	8.2
Yugoslavia	11.1	1.0	0.7	5.0
Japan	3.1	5.4	6.7	4.8
Israel	3.6	5.4	4.5	4.4
PLO	1.3	8.3	2.2	4.1
United Kingdom	4.9	0.5	6.7	3.7
France	3.6	1.5	2.2	2.5
Germany	3.6	1.5	1.5	2.3
India	1.3	2.0	3.0	2.0
Iran	0.4	3.9	1.5	2.0
Iraq	0.4	3.4	2.2	2.0
Turkey	0.9	1.5	2.2	1.4
Australia	2.2	0.5	0.7	1.2
Colombia	1.3	0.5	1.5	1.1
Italy	1.8	0.5	0.7	1.1
South Korea	0.4	1.5	0.7	0.9
Philippines	1.3	0.5	0.7	0.9
Other countries	31.3%	38.3%	19.7%	
Total stories	225	205	134	564
Number of countries covered	54	62	37	88
Percent of total countries[b]	31.9%	36.7%	21.7%	53.0%

[a]Entries include only primary countries that received coverage in all 3 years, thus eliminating time factor and country difference.

[b]The percentage denotes the proportion of all countries in the world covered on CCTV news in each of the 3 years, based on the 1992 UN membership ($N = 166$). UN itself was excluded.

In long-term world making, the CCTV spotlight evidently concentrated on a very few prominent countries or entities, such as the United States (11.7%), Russia (9.9%), UN (8.2%), Yugoslavia (5.0%), Japan (4.8%), Israel (4.4%), PLO (4.1%), and United Kingdom (3.7%) in foreign news when China stood as an observer on the world stage (Table

6.1). Although the proportion varied from year to year, the United States, Russia, and the UN remained among the top four countries and entities covered on the Chinese national news network. Other countries received less than 2% of coverage on CCTV in the 3 years combined. The findings in Table 6.1 display the picture of "world-making" by CCTV news according to the strength or ability of countries and entities to emerge on its news radar. As is shown in chapter 7, its worldview changed when China became engaged as a participant in foreign policy news.

The individual countries and entities on CCTV news flesh out the hot spots that stayed in the limelight from 1992 to 1998 on Chinese national television. They did not automatically lay out the larger landscape of which those countries constituted a part. For many years, China has claimed a membership of the Third World and pledged its support for countries in the developing world that are mostly in Africa, Middle East, Southeast Asia, and Latin America. It is therefore valuable to scan the big picture of the world reality that is more than the sum of its components on CCTV news. Table 6.2 details the proportions of news coverage devoted to each region of the world on CCTV. Unlike that of indi-

Table 6.2: Coverage of Regions in Foreign News on CCTV, 1992–1998[a]

Region	1992	1996	1998	Total
Eastern Europe/Russia	31.5%	11.2%	21.3%	21.9%
Middle East	8.5	35.7	18.1	20.4
Western Europe	20.0	8.4	18.1	15.4
North America	12.7	7.0	16.0	11.4
East Asia	4.8	18.2	9.6	10.7
South Asia	7.9	11.2	8.5	9.2
Africa	10.3	5.6	4.3	7.2
Australia/Oceania	3.0	2.1	1.1	2.2
South America	1.2	0.7	3.2	1.5
Central America	–	–	–	–
Total	165	143	94	402

$X^2 = 75.45$, $df = 16$, $p < .01$

[a]Entries include stories involving one clear region only. Excluded were stories with multiple regions or stories dealing with international organizations. Because of rounding, percentage total does not add up to 100.

vidual countries, coverage of regions denotes where the international actions may lie when more countries from the same regions show up in the news. The absence of it, of course, speaks otherwise.

On a yearly basis, the foreign news net on CCTV clearly is cast unevenly from region to region, indicating a fluctuation of contemporary events or issues taking place around the world that more or less caught the Chinese TV spotlight. From a long-range viewpoint, CCTV news had its lens fixated on some regions that have housed the world's economic, political, and military power centers, not to mention the frictions and disputes that arose from the cross-national encounters. During the study period, eastern Europe and Russia (21.9%) topped all regions on CCTV news, followed by the Middle East (20.4%), western Europe (15.4%), North America (11.4%), and East Asia (10.7%). South Asia, Africa, Australia and Oceania, and South America popped up occasionally on CCTV news while Central America was completely missing. A feasible explanation is that most countries in Central America still maintained diplomatic relations with the Republic of China on Taiwan, an arch-rival that China considers a renegade province when it split from the mainland in 1949 after the Chinese Communists defeated the Nationalists in the civil war. In the world of international high politics and cross national communication, Taiwan's friends became China's foes that did not even deserve to be recognized in the news.

Because the number of countries in each region covered on CCTV news varies considerably, the findings in Table 6.2 certainly would overestimate the prominence of some regions at the expense of other regions. A standardized comparison that took into account the number of countries covered in each region is reported in Table 6.3. This is tantamount to looking at the regions on a per-country basis by giving an equal weight to all regions according to the inclusion of countries in CCTV coverage of the regions. In other words, the distinction among regions is measured not by the relative size of membership of countries in each region, but by the ability or power of individual countries in each region to draw CCTV's news attention. With the prominence of regions equalized by the number of countries, a dissimilar world map emerges from the data that deviated from the one found in Table 6.2. To some extent, it is the underlying quality, not the quantity, of countries in a region that matters.

As is manifest, when gauged by a per-country equation, North America (5.7%) far outstripped all other regions on CCTV news, with East Asia (1.5%), eastern Europe and Russia (1.3%), Middle East (1.3%), and western Europe (1.0%) all trailing at a distance. On the average, each country in these regions that appeared on CCTV enjoyed at least 1% of foreign news coverage. The fact that North America and East Asia

Table 6.3: Coverage of Regions by All Countries in Foreign News on CCTV, 1992–1998

Region	All Countries[a]	Number of Countries Covered	Average[b]
North America	11.4%	2	5.7%
East Asia	10.7	7	1.5
Eastern Europe/Russia	21.9	17	1.3
Middle East	20.4	16	1.3
Western Europe	15.4	15	1.0
South Asia	9.2	13	0.7
Africa	7.2	11	0.7
Australia/Oceania	2.2	3	0.7
South America	1.5	4	0.4
Central America	–	–	–
Total	402	88	

[a]Entries represent coverage of all countries in the 3 years combined.

[b]Average refers to coverage of regions on a per-country basis. It is a standardized comparison, based on total coverage of each region divided by the number of countries covered in that region in the 3 years. Because of rounding, percentage total does not add up to 100.

ranked ahead of other regions on the Chinese national television marks the intrinsic magnitude of these two regions in the world stage. The former finds the world's largest economy and remaining superpower, the United States, after the collapse of Soviet Union in 1991, whereas the latter locates Japan, a regional political power and the world's second largest economy. By the sheer presence of these two countries, there should be little surprise that both regions embody the geopolitical spheres that loomed large on China's national TV news network, as they usually do in many other nations. For example, in a study of 38 countries, H. Wu (2000, p. 126) found that the United States "was the best-covered country" in 23 nations' international news coverage.

What is more explicit in Table 6.2 is that countries in South Asia, Africa, Australia and Oceania, and South America each garnered less than 1% of CCTV coverage of foreign news. Although 11 African countries and 13 countries in South Asia were reported on CCTV during the 3-year study period, their share of coverage was relatively small compared to that of other countries in North America, East Asia, eastern Europe/Russia, the Middle East, and western Europe. Moreover, Australia generated as much coverage as the whole African continent on CCTV news. It is unequivocal that when the Chinese national television surveyed the world as an observer, Africa for the most part did not exist. Neither did South Asia and Central or South America. The television-made world map in China is obviously skewed as a result of the unequal position each country finds itself in the community of nations. It is a global map drawn not by the cartographer, but by the CCTV news gatekeepers.

The world image on CCTV news altered further when the hot spots in each region are analyzed. During the study period, there were 18 countries that accounted for 20% of all countries covered by CCTV news. They amassed, however, 85% of the total foreign stories on the Chinese national television network. In light of the geographical hot spots (see Tables 6.1 and 6.4), the world of CCTV news was configured this way: the United States in North America; Russia and Yugoslavia in eastern Europe; Japan and South Korea in East Asia; Israel, PLO, Iran,

Table 6.4: Coverage of Regions by Hot Spots in Foreign News on CCTV over Time

Region	Hot Spots[a]	Number of Countries Covered	Average
North America	19.2%	1	19.2%
Eastern Europe/Russia	24.5	2	12.3
East Asia	9.3	2	4.7
Middle East	22.7	5	4.5
Western Europe	15.7	4	3.9
South Asia	4.7	2	2.4
Australia/Oceania	2.0	1	2.0
South America	1.7	1	1.7
Africa	–	–	–
Central America	–	–	–
$N =$	343	18	

[a]Entries are based on primary countries that were covered in all 3 years (see Table 6.1), thus eliminating time and country variation as contributing factors in coverage of geographical regions. Stories that involved the UN and secondary countries were excluded. Because of rounding, percentage total does not add up to 100.

Iraq, and Turkey in the Middle East; United Kingdom, France, Germany, and Italy in western Europe; India and the Philippines in South Asia; Australia; and Colombia in South America. The whole continent of Africa joined Central America as the only two regions that were invisible throughout the study period. In the study time frame, it is unimaginable that neither Africa nor Central America had produced no hot spots of any proportion unworthy of coverage on CCTV news. A realist and plausible explanation is that the omission of Africa and Central America from the Chinese national TV screen conveyed a sense of their insignificance as news objects.

As is shown later, for a variety of emphasis, each of the world's regions became visible on CCTV news in a particular fashion that underscored how it was perceived on Chinese national television. Thanks to the predominance of hot spots in the news, the mapping of regions on CCTV news reflects to a great extent their unspoken status as a news center. The consistent coverage and relatively high visibility of several primary countries or entities—the United States, Russia, the UN, and Japan—and some other nations over a period of 7 years cannot be easily dismissed as a sheer coincidence. A detailed examination of secondary countries or entities in the same story further suggests that some kind of "network" relationship exists among the countries reported on CCTV. Table 6.5 provide the findings.

Of all the nations that appeared on CCTV news, only five countries—the United States (65.2%), Russia (66.1%), Japan (77.8%), Yugoslavia (64.3%), and the United Kingdom (76.2%)—often became news by themselves in nearly two thirds of CCTV coverage. The United States stood as the sole country that was almost ubiquitous in stories dealing with multiple nations. From time to time, it showed up in stories about Russia, the UN, Yugoslavia, Japan, PLO, France, Germany, and many other countries that did not make the list of frequent coverage on CCTV. There is no denying that the United States was seldom out of sight, and for that matter out of mind, in CCTV foreign news coverage. To a lesser degree, Russia as the successor of the former Soviet Union still wielded a considerable amount of power to draw news attention from CCTV, especially when the former Soviet republics and the United States were present in the news. It probably testifies to the continuity of Russia as a viable and competing newsmaker in international mass communication.

In the world of China's news window, many countries or entities probably would not be mentioned had they not shared the spotlight with other countries, such as the United States, Russia, the UN, Israel, PLO, Germany, or France. These countries included Albania, Angola, Argentina, Azerbaijan, Bosnia-Herzegovina, Brazil, Canada, Cyprus, Egypt, Eritrea, Jordan, Kyrgysztan, Lebanon, Moldavia, Morocco,

Table 6.5: Primary and Secondary Countries/Entities in Foreign News on CCTV, 1992–1998

Primary	Secondary[a]	Frequency	Other Countries
United States (66)	–	43	Egypt, France, Germany, Iran, Iraq, Israel,
	Japan	4	Panama, Poland, Thailand, Eritrea
	Russia	4	
	Yugoslavia	3	
	10 countries	12	
Russia (56)	–	37	Argentina, Germany, India, Iran,
	United States	5	Kyrgyzstan, Moldavia, NATO, South Korea,
	11 countries	14	Yugoslavia, Ukraine, Independent States
United Nations (46)	–	10	Angola, Azerbaijan, Bosnia-Herzegovina,
	Yugoslavia	9	Cyprus, Israel, Kyrgyzstan, Moldavia,
	Ghana	5	Pakistan, PLO, Rwanda, Tanzania, United
	Iraq	3	States, Zaire
	14 countries	19	
Yugoslavia (28)	–	18	Russia, United States
	United Nations	7	
	2 countries	3	
Japan (27)	–	21	South Korea, Russia
	United States	4	
	2 countries	2	
Israel (25)	–	2	Egypt, Jordan, Lebanon, Syria
	PLO	17	
	4 countries	6	
PLO (23)	–	1	Egypt, Lebanon, United States
	Israel	18	
	3 countries	4	
United Kingdom (21)	–	16	Canada, France, Germany, Yugoslavia,
	5 countries	5	Eritrea
France (14)	–	7	Brazil, Iraq, Morocco, South Africa, United
	7 countries	7	Nations, United States
Germany (13)	–	3	Albania, France, Lebanon, Philippines,
	8 countries	10	Sweden, United Kingdom, United Nations,
			United States

[a]Entries include secondary countries that appeared in at least three stories with the primary country in the 3 years combined. Secondary countries that appeared in one or two stories with the primary country are listed under other countries. Multiple countries in a few stories were not listed.

Nigeria, Pakistan, Panama, Philippines, Poland, Rwanda, South Africa, Sweden, Syria, Tanzania, Thailand, Ukraine, and Zaire. The source of connection among these countries seems to be rooted in the international power balance (United States vs. Russia), missions of UN or regional conflicts. For example, PLO and Israel tended to appear in a symbiotic relationship or flanked by other countries in the region. Such linkage projects an international, rather than parochial, outlook on Chinese national television news.

The identification of countries on CCTV news tells the geographical origin of foreign stories, but says nothing about the nature of content that makes it newsworthy. Nor does it disclose why a particular region is portrayed in a certain way. Some important questions remain to be further explored: What kind of world is presented on CCTV news in terms of actors, topics, and visual images? How does it compare to the domestic news? Only through comparison can the world of China's window on the world be better understood and put into perspective.

WHAT KIND OF WORLD ON CCTV NEWS?

In international communication research, countries and regions are geographical units that tend to attract varying degree of recognition in the news, depending on their location or their mere size or both. Below the country level, there are individual or institutional actors who must face or handle events and issues that confront them in their specific environments. Who they are and what transpires in their surrounding denote the sources from which actions or concerns originate in a national or cross-national settings. Because sources make the news (Sigal, 1986) and what the news media cover is "a coherent narrative of the world that serves particular purposes" (Romano, 1986, p. 42), together they prioritize the reality in journalistic constructs that give order and meaning to an otherwise endless flow of events and issues around the world. Table 6.6 details the main actors in foreign news on CCTV.

From 1992 to 1998, about 75% of foreign stories on CCTV news came from four main groups of actors: head of state/government (31.5%), ministries/cabinet members (15.4%), public/public opinion (14.1%), and UN/international organizations (13.9%). Over time, public/public opinion as a group of actors seemed to be losing its appeal on CCTV news, dropping from 23.4% in 1992 to about 7% in 1998. In contrast, actors of head of state/government increasingly became highly visible, with their share of stories more than doubled from 21.2% to almost 50% within the same period. The cross-pattern confirms an unstated journalistic rule that for every news source selected for inclu-

Table 6.6: Main Actors in Foreign News on CCTV, 1992–1998

Main Actor[a]	1992	1996	1998	Total
Heads of state/government[b]	21.2%	34.7%	46.6%	31.5%
Ministries/cabinet members	11.7	22.8	12.1	15.4
Public/public opinion[c]	23.4	6.6	6.9	14.1
UN/international organizations	13.1	14.4	14.7	13.9
Military/public security/militia	9.5	7.2	4.3	7.5
Interest groups[d]	9.0	2.4	6.0	6.1
Congress/parliament	5.0	5.4	0.9	4.2
Political/party officials	2.3	3.0	5.2	3.2
Ambassadors/diplomats	2.7	2.4	2.6	2.6
Courts	1.8	0.6	–	1.0
Provincial/state governments	0.5	–	0.9	0.4
Local governments	–	0.6	–	0.2
Total	222	167	116	505

$X^2 = 71.78$, $df = 22$, $p < .01$

[a]Main actors refer to primary individuals, groups or other entities that do things or are affected by events in a way that is essential to the story. Actors may be individual, plural or institutional. Some individual actors held concurrent government positions and were coded in terms of either their highest positions or the position most relevant to the story. Other or unidentifiable actors were excluded.

[b]Heads of state/government include vice head of state and government.

[c]Public/public opinion mainly refers to nonofficial individuals. For instance, if peasants or citizens were interviewed about the market or harvest, they would be considered as the main actor and coded as public/public opinion.

[d]Interest groups include business, labor unions, companies, and mass organizations.

sion, another is excluded. It is part of the zero-sum equation inherent in any decision making in the newsroom.

On the Chinese national television news, what matters in the foreign world is high-ranking governmental officials, especially the top leadership, and leading world organizations, such as the UN. All other actors, including individuals and nonofficial entities and lower level state agencies, rarely turned up on CCTV news. The commission and omission of some actors in foreign news stood out when they were juxtaposed with those in the domestic news. As far as actors are concerned, CCTV news presents two different views of the world (see Table 6.7). Relatively speaking, the internal stories gave more exposure to such actors as ministries/ministers, interests groups, political/party officials, and local as well as provincial governments. The external stories, however, frequently featured heads of state/government, public/public opinion, United Nations/other international organizations, and diplomats/ambassadors. Actors like military/security, congress or parliament, and courts showed little variation between the domestic and foreign news.

The division of the worldview between here and there on CCTV displays China's longstanding effort since the early 1980s to add a foreign dimension to its world of television news. Although not directly related to the practices of domestic news, this attempt can nevertheless be inferred from CCTV's foreign news broadcast. In 1986, CCTV launched its English News Service (CCTV English News). According to the CCTV English News flyer, "Domestic viewers watch CCTV's English News Service for comprehensive and quality coverage of global events. Foreign television networks relay broadcasts for their authoritative reports that give insight into the Chinese perspective" (obtained from John Jirik,

Table 6.7: Comparison of Actors between Domestic and Foreign News on CCTV, 1992–1998

Main Actor	Domestic News[a]	Foreign News	Total
Heads of state/government	17.9%	31.5%	22.0%
Ministers/cabinet members	19.6	15.4	18.4
Interest groups	17.8	6.1	14.3
Public/public opinion	11.4	14.1	12.2
Political/party officials	10.2	3.2	8.8
Military/militia/security	8.4	7.5	8.2
UN/other international organizations	0.6	13.9	4.5
Congress/parliament	4.5	4.2	4.4
Local governments	4.8	0.2	3.5
Provincial/state governments	2.8	0.4	2.1
Diplomats/ambassadors	1.1	2.6	1.5
Courts	0.9	1.0	0.9
Total	1198	505	1,703

$X^2 = 266.19$, $df = 11$, $p < .01$

[a]For the purpose of compatibility, the category of "heads of state/government" in domestic news includes foreign policy and international relations between China and at least one other country.

CCTV consultant, personal communication). Because CCTV relies on a few major foreign news agencies to supply stories from overseas, but edited them for rebroadcast on its Xinwen Lianbo (see chap. 4), there should be little question that the selected foreign stories were expected in some way to bring out the Chinese viewpoint of what the world was and how it was to be seen. That viewpoint emerges more clearly in conjunction with the topics of foreign news covered on CCTV (Table 6.8).

It is evident that, of the various subject matters, CCTV devoted 69.1% of its foreign news segments to four major areas during the study period: diplomacy/government (21.8%), military/defense (19.0%), politics (16.1%), and economic-related topics (12.2%). Three other areas were relatively discernible from 1992 to 1998: sports (7.1%), social unrest

Table 6.8: Topics of Foreign News on CCTV, 1992–1998[a]

Topic	1992	1996	1998	Total
Diplomacy/government	16.0%	28.8%	21.9%	21.8%
Military/defense	21.7	20.0	13.8	19.0
Politics	18.4	17.1	11.3	16.1
Economic/trade/business	6.1	12.2	21.3	12.2
Sports	7.8	2.4	11.9	7.1
Social unrest	9.0	5.4	1.9	5.9
Disasters/accidents	2.9	7.8	7.5	5.7
Law/crime	3.3	2.0	3.8	3.0
Social service/health	2.0	2.0	2.5	2.1
Technology/science	4.9	0.5	–	2.1
Education/arts/culture	1.6	1.5	1.9	1.6
Human interest/lifestyle	2.5	–	–	1.0
Transportation/travel/tourism	0.8	0.5	1.9	1.0
Ecology/environment	1.6	–	–	0.7
Agriculture/forest	0.8	–	–	0.3
Entertainment	0.4	–	0.6	0.3
Religion	–	–	–	–
Obituary	–	–	–	–
Total	244	205	160	609

[a]The focus is on the main topic—what the story is mainly about. Excluded were other or unidentifiable stories.

(5.9%), and disasters/accidents (5.7%). The remaining topics—law/crime, social service/health, technology/science, education/arts/culture, human interest/lifestyle, transportation/travel/tourism, ecology/environment, agriculture/forest, and entertainment—were apparently unappealing to China's national television news. There wasn't much to see in these areas on CCTV news. Although not strictly comparable, coverage of foreign news on CCTV in the 1990s partly resembled the pattern in a previous study (e.g., Warren, 1988). In the mid-1980s, diplomacy/government—international relations in Warren's study—and military stories ranked among the top four categories, but economic stories were not.

Over time, a few changes in coverage of foreign topics on CCTV were worth noting. First, the proportion of foreign stories about military/defense and politics declined, whereas that of economic-oriented stories was on the rise. Without some external yardstick, it is difficult to assess whether the pattern was a realistic Chinese representation of the changing world fabric or a deliberate conceptual shift of journalistic focus. Second, when coverage of social unrest in foreign news decreased from 9% in 1992 to about 2% in 1998, reports of foreign disasters/accidents jumped from 3% to almost 8%. Given the negative nature of such stories, it may be argued that CCTV news was simply responding to the impulse and dynamics of an unpredictable world outside. Compared to that of domestic news, however, the world of foreign news on CCTV projected some sharp contrasting images that should be easily observed by the keen eyes. There was a penchant for dramatizing the down side, and by implication the problematics, of foreign countries in the news.

As is apparent from the comparison in Table 6.9, the world making of CCTV news moves along some topical divide, hence carving out unparalleled sectors of reality from within and without the Chinese geopolitical boundaries. To be sure, the world of foreign news witnesses more governmental, political, and military activities than the domestic one. Closer scrutiny reveals that, these stories generally conjure up tensions, negotiations, power contest, or confrontations in unilateral, bilateral or multilateral situations. Likewise, the world reality outside is more prone to disasters/accidents and social unrest than inside the Chinese territory. In fact, CCTV never reported any internal social unrest throughout the entire study period. The disparity of coverage of disasters and accidents between domestic and foreign news was also detectable in the mid-1980s.[3] The striking, but consistent contradiction

---

[3]Because of use of different categories, Warren's study could not be effectively compared to the current analysis. The comparison displayed in his data, particularly that involving disasters and accidents between domestic and international news, however, showed a consistent pattern over time.

Table 6.9: Comparison of Topics Between Domestic and Foreign News on CCTV, 1992–1998

Topic	Domestic News[a]	Foreign News	Total
Economic/trade/business	23.4%	12.2%	20.1%
Diplomacy/government	15.5	21.8	17.4
Politics	7.3	16.1	9.8
Military/defense	2.7	19.0	7.5
Law/crime	7.2	3.0	6.0
Transportation/travel/tourism	8.1	1.0	6.1
Education/arts/culture	7.8	1.6	6.0
Technology/science	7.5	2.1	5.9
Social service/health	4.6	2.1	3.9
Disasters/accidents	2.8	5.7	3.7
Agriculture/forest	4.8	0.3	3.5
Sports	1.3	7.1	3.0
Entertainment	2.6	0.3	2.0
Social unrest	–	5.9	1.7
Human Interest/life style	1.9	1.0	1.6
Ecology/environment	1.2	0.7	1.1
Obituary	1.2	0.8	
Total	1,473	609	2,082

$X^2 = 521.67$, $df = 17$, $p < .01$

[a]For the purpose of compatibility, the category of "diplomacy and government" in domestic news includes foreign policy and international relations between China and at least one other country. Religion had 0.1% in domestic news, but 0% in the overall distribution.

depicts a more intense and violent world beyond China's immediate confines. This appearance is best preserved in the visual dimension of CCTV news. Table 6.10 demonstrates that foreign news on CCTV is more likely than domestic news to be violence-oriented.

By contrast, the world of domestic news is full of stories of economic/trade/business, law/crime, transportation/travel/tourism, education/arts/culture, technology/science, social service/health, and agriculture/forest. Although the number of stories in many of these categories was relatively small, their presence on CCTV news often highlights the success of economic reforms in the forms of high productivity and prosperity, enforcement of law and order, construction or completion of major transportation infrastructures, breakthrough in technological and scientific advancement, improvement of living standards and

Table 6.10: Comparison of Image Between Domestic and Foreign News on CCTV, 1992–1998[a]

Visual Image	Domestic News	Foreign News	Total
Violence	1.2%	14.3%	5.9%
Non-violence	98.8	85.7	94.1
Total	1,047	573	1,620

$X^2 = 114.58$, $df = 1$, $p < .01$

[a]Stories with no video or films were excluded. Because of the small number (see Table 4.12), excluded also were foreign policy and international relations stories involving China.

health care, and enrichment of cultural life among the general population. Generally supported by factual data and visual images, these stories painted a more progressive and nonviolent world inside the Chinese geopolitical horizon (see Table 6.10).

Because the world outside China deviates significantly from that inside China on CCTV news, a compelling question to tackle is, under what circumstances did the various regions of the world get covered on CCTV over time? This analysis pertains to the investigation of enduring issues, prominent characteristics, or contemporary problems and practices that each region might encounter, signify, or commit on a long-term basis. They are certainly a function of the properties or behaviors, both national and international, of the countries located in the respective regions. Table 6.11 compares the news focus across seven regions on CCTV during the study period. Although the small sample size for certain regions calls for cautious interpretations of the findings, a clear-cut pattern can be established among the regions that offer some clues as to what made each region tick in the eyes of CCTV news.

Except for western Europe, where no single facet prevailed within and across regions on CCTV coverage of foreign news, each region apparently could be more or less characterized in one salient aspect: social unrest in Africa (34.5%), politics in East Asia (45.0%), military/defense in eastern Europe/Russia (27.1%), diplomacy/government in the Middle East (35.4%), disasters/accidents in North America (18.2%), and politics (44.4%) in South Asia. From a distance, the construction of foreign spectacles on CCTV news recounted a divergent makeup of the exterior world. Such differentiation generally

Table 6.11: Regions and Foreign News Focus on CCTV, 1992–1998[a]

News Focus	Regions						
	Africa	East Asia	Eastern Europe	Middle East	North America	South Asia	Western Europe
Diplomacy/government	13.8%	5.0%	15.3%	35.4%	4.5	13.9%	14.8%
Military/defense	17.2	7.5	27.1	21.5	4.5	22.2	4.9
Economic/trade/business	–	20.0	23.5	7.6	15.9	2.8	8.2
Education/arts/culture	–	7.5	–	1.3	4.5	2.8	4.9
Technology/science	–	2.5	1.2	–	11.4	–	1.6
Transportation/tourism	–	–	–	1.3	6.8	–	3.3
Social unrest	34.5	–	3.5	6.3	4.5	–	11.5
Agriculture/forest	–	–	–	–	–	–	3.3
Social service/health	–	2.5	2.4	1.3	4.5	2.8	3.3
Sports	3.4	5.0	1.2	2.5	2.3	–	8.2
Politics	24.1	45.0	20.0	15.2	9.1	44.4	14.8
Human interest/lifestyle	–	–	–	–	2.3	–	4.9
Disasters/accidents	–	5.0	5.9	5.1	18.2	11.1	4.9
Crime/law	3.4	–	–	2.5	9.1	–	6.6
Ecology/environment	3.4	–	–	–	–	–	4.9
Entertainment	–	–	–	–	2.3	–	–
N =	29	40	85	79	44	36	61

[a]Entries include regions that received at least 3% of total coverage on CCTV in the 3 years combined, excluding Australia/New Zealand/Oceania and South America.

holds true among regions, thus portraying the state of political affairs, social practices, or national and international undertakings in each region.

A more telling finding about foreign spectacles on Chinese national television is that CCTV devoted a higher proportion of stories to disasters/accidents in North America than in any other regions. If law/crime stories were counted, North America undoubtedly outpaced other regions in its share of stories about disasters/accidents and law/crime, which were largely jaundiced in nature. It should be pointed out, however, that this presentation of negative news in North America was accompanied by stories of its technological and scientific accomplishment or betterment. These mixed spectacles do not necessarily, in the words of Edelman (1992), "promote accurate expectations or understanding," but rather evoke a drama that objectifies hopes and vulnerability. Because stories about North America were mainly about the United States, chapter 8 expressly scrutinizes how the United States was seen through the Chinese national television.

FOREIGN SPECTACLES ACCORDING TO CHINA

Against the backdrop of social construction of reality, the point of theoretical departure in this study is that the ongoing market reforms and social reorientation to greater openness in China have led to a fundamental structural change that defies the earlier prescription of the mass persuasion and propaganda model. One key premise is that as a form of social knowledge, the news in China molds the external reality at large through the means of world-making that helps define the size and shape of the remote geopolitical landscape for the Chinese audiences. To investigate foreign news coverage in China is also to propose intellectual ways for handling the methodological problems that the inquiry has brought forward in the subject matter.

Although the samples were not randomly selected, the expanded study period at three points in time allows for a temporal comparative analysis between here and there. Through an analytical control, the focus on the CCTV permits a better examination of the constructed reality in the news as a short-term phenomenon and a careful determination of a more permanent worldview projected by some underlying policy concerns and social practices in China. Although the *process* of social construction of reality in the mass media cannot be adequately demonstrated by the content alone, the mediated reality as a *product* of that process certainly lies in the end result of journalistic practices—the news. If the form and content of foreign spectacles are consistently established over time, the impact of social structure on the formation and presentation of reality in the news become more plausible. This is especially true in China where the news media are firmly embedded in the larger sociopolitical system that places state interests above the public's rights to know. As a system of thought control over the world, the news about foreign countries on CCTV is not foreign countries as they are, but foreign countries as they have been manufactured.

Notwithstanding its undeniable improvement of economic well-being and apparent relaxation of ideological rigidity since the early 1980s, China today still adheres to the utopia of Communism superiority in its belief system and empirical exercise. Translated into practice is its unwillingness to renounce the state domination and intrusion—via the Communist Party and the government—in public and private spheres. Internally, the central authority therefore carefully monitors what and how the domestic reality might be presented in the news to the public. Externally, it stands vigilantly to screen the location from which the foreign reality originates and what component of it can be relayed to the Chinese people.

As the only national television news network, the worldview of China's window on the world is therefore bound by the Chinese range of vision that is largely determined by the logic of the views between here and there: "here" in the sense of China as a participant of what matters in the domestic world (see chap. 5 and chap. 7) and "there" in the sense of the country as an observer of what happens in foreign territories. It is unrealistic and conceptually unimaginable to expect that the two worlds would converge or display similar characteristics. The epistemological and sociological questions of sensitivity, reliability, and validity suggest otherwise. Consequently, the foreign spectacles reported on the CCTV news say as much about the properties of the reality itself as the propinquity of those who construct or put a finishing touch on it. The events or issues are not merely there, but a created battery of projections and a deliberated distribution of geographical awareness.

The findings in this chapter indicate not only quantitative, but also qualitative differential treatment of countries and regions in foreign news on CCTV from 1992 to 1998. The evidence strongly shows that in the process of news reporting, China's national television took certain aspects of the world reality to be relevant and others irrelevant to the domestic setting. Its worldview seems to follow the functional purposes that the news may serve and endorse the hierarchical structure embedded in the world landscape itself in various situations. With China being an observer, the Chinese TV surveys the reality beyond its own national borders by constructing foreign spectacles in ways that display how the world may take shape and what its constituting parts may be. Individually, countries in Africa and Central and South America did not fare well in foreign news. Collectively, these regions remained obscure on CCTV.

In the world of foreign news, CCTV was nonceremonial, conflict-laden and tactfully self-serving in that events or issues were packaged in a manner that would, when juxtaposed against the domestic news in the broadcast, create a subtle comparison between a stable and vibrant Chinese society and an antagonistic and strenuous world at large, hence showing a way of seeing and knowing China in relation to other countries. The short-term worldview in the news is often a response to the tension and sentiment outside China's own immediate environment. In the long run, the news configures the world map that hinges on a system of functional relevance or systemic typification. Like that in many other countries, the sketched external reality on Chinese television, therefore, does not deviate much from what has been true in the literature of international communication research. It focuses on some elite nations or hot spots that, due to the default structure of international power balance or regional conflicts and confrontations, often become news in the cross-national setting.

Under the structural constraints, the seemingly large spectacles on CCTV news feature only a few major international actors. Although the United States, Russia, and the UN clearly dominate foreign news on Chinese national television over time, it is their strategic location in the cross-national network structure that is more revealing. These three countries or entities not only represent a strong news center in their own right, but also become magnets linking directly or indirectly other countries from different regions in a news web. Although seldom alone in the CCTV newscast, many smaller and less powerful countries appear in the stories along with some "known" nations either because of their challenge to the powers that be or owing to their close alliance with them. This "foe or friend" differentiation on CCTV has been visible one way or another throughout the study period. That the world out there makes sense at all relies more on the CCTV itself than on the world at large. Although the manifest coverage and presentation of foreign countries might be characterized as less structured and more responsive to the social pulse and political forces of localities at any given point in time, the latent coverage and presentation were more or less stable and durable.

To a large extent, the international outlook on Chinese national TV news fuses an astute dimension to the dynamics of the world of foreign news that unfolds in China. Economically, China's door has been relatively wide open to the outside world as a result of the flow of goods and services, information, people, and capital since the reforms in the early 1980s. It is difficult, if not impossible, for the central authority to deny the Chinese people the opportunity to dig "into the world for valuable resources" (Gilder, 1990, p. 370) when new communication technology such as the Internet and other alternative means have made the foreign reality readily accessible and knowable to many people in China. Politically, however, for the huge majority of Chinese people who depend on television for a glimpse of that world, the "constructed window" on CCTV is rather limited in size and offers a choosy view of the external reality delimited by a narrow frame.

The scanning of the world on China's national television, while factual and timely, is highly selective, taking some constant snapshots from a few countries in areas closer to home, but leaving out vast regions unfocused or totally ignored. The foreign world that China's central TV news brings to the attention of the Chinese people dwells on the United States, the world's only superpower, in North America and Russia, the successor of another superpower before it collapsed in the early 1990s, in eastern Europe. A small number of countries prevail in some other regions: Japan and South Korea in East Asia, Israel and PLO in the Middle East, Britain, France and Germany in western Europe, and India and the Philippines in South Asia. By and large, the lineup of top foreign countries on CCTV news conforms closely to the distribution of its overseas bureaus around the world (see chap. 4). Compatible with U.S. TV network news (e.g., Epstein, 1973), it also indicates the impact of organizational resources and newsgathering structure on television news reporting in China. The assignment of CCTV foreign correspondents, of course, presupposes a calculated, if not entrenched, view of the world about what is to be pertinent to China's interests.

Although the Chinese leadership claims that "China will always belong to the third world" (H. Liu, 1999, p. 461), treatment of the Third World nations on its national television is no better than that by the First World countries in the process of international communication. Whether in terms of general coverage or hot spots, from a longitudinal viewpoint, the numerous countries in Africa, Central and South America simply do not exist on the national television in China. Against the backdrop of the nearly total absence of development related news in most of the Third World countries, such paucity of developing and underdeveloped nations on CCTV is a reflection of the Chinese government's increasing pragmatism in its approach to the outside world and the realism in its international diplomatic activities (see chap. 7). Of the foreign news stories, the Chinese preference centers around governmental and institutional affairs conducted by the national officials or organized groups from some selective countries.

As shown in chapter 4, although CCTV subscribed to overseas news services such as APTN and RTN for its foreign news spots, it did not necessarily identify the source in the stories. Basically, CCTV translated and edited the stories for its own broadcast with a Chinese touch. In major stories, it sometimes stated this practice at the end. Consequently, as far as foreign news is concerned in China, the mechanism of classification and typification (e.g., Tuchman, 1978) seems to be at work, offering definitions of the situation in a remote setting for the audience at home. A regular viewer of CCTV would have no difficulty associating Africa with the phenomenon of social unrest or eastern Europe/Russia and Middle East with issues of military and diplomatic nature. As to North America (essentially the United States), it seems to be more prone to natural disasters and accidents than any other regions in the world.

On the whole, foreign news on CCTV carried more violent visual images than domestic news. It means that as the last Communist superpower and an emerging economic power, China has oriented the Chinese society and people to aspects of its main concerns or steered them toward foreign events or issues that might make the country look good by comparison or by implication. It also implies that China is more assertive in its worldview regarding what it should perceive in the social reality and how it should construe it in the process of news production and presentation. The narrow range of foreign spectacles, both in the number of countries covered and in the scope of stories reported on Chinese national television news, lends support to the thesis that they are constructed to help evoke a sense of priority and expectation of either action or nonaction in China.

The focus of foreign news projects a world that differs clearly from that of the domestic one. The former is dominated by conflicts, tensions, and violence, whether real or perceived, whereas the latter peaceful, progressing, and caring. As such, the knowledge received and shared by the Chinese viewers based on these two types of news represents varying, perhaps unequal, access to the social reality. One is familiar and reassuring, the other uncertain and revolting. The fact that foreign and international news has been consistently ranked among the top of Chinese audiences' news exposure (T. Sun, Chang, & Yu, 2001) attests to the potential impact the sole TV news network may have on the enormous captive viewers. The pattern displayed on CCTV news hence opens a desired window on how the external world is to be seen and known by the people in China. Its implications for the interplay between China and the world are profound. Because of the manufactured worldview in the news, the world itself and all the countries involved are not necessarily a free body of information and knowledge, but rather a surrogate of images, narratives, and configuration of power among nations that may best serve the Chinese national interests.

CHAPTER 7

FOREIGN POLICY AFFAIRS AND CCTV NEWS: WORLD MAKING IN A CHINESE CLOSE-UP

Since the late 1970s, China's economic reforms have affected not only its domestic social, political, and cultural spheres, but also its foreign relations. The reform era throughout the 1980s and 1990s has transformed the once revolutionary and isolated country in the first three decades after its founding in 1949 into an emerging and outreaching force in international geopolitics. As the editors of *The China Reader* (Schell & Shambaugh, 1999) pointed out, "China is now a global actor, if not a global power" (p. 448). Unlike the first two decades before the reforms when Beijing was very much content to enmesh itself in radical political and social movements on the one hand and to instigate the Communism revolution in Asia on the other, China in the postreform and post-Soviet epoch seeks to foster its status as a contending power in the multipolar world system by shoving up its international connections and participation.

The demise of Communism in eastern Europe and the breakup of the former Soviet Union around the late 1980s certainly reshuffled the world's geopolitical panorama and forced China to reassess its own position in relation to other countries in the new international power structure that was once dominated by two rivaling superpowers. The repositioning of countries in the still unsettling external landscape poses both challenges and opportunities to China when its 20-year internal restructuring and openness have pushed the country further into the rules and demand of the world community of nations, especially in the global economic arena such as the World Trade Organization (WTO). To join WTO, for example, China faced tough conditions imposed by major countries like the United States and members of the Europe Union. It must first secure good trade relations by moving toward a free and democratic society and by improving its human rights records. Although Beijing's WTO membership was approved in 2001, the outside pressure is being felt inside China.

The last decade of the 20th century has witnessed China overcome, via the continuation of economic reforms and open-door policy, the consequences of foreign denunciations and retributions in the fallout of Beijing's brutal suppression and crackdown on the 1989 Tiananmen Square student democratic movement and the repercussion of Soviet dissolution concerning the legitimacy and viability of Communism as a viable form of governance. As Liu Huaqiu, director of the Foreign Affairs Office of the State Council, sized up in 1997, China has "withstood the impact from the drastic changes in Eastern Europe and disintegration of the Soviet Union, smashed Western sanctions, and developed [its] relations with developing countries," resulting in "multilateral diplomacy" (H. Liu, 1999, p. 460). This success is built on Beijing's aggressive diplomatic and international activities to woo foes and friends alike.

The world's political stage provides an ideal platform for China to assert its leadership role, whether real or imagined, and to peddle its own vision and formulation of the rules of game in international relations. From 1993 to 1997, for example, leaders of the Chinese Communist Party and the government made 124 visits to 143 countries, averaging 25 overseas trips per year and 2 per month during the 5-year period. At the same time, Beijing received 188 heads of state and government from around the world. Amid the diplomatic whirlwind, part of the fundamental tasks of China's foreign relations is "to secure a peaceful international environment," "strengthen solidarity and cooperation with large numbers of developing countries," and "maintain good relations" with surrounding countries (H. Liu, 1999, pp. 464–466). In all these processes, the Chinese news media are expected to play a key role and serve positive functions in promoting mutual understanding and bilateral cooperation among countries. Being part of the state apparatus in China, no medium can resist the pressure on it from the authority or from the ideological tradition in which it works.

The expectation was plainly spelled out by Chinese journalists in a 1998 conference on U.S. media coverage of China in Washington,

DC (for more information about this conference, see chap. 8). A galaxy of editors, journalists, academics, and policymakers from Australia, China, Britain, and the United States gathered together to discuss how U.S. and Chinese media covered each other and what factors might affect such coverage as well as the implications for Sino-American relations. "Throughout the conference, Chinese journalists impressed upon their Western colleagues the importance of including the improvement of relations between the United States and China among their perceived responsibilities" (National Committee on United States–China Relations, Inc., 1998, p. 4). For instance, Zhu Yinghuang, editor in chief of *China Daily*, said at the conference that the "Chinese media have given a great deal of coverage on world affairs, especially the United States." His view was echoed by Liu Zhengzhu, a CCTV Washington correspondent, and other Chinese journalists. Such a practice has grown out of a more and more specific sensitivity toward the geography of global politics.

As far as television news in China is concerned, the assessment of heavy reporting on international affairs was supported by the extant empirical evidence. How CCTV covered the world was documented in chapter 6, in that the United States clearly topped all countries reported in foreign news on CCTV from 1992 to 1998. Chapter 8 specifically investigates the extent to which the United States was portrayed on CCTV news during the study period. Following the perspective of social construction of reality outlined in the previous chapters as a framework, this chapter first looks at coverage of foreign policy news on CCTV and then compares it with that of foreign news to determine the variance, if any, of the reporting of international spectacles between different settings. Given China as a player in foreign policy and international relations, the world presented in foreign policy news on CCTV should be more likely to be affected by the Chinese actions and reactions as a result of its assessment and redefinition of situations with other countries around the world.

The fact that stories about foreign countries are packed together in one single segment at the end of CCTV news lineup suggests an evaluative judgment. The events or issues occur in locales outside China, not here. They are different types of news with no corresponding reality inside China. Because of the non-Chinese visual images, background, and location, foreign news is therefore a recognizable and distinctive formulation. Unlike foreign news, foreign policy news refers to international activities among nations that are intended to influence not only the actions of governments toward one another, but also the behaviors of nongovernmental organizations, business, and people toward the countries involved.

In this study, foreign policy news includes stories about China's diplomatic activities and international relations. As noted in chapter 4, the former deals with discrete governmental actions designed by the decision makers to sway the behaviors of international actors external to the Chinese polity, whereas the latter concerns foreign relationships, such as joint ventures, trade, and cultural exchanges between China and another country that do not necessarily implicate official activities. Whatever the setting, there is a direct political connection of China in the affairs of one or another country. Even though it is difficult to conceive of any cross-national deal not approved by the state, involvement on the part of China in international events or issues is thus a vital ingredient in shaping the way Chinese foreign policy news may be covered on television. If the representation is embedded in or intertwined with Chinese national interests and concerns besides the facts, then the "knowledge about" what is represented can never be unmediated or simply raw.

For one thing, when important actions or policies taken by other countries or the international community make life difficult for China, such as the global sanctions against Beijing in the wake of the 1989 Tiananmen Square crackdown, China could not possibly remain untouched or unscathed because it is part of the equation, if not the problem. In other words, if the external environment turns out to be hostile to the Chinese activities in a cross-national venue, the reporting of foreign policy affairs may indicate China's retreat from the international scene as indexed by its reduced range of foreign contacts or may stress its uneasy relationship with other countries as demonstrated by the increased Chinese attack on the nations involved. Either way, the mode of reporting and news focus tends to deviate from foreign stories that do not allude to China one way or another simply because Beijing stands detached.

Within the perspective of social construction of reality, this chapter completes what chapter 6 touched on only partially: the differentiation between the two types of news—foreign news versus foreign policy news—in international communication research. Conceptually and methodologically, both types have been used as an analytical device and as a journalistic way of seeing countries in different context. The uni-dimensional conception in many previous studies (e.g., Edelstein & Liu, 1963; Houn, 1961; A. Liu, 1971; K. Wang & Starck, 1972; F. Yu, 1964) could be attributed to three factors: (a) the monolithic view that the Chinese news media functioned in unison in their worldview, (b) a confusion over the proper domain of the concepts and their empirical indicators (e.g., Smelser, 1976), and (c) an epistemological failure to distinguish between where the Chinese news media locate themselves in the larger social structure and what they may observe from their unique position (e.g., Blau, 1975).

Against this backdrop, this chapter contends that in the reporting of international spectacles, China's position in the world is fundamentally grounded in its bilateral or multilateral interplay with other countries, not in its scrutiny of individual countries or collective entities out there uncoupled with Chinese domestic interests or foreign concerns. If, in the words of Said (1994, p. 332), "each age and society recreates its 'Others,'" then the contemporary China should be expected to construct an identity of itself and of other countries. As noted in chapter 6, the world-making ability of the mass media permits members of a given society to comprehend their national position or current conditions in a subtle comparison between here and there on the one hand and to draw their own conclusions or interpretations according to what and how the juxtaposed reality is constructed in the first place on the other.

In the domain of international relations, a well-established body of literature has long documented the role and functions of news media in the process of foreign policy decision making. The general view is that the news is a system of symbolic opportunities for making presentation and representation about other countries. In the realm of foreign policy, it is operated for a purpose, according to a particular bent and in a specific political, economic, and military context. A brief review of existing knowledge and findings should help illuminate the Chinese case, given that China's mass media are closely integrated into the political system and that not much is known about coverage of Chinese foreign policy in the news.

FOREIGN POLICY AND NEWS MEDIA

Foreign policy in any country is generally an extension of internal affairs and has domestic implications. By and large, it takes place within the boundaries of national concerns or expectations at the international level. Foreign policy news therefore adds a dimension that is usually not found in either domestic or foreign stories. From the production side, it implicates a definition of the situation in foreign relations with the identity of the country defining it. At the receiving end, it orients the audience toward cross-national events or issues that may require public understanding or support behind official activities. The success or failure of such awareness or backing hinges on the way national identity may be formulated or projected from a particular perspective in the news. Since the birth of the modern press in the West, the news media have hence long been considered a key factor in international relations (Douglass & Bomer, 1932), diplomatic activities (Coggeshall, 1934) or in cross-national disputes (Stowe, 1936). If nothing else, they are archives of information or a body of knowledge that is a useful substitute for an actual encounter with the reality.

Over the past decades, the relationship between the news media and foreign policy decision making has been extensively examined from a variety of perspectives and methodological styles by both academicians and journalists (e.g., Batscha, 1975; Berry, 1990; Bray, 1974; Chang, 1993; B. Cohen, 1963; Dorman & Farhang, 1987; Malek, 1997; Perlmutter, 1998; Reston, 1967; Seib, 1997; Serfaty, 1990). Whether empirical or impressionistic, most of these studies approach this area of intellectual inquiry with the assumption that no national policy, both domestic and foreign, can be successful without the necessary support of the people in the marketplace of ideas.

At one end of the spectrum is the belief that the news media stand as a watchdog, an independent observer, or an active participant in the process of foreign policy deliberations. The concept of an adversarial press, as is often prescribed in the Western democracy, best represents this line of thinking. Because of the authoritarian nature of the Communist system, the news media in China evidently do not assume the status of the Fourth Estate as they do in the West. Chinese journalists never hesitate to admit that their roles are, among other things, to assist the Party and government in creating awareness of official policies and building a socialist state (National Committee on United States–China Relations, 1998). Presumably, their journalistic work as "civil servants" to the central authority extends from the domestic to foreign affairs arena. No matter how competitive the media market is in China, the news media are first part of the state apparatus and second communication vehicles. In China, foreign affairs are to be viewed in a framework constructed out of political determinism and ideological assessment.

At the other end of the conception is the tenet that the news media are no more than a political pawn played by the powers that be in the geopolitical games between countries, whether authoritarian or democratic. This line of exploration is rooted in the symbiotic relationship between the news media and the power elites or the establishment in the making of foreign policy decision, as shown in many institutional and political economy analyses (e.g., Hallin, 1994; Herman & Chomsky, 1988). Unlike the normative perspective, this view considers the news media to be structurally subjugated to the authority and state power, often serving as an ideological apparatus in the implementation of foreign policy by supporting the status quo and existing political patterns (e.g., Altschull, 1995). In international politics, what matters most is that the news media could be regarded as the agent of the government as it attempts policy decisions vis-à-vis other countries

The hegemony thesis asserts that the capacity of news media in foreign policy realm is to manufacture public consent, not to contest the established order. As such, a certain concept of international reality is diffused via the news media throughout the society. In the totalistic sociopolitical structure in China, the news media apparently find themselves succumbed to the dictate and will of the state (see chap. 2). The dissemination of domestic policies and cultivation of public support represent the prescribed and accepted functions of the news media in Chinese society. Because of its reach and the monopolistic delivery of prime-time news, CCTV as the national window on the world, thus occupies an unrivaled position in shaping how the reality inside and outside China is to be perceived, processed, and retained. It is an agency for the articulation, dissemination, and implementation of official policies toward the world.

Chapter 5 details the attributes of domestic news and the differential treatments among various regions in China, particularly between the coastal and inland regions. The disparity between the domestic and foreign news as a result of social distance (e.g., geographical or psychological) separating China and other countries is discussed in chapter 6. This chapter focuses on another sphere that epitomizes China's openness and interaction in the world of international relations. Three main questions are addressed: What were the focus and general concerns in foreign policy news coverage on CCTV? Did the worldview of CCTV news alter when China's position moved away from being an observer to that of a participant? What are the implications of the discrepancy, if any, for understanding the relationship between the news media and foreign policy in the Chinese context?

THE SMALL WORLD OF FOREIGN POLICY NEWS ON CCTV

CCTV mixes foreign policy news with domestic stories in the top two thirds of its newscast, with foreign news slatted at the bottom one third. During the study period, CCTV carried 376 foreign policy stories. Compared to that of either domestic or foreign stories, the proportion of foreign policy news was much smaller. The length of foreign policy stories, however, tended to be longer and their placement in the lineup higher (see chap. 4), suggesting the importance attached to foreign policy news on CCTV. Technical matters aside, it is the symbolic world created in the news that gives television the power to articulate a preferred way of representing the reality. As noted earlier, news representation is a system of opportunities for making national statements about the world of international politics.

Because of possible variations due to the sampling selection, the explication of foreign policy news in this chapter looks at the long term or more permanent picture by focusing on those countries that consistently appeared on CCTV news over time. Like that in foreign news, this is equivalent to an analytical control over "seasonable" factors and country idiosyncrasies as the potential explanatory variables (see chap. 6 for more details). It is also tantamount to locating those countries to which CCTV's news antenna might be constantly turned. If, during the 7-year time span, certain countries showed up steadily one way or another on CCTV news, it is reasonable to expect that they assumed some underlying conceptual and practical significance in China's international and foreign relations. Because it is unrealistic, if not impossible, for any news medium to have a perfect representation of all the countries around the world, the reductive formula asserts a rationalization of systematic coverage and knowledge.

Using the 1992 UN membership as a baseline, Table 7.1 indicates how CCTV covered the world's countries and entities in foreign policy news. From 1992 to 1998, a total of 64 countries or entities received some coverage on CCTV news at one point in time during the study period. It accounted for a little more than one third of the world's nations (38.6%). On a yearly basis, however, the proportion of countries reported in foreign policy news on CCTV declined from about 26% in 1992 to 15% 6 years later, suggesting a shrinking window on the world. Although Chinese leaders had visited more than 140 countries between 1993 and 1997, the world as portrayed on China's national TV network fixed on some select countries.

Given the structural and organizational constraints, it is, of course, unfeasible for any television to survey the world as widely as possible (e.g., Epstein, 1973; Gans, 1979). Television worldwide must cast its news net in a way that helps construct the reality in a meaningful fashion by creating either shared experience (Tuchman, 1978) or common knowledge for the viewers (Neuman et al., 1992). As a media organization (Ball-Rokeach & Cantor, 1986), Chinese television, like its counterparts elsewhere, shares this characteristic: It works in a formal set of social, political, and cultural relations that affect the nature of its news product. In a sense, CCTV news could not deviate from China's contemporary geopolitical concerns and national interests. Although China's foreign relations have extended to various countries across all continents, it sets its priorities that are featured in the news.

Throughout the entire time span, only six countries or entities around the world managed to draw constant, albeit disparate, attention in foreign policy news on CCTV. The United States (26.2%) led the pack of countries, followed at a distance by Japan (7.4%), Russia (6.0%), United

Table 7.1: Countries/Entities in Foreign Policy News on CCTV from 1992–1998[a]

Country	1992	1996	1998	Total
United States	12.6%	8.3%	55.0%	26.2%
Japan	12.6	5.6	1.7	7.4
Russia	1.9	19.4	3.3	6.0
United Kingdom	3.1	4.2	3.3	3.4
United Nations	2.5	5.6	1.7	2.8
South Korea	1.3	1.4	1.7	1.4
Other countries	66.0%	55.5%	33.3%	
Total stories	159	72	120	351
Number of countries covered	44	23	26	64
Percent of total countries[b]	25.9%	13.3%	15.1%	38.6%

[a]Entries include only primary countries that received coverage in all 3 years, thus eliminating time factor and country difference.

[b]The percentage denotes the proportion of all countries in the world covered on CCTV news in each of the 3 years, based on 1992 UN membership ($N = 166$). The UN itself was excluded.

Kingdom (3.4%), the UN (2.8%), and South Korea (1.4%). The percentage of news that these six countries garnered in the newscast grew from one-third of CCTV foreign policy stories in 1992 to nearly double in 1998. Together, they took a lion's share of foreign policy news coverage on CCTV, leaving not much room for the rest of countries that more or less were included in the newscast. The latent pattern captured the essential components of China's foreign policy design (e.g., H. Liu, 1999).

Collectively, the make-up of the six countries underlines a constellation of factors China could not ignore in its foreign policy activities: geopolitical proximity (Japan, Russia and South Korea), regional power center (United Kingdom), global political theater (the UN), and the lone superpower in the world (United States). Individually, a foreign country's international status and its relevance to help improve China's standing as an emerging world power obviously played a major part in foreign policy news coverage on CCTV. For example, Russia (19.4%) out-numbered all other countries on CCTV news when it exchanged high-level official visits with China in 1996. As successor to the former Soviet Union, however, Russia apparently did not enjoy the kind of attention accorded to the United States (55%) on CCTV news in 1998 when President Clinton held a summit meeting with President Jiang in Beijing. The news indeed supplies differential pictures of countries, which says a great deal not only about those countries involved, but also about the politics of information and knowledge in Chinese foreign policy.

Unlike that of foreign news, the world of foreign policy news on CCTV was much smaller. Table 7.2 compares coverage of countries or entities between foreign news and foreign policy news on CCTV. When China stood as an observer, the spotlight on CCTV news evidently focused on a much larger number of countries. With varying degrees of coverage, the 19 countries and entities largely embodied China's proxi-mate neighbors (Russia, Japan, India, South Korea, and the Philippines), areas of perennial contention (Israel, PLO, Iran, Iraq, and Turkey), west-ern and eastern European powers (Yugoslavia, United Kingdom, France, Germany, and Italy), entities with global capability or authority (United States and the UN), and lesser regional powers (Australia and Colombia). From a long-term point of view, these countries or entities denoted the spots that habitually dotted foreign panorama on China's national TV screen. The reductive image is less a reflection of the com-plex reality, but more a function of the journalistic range of vision.

On a longitudinal basis, CCTV's worldview in foreign policy news changed drastically when China became involved as a participant in international relations. The setting in Chinese foreign policy was no longer remote because political relevance outweighed geographical dis-tance. In fact, geographical distance generally did not matter much in international communication, especially when interaction took place between countries (e.g., Chang, Lau, & Hao, 2000). The management of symbols in the news does not necessarily rely on the physical properties. The existence of countries per se can only be symbolically formulated and observed through words, terms, or their official identities. On the Chinese window of the world, not only did the number of countries sur-veyed perpetually drop from 19 in foreign news to 6 in foreign policy news, but also the presentation and interpretation of prominent coun-tries shifted between the two worlds.

During the study period, for example, Russia (9.9%), the UN (8.2%), Yugoslavia (5.0%), Japan (4.8%), Israel (4.4%), PLO (4.1%), United Kingdom (3.7%), France (2.5%), and Germany (2.3%) followed the United States (11.7%) as the top 10 countries in foreign news. In for-eign policy news, however, 5 of the top 10 countries (Yugoslavia, Israel,

Table 7.2: Comparison of Countries Between Foreign News and Foreign Policy News on CCTV, 1992-1998[a]

Foreign News		Foreign Policy News	
Country	Percent	Country	Percent
United States	11.7%	United States	26.2%
Russia	9.9	Japan	7.4
United Nations	8.2	Russia	6.0
Yugoslavia	5.0	United Kingdom	3.4
Japan	4.8	United Nations	2.8
Israel	4.4	South Korea	1.4
PLO	4.1		
United Kingdom	3.7		
France	2.5		
Germany	2.3		
India	2.0		
Iran	2.0		
Iraq	2.0		
Turkey	1.4		
Australia	1.2		
Colombia	1.1		
Italy	1.1		
South Korea	0.9		
Philippines	0.9		
Total stories	564		351
Number of countries	19		6
Number of other countries	69		59
Total number of countries	88		64

[a]Entries include only primary countries that received coverage in all 3 years, thus eliminating time factor and country difference.

PLO, France, and Germany) disappeared, with South Korea joining other nations to make a much shorter, more converged list. The fact that the United States outstripped all other countries in both categories of news on CCTV signifies the U.S. status as the remaining superpower in the community of nations after the collapse of Soviet Union and the growing importance of U.S.–China relations in the Chinese international geopolitical design and meanings. Chapter 8 closely monitors how the United States is seen through CCTV as a Chinese observation post and what its implications are for the two countries.

As a medium largely constrained by the requirements of time and space, let alone the visual imperative, television does not and cannot observe most of what it takes to be facts about countries. The findings in Table 7.2 display the picture of world-making on CCTV news according to a regular and fixed pattern of coverage. The brief roster of countries in foreign policy news on CCTV constructed international spectacles in a way that reflected either the arising position of China as a world power or its interests and concerns over matters closer to home. An obvious indication is that the worlds of foreign news and foreign policy news on the Chinese national television were not the same size or shape, mostly depending on where China might find itself in the scheme of things. The consistent coverage and relatively high visibility of a few select countries or entities (United States, Russia, Japan, the UN, and United Kingdom) on CCTV news over a period of 7 years could not easily be dismissed as sheer chance. There appears to be a formal structure embedded in CCTV's foreign news coverage. That structure is based on what Said (1997) called "certain rules and conventions to get things across intelligibly" (p. 49). It can be further detected through the representation of countries as part of a macro configuration.

THE PARTIAL WORLD MAP OF FOREIGN POLICY NEWS ON CCTV

As noted earlier, in its foreign policy activities, China claims international allegiance with developing countries around the world, especially the Third World nations. Because developing countries are located in regions other than North America and western Europe, an analysis of the distribution of regions in foreign policy news on CCTV supplies some clues as to the hierarchy of regional status in the Chinese foreign policy layout at the aggregated level. It is a composite world map that paints China's foreign relations by the intensity and diversity of countries encountered in each region. The more frequently China engaged a particular country or the more countries China contacted in its foreign policy activities or both, the higher the salience of the region involved should be. In news reporting, it is an efficient rule to reduce an apparently unmanageable distant reality into some kind of stories that are accessible and understandable to the audiences. Table 7.3 shows coverage of the world's various regions on CCTV over time.

To avoid inflating the visibility of some regions due to any historical connection among countries or entities (e.g., colonial relationship between Britain and Hong Kong) or the involvement of international organizations (e.g., the UN), the data in Table 7.3 exclude foreign policy

Table 7.3: Coverage of Regions in Foreign Policy News on CCTV, 1992–1998[a]

Region	1992	1996	1998	Total
North America	8.8%	9.8%	59.1%	28.9%
East Asia	34.4	29.4	4.3	21.6
Africa	21.6	17.6	4.3	14.1
Eastern Europe/Russia	7.2	29.4	14.8	14.1
Western Europe	12.0	–	8.7	8.6
South Asia	9.6	5.9	3.5	6.5
Middle East	–	3.9	4.3	2.4
South America	4.0	2.0	–	2.1
Australia and Oceania	2.4	–	–	1.0
Central America	–	2.0	0.9	0.7
Total	125	51	115	291

$X^2 = 138.61$, $df = 18$, $p < .01$

[a]Entries include stories involving one clear region only. Excluded were stories with multiple regions or stories dealing with international organizations.

stories dealing with multiple countries or entities in different regions. The exclusion of multiple regions from the analysis pinpoints more precisely where CCTV spreads its news net in the world of China foreign relations and what profile that world may be from the Chinese vintage point of view. If the world map could be considered a big zigzag puzzle made up of 10 pieces of regions, as shown in Table 7.3, it was a partial one, with missing pieces here or there over time.

Unlike that in foreign news coverage where only one region—Central America—never appeared on CCTV during the study period (see Table 6.2), five regions around the world (Western Europe, Middle East, South America, Australia and Oceania, and Central America) were left out of the larger picture at one point in time from 1992 to 1998 in foreign policy news on CCTV. Except for western Europe (8.6%), these regions also received relatively little coverage throughout the whole duration. North America (28.9%), East Asia (21.6%), Africa (14.1%), eastern Europe/Russia (14.1%), and to a lesser extent South Asia (6.5%) rounded up as the regions that more or less received continual attention in CCTV coverage of Chinese foreign affairs. Roughly speaking, they highlighted the locale where China's international activities were given higher priority in the news. CCTV news inevitably reported on the outside world inside a framework delimited by the government policy in China.

Because the proportion of newscast and amount of time devoted to foreign policy news on CCTV were limited (see chap. 4), the logic and structure of news inherently governed the process and product of its selection and presentation (Galtung & Ruge, 1981; Roshco, 1975). The zero-sum rule in news time or space portends that an increase in coverage for one area will result in a decrease in exposure for another area because of the structural constancy involved in newsmaking. This phenomenon was noticeably discernible in foreign policy news on CCTV. Over time, when both North America and eastern Europe/Russia obtained more coverage, they surged at the expense of the other three regions—East Asia, Africa, and South Asia, all of which saw their share of foreign policy news cut a great deal from 1992 to 1998. The rearrangement of news proportion conferred an unspoken pecking order of regional importance on CCTV. Obviously, a set of political and ideological calculations comes into play.

The hierarchical standing of regions on CCTV did not change when a standardized comparison was used based on the number of countries in each region that were reported in foreign policy news. It is an unambiguous indication that a formal structure and logic existed in the way the Chinese national television network put China's international affairs on the world map. Table 7.4 describes the results. On a per-country basis, North America (9.6%), East Asia (3.6%), eastern Europe/Russia (1.4%), and Africa (1.2%) each generated a relatively high proportion of foreign policy news on CCTV during the study period. All other regions—Middle East, Central America, South Asia, South America, western Europe, and Australia and Oceania—barely made a beep on the CCTV radar screen. In a holistic outlook, each of these regions as a whole fares poorly as zones of news interest in the realm of China's foreign policy.

As much as China asserts its determination to develop friendly relations with all countries in the world, there are areas that may either contribute to or pose potential threats to Beijing's aspirations to be a global power (H. Liu, 1999). To a great extent, these sectors constitute the hot spots that China cannot afford to overlook in its international interactions one way or another. The Chinese news media not only follow these contours, but also intensify the national interests China has over there. Table 7.5 presents the worldview of CCTV as confined by the select few countries that made some regions more macroscopic than other regions.

In a parochial view, the spectacles of Chinese foreign affairs on CCTV news fluctuated dramatically. Africa dropped out of the CCTV news coverage, whereas western Europe joined North America, Eastern

Table 7.4: Coverage of Regions by All Countries in Foreign Policy News on CCTV, 1992–1998

Region	All Countries[a]	Number of Countries Covered	Average[b]
North America	28.9%	3	9.6%
East Asia	21.6	6	3.6
Eastern Europe/Russia	14.1	10	1.4
Africa	14.1	12	1.2
Middle East	2.4	3	0.8
Central America	0.7	1	0.7
South Asia	6.5	10	0.7
South America	2.1	3	0.7
Western Europe	8.6	14	0.6
Australia and Oceania	1.0	2	0.5
Total	291	64	

[a]Entries represent coverage of all countries in the 3 years combined.

[b]Average refers to coverage of regions on a per-country basis. It is a standardized comparison, based on total coverage for each region divided by the number of countries covered in that region in the 3 years.

Table 7.5: Coverage of Regions by Hot Spots in Foreign Policy News on CCTV over Time

Region	Hot Spots[a] Covered	Number of Countries	Average
North America	59.0%	1	59.0%
Eastern Europe/Russia	13.5	1	13.5
East Asia	19.9	2	10.0
Western Europe	7.7	1	7.7
Africa	–	–	–
Australia and Oceania	–	–	–
Middle East	–	–	–
Central America	–	–	–
South Asia	–	–	–
South America	–	–	–
Total	156	5	

[a]Entries are based on primary countries that were covered in all 3 years (see Table 7.1), thus eliminating time and country variation as contributing factors in coverage of geographical regions. Stories that involved the UN and secondary countries were excluded. Because of rounding, percentage total does not add up to 100.

Europe/Russia, and East Asia as the regions most pertinent to China's foreign policy. These four regions comprised only five countries that received persistent attention (United States, Russia, Japan, South Korea, and United Kingdom). The constricted locus reveals some structural composition in foreign policy news coverage on CCTV. Together, the small number of countries and the array of these nations furnish a Chinese official image of foreign relations reality that has a recognizable coherence. An examination of secondary countries or entities in the same stories confirms that there exists a kind of formal network among the countries reported on Chinese national television news.

As shown in Table 7.6, the relationship between China and other countries in foreign policy news on CCTV was mostly depicted on a one-to-one basis. When they appeared in the news, the United States (88%), Hong Kong (64.3%), Japan (88.5%), and Russia (85.7%) often stood in the limelight by themselves because of their bilateral relations with China. They also led CCTV coverage of all countries in China's foreign affairs during the study period, followed by the United Kingdom, Tunisia, United Nations, Taiwan, Ivory Coast, Germany, and Kazakhstan. The UN (70%), of course, provided an international forum through which China as a permanent member of the Security Council was able to express its concerns over world affairs. It is a worldwide platform that allows Beijing to inject itself as a power to be reckoned with in a multinational setting.

Like foreign news on CCTV, many countries probably would not receive any coverage if they had not shared the spotlight with other more prominent nations in China's foreign affairs relations. These countries included France, Netherlands, North Korea, Thailand, Yugoslavia, Mongolia, Saudi Arabia, PLO, Brazil, Egypt, Iraq, the Philippines, and Morocco. In other words, foreign policy news on CCTV seems to be functional in that inclusion of other countries serves some useful purpose in multilateral situations. Two cases are exemplary here: Taiwan and Hong Kong.

Taiwan, whose Nationalist government lost to the Communists in the Chinese civil war in 1949, was brought into the foreign policy equation to reaffirm China's claim of its sovereignty over the island nation. This phenomenon occurred in CCTV coverage of China relations with the United States, Hong Kong, and Russia, not to mention Taiwan itself. Taiwan was often characterized in the news as part of the "one China" reality through either the pronouncements of Chinese officials or words of support from foreign officials. The same is true for Hong Kong. The transfer of sovereignty between Britain and China put the colony high on the CCTV foreign policy news agenda. In addition to its own reports, Hong Kong showed up in foreign relations stories involving

Table 7.6: Primary and Secondary Countries/Entities in Foreign Policy News on CCTV, 1992–1998[a]

Primary	Secondary	Frequency	Other Countries
United States (93)	–	82	France, Germany, Netherlands,
	Japan (26)	4	North Korea, Taiwan, Thailand,
	7 countries	7	Yugoslavia
Hong Kong (28)	–	18	Macao, Russia, United States
	Taiwan	4	
	United Kingdom	3	
	3 countries/entities	3	
Japan (26)	–	23	France, Germany, United States
	3 countries	3	
Russia (21)	–	18	Hong Kong, Mongolia, Taiwan
	3 countries	3	
United Kingdom (12)	–	7	Japan, United States
	Hong Kong	3	
	2 countries	2	
Tunisia (11)	–	9	Saudi Arabia, PLO
	2 countries	2	
United Nations (10)	–	7	Brazil, Egypt, Iraq
	3 countries	3	
Taiwan (10)	–	6	Philippines
Hong Kong		3	
	1 country	1	
Ivory Coast (8)	–	7	Morocco
	1 country	1	
Germany (7)	–	2	France, Japan, South Korea,
	4 countries/entities	5	Hong Kong
Kazakhstan (7)	–	7	

[a]Foreign policy news refers to international relations and foreign policy activities between China and another country. Entries include primary countries that appeared in at least 2% of stories in the three years combined. Multiple countries in a few stories were not listed.

Russia, United Kingdom, Taiwan, and Germany. Such evidence supports the thesis that social construction of political spectacles in the news is grounded in the larger process of definition of the world (Edelman, 1988). In foreign policy news on CCTV, both Taiwan and Hong Kong were largely defined from China's point of view. To speak of Taiwan and Hong Kong in stories of Chinese foreign affairs is to forge a national identity and trajectory that underscores what the received interpretations of reality might be.

These findings indicate a differential treatment of countries or entities in foreign policy news on CCTV from 1992 to 1998, suggesting that in the process of foreign affairs reporting, the Chinese national television took certain parts of the world reality to be relevant and others to be irrelevant to China's worldwide diplomatic activities. This changing worldview seems to comply with the logic of the range of vision that is bound more by a psychological engagement than by the geographical distance between China and other countries. It provides the clues as to how the reality might be reduced to a presentable version in the news according to rules, perspectives or conventions. Tables 7.7 and 7.8 fur-

Table 7.7: Comparison of Regions by All Countries Between Foreign News and Foreign Policy News on CCTV, 1992-1998[a]

Region	Foreign News		Foreign Policy News		
	Coverage	All Countries[b]	Coverage	All Countries	Total
North America	11.4%	2	28.9%	3	18.8%
Eastern Europe/Russia	21.9	17	14.1	10	18.6
East Asia	10.7	7	21.6	6	15.3
Middle East	20.4	16	2.4	3	12.8
Western Europe	15.4	15	8.6	14	12.6
Africa	7.2	11	14.1	12	10.1
South Asia	9.2	13	6.5	10	8.1
Australia and Oceania	2.2	3	1.0	2	1.7
South America	1.5	4	2.1	3	1.7
Central America	–	–	0.7	1	0.3
Total	402	88	291	64	693

[a]Entries include stories involving one clear region only, based on countries covered in all 3 years. Excluded were stories with multiple regions or stories dealing with international organizations.

[b]Entries denote number of countries covered in each region.

Table 7.8: Comparison of Regions by Hot Spots Between Foreign News and Foreign Policy News on CCTV, 1992-1998[a]

Region	Foreign News		Foreign Policy News	
	Coverage	Hot Spots[b]	Coverage	Hot Spots
North America	19.2%	1	59.0%	1
Eastern Europe/Russia	24.5	2	13.5	1
East Asia	9.3	2	19.9	2
Middle East	22.7	5	–	–
Western Europe	15.7	4	7.7	1
South Asia	4.7	2	–	–
Australia and Oceania	2.0	1	–	–
South America	1.7	1	–	–
Africa	–	–	–	–
Central America	–	–	–	–
Total	343	18	156	5

[a]Entries include stories involving one clear region only, based on countries covered in all 3 years. Excluded were stories with multiple regions or stories dealing with international organizations.

[b]Entries denote number of countries covered in each region.

ther compare how the various regions are configured in the world map between foreign news and foreign policy news on CCTV during the entire study period.

FOREIGN NEWS VERSUS
FOREIGN POLICY NEWS ON CCTV

From 1992 to 1998, if foreign news and foreign policy news on CCTV were combined into one single category, regions of the world ranked in the following order (Table 7.7): North America (18.8%), eastern Europe/Russia (18.6%), East Asia (15.3%), Middle East (12.8%), western Europe (12.6%), Africa (10.1%), South Asia (8.1%), Australia and Oceania (1.7%), South America (1.7%), and Central America (0.3%). A reasonable conclusion could be that these regions, at least among the top six, were more or less notable in both foreign news and foreign policy news on the

Chinese national television. The pecking order of regions somehow stresses certain pictures of the world reality: There are tiers of descending geopolitical significance in the news, with North America and eastern Europe/Russia sitting on the top.

As is clear in Table 7.7, however, mixing these two different concepts in international communication obfuscates, rather than illuminates, the incompatible world maps sketched in both foreign news and foreign policy news. Individually, countries in some regions might fare well in the news on CCTV, but collectively their regions would remain obscure. North America was a case in point. Furthermore, regions that were conspicuous in foreign news did not necessarily turn out to be so in foreign policy news. In fact, there was a reversed relationship of coverage of regions between the two categories of news on CCTV: High coverage in foreign news tended to be accompanied by low coverage in foreign policy news, and vice versa. This phenomenon shows the dual lens of Chinese television ground by China's external interests. The picture of the world reflects the Chinese concerns served by the state-owned media.

Considering all countries reported on CCTV during the study period, the data in Table 7.7 delineate an extended worldview that identifies some broader geopolitical areas deserving China's constant news watch, rather than ephemeral snapshots that are subject to temporal changes. Eastern Europe/Russia (21.9%), Middle East (20.4%), western Europe (15.4%), and to a lesser extent South Asia (9.2%) were more prominent in foreign news when China surveyed the world as an observer than otherwise. Except for South Asia, these regions each had the largest number of countries covered and enjoyed more news attention than other regions. In eastern Europe/Russia, China found many of its former Communist allies. The Middle East remained a volatile region where military confrontation and political tension could easily spread across national borders. Western Europe represented a rising world news leader in international communication (Tunstall, 1992). Given these factors, it would be difficult for China's window on the world to ignore the three regions in its news reports.

When China became a participant in international relations, CCTV news eyes clearly focused more on North America (28.9%), East Asia (21.6%), and Africa (14.1%) than on other regions. Although eastern Europe/Russia, the Middle East, and western Europe each saw their share of news diminished significantly from about 20% in foreign news to 8% in foreign policy news, North America, East Asia, and Africa all doubled their proportion of coverage from foreign news to foreign policy news on CCTV. As noted earlier, these three regions corresponded closely to China's concerns and commitments to international relations.

On a per country basis, CCTV news portrayed a divergent world map between foreign news and foreign policy news that was fundamentally outlined by the hot spots found in each region (Table 7.8). In foreign news, eight regions—North America, eastern Europe/Russia, East Asia, Middle East, western Europe, South Asia, Australia and Oceania, and South America—each at least had one country that more or less managed to attract news attention on CCTV during the study period. Africa and Central America were the only two regions that failed to produce any hot spots over time to draw CCTV coverage from 1992 to 1998. The shrunken world was even more vivid in foreign policy news when four more regions (Middle East, South Asia, Australia and Oceania, and South America) joined Africa and Central America to vanish from the CCTV screen that did not feature any single country worthy of long-term reporting. This latent pattern of coverage indicates a reductive tendency to organize and promote a specific kind of information and knowledge for the Chinese TV viewers.

FOREIGN POLICY NEWS AS INDICATION OF CHINA'S CURRENT PRACTICES

In international communication, regions get covered not because of their sheer size, but because of things actors, both individual and institutional, do, especially when a country's foreign affairs are concerned. Since its external opening in 1978, China has been quite active in cultivating bilateral relations in the family of nations. Because diplomatic and governmental activities naturally made of the thrust of foreign policy news, it is understandable that heads of state/government (44.7%) and ministries/cabinet members (17.5%) accounted for nearly one third of China's foreign affairs stories on CCTV during the study period (Table 7.9). This evidence is in line with the high-level international activities conducted by the Chinese leadership between 1993 and 1997 (H. Liu, 1999). It is a visual presentation of top Chinese officials a work, designed to project the images of current national commitment and practices.

Other actors below the ministerial or cabinet level, such as public opinion, congress, political party, diplomats, and international organizations generally played an insignificant part in Chinese foreign policy news on China's window on the world (Table 7.10). In foreign news, however, some of these actors (public opinion, UN/international organizations and military/militia/security) evidently had more coverage than their Chinese counterparts in foreign policy news. The fact that interest groups—business and companies that dealt with joint ventures between China and other countries—appeared more often in foreign

Table 7.9: Main Actors in Foreign Policy News on CCTV, 1992–1998[a]

Main Actor	1992	1996	1998	Total
Heads of state/government	32.6%	49.3%	56.3%	44.7%
Ministries/cabinet members	16.7	26.7	12.6	17.5
Interest groups	19.4	1.3	5.9	10.7
Public/public opinion	9.7	2.7	5.9	6.8
Congress/parliament	4.2	6.7	6.7	5.6
Political/party officials	6.3	6.7	3.4	5.3
Ambassadors/diplomats	3.5	2.7	5.0	3.8
Military/public security	1.4	4.0	2.5	2.4
UN/international organizations	3.5	–	1.7	2.1
Local governments	2.8	–	–	1.2
Total	144	75	119	338

$X^2 = 49.77$, $df = 18$, $p < .01$

[a]Foreign policy news includes stories about both foreign policy and international relations. Foreign policy refers to discrete governmental actions intended by the decision makers to influence the behavior of international actors external to the Chinese polity. International relations concerns foreign relationships, such as joint ventures, trade and cultural exchanges between China and at least one other country. It does not necessarily involve governmental activities.

Table 7.10: Comparison of Actors Between Foreign and Foreign Policy News on CCTV, 1992–1998

Main Actor	Foreign News	Foreign Policy News	Total
Heads of state/government	31.5%	44.7%	36.8%
Ministers/cabinet members	15.4	17.5	16.3
Public/public opinion	14.1	6.8	11.2
UN/other international organizations	13.9	2.1	9.1
Interest groups	6.1	10.7	7.9
Military/militia/security	7.5	2.4	5.5
Congress/parliament	4.2	5.6	4.7
Political/party officials	3.2	5.3	4.0
Diplomats/ambassadors	2.6	3.8	3.1
Courts	1.0	–	0.6
Local governments	0.2	1.2	0.6
Provincial/state governments	0.4	–	0.2
Total	505	338	843

$X^2 = 77.83$, $df = 11$, $p < .01$

policy news than in foreign news on CCTV indicates that to some extent the former manifests Beijing's prevalent undertaking in domestic affairs.

Since the late 1970s, internal economic reforms and open-door policy have been China's established guiding principles. Both categories of activities were well programmed on the Chinese window on the world. In domestic news, economic related stories generally ranked high on the CCTV newscasts in terms of their proportion, placement and length (see chap. 5). In foreign policy news, stories concerning governmental interactions and business-oriented international visits between China and other countries were unquestionably the main stable on CCTV. As shown in Table 7.11, about 8 out of 10 stories on CCTV during the study period dwelled on diplomacy/government and economic/business/trade between China and other countries (78.4%).

Table 7.11: Topics of Foreign Policy News on CCTV, 1992–1998[a]

Topic	1992	1996	1998	Total
Diplomacy/government	45.2%	73.7%	77.6%	62.1%
Economic/trade/business	22.6	7.9	12.8	16.3
Social unrest	9.0	5.4	1.9	5.9
Education/arts/culture	10.1	1.3	1.6	5.4
Politics	2.4	14.5	0.8	4.3
Technology/science	8.9	–	–	4.1
Military/defense	1.2	1.3	3.2	1.9
Social service/health	2.4	–	1.6	1.6
Transportation/travel/tourism	3.0	1.3	–	1.6
Human interest/lifestyle	2.5	–	–	1.0
Entertainment	–	–	1.6	0.5
Law/crime	0.6	–	0.8	0.5
Sports	1.2	–	–	0.5
Agriculture/forest	0.6	–	–	0.3
Disasters/accidents	0.6	–	–	0.3
Ecology/environment	0.6	–	–	0.3
Obituary	0.6	–	–	0.3
Total	168	76	125	369

[a]The focus is on the main topic—what the story is mainly about. Excluded were other or unidentifiable stories.

Compared to foreign news (see Table 7.12), foreign policy news on CCTV indeed was much more concentrated on stories about China's official protocols and its economic interests across national borders. For the Chinese national television viewers, two aspects of foreign policy news were paramount: what China's leadership was doing in a global context and how the country could benefit from economic, trade, or business—not to mention diplomatic—opportunities that arose from such contacts. The appearance of economic stories in CCTV's foreign policy news clearly suggests a connection between the complexity of China's evolving external socioeconomic conditions and its potential impact on the internal development.

In foreign news, however, the Chinese viewers could be exposed to a much wider array of events and issues that did not implicate China, such as military/defense, politics, sports, disasters/acci-

Table 7.12: Comparison of Topics Between Foreign and Foreign Policy News on CCTV, 1992–1998[a]

Topic	Foreign News	Foreign Policy News	Total
Diplomacy/government	21.8%	62.1%	37.0%
Economic/trade/business	12.2	16.3	13.7
Military/defense	19.0	1.9	12.6
Politics	16.1	4.3	11.7
Sports	7.1	0.5	4.6
Disasters/accidents	5.7	0.3	3.7
Social unrest	5.9	–	3.7
Education/arts/culture	1.6	5.4	3.1
Technology/science	2.1	4.1	2.9
Law/crime	3.0	0.5	2.0
Social service/health	2.1	1.6	1.9
Transportation/travel/tourism	1.0	1.6	1.2
Human interest/lifestyle	1.0	–	0.6
Ecology/environment	0.7	0.3	0.5
Entertainment	0.3	0.5	0.4
Agriculture/forest	0.3	0.3	0.3
Obituary	–	0.3	0.1
Total	609	369	978

$X^2 = 273.73$, $df = 16$, $p < .01$

[a]The focus is on the main topic—what the story is mainly about. Excluded were other or unidentifiable stories.

dents, and social unrest. As far as content was concerned, the two worlds on CCTV news were inescapably instrumental: foreign policy news directed the Chinese people toward China's aspirations and attainments in the community of nations, whereas foreign news guided them toward a world of conflicts and tension. It is a creation and presentation of international political situation that tends to pit a friendly, stable China against a hostile, chaotic world out there.

THE INCOMPATIBLE WORLD MAPS
FROM HERE AND THERE

Following the general theoretical framework—social construction of reality—outlined in the two previous chapters, this chapter aims to identify, through a comparative analysis between foreign news and foreign policy news on CCTV, how the world outside China's immediate geopolitical horizon might be socially constructed and articulated in the news. The central thesis argues that the world map changes according to the relative positions from "here"—China's involvement in foreign affairs—and "there"—the world at large. Consequently, the Chinese national television may place certain parts of the world reality higher in the hierarchical domain of news, according to a functional system of relevance or significance associated with the countries involved within a particular context. From a long-term point of view, countries do not necessarily assume or command similar entry points into the world of mediated reality in China.

From 1992 to 1998, only a core of very few select countries or entities consistently makes up the list of foreign policy news on CCTV. It is a world that differs significantly from that of foreign news in both quantity and quality. Quantitatively, the CCTV news net tends to be cast wider and farther in foreign news, whereas it is narrower and closer to home in foreign policy news. Qualitatively, a nexus of network of countries is configured around different sets of national or international concerns in the realm of foreign news or foreign policy news or both. The Chinese central television often recognizes the prevalent societal experience and domestic interests to the extent that the world of foreign affairs is likely to be viewed from a limited conceptual range of vision.

On a comparative scale between foreign news and foreign policy news, the world's hot spots on CCTV TV news seem to be organized by systematic means that give more weight to some regions than other regions. It means that as a social transcript in China, CCTV news takes and records certain sectors in its immediate and remote environment as information and knowledge. Such presentation and representation have testified to a penchant for dividing the world into an ethnocentric (China centered) and reductive (a simplistic external reality) distinction. To a great extent, CCTV thus functions as part of the knowledge-cumulating institutions in China, allowing the public to make sense of the spirit and practices of its own world and the land beyond.

Longitudinally, the world that China's central TV news brings to the attention of the Chinese people is one that largely lies within or has implications for its sphere of influence: North America, eastern Europe/Russia, and East Asia. The narrow scope indicates that international spectacles are constructed to help portray a sense of immediacy or currency—Chinese national concerns and social practices. Ethnocentrism in international communication is thus a matter of degree, not kind. The binding factors are usually socially bound and politically delimited, manifesting a country's typification or formation of another's image that is rearranged in this or that perspective, based on the demand of context and continuity.

On a conceptual and methodological note, the two worlds of CCTV news—one in foreign news and the other in foreign policy news—point out the necessity of sound conceptualization and appropriate analytical approach in international communication research. Without such differentiation between the two concepts, the nuance in the differing worldviews, as exemplified by China's national television news, may be lost. Mixing the two, at best, will cancel out each other, obscuring the true, opposite phenomenon. At worst, it may result in erroneous conclusions and unwarranted interpretations of a skewed relationship between variables.

Amid the extraordinary global political, social, and economic changes, an understanding of the role of Chinese news media in sorting out the "risks and opportunities" (Hoge, 1993) and in redefining the worldview is crucial in the post-Cold War world, both inside and outside of China. If the evidence in this chapter is any indication, the processes of foreign news reporting and foreign policy news coverage in China do not necessarily originate from the same location; nor are they likely to follow the same trajectory. How each may end can be largely determined by where the state in China wants it to be and what it may bring out along the way. The incompatible world maps on CCTV demonstrates that it is inadvisable to approach the multifaceted Chinese worldview in the news through a single and simple prism. The standardized vision reduces the complex reality in China into an illusion that fails to distinguish what there is to observe inside the Middle Kingdom.

CHAPTER 8

UNITED STATES IN THE EYES OF CHINESE TELEVISION: A SUBTLE NEWS PRISM WITH A PREFERRED MESSAGE

In a speech given on January 18, 2000, Li Zhaoxing, Chinese ambassador to the United States, flatly rejected the U.S. call for China to change its authoritarian behavior and repressive policy toward dissidents in order to improve the relations between the two countries. Insisting that "China already practices democracy and respects human right," he argued, "there is nothing China needs to change—except *inaccurate impressions* of China created by some U.S. politicians—to smooth the way to warmer U.S.–China relations" (Black, 2000, p. A5, italics added). He criticized all those who alleged that China violates the human rights of its citizens and dismissed such perceptions as groundless creations by some U.S. politicians. Although Li did not single out U.S. news media, his remarks left little doubt that they were one of the culprits responsible for China's bad image in the United States.

The Chinese ambassador's accusation against the false representation of China in the United States echoes a series of charges of "demonizing China" that have long been brewing in the Chinese news media, especially since the mid-1990s. In 1996, several Chinese journalists and scholars published a book titled *The Background of Demonizing China*, alleging that the U.S. government and news media have waged a conspiracy to smear or demonize China in the United States and around the wórld (X. Li et al., 1996). The book was well received and the allegation of demonization has since become a standard Chinese explanation of how and why U.S. news media cover China and its people the way they do.

The scathing Chinese indictment against U.S. news media prompted the School of Communication at American University, the John F. Kennedy School of Government at Harvard University, and the National Committee on United States–China Relations to co-sponsor a conference on "U.S. Media Coverage of China" in 1998.[1] A group of journalists, academics and policy makers from Australia, China, Britain, and the United States was invited to discuss how American and Chinese news media covered each other and what factors might affect such report as well as the implications for Sino-American relations. It was the first time since China and the United States established formal diplomatic relations in 1979 that journalists and scholars from both sides gathered to address issues and concerns involving contemporary journalistic spirit and practices between the two countries.[2]

The Chinese journalists and officials included Liu Zhengzhu, CCTV's correspondent in Washington, DC; Shao Wenguang, former minister-counselor for Congressional Relations, Embassy of the People's Republic of China; Xiong Lei, senior writer and managing editor of *China Features* at Xinhua News Agency; Cui Tiankai, minister-counselor for PRC Mission to the UN and former deputy spokesperson of Ministry of Foreign Affairs; Zhu Xingfu, Washington, DC bureau chief of *Wenhui Bao*; Zhu Yinghuang, editor in chief of *China Daily*; and Li Yunfei, Washington, DC bureau chief of *People's Daily*.[3] Xiong Lei and Zhu Yinghuang were the only two who flew directly from China to participate in the conference.

Xiong was one of the authors of *The Background of Demonizing of China*. At the conference, she and her colleagues were reassured by U.S.

---

[1]The first author was invited to attend as a panelist for the conference held at the American University in Washington, DC. Chaired by Stephen R. MacKinnon, professor of history at Arizona State University, the panel on "Chinese coverage of the United States" included Orville H. Schell, dean of Graduate School of Journalism at University of California at Berkeley; Zhu Xingfu, Washington, DC bureau chief of *Wenhui Bao*; and Zhu Yinghuang, editor in chief of *China Daily*.

[2]In November 1982, a group of U.S. journalists, historians, and China experts gathered in Scottsdale, Arizona, for a 2-day conference on the war reporting of China in the 1940s, focusing on the last phase of the Chinese civil war between the Nationalists and the Communists. For a detailed discussion of this conference, see MacKinnon and Friesen (1987).

[3]For a list of other participants from Australia, Britain, and the United States, see the conference report published by the National Committee on United States–China Relations in June 1998.

journalists and officials that there was no such thing as a conspiracy between the U.S. government and the news media to castigate China. The U.S. conferees indicated that, unlike Chinese journalists, U.S. journalists were independent and autonomous of official intervention or outside interference. Other Western journalists concurred, asserting that U.S. society, mass media and business interests were far too varied for the government to exercise any monolithic control over the content of the news media. This line of explanation apparently did not register with those journalists from China whose news media have been dominated by the state interests and official ideology and who have different views of the press-state relationship.

Unpersuaded, Xiong returned to Beijing more convinced that there has been indeed a tendency in the U.S. news media to "demonize" China. The responses from the U.S. journalists were simply defensive. She later wrote in an article that "none of American journalists would admit there was a bias in their reports about China; they repeatedly insisted that there was no attempt to demonize China in the U.S. news media. If there was any negative report about China, it was China's own fault" (Xiong, 1998, p. 12). She concluded by questioning whether the U.S. news media have truly enjoyed press freedom if they harbored an anti-Communism mentality and a narrow conceptual fixation toward different countries and cultures. Her belief resonated with that of other Chinese journalists. In fact, there was a consensus among the Chinese panelists that U.S. journalistic practices could undermine the relationship between China and the United States.

The 1998 Washington, DC conference took place shortly before President Clinton was to visit China in late June. The upcoming presidential trip triggered heated debates between Chinese and U.S. journalists over what and how their respective news media should cover the Clinton–Jiang summit and, for that matter, the two countries from a long-term point of view. At the conference, Chinese journalists maintained that coverage of the United States in China was much more extensive and objective than U.S. reports on China. They urged their U.S. counterparts to help improve Sino–American relations through unbiased and nonprovocative style in their news reporting and writing about China. To them, the news media were to be a means to an end, the outcome of which should be predicated on the merits of its social values and political utility.

Among other things,[4] Chinese journalists argued that while China and the United States were working hard to cultivate a good rela-

---

[4]The Chinese journalists' comments and statements were borrowed heavily from the conference report released by the National Committee on United States–China Relations in June 1998.

tionship, the news media in both countries should play a more positive and constructive role by creating a friendly atmosphere for President Clinton's visit to Beijing. They specifically emphasized that the Chinese news media would refrain from reporting U.S. domestic political scandals such as the Clinton–Lewinsky affair since they were essentially "internal matters" and thus irrelevant to the Sino–American relations. One Chinese journalist even predicted that during the presidential visit, the news media in China would be courteous and nonconfrontational, but U.S. reporters would likely ask uncomfortable and provocative questions. By implication, they challenged U.S. journalists to reciprocally steer clear of intruding into Chinese domestic affairs like the 1989 Tiananmen Square democratic movement in which many students were killed in a brutal military crackdown. In the official verdict, the incident was branded as counterrevolutionary and the Chinese government had acted appropriately to suppress the social disturbance.

The Chinese journalists contended that the news media in China have become more open, impartial, and friendly toward the United States since the two nations embarked on the process of normalization in the early 1970s. The quality of U.S. news coverage in the Chinese media, they claimed, has greatly shifted away from the era when the two countries were entangled in the Cold War under which the reporting of the United States tended to highlight the "decadent, rotten sins of capitalism." Any disparagement against the United States in the Chinese media accordingly was "retaliatory" in nature and occurred only when China perceived that it was being unfairly attacked by the U.S. news media. As one Chinese journalist said, "You bash us 100 times, we only bash you once." In other words, the variance of news reports between China and the United States is a matter of degree, not kind. What is unspoken, of course, is that the Chinese news media are nationally responsible and internationally responsive. In terms of media ideology, they do not necessarily see the world the way the U.S. media do, especially when China and the United States see each other.

CHANGING IMAGES OF THE UNITED STATES IN CHINA'S NEWS MEDIA

The philosophical differences about the role and function of news media in the U.S.–China relations aside, the blunt and spirited dialogue between Chinese and U.S. journalists at the 1998 conference raised serious questions regarding how China and the United States have reported each other over the past decades, particularly since China opened its door to the West in the late 1970s. These questions are not only theoretically important, but also empirically noteworthy. They have attracted increasing journalistic and scholarly attention to the performances of news media in both countries. The Chinese thesis of a U.S. conspiracy is certainly a conceptual attempt to make sense of the way China is covered in the U.S. news media.

On the U.S. side, as communities of interpretation (e.g., Said, 1997), the press has been extensively examined in terms of its form and content of coverage of Sino–American relations over time (e.g., Chang, 1993; Goodman, 1990, 1999; Lin & Salwen, 1986). As far as China policy news was concerned, Chang found that since 1950 the U.S. press unquestionably helped perpetuate an illusion of U.S.–China relations that bore little resemblance to the underlying reality. At best, it was "a press reality filtered through a conceptual lens ground by policy makers sitting on top of official Washington" (Chang, 1993, p. 247). The entire Winter 1999 issue of *Media Studies Journal* on "Covering China" represents a more recent effort to see China "from as many perspectives as possible" (Giler & Snider, 1999, p. xiv). It is a testament to the complex and intriguing position China holds in American journalism (see also MacKinnon & Friesen, 1987). As noted in the previous chapters, the multifaceted or pluralistic approach helps shed greater light on the Chinese reality.

On the Chinese side, being part of the Communist ideological state apparatus, the news media are intricately woven into the political structure and social fabric in China, serving as educator, catalyst, and mobilizer for the Party and government in their attempt to build a socialist country. A well-established body of literature has closely documented the changes and continuities of Chinese mass media since China launched its economic reforms and open-door policy to the West in the late 1970s (e.g., Chinoy, 1999; C. Lee, 1990a, 1994, 2000; Schell & Shambaugh, 1999; Zhao, 1998). Whether journalistic accounts or academic studies, these recent works have provided new knowledge and insightful analysis of the Chinese news media through a historical or political economic point of view. From the perspective of sociology of knowledge, little is known as to how the Chinese mass media construct the reality in the news. Given the tensions and the uneasy relationship between China and the United States, the way the latter has been covered in Chinese mass media, especially on television since the 1980s, should serve as clues of news construction of social reality in the former.

Since the 1970s, a few sporadic studies have looked at images of the United States in the following major Chinese national media: *People's Daily* and *Peking Review* in the 1960s (Edelstein & Liu, 1963; Oliphant, 1964), Peking Television (later CCTV), *Peking Review*, *People's Daily*, *Enlightenment Daily*, and China's external propaganda materials in 1970s (K. Chen, 1987; L. Chu, 1978; Y. Lee, 1981; Y. Liu, 1974; Tretiak, 1971; K.

Wang & Starck, 1972), *People's Daily, Enlightenment Daily, Southern Daily*, and CCTV in 1980s (K. Chen, 1987; C. Lee, 1981, 1982; Warren, 1988), and CCTV in 1990s (Chang et al., 1994). Although these outlets represent only a small number of Chinese news media, they stand as the most authoritative observation posts in China, supplying both information and interpretation about the outside world. With varying conceptual sophistication and methodological vigor, the few studies have offered some useful baseline for comparison of the changing Chinese views toward the United States in the news media throughout the process of China's pursuit of domestic economic liberalization and open-door policy (see also Cunningham, 1999; M. Zhang, 1999).

Whether in print or in broadcast media, the historical presentation of the United States in China invariably followed the tensions, conflicts, and cooperations between the two countries as well as international relations that had profound implications for Sino–American interaction, such as the Korean War and Taiwan Strait Crises in the 1950s, the Vietnam War in the 1960s and 1970s, and the U.S.–Soviet Cold War confrontation. China's own domestic politics and social movements (e.g., the Cultural Revolution from 1966 to 1976), of course, have always been inextricably linked to its international behaviors, including its worldview and rhetorics toward other countries. The Chinese news media epitomize the manifestation of the United States as both a symbol and an issue in China's internal purposes and external considerations. There is an ideological need over time to impart a more or less standardized portrayal of the United States in the news.

In the late 1950s and early 1960s, as shown in the *People's Daily* (Edelstein & Liu, 1963) and the *Peking Review* (Oliphant, 1964), the United States was branded an imperialist and the major enemy of the worldwide Communist revolution. The ideological and militant overtone intended to pin the United States as the driving force of Western imperialism and the stumbling block of the proletariat movement toward Communism utopia. Derived from such functional calculation, the Chinese news media were determined to expose the decadent and exploitative nature of U.S. capitalism. The economic woes (e.g., unequal distribution of wealth and high unemployment) and social ills (e.g., crimes and racial tension) were therefore the staple of news coverage of the United States in China. It was a fragmented, circumscribed, and stereotyped typification.

When China and Soviet Union openly split in the mid-1960s over Soviet's revisionist approach to the Communist international strategy and its invasion of Czechoslovakia, Beijing faced an uneasy ideological dilemma between the Soviet socialist imperialism and U.S. capitalist imperialism. Struggling to ascertain the lesser of two evils, China began to mitigate its animosity toward the United States at the expense of Soviet Union. As revealed in the *Peking Review* from 1966 to 1969, Chinese news media gradually softened their bellicose rhetorical assault against the United States on the one hand and hardened their criticism of Soviet Union on the other (Tretiak, 1971). Instead of being the world's foremost imperialist, the United States was now paired with the Soviet Union as the two evils threatening the Third World. The public image of the United States in China was still rooted in a confrontational equation in the new geopolitical setting, however.

The instrumental prerequisite in China's dealings with the United States was most visible in the news when the relationship between the two countries started to thaw in the early 1970s. In April 1971, China invited the U.S. ping pong team for a friendship tour. During the U.S. team's visit, Chinese news media temporarily withheld their hostile verbal attack against the United States (K. Wang & Starck, 1972). The ping pong diplomacy was followed in June 1971 by the U.S. lift of a 21-year-old trade embargo imposed on China after its entry into the Korean War in 1950. In December 1971, President Nixon announced that he would visit China in February 1972. Notwithstanding the U.S. friendly posture, the *People's Daily* and the *Enlightenment Daily* continued to label the United States as imperialist for its external behavior and to portray U.S. domestic situation as mired in economic and social crises (K. Chen, 1987; A. Liu, 1974). The negative images of the United States were often total and unwavering. Such representation of U.S. society imposed an unmistakably conception of anti-America and anything it reflected and served.

The end of Cultural Revolution and the return of Deng Xiaoping to power apparently shifted China's social practices and policy commitments from the ideological class struggle to the pragmatic market orientation in the late 1970s. Accompanying the internal reforms was an open-door policy that not only changed China's worldview in general, but also transformed its perception of Sino–American relations in particular. Useful as it might be, coverage of the general news in Chinese national media does not necessarily allow for a detailed examination of the linkage between China's domestic aspiration and its orientation toward a specific country, which may better explain how the news as a form of social knowledge is articulated and circulated in society over time.

Lee's 1979–1980 study of U.S. images in the *People's Daily* thus provides some meaningful illustration. Using it as a yardstick helps determine how the Chinese knowledge of the United States evolves from the early phase of China's modernization process through the reform years. According to C. Lee's (1981) data, during 1979–1980 about one third of U.S. stories in the *People's Daily* involved U.S. internal prob-

lems, such as economic and social crises. Lee speculated that "the prominent display of U.S. domestic problems was partially warranted because
of U.S. economic and social mismanagement" (p. 97). He also noted that
"there was a substantial increase [from 1979 to 1980] in the proportion of
admiring mentions about advanced U.S. science and technology" (p. 97).

     As demonstrated in the *People's Daily, Southern Daily,* and the
Enlightenment Daily (K. Chen, 1987; C. Lee, 1981, 1982; Y. Lee, 1981),
from the mid-1970s through the early 1980s, the United States appeared
either more favorably or less negatively in the Chinese news media. In
"almost all dimensions (except government/politics and
military/defense)," for example, "images of America" in the *People's
Daily* and the *Southern Daily* were "overwhelmingly favorable" in 1980
(C. Lee, 1982, p. 70). Although no such phenomenon was found in 1981,
the *People's Daily* and the *Enlightenment Daily* both nevertheless cast the
United States in an apolitical and neutral light (K. Chen, 1987).
Compared to the previous decades, the turnaround of U.S. identification
in the Chinese news was striking. What has changed in the transformation is not necessarily the United States per se, but rather China itself
and the context in which it placed the United States as an object of observation and interpretation.

     Among the few previous studies examining U.S. images in the
Chinese news media, for obvious rationale (e.g., easy access and comparison purpose), most have focused on the content of daily newspapers
or weekly magazines in China. Although they have more or less charted
a consistent pattern of verbal portrayal of the United States in some
major Chinese print media, how the United States is visually perceived
and conveyed on television throughout China remains sketchy and
undetermined. To be more specific, Chinese national television news is
rarely explored systematically. One key reason is certainly the difficulty
in collecting the actual video cast of Chinese national television news for
analysis. As far as English sources are concerned, some earlier journalistic accounts reported impressionistic, but anecdotal snippets. Only two
systemic, albeit limited, studies on China's national television news in
the 1980s could be found in the literature (J. Chu, 1978; Warren, 1988).
This deficiency of intellectual inquiry leaves a huge gap to be filled in
the understanding of Chinese television news coverage of the United
States over time.

CHINESE TELEVISION AND THE UNITED STATES

As noted in chapter 1, television has now become the leading source for
news in China, reaching every province and autonomous region as well

as more than 90% of the Chinese population. With its humble begin-nings in 1958, Chinese television suffered significantly in both the quan-titative growth of stations and the qualitative diversity of content during the 10-year Cultural Revolution (1966–1976). Understandably, nothing much about the outside world was shown on television in China, other than the standard presentation of Chinese struggle against Western imperialism and hegemony. For the United States, it "appeared as a place of riots, crime, poverty, and other man-made and natural disas-ters" (Chang, 1989, p. 222). The rationality embedded in these images was certainly recognizable: the United States was nothing but trouble.

Shortly after the end of the Cultural Revolution, BTS established itself as the nation's most authoritative TV network in 1978 when it was renamed CCTV. A small-scale study of international news flow on BTS conducted by J. Chu (1978) in September 1977 somehow captured the form and content of China's window on the world at the beginning of its expansion. Although confined in scope and depth, the analysis of 6-day evening newscasts more or less recorded how the world and its various countries were reported on Chinese television news.

A year before China embarked on its ambitious economic reforms and open-door policy, the snapshots of BTS news in 1977 served as a useful benchmark for the changing TV landscape in later years, even though the comparison should be exercised with caution because of discrepant measures. First, a majority of international stories on BTS involved politics. Second, whether in domestic or in international news, BTS never carried any stories about crimes or disasters. Third, nine Third World countries led all the countries mentioned in the internation-al news, followed by five Western nations. The United States was nowhere to be found. The last two points contrast sharply with the find-ings displayed in the previous chapters and those to be seen in this chapter later.

By the mid-1980s, Chinese television had developed quickly fol-lowing the footsteps of economic reforms. Both the number of TV receivers and audiences jumped dramatically from the decade before (e.g., Bishop, 1989; Huang, 1994; Rogers, Zhao, Pan, & Chen, 1985). Coverage of foreign news became a regular fixture of CCTV, the only national network of its kind in the country. In 1985, Warren (1988) ana-lyzed 20 CCTV newscasts randomly selected between October and December to compare its foreign and domestic news content. The typical analysis yielded a very brief account regarding how the United States showed up on CCTV news. "The U.S. was the source of the largest num-ber of stories (24); this was 10 more than either the United Kingdom or the Soviet Union" (Warren, 1988, p. 220). Unfortunately, like L. Chu (1978), Warren missed a good opportunity to probe deeper into how the

Chinese television reduced the dynamic U.S. reality to symbolic, rhetorical, and visual elements in the news. Other than frequency, not much else could be learned specifically from the two studies.

Since its reforms and external openness in the late 1970s and early 1980s, China has unambiguously reexamined its position vis-à-vis that of the world in general and the United States in particular in political, social, economic, and cultural dimensions. The foreign sanctions against the 1989 Tiananmen Square crackdown that brutally crushed a pro-democracy student movement has not detracted China from pursuing high-level external relations. President Jiang Zemin's visit to the United States in October 1997 and President Clinton's trip to China in June 1998 highlighted China's efforts to seek U.S. support for its domestic and foreign behaviors in the community of nations. The release and exile of the most known Chinese dissident Wei Jingsheng to the United States about 2 weeks after the Jiang–Clinton Washington summit unequivocally underscored China's interactive strategy and communication skills in response to the international pressures on its human rights record.

In the post-Cold War international landscape, the United States, the world's remaining superpower, and China, the last Communist stronghold and the world's most populous country, are often brought into the power equation either by design or by default. Because of the dynamics and complexity of changing geopolitical structure, the "absence of clear, steady cues from Washington" makes the U.S. news media's reporting task more difficult (Hoge, 1993, p. 2). In China, as shown in earlier studies (e.g., Chang et al., 1993), "old constructs are inadequate" in that the unpredictable society requires "a flexible and sophisticated journalistic perspective" (Tefft, 1993, p. 62). In international communication, how countries scrutinize the world and one another thus has practical and theoretical significance in the post-Cold War news flow across national borders (e.g., Chang, Wang, & Chen, 1998).

As mentioned earlier, this study represents the most comprehensive analysis of Chinese national television news over time and across space. Following the perspective of social construction of reality discussed in the previous three chapters, this chapter aims at detailing the way the United States is conceived, depicted, and treated, both quantitatively and qualitatively, on CCTV news from 1992 to 1998. Several questions are especially addressed: What was the international imagery of the United States as seen on Chinese national television news? How did the TV representation of the United States compare to that of the world in China? How was the discourse about the United States on CCTV news socially constructed? What are the implications of U.S. images in China for better understanding of Sino–American relations?

CONSTRUCTING THE UNITED STATES ON CHINESE TELEVISION NEWS

Chapters 6 and 7 documented that the United States constantly ranked among the top on CCTV coverage of foreign and foreign policy news. This phenomenon generally agreed with an earlier finding that in 1985 the United States outnumbered all other countries in foreign stories on CCTV (Warren, 1988). It suggests that, unlike in the 1970s (e.g., L. Chu, 1978), the United States has enjoyed an overriding presence on Chinese national television since the mid-1980s. In different ways, the United States also stood as the core country that linked various countries in a network pattern on the Chinese window on the world. The meanings of such consistent U.S. domination, both as an object when China is a spectator and as a counterpart when China is a participant, have yet to be unraveled. What has been left unexplained is the sort of information and knowledge as well as their relationship that underlies the prevalent mode of TV news coverage of the United States in China. It is an essential part of the intellectual pursuit involving the news as a form of knowledge.

During the 1992 to 1998 study period, 159 stories (15.9% of all foreign and foreign policy news) related directly or indirectly to the United States appeared on CCTV, with 93 items (58.5%) in foreign policy news devoted to Sino–American relations and 66 stories (41.5%) dealing with U.S. domestic matters or foreign affairs that did not concern China. No other countries came closer to sharing the spotlight with the United States on CCTV news. The prominence of the United States on CCTV lay not only in the large proportion of news among all countries, but also in the wide distribution of newscasts across time. Of the combined 78 daily newscasts in the 3 years under study, the United States turned up in 61 newscasts (78.2%), averaging nearly three stories per appearance (61/159) and two stories per day (78/159). Again, such status was unmatched by any other country. The quantity of U.S. coverage needs to be further viewed in the context of quality.

Table 8.1 presents coverage of U.S.-related stories on CCTV from a technical point of view: timeliness of news. Between foreign news and foreign policy news on CCTV, there was an apparent discrepancy in how timely stories involving the United States were scheduled in the newscast. In foreign policy news where China was engaged in Sino–American relations one way or another, most stories (40.2%) concerning the United States were reported "today," whereas only 3% of such stories in foreign news where China was a bystander appeared on the same day of newscast. In fact, almost 85% of stories about U.S. domestic matters and other foreign affairs on CCTV took place either "yesterday" (66.7%) or "recently/this week" (18.2%).

Table 8.1: Timeliness of United States Related News on CCTV, 1992-1998[a]

Timeliness	Foreign News[b]	Foreign Policy News[c]	Total
Yesterday	66.7%	30.4%	45.6%
Today	3.0	40.2	24.7
Recently/this week	18.2	9.8	13.3
Unidentified	9.1	15.2	12.7
Last week	–	2.2	1.3
Last month	1.5	–	0.6
Total	66	92	158

$X^2 = 38.70$, $df = 6$, $p < .01$

[a]Entries include stories involving the United States as the primary country only. Excluded were stories concerning the United States as a secondary country.

[b]Foreign news deals with stories concerning U.S. domestic news and U.S. foreign relations that does not involve China.

[c]Foreign policy news refers to stories about Sino–American relations, either from Chinese or U.S. point of view.

Given the location of the two countries in different time zones, it might be argued that the disparity of timeliness between these two types of stories could be partly explained by the transmission and broadcast delay of foreign news from the United States to China. A close reading of U.S.-connected stories, however, indicated that timeliness in foreign policy news resulted mostly from the propensity of CCTV news to place the United States within the domain of China's contemporary commitments and current practices, such as economic joint ventures, U.S. trade investment or Chinese receptions of American officials and business delegations. Since the settings of Sino-American relations were mostly domestic, foreign policy stories about the United State therefore had greater Chinese interests and relevance than foreign news. Their timely reports were obviously expedient. As is discussed later, President Clinton's visit to China in June 1998 represented an ideal opportunity that allowed CCTV news to reconstruct an opportune foreign relations event into a desirable domestic and international spectacle.

Timeliness in news is naturally a matter of technical rationality driven largely by the logic of technology and journalistic professionalism. CCTV is no exception (see chap. 4). The news content itself, however, has to go through a series of editorial decision making that is fundamentally delimited by the social position and organizational structure of the mass media in any society, regardless of the nature of its political system (e.g., Ball-Rokeach & Cantor, 1986). In international communication, the selection and presentation of news topics, therefore, constitute the ways of seeing and knowing the world. Depending on the location and degree of involvement of the observer, the results may indicate areas of interests, locales of problems, or spheres of activities. Whether individual or collective, what counts as knowledge accordingly hinges on only what they have made.

Like news programs with a fixed amount of time in any country, the prime-time newscast of CCTV could not realistically scan and equally introduce a wide range of topics that might appeal to its viewers. By default, the network news of CCTV must, therefore, choose from a myriad of daily events and issues to fill its screen. By design, it can decide in the selection process to include or exclude particular types of events or issues as ingredients of its news menu. Either way, the chosen stories become part of the discourse that tells something about the objects, people or countries under observation. It is, in essence, a form of social construction of reality in the news that takes and records certain features in the immediate and remote environment as information and knowledge. On CCTV news, the United States emerged as a country that fluctuated its distinct images according to the episodes and agencies from context to context.

THE TWO FACES OF UNITED STATES ON CCTV NEWS

As is evident in Table 8.2, the United States was cast on CCTV news against two sets of topical backgrounds. By its very nature, foreign policy news regularly centers around bilateral activities between countries, including diplomatic contacts, governmental reactions, and other international relations that do not openly necessitate the official participation.[5] In China, it is common knowledge that any international interaction with other countries through nonofficial channels such as business ventures, institutional exchanges, or private interests explicitly or implicitly carries some sort of official endorsement from the central to local levels. During the study period, the United States showed up predominantly on CCTV news in diplomatic and governmental activities (61.1%), with economic/trade/business (15.6%) and technology/science (8.9%) stories trailing far behind. It had little visibility in other categories of news.

---

[5]Foreign policy news in this study is broadly defined to include stories about China's foreign policy and international relations. For further definition, see chapter 4.

Table 8.2: Coverage of Topics in United States Related News on CCTV, 1992–1998[a]

Topics	Foreign News	Foreign Policy News	Total
Diplomacy/government	12.9%	61.1%	41.4%
Economic/trade/business	19.4	15.6	17.1
Technology/science	9.7	8.9	9.2
Disasters/accidents	12.9	–	5.3
Military/defense	6.5	4.4	5.3
Crime/law	9.7	1.1	4.6
Politics	9.7	1.1	4.6
Education/arts/culture	3.2	4.4	3.9
Transportation/travel/tourism	4.8	1.1	2.6
Social service/health	3.2	1.1	2.0
Social unrest	3.2	–	1.3
Entertainment	1.6	1.1	1.3
Human interest/life style	1.6	–	0.7
Sports	1.6	–	0.7
Total	62	90	152

$X^2 = 53.30$, $df = 13$, $p < .01$

[a]Entries include stories involving the United States as the primary country only. Excluded were stories concerning the United States as a secondary country and other topics.

In foreign news on CCTV, when China stood from a distance, the backdrop of the United States deviated significantly from that of foreign policy news. Although the number of U.S.-related stories was smaller, CCTV put the United States in a variety of milieu, ranging from economic/trade/business (19.4%), diplomacy/government (12.9%), disasters/accidents (12.9%), technology/science (9.7%), crime/law (9.7%), politics (9.7%), military/defense (6.5%), and other occasional settings. Unquestionably, when China was an onlooker in foreign news, the United States came to be perceived in variegated hues and behavioral dimensions. What is more revealing perhaps is the Chinese TV projection and interpretation of U.S. domestic dysfunctions. They allow the viewers in China to make normative judgment of everyday life in the United States.

In 1977, L. Chu (1978) found no coverage of crimes and disasters about China or other countries on BTS (the predecessor of CCTV). The diversification of news, and thus the expansion of social knowledge, on the Chinese national television apparently grew with the passage of time throughout the reform years. During the study period, crime and disaster stories appeared on CCTV. If stories about the social unrest and crime/law in the United States were added to the category of disasters/accidents, the despicable side of U.S. society would loom much bigger. One in every four stories (25.8%) had a negative connotation for the United States.

The lack of such stories on CCTV in the late 1970s might arguably be due to the small sample of Chu's 1977 study. It was difficult, however, to imagine that no crime or disaster ever occurred in China, the United States, or around the world during a 1-week period. The answer to the absence of crime and disaster stories on Chinese television therefore lay elsewhere. A review of Chinese publications (e.g., X. Sun, 1992) on the functions of mass media in China suggests that the news serves both descriptive and prescriptive purposes, one of which is to add insights into the Chinese perspective. In other words, countries see themselves in relation to the images, whether real or perceived, they create for other nations. It is an ethnocentric penchant to divide the world into a pro-self and anti-other configuration that benefits the observing country.

The dissimilar news orientation resulting from the different range of vision and diverse sectors of U.S. reality on the CCTV network also becomes discernible when actors were brought into the picture (Table 8.3). In foreign policy news on CCTV, the presence of U.S. actors was clearly tied to the prevalent Chinese national concerns and political engagements at the highest level. For the most part, heads of state and government (51.2%) from both countries outnumbered all other actors. From the Chinese perspective, it means China heavily relied on its top leadership to court U.S. players who included President Clinton, business representatives, and individual Americans (e.g., retired officials and media people) during the study period. To a much lesser extent, U.S. actors in nonofficial capacities—public/public opinion and interest groups—made their way to China's international relations on CCTV news, too.

Again, the status of U.S. actors changed notably from foreign policy news to foreign news on CCTV. Among all U.S. actors during the study period, President Clinton did not command the highest attention when CCTV sized up U.S. internal matters and external affairs that had no relevance to China. Consistent with the greater emphasis on nondiplomatic and governmental events and issues (see Table 8.2),

Table 8.3: Coverage of Actors in United States Related News on CCTV, 1992–1998[a]

Actors	Foreign News	Foreign Policy News	Total
Heads of state/government	20.4%	51.2%	39.7%
Public/public opinion	28.6	12.2	18.3
Interest groups	22.4	14.6	17.6
Ministers/cabinet members	8.2	11.0	9.9
Congressional members	4.1	4.9	4.6
Ambassadors/diplomats	4.1	3.7	3.8
Courts	6.1	–	2.3
Military/security	2.0	2.4	2.3
Political/party officials	4.1	–	1.5
Total	49	82	131

$X^2 = 21.58$, $df = 8$, $p < .01$

[a]Entries include stories involving the United States as the primary country only. Excluded were stories concerning the United States as a secondary country and other/unidentifiable actors.

CCTV gave more foreign news frequency and time to individual and collective actors in the categories of public/public opinion (28.6%) and interest groups (22.4%) than any other actors.

Considering the findings in Table 8.2 and Table 8.3 together, these two aspects of news about the United States—disproportionate coverage of topics and actors between foreign news and foreign policy news—are likely to transmit specific knowledge to the Chinese society. To paraphrase Mannheim (1936), in any given social setting, the presence or absence of certain conceptual objects (e.g., disasters/accidents) implies very often not only the presence or absence of certain points of view of the reality, but also the presence or absence of a definite drive to come to shape certain problems in society. In the symbolic world about the United States on CCTV, it could be argued that the typification of some types of adverse news implies the referents of those events and issues actually existed and were thus problematic. This typification not only focused observation, but also organized knowledge. It was more acute when the United States was pitted against the whole world on CCTV news.

THE UNITED STATES VERSUS
THE WORLD ON CCTV NEWS

From 1992 to 1998, in addition to the United States, CCTV reported 256 stories pertaining to 63 countries or entities in foreign policy news during the study period, with an average of four stories per country or entity (Table 8.4). The United States alone had 90 stories on CCTV, far outdistancing all other countries. Using the United States as a point of reference, on a per newscast basis on CCTV (78 newscasts in the 3-year sample), for every 22 foreign policy stories about the United States, 1 was devoted to another country. The eminence of the United States in foreign policy news on the CCTV was numerically unrivaled by any individual country or all other countries combined.

As for the scope of foreign policy and international relations, however, no conspicuous discrepancy existed between the United States and the rest of the world (Table 8.4). Without exception in foreign policy arena, CCTV attended to the United States and the world in a roughly identical manner: predominance of diplomatic and governmental activities, augmented by economic/trade/business stories. In the world of China's geopolitical relations on CCTV news, there is a convergent, if not tunnel, vision as to what countries generally do in the company of others. The performance of United States in the news of Sino–American interplay mimics that of a broader Chinese interchange with the world, of which it is a part.

This is not the case in foreign news on CCTV. During the study period, besides the United States, CCTV registered 484 stories covering 87 countries/entities in foreign news, averaging about 6 stories per country/entity from 1992 to 1998 (Table 8.5). The United States itself accounted for 62 stories on CCTV, again far outstripping all other countries. On a typical CCTV newscast, the ratio of foreign stories between the United States and individual countries of the world was 10 to 1, much smaller than the 22–1 mark in foreign policy news. The closer gap still pointed out the lead role of U.S. affairs on CCTV news. Unlike foreign policy news, the U.S. appearance in foreign news contrasted pointedly with that of the rest of the world.

In Table 8.5, the juxtaposition of "what happened" in the news between the United States and the world on Chinese television illuminates how the former has been identified and projected in China as a result of journalistic selection process over time. Compared to the world as a whole on CCTV news, the United States outpaced other countries in stories about economic/trade/business (19.4% vs. 10.5%), disasters/accidents (12.9% vs. 4.8%), crime/law (9.7% vs. 2.5%), technology/science (9.7% vs. 1.4%), and transportation/travel/tourism (4.8% vs. 0.6%).

Table 8.4: Topics of US and the World in Foreign Policy News on CCTV, 1992–1998

Topics	United States	The World[a]	Total
Diplomacy/government	61.1%	61.3%	61.3%
Economic/trade/business	15.6	16.8	16.5
Education/arts/culture	4.4	5.5	5.2
Politics	1.1	5.9	4.6
Technology/science	8.9	2.7	4.3
Military/defense	4.4	1.2	2.0
Transportation/travel/tourism	1.1	2.0	1.7
Social service/health	1.1	1.6	1.4
Crime/law	1.1	0.4	0.6
Sports	–	0.8	0.6
Entertainment	1.1	0.4	0.6
Agriculture/forest	–	0.4	0.3
Disasters/accidents	–	0.4	0.3
Ecology/environment	–	0.4	0.3
Obituary	–	0.4	0.3
Total	90	256	346

$X^2 = 16.46$, $df = 14$, p = n.g.

[a]The total number of foreign countries or entities is 63. Excluded were international organizations, except for the United Nations, and other topics.

These contradictions were remarkable in that the United States was stacked up against 87 other countries around the world on CCTV news. The U.S. stories were not all rosy.

Despite the prominent presence of neutral reporting of U.S.-related issues, CCTV carried a relatively higher proportion of stories about disasters, accidents, law enforcement, and criminal activities in the United States. When flanked by all other countries shown on the Chinese national television, the crises and woes in U.S. society tended to receive more than their "fair share" of attention in foreign news. On a per country basis, this disproportionate treatment of the United States was even more glaring. For whatever reason, the dark side of the U.S. society simply did not escape the eyes of CCTV. As is discussed later, the combination of divergent news stories on CCTV demonstrated a subtle Chinese approach to molding the United States in a mixed mode of identity: the good, the bad, and the ugly.

**Table 8.5: Topics of US and the World in Foreign News on CCTV,
1992–1998**

Topics	United States	The World[a]	Total
Diplomacy/government	12.9%	22.3%	21.2%
Military/defense	6.5	22.3	20.5
Politics	9.7	19.0	17.9
Economic/trade/business	19.4	10.5	11.5
Social unrest	3.2	6.4	6.0
Disasters/accidents	12.9	4.8	5.7
Sports	1.6	4.5	4.2
Crime/law	9.7	2.5	3.3
Technology/science	9.7	1.4	2.4
Social service/health	3.2	1.9	2.0
Education/arts/culture	3.2	1.7	1.8
Transportation/travel/tourism	4.8	0.6	1.1
Human interest/lifestyle	1.6	1.0	1.1
Ecology/environment	–	0.6	0.5
Agriculture/forest	–	0.4	0.4
Entertainment	1.6	–	0.2
Total	62	484	546

$X^2 = 66.92$, $df = 15$, $p < .01$

[a]The total number of foreign countries or entities is 87. Excluded were stories about international organizations, except for the United Nations, and other topics.

What was covered about the United States on CCTV news, of course, was first made possible by the things individual and institutional actors did or the way they reacted to the scheme of things in the immediate and remote environment. The extent to which these various actors were accorded a spot in the news limelight certainly could not be separated from the context in which they found themselves. Nonetheless, the parade of actors in the United States and the world on Chinese national television hinted at the scope and standing of these actors the news net hoped to reach, particularly when China was a participant, not an observer in the process. Comparatively speaking, because of the delicate situation in Sino–American relations and China's desire to maintain a leveled playing field in the community of nations (e.g., H. Liu, 1999), the United States and the world entered the Chinese TV theater with an unparalleled cast of actors in a unique pecking order.

Table 8.6 lists the U.S. actors and those of the rest of the world in foreign news on CCTV during the 1992–1998 study period. For the world in general, heads of state/government (32.9%) led all other actors in a lopsided fashion, with ministers/cabinet members (16.9%), public/public opinion (13.4%), UN/international organizations (12.4%), and military/militia/security (8.8%) rounding up as the top five players in the news. Excluding those belonging to the general category of "public/public opinion," the other four groups of actors all performed in some official capacities and garnered more than 70% of the foreign stories on CCTV. It is an indication of who or what matters most in the Chinese perception of the world.

By contrast, in the lineup of U.S. actors in foreign news, those with nonofficial status—public/public opinion (28.6%) and interest groups (22.4%)—ranked among the top two groups, accounting for more than 50% of U.S.-related stories on CCTV during the study period. President Clinton and his cabinet members made up the rest of the leading cast. In foreign news, when China stood as an onlooker, the hierar-

Table 8.6: Actors of US and the World in Foreign News on CCTV, 1992–1998[a]

Actors	United States	The World[b]	Total
Head of state/government	20.4%	32.9%	31.6%
Ministers/cabinet members	8.2	16.9	16.0
Public/public opinion	28.6	13.4	15.0
UN/International organizations	–	12.4	11.1
Military/militia/security	2.0	8.8	8.1
Interest groups	22.4	4.5	6.4
Congress/parliament	4.1	4.5	4.5
Political/party officials	4.1	3.1	3.2
Ambassadors/diplomats	4.1	2.1	2.4
Courts	6.1	0.5	1.1
Provincial/state government	–	0.5	0.4
Local government	–	0.2	0.2
Total	49	419	468

$X^2 = 55.89$, $df = 11$, $p < .01$

[a]Entries include stories involving primary countries only. Excluded were stories concerning other or unidentifiable actors.

[b]The total number of foreign countries is 87.

chy of actors or their authority in decision making in the United States did not seem to be as substantial as those from around the world. To some degree, CCTV news was more receptive to actors in the private sectors from the United States than from the remaining countries. When judged on a per country standard, President Clinton as a major actor surely outplayed all other heads of state/government on CCTV news. Whether individual or collective, U.S. actors remained dominant players in the Chinese national television news scene.

The discrepant distribution of actors between the United States and the world held up in foreign policy news, but with a different twist (Table 8.7). When the United States became part of the picture in Sino-American relations, President Clinton and his counterpart in China together (51.2%) drew more attention on CCTV news than the joint exposure of heads of state/government from countries around the world (41.7%). With a smaller share of stories than that in foreign policy news, actors in the categories of interest groups (14.6%) and public/public opinion (12.2%) in the U.S.-related foreign affairs and international relations continued to outshine those from all other nations (9.8% and

Table 8.7: Actors of US and the World in Foreign Policy News on CCTV, 1992–1998[a]

Actors	United States	The World[b]	Total
Heads of state/government	51.2%	41.7%	44.2%
Ministers/cabinet members	11.0	19.6	17.4
Public/public opinion	12.2	5.1	6.9
UN/International organizations	–	1.7	1.3
Military/militia/security	2.4	2.6	2.5
Interest groups	14.6	9.8	11.0
Congress/parliament	4.9	6.0	5.7
Political/party officials	–	7.7	5.7
Ambassadors/diplomats	3.7	4.3	4.1
Local government	–	1.7	1.3
Total	82	235	317

$X^2 = 18.79$, $df = 9$, $p < .01$

[a]Entries include stories involving primary countries only. Excluded were stories concerning other or unidentifiable actors.

[b]The total number of foreign countries is 63.

5.1%, respectively). Ministers or cabinet members in stories about Sino–American relations (11.0%) lagged those in the world (19.6%) in news coverage on CCTV. For the most part, U.S. actors prevailed in Chinese TV news.

From foreign news to foreign policy stories on Chinese national television, the preferred showing of certain aspects of U.S. society and actors over those of the rest of the whole world, not to mention the frequent screening of the United States over time (see chaps. 6 and 7), categorically confirmed the unambiguous U.S. news leadership in the symbolic world of China's central TV network. Although no recent comparison was available, a previous study indicated that although CCTV paid most attention to the United States in foreign news coverage in 1992, ABC did not report anything about China during the same time span, other than mentioning it in passing in one single story about U.S. POWs in the Korean War. "On ABC's news radar, China, with all its international activities, simply could not be found" (Chang et al., 1998, p. 291). The empirical evidence illuminated the politics of presenting and interpreting the reality in international journalism between China and the United States.

Within the conventional thinking of a balanced or reciprocal flow of news among nations, such as the New World Information and Communication Order (e.g., Masmoudi, 1979), the largely one-way traffic of news between China and the United States was problematic. It might be attributed to the structural inequity in international communication (e.g., domination of the West over the rest) and could be interpreted as a form of Western media imperialism or hegemony (e.g., Meyer, 1989). It is difficult, however, to conjecture that China as another power in the Sino–American equation would concede U.S. predominance in the news. Such reasoning of an imperial or hegemonic structure in the Chinese TV case is thus unsatisfactory. There must be other more compelling and qualitative explanations that lay behind the quantitative coverage of the United States on Chinese national television. The narration of U.S.-related stories on CCTV over time constitutes a system of discourse in the public sphere. Through the plot, the characters, the rhetoric, and the genre underpinning the U.S. news in China, the narratives help the Chinese understand the United States as an "imagined community" in a distant context.

UNITED STATES IN A CHINESE TV NEWS CLOSE-UP

From the U.S. standpoint, the 159 stories about the United States on CCTV news during the study period could be classified into three categories: China–U.S. relations (58.5%), domestic matters (28.3%), and foreign affairs (13.2%). The Chinese narrative of these stories painted the United States as a multifaceted country of progress, potentials, and problems, depending on how China positioned itself in relation to the United States and what profile it might expect to generate about the U.S. society in political, economic, and technological dimensions. From 1992 to 1998, many stories covering a wide range of texts put together a composite picture of the United States that conveyed layers of meanings.

On CCTV, nearly 60% of the stories concerning the United States revolved around two salient themes: high-level governmental exchanges and the U.S. role in China's economic reforms. The themes were not necessarily mutually exclusive and echoed the Chinese government's policy initiatives and practices in foreign affairs. In stories about U.S.–China relations over time, U.S. actors included current officials (White House, House of Representatives, U.S. consulate in China, Department of Commerce, National Security Council, Department of State, and military personnel), former officials, journalists (the *Philadelphia Inquirer* and *Newsweek*), cultural groups (New York Orchestra), individuals and companies (bankers and business executives). The settings took place in either China or the United States.

The stories about U.S. government and diplomatic activities on CCTV had a clear Chinese interest. Many lengthy stories documented official meetings between Chinese leaders and U.S. visitors, including President Clinton's visit to China. A detailed textual examination of these stories revealed that they were driven by China's current domestic agenda and considerations, especially those that occurred in the realm of Chinese national framework. The latent knowledge in the news is that China's economic reforms required the country to maintain a mutually beneficial and close working relationship with the United States.

For example, in a 1992 meeting with former U.S. Secretary of State Alexander Haig, Jiang Zemin (secretary general of the Communist Party, later the party Chairman) touted Haig as an old friend of the Chinese people and highly praised his contribution to the development of the Sino–American relationship. He also expressed high hopes for more cooperation and exchange between the two countries in order to foster better mutual understanding. The report continued with Haig's favorable assessment of the economic reforms undertaken in China and his emphasis on the importance of upholding good U.S.–China relations. This story was void of any confrontations or difficulties that would seem to strain relations. The tone and theme ran through many similar stories, as is seen later in the discussion of President Clinton's 1998 visit to China.

Attracting foreign investment appears to be an integral part of the Chinese economic development strategy that tends to become a selling point on CCTV news. In economic news, CCTV often identified the United States as a major source of foreign investment in China. When Premier Li Peng met a delegation of U.S. bankers in 1992, for instance, he promoted foreign investment in China and Chinese economic ties to the United States by emphasizing the significance of cooperation in banking and finance between the two countries. In return, U.S. bankers saluted recent Chinese economic reforms and promised to do their best to expand business interaction with China. This meeting underscored a recurring theme of reforms in China's domestic economic sector and continued consolidation of bilateral Sino–U.S. relations in the international arena. Similar stories abound during the study period. Positive evaluation of China and its current practices on the part of U.S. commentators, especially the president, apparently lent some sort of legitimacy to the Chinese authority and justification to its policies.

The context in which interactions with the United States transpired added something to the text itself in the stories. For one thing, it injected a sense of importance or significance to the parties involved. In China, U.S. actors got to meet with the top Chinese leadership, including President Jiang Zemin, Premier Li Peng (later chairman of the National People's Congress), high-ranking officials of the Ministry of Foreign Affairs, Defense Minister Chi Haotien, Chairman of the National People's Congress Qiao Shi, Foreign Trade Minister, and Premier Zhu Rongji. Nonofficial U.S. individuals, companies, and general reference of the United States often showed up in news that implied some form of U.S.–China economic and technological cooperation.

The appearance of United States in stories about China's economic progress on CCTV clearly suggests a connection between the international structure and national construction of social reality. This linkage would certainly help the Chinese public to become aware of the complexity of China's evolving external socioeconomic conditions and its potential impact on the internal development. Such emphasis on economic activities in stories about Sino–American relations reflects existing social practices and commitments in China. Although the news of U.S. social and economic crises was less frequent (see later), its presence on CCTV nevertheless fell in line with the general pattern identified in previous research (e.g., C. Lee, 1981), serving as a reminder of the social affliction of U.S. capitalist system. This is especially true when negative coverage of the United States was examined against the backdrop of a broader world landscape.

Within the framework of sociology of knowledge, the circulation of economic news, including those concerning Sino–American relations, in the Chinese society insinuates that its members would be able to understand and thus participate in China's economic reforms and social reconstruction. Luo (1993), for instance, reported that the economic and trade news in the mass media has increased communication and sharing of knowledge between China and Taiwan. This kind of knowledge eventually helps orient the public mind and, by implication, the collective act in China's march toward modernization. News as a form of knowledge, in Park's (1955) view, has an interest that is "pragmatic rather than appreciative" (p. 82).

The second group of stories about the United States on CCTV dwelled on U.S. domestic events and issues that, unlike news about Sino–American relations, bore no immediate relevance or currency to China. Although the domains of coverage seem to be relatively wide, the stories formed some core images of the United States as a place of contradictions of technological development or scientific achievements, social disorder or economic injustice and natural or man-made disasters. They were a mixture of positive and negative reports. Together with other minor aspects of domestic scene, these stories on CCTV sought to develop a relatively comprehensive picture of or a conceptual way of seeing and knowing the United States.

The positive news included such stories as discovery by U.S. astronomers, space shuttle programs, launch of satellites, maritime projects, medical research and practices, and the telecommunications industry and its market structure. These stories were general and did not refer to any specific geographical location in the United States. The highlight of U.S. technological and scientific achievements became more significant when compared to a few of such stories (1.4% of 484 items) involving all other countries reported on CCTV news (see Table 8.5). It signified a particular aspect of the U.S. society that invites international attention.

The high proportion of U.S. technology-related stories on CCTV news probably illustrates the Chinese government's desire to emphasize the importance of science and technology in China's road to modernization. It at least demonstrates the fact that the Chinese authority was more receptive to U.S. technology than U.S. ideology. The former is certainly practical and conducive to the ongoing campaign of technical and economic rationality in China. Since the late 1970s, China has been in serious need of Western technological know-how, knowledge, and expertise to help reform the infrastructures in various sectors. To pave the way for the fundamental social change, it becomes critical for the public to understand China's changing face and its relevance to the Chinese daily experience. Knowing the familiar practices and social orientation should make it easier for the people to understand and act in the world accordingly. At the collective level, the news narratives hence stands as an ideal starting point to construct the preferred identity and to initiate the potential action.

When CCTV reported a successful transplant operation performed by U.S. physicians, a new discovery made by U.S. astronomers, and the landing of the space shuttle Columbia on three consecutive nights, and other media research advances, it was evident that the achievements of U.S. scientists were being tactically recognized. These stories could be treated as a summation of the common knowledge about the merits and strength of U.S. technology and science. They also constituted an effective means to accomplish pragmatic orientation to the existing national policy design. The availability of such knowledge then was functional, providing a rationale for the U.S. involvement in the Chinese domestic economic development.

During the study period, however, the positive display of U.S. technological and scientific accomplishments was counterbalanced by a negative depiction of U.S. society, such as protests, riots, or natural and human disasters. Amid the array of news about the good America, CCTV news dotted the U.S. landscape with the bad and the ugly: the riot in New York, the investigation of White police killing Black people in Los Angeles, a Green Peace protest in Nevada, the indictment of former Secretary of Defense Weinberger for his alleged misconduct in the Iran-Contra scandal, the railroad workers' strike, an earthquake in Los Angeles, the pollution of river caused by a train accident in Minnesota, the unemployment concerns, fires in New York and Florida, a historical record of bankruptcy in the United States, the bombing case in Atlanta, the crash of a cargo ship in New Orleans, a snow storm in the midwest, and a tornado in Oklahoma. In news reporting, these stories are often considered more newsworthy or appealing because of the graphic presentation. The visual element, however, is the necessary, but not the sufficient condition in TV news coverage.

Within the context of the United States, many of the stories were plainly local. They clearly had no ostensible bearing on Sino–American relations; nor did they pose any direct or indirect concern for the Chinese national TV audience. Geographical proximity or psychological relevance, therefore, could not satisfactorily explain why those stories were picked up by CCTV news several thousand miles away from the scenes. The answer does not necessarily lie in the nature of event or issue itself, either. The reporting of this kind of U.S. news in China became more illuminating when juxtaposed with the rest of the world. As shown in Table 8.5, the proportion of disasters/accidents or social unrest stories about the United States alone far exceeded that of all other countries combined. A comparison of top countries identified on CCTV news also demonstrated a skewed account of the United States.

Among the most covered countries in foreign news on CCTV (U.S., Russia, Yugoslavia, Japan, Israel, PLO, and the United Kingdom), other nations rarely appeared in the disaster or social unrest news while the United States emerged in 16% of such stories. The use of footage portrayed the U.S. society as violent and turbulent. In the New York riot, for example, the footage showed nothing but the riot scene (e.g., burning fire, people running wild in the streets, confrontation between the police and rioters). The narration explained the cause, but carried no clips of the police or the victim's family despite more detailed reference to them in the story telling. Throughout the whole report, the focal point was clearly the dominant violent visual image.

Because foreign news was edited by its own staff within the parameter of Chinese perspective (see chap. 4), CCTV thus created a symbolic social reality about the United States that was based on facts, yet regimented according to the Chinese political purpose and point of view. Take the 1992 train accident in Duluth, Minnesota. Of all the U.S. cities, Duluth could hardly be considered a major metropolitan city and would not rank high in its status and ability to draw news attention from the U.S. TV networks, not to mention international coverage. By any measure, the incident was a local, not national, catastrophe. Yet, CCTV spent twice as much time (46 seconds) covering this U.S. domestic disaster as ABC did (22 seconds). This case demonstrates that the form and content of specific news in a given social structure might be determined by its national or international context. A comparison between CCTV and ABC newscasts supported this observation in that the two national TV networks did not see eye to eye with regard to the critical events and issues of the world reality (Chang et al., 1998).

The last group of U.S.-related stories on CCTV dealt with U.S. foreign, economic, and military relations concerning some hot spots and general problems around the world. They included the monetary, economic, and trade relationship with Japan, President Bush's visit to Poland, a Russian agreement on reduction of nuclear power, economic assistance and aid to Russia and Sarajevo, a treaty on biological weapon restriction, the reaction to Israeli settlement, economic relationship with Thailand, Iran affairs, and the military support in Kosovo. Although none of these stories had anything to do with China, they nevertheless tacitly alluded to the Chinese closeness in the larger scheme of U.S. foreign relations. For example, those countries (Japan, Russia, Thailand, Yugoslavia, Bosnia and Herzegovina, and Iran) that were closer to China, either geographically or ideologically, often became more visible in U.S. foreign affairs news than other countries. This structural connection in the presumably unrelated stories underscores the news as a form of systematic knowledge derived from a particular narrative, explanation or interpretation.

As in the study of the *People's Daily* (Chang et al., 1994; C. Lee, 1981), the general pattern on CCTV news looked at the United States from a structural point of view, describing U.S. social issues and economic development not as isolated and self-contained units, but as part of a larger capitalist system with its inherent ills or problematics. In this sense, the most authoritative Chinese national television was consistent in cultivating a type of mixed knowledge about the U.S. society. This knowledge as daily communication in the news becomes an empirical domain into which the readers could be socialized. A common source of shared "experience" with a remote reality is hence systematically and formally created and maintained in the everyday life in China throughout the years.

The "typification" of U.S. stories free of ideological attachment was a significant departure from an earlier Chinese practice that often identified the United States as an imperialist. Although the label *U.S. imperialism* has fallen into oblivion on the Chinese national television, its absence nevertheless does not signify a total change of heart by the Chinese government, whose view of the United States is not altogether positive. Apparently, an outright antagonism toward the United States has been eliminated, but repugnance toward U.S. system and some aspects of its political culture has taken on a different and more subtle shape.

This style of reporting about the United States manifests the ambivalence or uneasiness of CCTV, and in a broader sense the Chinese government, in handling news reports about the United States. On the one hand, it acknowledges the importance of the United States in China's economic reforms and foreign relations. On the other hand, it tries to avoid presenting the Chinese people with too rosy a picture, and thus a seeming approval, of the U.S. ideas and behaviors. The image and subsequent knowledge of a friendly America with advanced technology and science was counterpoised by the depiction of its social injustice and environmental disaster.

Despite the absolute amount of coverage the United States received on CCTV, the presentation of news precluded the Chinese audiences from getting as much knowledge as the quantity of coverage might have promised. When reporting on the United States, CCTV mainly utilized foreign video footage accompanied by the anchorperson's voice-over narration. A closer viewing and examination of the news reveals that the narration and footage were often not well connected. Obviously, the use of narratives allowed Chinese gatekeepers some degree of freedom to rearrange social facts about the United States according to their vantage point of view. As suggested by Park (1955, p. 74), the news is a form of social knowledge that is "ranged in this and that perspective" of the investigator. It could be expected that such incongruity might hamper the reception of information and formation of knowledge among the viewers.

In the story on the 1992 Democratic National Convention, for example, the narration on CCTV was loosely related to the footage. The anchorperson reported the opening of the convention in New York, followed by a brief analysis of the serious problems facing the United States, ranging from the gloomy economy to the tense racial relations and the public's apathy toward politics. It ended with the Democrats' belief that they would have a chance to take over the White house in 1993. The footage, however, told another story.

Beginning with a quick shot of Bill Clinton, the footage changed to a medium-distance shot of Al Gore. The rest of it focused on other Democratic presidential contenders Paul Tsongas and Jerry Brown. None of them was identified by the narration except for Brown with a caption. Interestingly enough, a clip taken from the ABC *Good Morning America* contained a close-up shot of the host's interview with Brown. In the narration, Ross Perot's bid for the White House was mentioned without any footage. There was also no footage in the report about Gore being selected as the vice presidential candidate. Regardless of the timeliness and reasonable length of the report, one could hardly catch sight of the convention itself, nor could one recognize the leading news actors associated with the story (i.e., Clinton and Gore). As such, CCTV viewers of the story would have a hard time sorting out who was who in the news.

Qualitatively, this kind of disconnection between the narration and footage casts serious doubt on the amount of information, or "knowledge about," Chinese viewers might take in. The loose linkage could be attributed to the limitations of available footage or lack of knowledge on the part of the reporter. Given the official need and attempt to channel the direction of public opinion (e.g., Gan, 1992; Y. Sun, 1993), it was more likely to be the result of a deliberate manipulation by the television station to range and rationalize certain foreign news.

It would be counterproductive, or perhaps even detrimental, to the Chinese government to show scenes replete with enthusiasm and vigor displayed by the convention participants, because CCTV viewers would then have been in a position to make immediate comparison with the tedious Communist Party's national meeting. A total blackout of the event on CCTV would have been too obvious an official censorship of important information and an injudicious judgment in terms of Chinese foreign policy toward the United States. An incomplete and superficial report of the Democratic convention built around Chinese domestic needs thus struck a compromise in favor of the central knowledge dictated by the authority's political consideration. Such effort could be best observed in CCTV coverage of President Clinton's visit to China in June 1998.

PRESIDENT CLINTON AS SEEN THROUGH THE EYES OF CCTV

At the invitation of President Jiang Zemin, President Clinton visited China from June 25 to July 4, 1998. The 9-day state visit took Clinton and his entourage through four Chinese cities—Xian, Beijing, Shanghai, and Guilin—and a special administrative region Hong Kong. In addition to diplomatic protocols (e.g., welcome reception and departure sendoffs at the airports as well as state dinners) and sightseeings, CCTV reported that Clinton held a summit meeting and an unprecedented live press conference with Jiang; met with Chinese Premier Zhu Rongji; visited a village, a school, a housing project, and the Shanghai stock exchange; toured the tomb of Qing Emperor, a library and a park; held talks with small groups of ordinary Chinese citizens at several locations and over a radio talk show; and gave speeches at Beijing University, an elementary school, and American Chamber of Commerce in Shanghai and Hong Kong.

Throughout the whole trip, other than the routines, President Clinton and the United States were reported on CCTV news in a specific plot and subject area. As a structural component of narratives (e.g., Jacobs, 2000), a plot "is concerned with the selection, evaluation, and attribution of differential status to events" (p. 10). Categorically missing from the plot on CCTV, however, was the Clinton–Lewinsky affair during the entire presidential visit. Although the White House scandal had kept the U.S. media preoccupied for some time, there was no reference or hint whatsoever about this sexual encounter in the Oval Office on CCTV. Such coverage free of the embarrassing and troublesome episode of the Clinton presidency on the national television in China confirmed Chinese journalists' prediction and expectation. As mentioned earlier, at the May 1998 Washington, DC conference, Chinese journalists assured their U.S. counterparts that the news media in China would never raise Clinton's escapade with an intern when he went to Beijing in June. This was more than a month before it happened.

Given the a priori nature of Chinese journalists' assurance, the absence of any allusion to the Clinton's disgrace was apparently not a coincidence. It testified to the acceptance and common understanding among Chinese journalists of what was possible and permissible in the news media in China at the collective level, especially when

Sino–American relations was involved. In this case, the unreported story on CCTV spoke as much about China's worldview as those that were ostensibly featured in the news. The unifying tenet appeared to be a deliberate effort to forge a coherent body of knowledge about President Clinton's visit to China and its implications for the world at large. A close analysis of the more than 30 stories of Clinton's China trip indicated a consistent pattern of presentation and interpretation of some major themes about the president and Sino–American relations. The plot and the careful use of characters as well as the rhetoric were organized in a way to elicit a certain reading of the stories.

From the beginning (June 25), President Clinton's visit to China was unequivocally touted as an important step in the right direction of Sino–American relations. His arrival in Xian, Shaanxi Province, however, was briefly announced in the middle of newscast with no live coverage nor visual. The 14-second announcement was placed two stories behind the news about the performance of the New York Orchestra in Beijing in which Chinese Premier Zhu Rongji attended. It was followed by an 88-second piece by a CCTV correspondent in Washington, DC, which interviewed former Secretary of State Alexander Haig and some congressmen in terms of their assessment of Clinton's visit. With voice-over, the report framed the presidential trip as a significant act that would improve Sino-American relations in all areas and benefit mutual interests, setting up the basic tone and preferred thematic focus for the journey to come.

The story included a short segment of Chinese President Jiang Zemin's state visit to the United States in October 1997. In his interview with CCTV, Haig praised Jiang's U.S. tour as successful and considered Clinton's China trip timely and important. The story also reminded viewers that Clinton's reciprocal trip to China received heavy coverage and comments by Chinese language newspapers and major dailies in the United States, such as *The New York Times* and the *Washington Post*. The public responses from both officials and civilians alike in the United States as well as governmental and media reactions from around the world formed a coherent articulation of the upcoming CCTV coverage of the imminent Jiang–Clinton summit.

On the second day of Clinton's arrival in China, CCTV moved the story to the third spot in the lineup. It first showed footage of Air Force One taxiing at the Xian International Airport and Chinese officials welcoming the Clinton delegation the night before. In addition to his itinerary, the narrative indicated that Clinton was the first incumbent U.S. president to visit China since the 1980s. The story then switched to Clinton's tour of a village in Xian and his conference with six villagers. Outside the door of a house, they sat neatly in a prearranged half circle facing the camera. The visual showed them talking with Clinton.

However, none of the participants, including a college student, an elementary school teacher, a doctor, and the head of a nursery home, was heard directly on CCTV news. With a voice-over, the 63-second story told of casual exchanges between Clinton and the village folks.

It was at an elementary school in the village that President Clinton gave his first public speech in China. With hundreds of students and teachers in the audience, he praised the economic success of the village and underscored his trip to China was to strengthen the friendship between the two countries. Via the voice of the narrator, Clinton was heard saying that China has changed a lot during the past 40 years and the village is like a window that introduces China's achievements to the world. He wished the village more success and a brighter future. Later, the scene changed to the Clintons standing amid the terra cotta soldiers in the Qing Emperor's tomb. The story said Clinton was the second U.S. president to tour the tomb since 1974. It ended with Clinton's departure from Xian for Beijing.

The segment lasted for more than 1 minute and 40 seconds, followed immediately by a pre-prepared story of a nearly equal length about the United States investment in Shanghai. The gist of the piece emphasized the increasing role played by U.S. companies in Shanghai's cross-national corporations in banking, high-tech, auto manufacturing, and insurance sectors. The day's domestic lineup concluded with a 26-second promo for a special report on the *News Investigation*. Titled "The Handshake of Great Nations," the short clip lauded Jiang's 1997 U.S. trip as successful and proclaimed that the reciprocal visits by leaders of China and the United States would permanently enter the record of history as profound events. Although brief, this preview set the stage for an extravagant and extensive coverage of Clinton's visit the next day.

On the third day of Clinton's visit, CCTV gave its viewers a heavy dose of what Sino–American relations was all about. In the top six stories, CCTV devoted more than 18 minutes to the full agenda of Clinton's meetings with Jiang Zemin and Zhu Rongji in various settings. It started with a welcome ceremony at the Tiananmen Square that included reading an extensive list of names of high-ranking Chinese and U.S. officials. While the national anthems of both countries were playing, the camera moved from left to right and back, showing Chinese and U.S. officials standing with full attention. Jiang and Clinton then left the podium to review the honor guards of Chinese armed forces. The video was interrupted by a still photo of Clinton, with a chronicle of his biography rolling up from the bottom of the TV screen, describing in detail Clinton's birth, education, and public services. It noted Clinton's achievements as governor of Arkansas and his election to the U.S. presidency in 1992 and 1996, but did not mention anything about his sexual affair with Monica Lewinsky. This opening story ran more than 6 minutes. The plot was straightforward and the rhetoric purely factual and nonjudgmental. The historical recount of Clinton's life was more than enough for the Chinese to know him as a person and a politician, but left no room for imagination about his personal conduct or political misbehavior.

The second story got down to serious business and the nitty-gritty of Sino–American relations. CCTV news showed Jiang and Clinton meeting in the afternoon in the People's Hall, attended by key governmental officials from both sides. There were seen, but not heard in their own words. Through the narrator's voice, the two presidents first expressed their valuation of the opportunity for China and the United States to better understand each other and their firm belief of the inevitable improvement of the relationship between the two countries. The story quickly zeroed in on a lengthy reading of Jiang's remarks that touched on the importance of mutual understanding and cooperation, world peace and nonproliferation of massive destruction weapons, the problem of Taiwan and noninterference with domestic affairs between China and the United States. Clinton was heard via a Chinese narration to reiterate the U.S. position on the Taiwan issues, U.S.–China strategic cooperation and U.S. support of China's WTO membership. In the plot, the leading characters were shown, with a voice of not their own.

During the exchange, the narrator alternated between Jiang's remarks and those of Clinton's. Near the end, the story indicated that both sides agreed that the Taiwan problem was the most important and sensitive issue in Sino-American relations. To accommodate the nearly 7-minute recitation of statements from Jiang and Clinton, the TV camera took shots between Chinese and U.S. delegations, focusing on the two leaders from time to time. Because of the limited angles of the conference room and the inability to zoom in and out freely, the visual images ended up repeating identical pictures of Jiang and Clinton while the voice-over recounting continued to unfold. When the camera seemed to have run out of fresh shots, one segment displayed flags of the two countries with no one from either side in sight.

This story clearly indicated the insignificant or secondary nature of visual elements in foreign policy stories on CCTV. In the case of Sino–American relations, especially in the Jiang–Clinton summit at the People's Hall, the visuals served as a background or mechanism that helped to extend the textual part intended by the Chinese host to convey desirable messages to the CCTV viewers. What matters in the story telling is thus not the visual imperative, as is often pursued by U.S. television networks, but rather the favored articulation of a precise point of view. This could only be accomplished via the carefully constructed news narratives.

Take the Taiwan problem. It was mentioned three times in different parts of the story, through either Jiang's remarks or those of Clinton's. Anyone who watched the Clinton–Jiang meeting in Beijing would have no difficulty learning from the narration that Taiwan was part of China's sovereign jurisdiction and that the United States acknowledged the Chinese position. As a matter of fact, the Taiwan issue would become one of the key themes that often popped up in Clinton's talks at the Beijing University and in Shanghai on two consecutive days. Taiwan as a presumed third party to the Sino–American diplomatic dialogue was written into the script, with no role to play on its part.

The only time that the two presidents' voice could be heard directly on CCTV news occurred in a 3-minute piece after the Jiang–Clinton summit meeting in the People's Hall. After announcing that Jiang and Clinton together met with Chinese and foreign reporters following their meeting, the story let the two presidents speak for themselves. Reading from a prescripted text, Jiang said that the cooperation between China and the United States was good for peace in Asia-Pacific and the world. He said the two countries had agreed not to target nuclear weapons at each other. He hoped the two countries would join hands in fighting against international terrorism and drug trafficking and in protecting the environment for the sake of world peace and progress. His opening remarks did not deviate from the main ideas he laid out in the morning meeting with Clinton. Jiang got the best part of this story, taking the lead and doing the most talk.

For his share, Clinton spoke in his own voice and an American translator provided the Chinese version. His portion in the story was much shorter than Jiang's, however. Clinton pointed out that since the early 1990s, he and Jiang had met seven times and praised that Jiang's leadership has transformed China and U.S. relationship for the future. He then said that "a stable, open and prosperous China shouldering its responsibility for a safer world is good for the United States." This statement was repeated in Chinese by the American translator. The piece ended with the anchorperson's voice-over, indicating that Jiang and Clinton also answered questions raised by reporters at the press conference. An American reporter could be seen in the picture asking questions, with the sound deleted. Clinton was last heard saying in the background that both countries agreed not to target nuclear weapons against each other.

For any casual viewer, other than the two leaders' own voice, this story did not differ much from the rest of all stories in terms of form and content about Clinton's visit to China. The news was bland and talked about familiar topics. For those who happened to watch at midday the live broadcast of Jiang–Clinton press conference on CCTV-1, there was much more than meets the eyes in the edited version. The story never mentioned that Jiang and Clinton held an hour-long press conference that was broadcast live in its entirety all over China. In fact, the joint news conference was not listed anywhere on the TV schedules or otherwise advertised in advance. How many Chinese viewers actually watched the lively press conference was difficult to determine. But *The New York Times* reported that more Chinese would have tuned to the press conference if only they had known. Whether the live press conference was part of the original plot remains an interesting puzzle yet to be solved.

The Jiang–Clinton live press conference was the first ever done on CCTV news. It was hailed as a breakthrough both inside and outside of China in international communication. By all accounts, the live broadcast was indeed remarkable and unprecedented in the history of Chinese national television. During the hour-long live political debate, President Clinton and President Jiang covered a wide variety of sensitive topics, ranging from human rights to Tibet. They argued over the arrest of dissidents in China and the Chinese government's crackdown on the 1989 student demonstration at the Tiananmen Square as well as their merits. Clinton specifically stated that the "tragic loss of life" at the Tiananmen Square was "wrong." An American reporter pointedly questioned the detention of four dissidents in Xian and 2,000 other dissidents who were taken to jail before Clinton arrived in China. The questions and answers were intense.

None of these sensitive subjects and other controversial issues was included on the CCTV 7 p.m. prime-time news. A 60-minute debate apparently could not fit easily into a shortened 3-minute segment. The gatekeepers in the TV newsroom had to decide what and how much to report. In the editing process, a lot of informative and invigorating stories, including those that might be detrimental to the image and authority of the Communist Party and government, were denied to the Chinese viewers. Although China's national TV network has become relatively open in recent years than before (see chap. 1), the handling and treatment of Jiang–Clinton news conference followed a well-known pattern in Chinese journalistic practices: the presentation of scripted events and deletion of touchy issues on television.

This was exactly what happened to the remaining stories on the third day of Clinton's stay in China. After the brief account of the press conference, Clinton was shown meeting with premier Zhu Rongji for a working lunch. The 49-second clip announced that Clinton and Zhu talked about the Asian economy and China's economic reforms and openness. A much shorter story next showed Air Force One arriving at the Beijing International Airport the night before, with the Chinese vice president leading the welcome reception at the airport. The broadcast then switched the location from China to the United States. The characters included in the segment did not speak directly, but were brought in to provide additional rhetoric in the narratives.

A CCTV Washington correspondent did a piece on reactions to Clinton trip from political and academic circles. Although these U.S. characters never spoke in the own voice, they were used as a general attribution in the news. Again, the voice-over said that the Beijing summit was mutually beneficial to both China and the United States and the U.S. public response was positive. The item concluded with comments by the State Department spokesperson James Rubin who said that Sino–American relations had moved from the low point several years ago to the right track and the Clinton visit fulfilled the fundamental interests of the two countries. The message was: It was not just the Chinese, but Americans too, making a positive appraisal about the presidential trip.

Near the end of the day's domestic segment and before the sport portion, an anchorperson announced that CCTV had just received the news that Jiang and Clinton met at a state banquet at 7 p.m. The voice-over individually introduced key Chinese leaders present at the dinner. The 44-second news was clearly not a live report, but rather a delay taped clip because by the time it was announced, CCTV was already 23 minutes into its newscast. This short piece further confirms an unspoken general rule in television coverage of important political events and issues in China: They must be taped, edited and shown later. The purpose, of course, is to carefully present major events and issues in a fashion that would not turn into an impromptu debate or invite spontaneous questions. The Jiang–Clinton live conference was the exception, not the norm.

On Monday, June 29,[6] CCTV began in a short story that showed Jiang bidding farewell to the Clinton entourage at the Zhongnanhai compound where the Chinese top leadership lives and works. Major participants from both sides were introduced individually. This reading of names appeared to affirm the status and authority of the Chinese leadership more than the U.S. counterparts. The narrator said Clinton thanked Jiang for the warm and friendly reception and indicated that the U.S.–China relations would improve into the 21st century. Two stories later, Clinton was shown talking to more than 600 students at the Beijing University. The visual displayed a well-packed auditorium with many students standing in the side aisles.

---

[6]The CCTV newscast on Sunday, June 28 was missing due to technical difficulty in taping during Clinton's visit in Beijing. Because it was Sunday, it should be reasonable to expect that no official activities took place between the two sides.

With a voice-over, this story ran nearly 3 minutes and was the longest piece for the rest of Clinton's schedule in China. Clinton told the students that the United States admired China's contribution to culture, religion, literature, and philosophy and highly appreciated the measures China took during the Asian economic crisis. He indicated that the United States intended to develop a full relationship with China through direct communication and mutual cooperation. In answering questions from the students, Clinton addressed the U.S. "one-China" principle, the Taiwan problem, and issues of Asian and U.S. economies. He emphasized that the U.S.–China partnership was important and China's economic progress was vital in the Asian economy. As in previous stories, the Taiwan problem was brought up and Clinton was quoted as saying that the United States would adhere to the "Three Nos" policy toward the Taiwan issue: no support for the Taiwan independence, no support for the idea of "one China, one Taiwan" or "two Chinas," and no support for Taiwan in any world organization that requires statehood. Whether economic affairs or international relations, the linkage of characters and issues and the genre of politics in command were unequivocal on CCTV news.

Three more stories completed Clinton's China visit on the day presented in the domestic segment on CCTV. All were essentially customary and protocal, portraying representatives from both countries signing agreements on economic, trade, nuclear technology, and health issues. The narrative indicated that China was the second largest trade partner to the United States, whereas the United States was the fourth largest trade partner to China. The seven economic and trade agreements signed between the two countries were worth $2 billion, signaling the positive outcome of Clinton's trip to China. A brief piece said Clinton and his delegation left Beijing for Shanghai on his next stop. The first story in the foreign news segment spent 75 seconds, an unusual amount of time in that portion of CCTV newscast, describing what ordinary Americans thought of Clinton's trip to China.

The visual showed a CCTV Washington correspondent interviewing four women and two men at what looked like a social gathering where many people could be seen in the background. None of the six respondents were heard in their own words. The narrative said the U.S. public responded positively to the Jiang–Clinton summit in Beijing. Through the narrator's voice, the respondents noted that China was an important and influential country in the world affairs and Clinton's trip to China was a right decision. One American said that because of different history, social system, and cultural idiosyncrasies, it was natural for the United States and China to have disagreements, but there were more common similarities than differences. Relying on U.S. reactions, this piece not only explicitly repeated the approving themes that were found in previous stories on CCTV, but also subtly defended Chinese approaches to unidentified internal issues that might not be well received on the American side.

Clinton's tour of Shanghai did not raise any new topics that were unreported on CCTV news before. His visit no longer commanded top attention and the two stories were relegated to the middle of the news lineup for about 3 minutes. The narration on CCTV, however, made the most of Clinton's remarks to score political points. Via the narrator's voice, Clinton said that a strong, open, and prosperous new China was emerging and that the two countries should improve relations through dialogue and cooperation to enhance mutual understanding. The U.S. "Three Nos" policy toward Taiwan were again stressed in the CCTV report. In a talk with representatives from various professions, the voice-over restated Clinton's call for a better relationship between China and the United States. It accentuated Clinton's statement that the United States should be more positive in China's modernization by way of scientific and technological cooperation and transfer of environmental skills and techniques to China.

As on the previous day, the foreign news segment included a piece about reactions to Clinton's China trip from countries around the world. With no visuals, the narrative said news media in Thailand, Britain, Australia, Finland, Cuba, and France highly praised the summit meeting between Jiang and Clinton. The candid exchange between the top leaders, according to foreign news media, was a breakthrough and ushered in a new era in Sino–American relations. As retold by CCTV, foreign news media believed that the two countries made a giant step in Beijing for a long-term strategic cooperation between China and the United States. In the eyes of foreign news media, CCTV said, Sino–American relations had a significant impact on world peace and stability. Quoting foreign sources, the narration said, "China is emerging. Without China, it is impossible for the world economy to be stable." This 68-second report left little doubt about how China wanted to shape the perception and interpretation of U.S.–China relations. The point of China's influence in the world was recounted on the last day of Clinton's stop in Shanghai.

Two major anniversaries fell on July 1, 1998: the first anniversary of the return of Hong Kong sovereignty from Britain to China and the 77th anniversary of the founding of the Communist Party in China. Three stories for about 12 minutes topped the CCTV news lineup that day. President Clinton appeared in two stories in the middle of the domestic segment for nearly 4 minutes. Interviewed by two CCTV reporters in Shanghai, Clinton said in the narration that the mutual trust between the two great nations was instrumental in the stability and security of the Asia-Pacific. The U.S. president indicated that he was highly impressed with China's development and was hopeful about the common interests of Sino–American relations in the areas of economy, trade, energy, and technology.

In the breakfast talk at the American Chamber of Commerce in Shanghai, the recounting on CCTV recited Clinton as stating that China's economic reforms would affect the Asian and world economies. He said that China should not be excluded from the WTO because its interests were tied to the world interests. The second piece also included portions of Clinton visiting the Shanghai Stock Exchange and a housing project in the city. Naturally in the news reports, Clinton was impressed with the housing condition in Shanghai and the general living condition in China. It was evident that Chinese economic success was the focal point in the narratives.

Consistent with the earlier practices, the day's newscast in the foreign news section again presented overseas reactions to the Clintons' China visit. With more than 1 minute, the story cited responses from governments in Vietnam, Pakistan, and Japan, saying that they welcomed the summit meeting between China and United States. They held that Sino–American relations would contribute to the stability, peace and prosperity in Asia and around the world. It also mentioned that news media in the United States, Germany, Malaysia, Britain, and Russia all expressed positive assessment of Clinton's trip to China. The story clearly put China at the center of world attention and the narration had an air of pride. The foreign reports therefore reinforced the domestic depiction of relationship between China and the United States.

The news about Chinese President Jiang Zemin's visit to Hong Kong dominated the CCTV lineup on July 2. One story about President Clinton was buried at the bottom of the domestic segment. It told of Clinton leaving Shanghai and arriving in Guilin, Guangxi. A brief welcome reception at the airport in Guilin was followed by Clinton standing at a podium in a park. A voice-over narrated the story. With a beautiful rock formation in the background, Clinton talked about environmental policy protection and applauded Chinese civilization and efforts of China's scientists and citizens in protecting the environment. Through the recitation, Clinton encouraged the Chinese and American people to work together to preserve the environment in order to give themselves a brighter future and to protect the future for the young generations to come. Free of political undertone in the news, there was no foreign comment.

The total calculation and symbolic treatment of Clinton's visit to China were most visible when the U.S. president delegation left Guilin for Hong Kong. Ostensibly, the major stories on the day had nothing to do with the United States. Any keen observer, however, should have little difficulty in detecting the astute connection between the arrangement of meetings with China's close allies in the former Soviet camp and Clinton's departure for Hong Kong on the same day. On CCTV, the top four stories devoted more than 11 minutes to Chinese President Jiang's meetings with leaders from Russia and four other former Soviet republics. The five leaders talked about military cooperation and issued communiqué pledging closer relations in a wide range of areas. Undeniably, these meetings were prearranged and timed to occur on that day. The plot and a different cast of characters were apparently set up to articulate China's even-handed strategy in foreign relations. The message was perhaps directed more toward the United States than to other countries.

Later in the newscast on CCTV, for more than 4 minutes, three stories showed Clinton meeting with Hong Kong's Chief Executive Tung Chi-hwa, giving a speech at the American Chamber of Commerce and holding a press conference. As in most of previous stories, Clinton was never heard directly. In his dinner party with Tung, Clinton commended the success of China's "one country, two systems" policy and said his China trip was very successful. He indicated that close Sino–American relations brought hope to peace, stability, and prosperity in Asia and around the world. The same thesis was reiterated in Clinton's talk at the American Chamber of Commerce. A general summary of Clinton's 9-day visit to China was recapped in his press conference in Hong Kong.

The piece was loaded with upbeat messages and admiration of China. Through the narration, Clinton again stressed that his trip was very successful. He indicated that during his stay he saw enormous changes in China and China was a great nation. As such, it was impossible for the United States and the world not to work with China, he said. Clinton also spoke of the grand vision President Jiang Zemin and the Chinese leadership had that would take China forward into the 21st century. He pointed out that the United States hoped to foster a strong "strategic partnership" with China and expand areas of cooperation between the two countries. He said the U.S. policy was not to contain China, but to cooperate with China. In light of Jiang's earlier meetings with leaders from Russia and other four neighboring countries in the same newscast, this story therefore tacitly acknowledged China as a powerful player in the world politics.

Clinton's visit to China officially ended the day when he left Hong Kong for the United States on July 4. Three short stories at the bottom of the domestic segment on CCTV wrapped up the complete coverage of Clinton's sojourn on the Chinese soil. The first two items showed Clinton leaving Hong Kong and arriving at the Andrew airforce base in Washington, DC. They noted that Clinton was the first U.S. president to visit Hong Kong and his trip to China was very successful. On his arrival in the United States, the story mentioned that Clinton had positive evaluations of the huge changes he saw in China and complimented the ability of the Chinese leadership to govern the country. Although routine, these clips certainly put a final touch on a well polished story during the past nine days. A more illuminating moment appeared in the last story about reactions from political, academic, and economic circles in the United States.

Without identifying those interviewed for the story, the piece showed four Americans talking to the CCTV Washington correspondent. In the story, the narrator simply used the general terms, such as "they," "many of them," or "many ordinary Americans," to refer to the public responses. It stated that many people believed Clinton's China trip was a success and would increase trust, friendship, and understanding between the two countries and peoples. In the news, the Americans were further quoted as saying that China's openness was good for the U.S. business interests and that the development of Sino–American relations had a great influence on peace and stability of the world. Summing up the reactions, the story concluded with this statement: "Many ordinary Americans indicated that as seen during Clinton's visit, China and the Chinese people were nothing like what was reported in the U.S. news media before." The last comment really gave away how CCTV attempted to shape Clinton's visit to China and what it might hope to achieve in constructing the reality in the news. Throughout the whole presidential trip, the central plot, the arrangement of a variety of characters and the rhetoric in the narratives on CCTV news were packaged coherently to make China look good, to advance its international status, and to mold the worldview based on the Chinese specifications.

A SUBTLE VIEW OF THE UNITED STATES WITH A PREFERRED MESSAGE

Since the beginning of economic reforms in the late 1970s, the news as a form of social knowledge in China has performed a crucial function in orienting the Chinese people and society toward aspects of the world reality that are most relevant and familiar to the Chinese experience. The news about the United States is not only quantitatively determined by the technical logic that requires speedy transmission and broader distribution of information and knowledge in China, but also qualitatively designed to put U.S. reality into perspective within the Chinese context. To a great extent, the U.S.-related stories on Chinese national television serves as a vehicle or mechanism to help define and redefine how the world out there is to be seen in China.

Throughout the study period (1992 to 1998), based on the findings in this chapter, the significance of U.S.-related stories on Chinese national television, like the stories about President Clinton's visit to China, probably lies not in their content, but the symbolic form they take in framing the United States in a particular formulation or in a preferred reading. The structural connection of this kind of news approach becomes clearer when coverage of the United States is pitted against that of the rest of the world, thus bringing out China's perspective and its journalistic tendency or practice toward the United States. From the Chinese point of view, many stories about the United States on CCTV are essentially U.S. domestic affairs, having nothing to do with China. Within a comparative context, the world of the United States created on CCTV apparently is cast according to not only the logic of views of the landscape between "here and there," but also the functional consideration of the news in the larger Sino–American geopolitical structure.

As China's window on the outside world, the relatively extensive coverage of U.S.-related news in the realm of both foreign matters and foreign policy affairs on CCTV signifies the centrality of the United States as a major news center in the world of Chinese TV news. As far as television content is concerned, it means that quantitatively the United States leads other countries in Chinese TV programming from entertainment (see chap. 3) to the news. Qualitatively, despite the fact that Chinese TV reporting of U.S.-related stories appears to be neutral, it does carry a higher proportion of stories about social ills or disorder, such as disasters, accidents, and crimes in the United States.

When flanked by all other countries, the crises in the United States tend to receive more than their "fair share" attention. From the sociology of knowledge perspective, this means that presentation of U.S.-related stories on the Chinese national television is determined not so much on the properties of the news itself, but rather on its place in the broader Sino–American relations. From the 1970s to the 1990s, the changing Chinese worldview about the United States, as sketched on CCTV and transmitted by it throughout China, represents the kind of information and knowledge that results from the interaction between the objective reality and China's own practical and social commitments.

Internally, the knowledge conveyed on Chinese national television stresses the government's current undertaking of economic reforms and practices of social restructuring (see chaps. 5 and 7). In this regard, the United States with its status as the largest economy and the most power country in the world becomes an important factor that China simply cannot ignore. In the process of international communication, the Sino–American interaction helps add a sense of legitimacy and authority of China as a major news maker.

Externally, the knowledge reinforces the continued desire of the central authority in China to open up the Chinese window on the world on the one hand and its attempt to limit the scope of public understanding and perception of the world on the other hand (see chap. 6). As shown in this chapter, the way the United States has been treated on the Chinese national TV network follows an uneasy dilemma facing the news media in China: how to cover international and foreign news in a factual and fair manner without losing China's own point of view. After shedding the Communist ideology that was once embedded in all news reports with a downright China slant from the 1950s through the 1970s, the Chinese news media in the 1990s have become more professional and savvy in their coverage of other countries. The result is a representation and interpretation of the United States in the news that carries a subtle message in the narratives.

In the symbolic world of television news in China, the United States is both an object of interest and a subject of importance. In the former, no longer being cast as an imperialist in the world politics, the United States appears to be multifaceted: politically powerful and technologically advanced, but prone to economic misery and social disease. In the latter, no more being touted as the main enemy of communism in the Chinese official narration, the United States emerges as a strategic partner that holds the key to China's success in domestic and international settings as well as its global status. Either way, the news about the United States in China provides the Chinese people with the basic knowledge to forge a shared view and common experience about the perception and direction of Sino–American relations. Despite the fact that CCTV news occurs in a more localized space than international communication, its narratives about the United States are very much affected by the Chinese official considerations of cross-national geopolitics and the rationalization of central knowledge in China.

CHAPTER 9

LOOKING THROUGH CHINA'S WINDOW ON THE WORLD: CONCLUSION AND DISCUSSION

There is no denying that since the late 1970s China has undergone dramatic changes in economic, political, social, and cultural aspects. Economically, the consumer revolution (Davis, 2000) has gradually spread from urban to rural China. Chinese living standards have improved significantly from the 1970s through the 1990s in terms of lifestyle, daily necessities, and luxury consumer goods and services. Politically, China has emerged unscathed from the backlash of 1989 Tiananmen Square crackdown in Beijing, the failure of Communism in eastern Europe, and the disintegration of Soviet Union. Although the Communist Party is unyielding in its hold on the absolute power and the state still omnipresent, the Chinese polity has become more pluralized and less unitary (Schell & Shambaugh, 1999).

Socially and culturally, China has transformed itself from a rigid and monotonous land to spawn greater flexibility and diversity in life experience and public practices for the people. The Chinese scene cannot be captured via single lenses (Chinoy, 1999). All these metamorphoses do not take place in a vacuum or go unnoticed. They are more or less recorded in the Chinese social transcript—the news itself. Whether democratic or authoritarian, the news media in any system function one way or another as a mediating agent that takes certain part or sector of social reality in either the immediate or remote settings as relevant, while ignoring other segments as irrelevant in the process of selection, presentation, and interpretation. In China's modernization, the mass media are both an index and a catalyst of social change.

Like the country itself, the mass media in China have also evolved from the state-controlled propaganda machines to the market-driven commercial vehicles. Although the Chinese mass media today are still subject to the state ownership and the guidance of Communist Party, most of them nevertheless no longer receive financial subsidies from the governments at various levels. They now have to compete in the marketplace for audiences and advertising revenue in order to succeed and survive. The arrangement creates a state-market configuration—the so-called socialist capitalism system with a Chinese characteristic—that allows the mass media to be economically self-reliant, but politically handicapped.

Under such circumstances, one of the main strategies of Chinese mass media is to court the huge number of potential consumers by navigating "between the party line and the bottom line" (Zhao, 1998). In the process, the media content represents the most visible site where the struggle ostensibly takes place. Insofar as it does not challenge or question the authority and legitimacy of the Communist regime, the content of all forms of mass media in China, whether news or otherwise, has in recent years become more innovative and aggressive in their appeal to a wider and bigger audience. Commercialization and conglomeration have hence caused both expected and unexpected consequences in political control and media management in the marketplace of ideas (e.g., Zhao, 2000).

Regardless of how it is called in China, the logic of market-oriented economy has obviously opened many opportunities for the mass media to present, and for that matter to experiment new ways of presenting, the world through factual and fictitious accounts to the Chinese people in order to carve up a niche in the competitive environment. Because of the division of labor in the media system and the state's political consideration over the definition and presentation of reality, however, the news in China does not necessarily enjoy as much leeway or freedom as that of other realms of media content. This is especially true for the news media at the national level where the central authority exercises a tight grip of organizational management and editorial supervision.

As China's window on the world, CCTV epitomizes the processes and structure of Chinese mass communication as well as the state–media relationship in the Middle Kingdom. Although the *People's Daily*, Xinhua News Agency, and *People's Liberation Army Daily* each maintain a central and commanding status in the political hierarchy of

Chinese mass media, none can rival the accessibility and immediacy of the *Xinwen Lianbo* on CCTV throughout the country in view of geographical coverage, audience size and visual imperatives. By any measure, CCTV Channel 1 has increasingly become the dominant and most authoritative source of news, information, and ideas from the coastal to the inland regions of China. Its antenna extends far beyond the Chinese geopolitical sphere.

In the age of telecommunication and satellite broadcasting, CCTV news thus stands at the forefront of surveying and portraying the world, both domestic and foreign, to the vast majority of Chinese people. Its success so far and future aspirations hinge on the extent to which the interplay between the state and the market in China strikes a structural balance concerning its inherent standing as part of the state political apparatus and the ever growing momentum of market demand and competition set in motion by the economic reforms. What that balance is and how it may take shape require a systematic and longitudinal examination of CCTV that involves, among other things, historical, legal, and economic dimensions.

In many ways, the analysis of form and content of news on CCTV as well as its regulatory control serves as a microcosm through which the journalistic spirit and practices of Chinese news media and their implications for social knowledge in China and international communication across national borders can be better understood. They pertain to the empirical and theoretical questions that have attracted mounting intellectual inquiry within and without academic circles into the still evolving Chinese sociopolitical system and its impact on the media subsystem. This chapter recaps the key findings discussed in previous chapters in the context of the larger sociopolitical landscape in China and speculates the direction the Chinese national television may be heading and its implications for social understanding.

THE POLITICS OF CHINESE TELEVISION

Ten years after the founding of the PRC in 1949, Chinese television was born in 1958 with a twofold political mission: to move one step ahead of the Nationalist Party's plan to launch TV service in Taiwan and to lay the groundwork for establishing a nationwide broadcasting network that would unite the whole country under the leadership of Communist Party. The former objective was mostly symbolic because television on both sides of the Taiwan strait did not play any major role in the power struggle between the Communists and the Nationalists following the split of China and Taiwan after the Chinese civil war. The latter goal was more substantive because television in China has grown since the 1960s from a meek local station in Beijing into a formidable conglomerate that strives to be a world class network in the 21st century.

The historical trajectory of Chinese television is laden with political consideration, technological innovation, and international projection in both news and noneditorial programming. Throughout the path, television in China has witnessed and been shaped by the tremendous revolution and evolution of infrastructure in the country's march toward economic modernization and ideological purification. The tension between the push and pull of these two forces and their categorical incompatibility, let alone China's isolation during the Cold War era, made it difficult for Chinese television to materialize in the nascent years as the leading vehicle of news, information, and entertainment for the masses who constituted the backbone of Communist ascendancy to power earlier and the base of government's general support.

The 1960s saw China mired in destructive social movements and political turmoils, especially the Cultural Revolution, that subjugated Chinese television strictly under the state's total dictation and manipulation in pursuit of the Communist utopia and re-creation of a new country free of the perils of domestic feudalism, external imperialism, and decadent Western capitalism. Although television proceeded haltingly on the technological and technical fronts during this period, it inevitably suffered great setbacks in the production, distribution, and presentation of programming in all realms of content, including the already limited foreign contact and exchange with countries of the former Soviet block.

As a victim of chaotic circumstances and deliberate calculation, Chinese television became an ideologically charged instrument that was forced to cultivate a narrow range of social reality and foster a mandatory consensus among the populace as to what really happened at home and from abroad. Because of lack of direct evidence and inaccessibility of empirical observation, it is difficult to determine the scope and size of TV's influence on how the Chinese viewers might have perceived the world and acted on it accordingly. Given the sporadic anecdotal accounts in the literature, suffice it to say that television programming in the 1960s, when it functioned at all, was more persuasively oriented than informatively inclined, leaning heavily toward the reproduction of official knowledge and preferred images of society.

The first half of the 1970s rounded up the disastrous Cultural Revolution, during which Chinese television attained the milestone of creating a national broadcasting network through the installation of microwave trunk lines. The linkage among the majority of provinces, municipalities and autonomous regions across China eventually paved the way for the formation of CCTV's network news in the late 1970s and early 1980s. Technological achievement aside, the 10-year devastating campaign also planted seeds for the reform-minded leadership of the Communist Party, notably headed by Deng Xiaoping, to ascend and steer the country away from the fanatic class struggles to the pragmatic approach to the everyday life in China, particularly economic restructuring and social openness.

Relatively relieved of outright propagandistic prerequisites, Chinese national television, like other news media, was entrusted to promote and justify the new ways of thinking, seeing, and doing things in China, which departed dramatically from the inflexible totalistic command system under Mao Tse-tung. The dual reforms meant a rising need on the part of CCTV to monitor and index the changing environment both internally and externally. In addition to other types of programming, CCTV began to expand its news programs in the 1980s at a pace that was unimaginable just a decade before. The rapid appearance of TV stations at the provincial, metropolitan, and county levels as a result of deregulation during this period further consolidated the network foundation of Chinese television system, with CCTV sitting on top of the hierarchy. By the 1990s, the complex broadcasting web allows CCTV news and other popular shows to enter into hundreds of millions of Chinese households in nearly every corner of the country.

Although the structural domination of CCTV remained unchallenged in the television industry, competition for audiences and market shares reached a turning point in the early 1990s when provincial TV stations started using telecommunication satellites to transmit signals across regions, thus breaking the limitations on the choice of channels within certain geographical confines. In response to the regional competition, CCTV not only broadened its content diversity, but also depoliticized the programs in order to cater to the needs and wants of potential viewers and consumers (J. Yu, 2000). Its 11 channels now encompass a full spectrum of programming that ranges from current affairs to variety shows. The audience reach has moved beyond China's national boundaries into the cross-national sphere.

The assorted news programs on the flagship channel, CCTV-1, each pose a substantial size of domestic viewership across different segments of the Chinese population. CCTV's goal, however, is to become an international player in global communication. One strong indication of that ambition lies in the fact that CCTV has been setting up foreign news bureaus in major cities in Asia, Australia, Europe, Latin America, and North America. Because of its ability to define the situation and shape the reality, the news on CCTV exemplifies the most important component of China's window on the world. There should be no doubt that it would be closely scrutinized by the powers that be in China. Although the state continues to dominate the operation and function of the news media, it has relaxed its central command mechanism through decentralization.

In many aspects of Chinese political and social processes, decentralization does not automatically lead to a self-organization free of the official supervision or a full autonomy of organizational decision making and independence of state interference in the mass media industry. For television, decentralization has introduced a greater leeway of self-management in the development, creation and scheduling of programming. Its institutional structure, cultural undertaking, and standard operating procedures, however, are very much organized around a series of legal actions designed primarily to keep the spirit and practices of television within the acceptable political and governmental limitations.

Rather than the brute disposition that was often contingent on the whims of individual leadership or personal inclination (e.g., Mao during the Cultural Revolution), the upshot of legal rationality in television regulations in China affirms the state's legitimacy and authority in placing this pervasive medium under the central government's jurisdiction. It also spells out the dos and don'ts of television execution from the domestic content to external contact, forming a far ranging complex of stipulations for TV practitioners to comply.

LEGAL RATIONALITY OF CHINESE TELEVISION

The overarching legal and political framework for mass communication in China is that the state owns and controls every forms of mass media from the national to local levels. Both the Communist Party and the government supervise and operate a variety of mass media at the national level that assume different positions in the state–media relationship and follow a strict division of labor in their mission and journalistic practices. Because of the accepted status of mass media as part of the state ideological apparatus subsumed under the official leadership, as specified in the Chinese constitution, there had been little legalistic and legislative necessity to regulate the media of mass communication in China from the 1950s through the 1970s.

Unlike the media system in many other countries, the submission and subservience of Chinese mass media to the state purposes and official interests as manifested by the Communist Party's dictatorship and the government's monopoly of power to distribute communications resources were indisputably expected from the central authority, leaving no room for negotiation or public deliberation. Given that television in China was limited in content production, audience reach and external programming exchanges during the first two decades of its existence, not to mention the setbacks caused by the frequent social and political movements, its regulation in any formal legal-rational format required no pressing attention or seemed to be minimal.

When television joined other mass media as ideologues to wage massive campaigns against the class enemies in Chinese society and abroad, such as during the 10-year Cultural Revolution from 1966 to 1976, by way of the Party or the government, the state held, by default, an undiluted ideological and administrative power over the organizational, managerial, and programmatic aspects of the monolithic television in China. To propose any lawful framework for the mass media in times of chaotic or anarchic social conditions apparently was beyond imagination and implementation. The rationality of Chinese television in terms of efficiency, legality, and operational boundaries became crucial when the market emerged in a competitive fashion, the technology was more sophisticated, and the content turned out to be diversified.

In the wake of economic reforms and social openness, the revival of television in China picked up momentum in the mid-1980s when it successively spread across the country and institutionalized itself as a common fixture in the Chinese social and household fabric. The fierce market competition for audience shares and advertising revenues in the television industry brought unprecedented challenges to the existing order and posed substantial threats to the centralized mechanism through which the state could no longer effectively extract political acquiescence and collective allegiance in the broadcasting sector. What is clearly needed is a set of rules of the game that would be legally compulsory and practically enforceable. This process of rationalization supersedes the longstanding exigency for indoctrination to the extent that subsequent regulatory measures permeate the entire array of television operations.

Other than explicit consideration of the scarcity of air waves and distribution of resources, like those of other mass media in China, regulation and control of television have long rooted in the Party's and the government's implicit belief and concern over the persuasive capability of mass communication and their powerful effects on individuals and society. An unambiguous indication of such faith in the power of news media to mold public opinion and shape behaviors can be found in the ubiquitous presence of a propaganda unit throughout the Communist Party and governmental agencies from the national to local levels. The Chinese concept of "propaganda" does not necessarily carry any negative connotation as it does in the Western usage. In China, to propagate is to use all means of communication to publicize the news, information and policy that the authority deems important in the people's everyday life.

Thanks to the state's conception of the mass media as agents of information, education and mobilization, no private ownership of any medium in any form currently exists in China. Although the mass media have been decentralized and depoliticized as a result of more than 20-year economic reforms and social openness, an independent and autonomous media system free of the state's subjugation has yet to find a legitimate grounding in the Chinese legal and bureaucratic thinking. At most, the mass media in China serve as state managers, tending the business of news reporting and other activities (e.g., entertainment and advertising) with more specific knowledge, greater executive skills and better technical standards. Various governmental agencies and party organs retain, however, the mandate to oversee media performance and to provide editorial guidance whenever the situation calls for.

In the television industry, the NBRFT, under the State Council, is the highest authority in the broadcasting sector and wields a considerable amount of power. It is not alone in exercising control over TV, however. Other governmental and Party agencies in the areas of security, business, education, and politics have one way or another certain vested interests in tempering the process and products of television. The involvement of Ministry of Justice, Ministry of Public Security, National Secrecy Bureau, and Ministry of State Security in television regulations points out the governmental determination and realization of cross-surveillance of mass media activities in China.

Since the mid-1980s, a significant number of rules, orders, directives, laws, and provisions have been issued independently or jointly by NBRFT and other bodies, covering nearly every facet of Chinese TV production, dissemination, reception, and consumption. From security of facilities to staff hiring and training, there are at least some guideline as to the dos and don'ts of television. The trepidation over secrecy, safety measures, and personnel in the television industry unequivocally speaks of the state's emphasis on placing the broadcasting media under stringent official scrutiny owing to their far-reaching capacity and influences.

Along with the comprehensive framework for TV's new role in the Chinese version of market economy lies the reassessment of television as a mass entertainer and an opinion leader. In the former, the dynamics of the market often opens opportunities for television to navigate through a wide scope of programming options sanctioned by the state, including cooperative ventures with counterparts in Hong Kong and Taiwan and imports from Western countries, particularly the United States. A key requirement is that domestic and foreign TV entertainment programs must not damage the image, integrity, and sovereignty of China and its social, political, and cultural values; nor should it undercut China's international relations and foreign activities. This applies to the transborder satellite broadcasting, too (e.g., Hao, 2000).

If the fictitious world on Chinese television has to uphold the larger purposes of Beijing's internal and external missions, obviously the world of real events and issues in television news would not have more degree of freedom to deviate from what might be feasible or permissible in its presentation and interpretation of the reality out there. Although foreign capital and interests have entered many economic and business sectors in China, news broadcasting remains one domain where nondomestic media practices in any shape and size are strictly prohibited. When the production of noneditorial programming (e.g., dramas and variety shows) has increasingly been shifted to outside producers under a contractual system with TV stations across the country (B. Zhang, 2000), TV news programs, because of their immediacy and centrality in the information flow, are firmly entrenched to be an in-house operation with a built-in filtering device connected to the national prism.

In the process of TV regulations in China, as marked by the extensive web of binding mechanisms to curb the genesis, access and traffic of broadcasting messages, the state occupies a dominating position that is generally unrivaled by that in many other countries. Although these procedures turn out to be intimidating and punishments for violations could be overwhelming (e.g., the purge of journalists and media practitioners in the aftermath of the 1989 Tiananmen Square crackdown), it does not unavoidably imply that the market itself, albeit limited in some sense by the official imposition of a "socialist character," could not ensue its own logic and carve out a niche that is intolerable to the state authority. The diversification and proliferation of foreign imports of television programming in China are exemplary.

FROM FRIENDS TO FOES: FOREIGN TV PROGRAMMING IN CHINA

Except for trade and tourism, one of the barometers of China's open-door policy to the outside world is the pragmatic use of media products from abroad and their symbolic representation. The Chinese openness, of course, did not occur overnight. Its venue, however, took place largely in the realm of mediated reality because of Beijing's isolation from most countries in the community of nations during the first three decades after the founding of the PRC. There is no other medium than television that could better depict in visual format the striking transformation of China from a dull, ideologically focused political arena to a vibrant, commercially oriented consumer society. The origin and content of imported TV programs symbolize China's reevaluation and adjustment to the shifting reality in the domestic and overseas environments.

Importation of foreign TV programming has been an ingredient of the long process of media internationalization in China, the objective of which is to prepare Chinese television to compete in the surging global market of news and entertainment in order to harness the impact of globalization within manageable parameters. It began with a rather parochial and dogmatic predilection toward countries in the former Soviet block. The Cold War mentality and its corollary, such as the devotion to the Communism international movement and the distrust of Capitalist nations, apparently restricted the gamut of cultural products, especially those from the United States and western Europe, to which China would want to expose its citizens. Another reason was the nationalistic pride and xenophobia when China turned inward for self-reliance in its stride for modernization and nation building.

It was not until pragmatism of market reforms replaced fanaticism of Communism revolution in the late 1970s that China broadened its vision of the world and opened up its window on national television accordingly. What decentralization, depoliticization, and legal rationality entailed in the media control was a sensible response to the domestic request for a greater autonomy in broadcasting decision making and a tacit recognition of multiplicity of TV programming in the international marketplace. As far as the import of foreign programs is concerned, the liberalization of social task of television in China could be characterized as moving away from the role of a class ideologue to that of a state manager delegated with more industrial management and less ideological procurement. The ostensible outcome is a remarkable reconfiguration of entries of foreign TV menu from which the Chinese viewers could choose.

The changes in acquisition of foreign TV programming were evident in both quantity and quality. Quantitatively, before the end of Cultural Revolution in 1976, foreign imports accounted for only a very small proportion of the total programming on Chinese television. In fact, during the first two decades of its existence, television in China rarely carried any type of foreign programs that did not directly or indirectly promote the Communist tenets or interpreted the world based on the Marxist point of view as the country stumbled through successive large-scale campaigns in a revolutionary mode initiated by Mao Tse-tung. The 1980s and 1990s registered the rise and fall of foreign TV programming in China, signaling the maturity of local broadcasting production capability and audience preference for domestic taste.

Qualitatively, movies from a few select Communist countries—the former Soviet Union, North Korea, and Albania—appeared sporadically on Chinese television in the 1970s. No foreign programs from non-Communist nations helped fill the TV time in China as if nothing else for television was ever produced or was worthy of inclusion from abroad. The absence of varying shows denied the Chinese viewers the opportunities to map out the divergent content and set-up of alien TV programming that might, by comparison, undermine the state's marching order for self-dependence and its claim of the socialist superiority in individual and collective life.

Partially open, China's window on the world of entertainment was further fixated on a small part of it when the country stayed isolated from many nations outside its own sphere of influence. Integration of the Chinese market into the worldwide economic system ultimately led to an influx of Western television programming. A full listing of imported programming became available in the 1980s and 1990s, offering not just movies, but every conceivable type of enlightening and entertaining content for all age groups. This conspicuous turnaround of foreign TV schedules in China correlates highly with the expansion of Chinese external economic exchanges, indicating a positive relationship between the international flows of trade and media-cultural products.

Although the inflow of foreign TV programs in China increases over time, their circulation across the country exhibits signs of regional differentiation as each province responds to the economic decentralization and development differently due to an unequal access to national decision making and endowment of natural resources. The disparity of frequency and amount of foreign TV programming between coastal and inland regions demonstrated the upshot of uneven financial ability and power status among the Chinese provinces to draw attention to their social circumstances and to bring the leisure aspect of the outside world closer to home. This discrepancy also translates into how the provinces and autonomous regions were technically reported on China's national television news network.

TECHNICAL RATIONALITY AND TV NEWS PROFESSIONALISM

Of the 11 channels on CCTV, CCTV-1 has been the flagship channel in both its authority and rank in the Chinese TV broadcasting industry. Amid the ever expanding programming capacities of CCTV and rising popularity of some programs (e.g., investigative reports and drama series) around the country, the 7 p.m. *Xinwen Lianbo* on CCTV-1 has built a tremendous power base in terms of its exclusiveness and authoritativeness in presenting and interpreting the national and international realities to hundreds of millions of Chinese people on a daily basis. With no commercials packed in between the domestic and foreign news segments, this primetime newscast ranks among the most watched TV programs across different age groups in China.

The ban of commercials during the broadcast of *Xinwen Lianbo* naturally should give CCTV news greater time to include more stories about events and issues from inside and outside of China that might be of interest to the Chinese society at large. In fact, during the 1990s, the number of stories per newscast and the proportion of news in either domestic or foreign news segment showed a noticeable pattern of decline over time. The waning amount of air time often came at the expense of foreign news and the trend continues in the 21st century. In the 1990s, the average length of time for the foreign news segment on CCTV news was 5 minutes. That amount was further cut to below 5 minutes in the early 2000. Because of the consistent attractiveness of foreign and international news (e.g., T. Sun, Chang, & Yu, 2001), there has been some misgiving over the loss of time in this realm (Pei, 2000).

The reallocation of amount of time from foreign stories to domestic and foreign policy news on CCTV indicates an apparent need and preference on China's sole national television network to concentrate on matters more closely related or relevant to the shared experience and common knowledge of the Chinese people. Accompanied by this tendency is the necessity of speed to shorten the gap between the occurrence of events or issues and the timing of their reports. In the age of information technology and global competitiveness, the imperative of timeliness in news reporting therefore becomes one of the requisite tasks of Chinese journalism reforms. Most of the stories on CCTV news, whether domestic or foreign, were reported in a more timely fashion in the late 1990s than before.

This phenomenon evidently suggests the improvement of transmission technology and dedication to journalistic professionalism in China. What has yet to be realized on CCTV news is live coverage of events during the primetime newscast. During the study period (1992–1998), not a single story was ever broadcast live. As a matter of fact, the 7 p.m. network news on CCTV has been edited and pretaped before it is aired. The raison d'être has more to do with political constraint than lack of technical sophistication. It is impossible to censor the content properly or to present and interpret the news in a favored manner if the story is covered spontaneously. The pre-packaged newscast unquestionably guarantees that the script and images on CCTV news conform to the official standpoint as to what and how the world should be reported in China.

The use of videos in CCTV news, especially foreign videos, thus tells stories of their own, casting the Chinese leadership, and by implication China itself, as being responsive to the domestic welfare on the one hand and responsible for the international order and peace on the other hand. In domestic videos, high-ranking officials were frequently seen in important political meetings, field investigations and social and cultural gatherings that involved decision making, fact-finding, and personal interaction with the Chinese people from all walks of life. In foreign videos, China's leadership and its representatives generally appeared in bilateral or multinational context that attached a powerful status and influential role to the country in the global community of nations.

Such imagery could only be made possible with careful writing and editing of narratives in the news. From the domestic scene to the foreign landscape, CCTV news presents not just simply factual, speedier, and visual accounts of "what happened" in China and around the world, but a signpost, an attitude, and a way of seeing and thinking, the totality of which constitutes a paradigm of knowing and helps make sense of the changing reality within the Chinese perspective. Whether internal or external, no sector of the real world is ever unchanged or unchanging. In China, the social change is even more sweeping and its ramification profound. Since the late 1970s, the Chinese society has experienced an unparalleled metamorphosis that defies conventional wisdom. On the national network, it is a tale of social progress and economic success that has graced the TV screen across the country.

CHINA ON THE MOVE AND THE PICTURES IN THE NEWS

Unlike the earlier traditional belief that looked at mass media in China as the means of propaganda and persuasion in the ideological sense, this book contends that the news in China has represented a form of social knowledge, constructing the world of everyday life for the Chinese people and distributing it at all strata in society. By way of effective and efficient mass communication, this socially constructed and culturally bound knowledge assists in forging an awareness or recognition among the Chinese public of being members of what Anderson (1991) called "the imagined community." A community's ability to do actions and accounts of its conduct obviously relies on its stock of social knowledge. Like that in other countries, the news as social knowledge in China records and recapitulates only some segments of the total reality as pertinent to the contemporary Chinese national practices and policy commitments.

In the area of domestic affairs, the social construction of reality in the news hence selects and projects from a myriad of events and issues a relatively small proportion about what is to be known, how it is to be perceived and why it is so within the prevalent boundaries of

China's social structure. As delimited by some general categories of common experience, the news in China either informs the Chinese people of what to expect from their social life or establishes a social frame of reference based on normative measures and bureaucratic guidelines set forth by the dominant worldview. It is implausible, if not naïve, to believe that in the face of persistent and broad economic reforms in China since the early 1980s, Chinese national television news could not attest the pulse and magnitude of such societal transformation.

On the contrary, television in China organizes the prevailing experience and general routines through the recursive mobilization of social knowledge at the national level. Throughout the 1990s, CCTV news could be understood as a continual documenting and displaying instrument that makes social reality in China conceivable and accessible. One main manifestation is the identification of the existence of knowledge of how things are to be done on the part of major actors from the central to local governments in China and their authority and capabilities to carry out the task as required by the rules of governance and hierarchical positions. The characters were carefully screened, the plot well designed and the narration tightly scripted. Who speaks in what context on the Chinese national television news denotes to a great extent the location and degree of centrality of the actors in the world of China's day-to-day activities that are closely associated with existing policy concerns.

Similar to what has been observed in the United States (e.g., Gans, 1979), the top echelon of Chinese leadership, mostly the president, the premier and leading ministerial and Communist Party officials, dominated the CCTV news either by their perpetual appearance or by the prominent treatment in the newscast. In stark contrast with U.S. television news, however, CCTV slated a plethora of endless stories about meetings by major governmental agencies and mass organizations that tended to put the spotlight on the presiding leaders giving a lengthy speech or reading a long report over a stale and boring video background. The excessive "meeting news" was recently criticized by a former head of CCTV as one of the three "too manys" of TV programming that irked the Chinese people. The other two are "too many commercials" and "too many extravagant ceremonial evening shows" (B. Li, 2000). There is little sign that any of the three "too manys," particularly the meeting stories, is likely to be reduced any time soon. For the leadership at various levels, the "meeting news" is not merely instructive of what is happening, but indicative of who is in charge.

Over time, the visibility of various actors, particularly those less known, unfamiliar or collective in nature (e.g., factories and companies), gradually faded with the institutionalization of economic reforms and social depoliticization. Unlike its U.S. counterpart, the military in China, although not as noticeable as the high-ranking officials in other state units, markedly held a consistent presence and positive profile on the national television. It conveyed a subtle acknowledgement of the PLA as an indispensable pillar in upholding the state power and as a stabilizing force in maintaining the social order. The news media and the military are traditionally the two barrels that the Communist Party has utilized heavily for its own legitimacy and authority.

The PLA's affirmative image on CCTV was part of the larger picture that painted the domestic world in China as economically successful, socially harmonious, and politically progressive. In story after story, the Chinese society came across as dynamic and diversified, moving forward toward better living standards, more access to national resources and greater social responsibility in many different fronts. This pragmatic approach in television news reports departed from the earlier style in the 1970s by dwelling on factual and nonideological issues and events that ritually underscored the government's attention and actions involving the routine and urgent problems facing China. It recognized social ills and disorders caused by the dysfunctions of human and natural factors across the country, but countered with the state's resolve and reaction to address them quickly and decisively.

The news in China, therefore, produces a certain kind of knowledge that tends to normalize and rationalize the world in which the Chinese people may find themselves. Notwithstanding the constructive and functional representation of the domestic world in the news, like the mass media in other countries, CCTV could not possibly and realistically cover the contours and elevations of the country as completely or perfectly as it might hope for. The map making of the Chinese reality in the news on the national TV network is therefore simplified and bound to be a distorted projection of what is out there. Whether it is a metropolitan or a province, to be constantly on the news radar of CCTV is to signify its geopolitical and sociocultural weight as a center of focus in China. It is indicative of where the action may be, what the Chinese audiences can be expected to see in the spotlight and how the part may fit into the whole.

The reconfigured atlas in the news consequently contains a simplified version of a much more complicated reality that generally highlights some areas of predetermined importance in the vast territories of China. Without any question, Beijing as the most significant news center in China is full of activities that bear political, social, cultural, and economic insinuations for the rest of the country. In the 1990s, of the 32 provinces, municipalities, and special regions, none received as high a proportion of news coverage on CCTV as that of Beijing or even came closer comparably, indicating the latter's supreme status and unsurpassed ability to generate a near monopoly of newsmaking in China. Outside the capital, there was also an indisputable divide in the news that separated coastal provinces from inland regions in relation to their drawing power.

The fact that Hong Kong ranked as a distant second in the overall reports on CCTV news after its reversion from the British to the Chinese rule accentuated China's attempt to showcase the mastery of the "one country, two systems" principle. Like the multidimension of stories, ranging from more of the once tabooed news of disasters, accidents, and crimes to less of the ideologically loaded news, the priority accorded to Hong Kong coverage on CCTV throughout the 1990s gave away the unspoken Chinese conviction at the national level that the news should familiarize the audiences with current concerns and impending solutions. The Hong Kong case is not simply a media event, but rather an ideal opportunity to tell stories as Beijing sees fit.

After all, the news is not merely an assortment of facts, but an accumulation of knowledge that helps socialize the public in its understanding and interaction with the environment. For the remote settings, whether in China or elsewhere, the dependency on the news media for contact with the outside world should be more acute when it is further removed from the personal experience or direct observation. As seen through CCTV at a distance, the foreign spectacles represent a condensed montage of the world in general that is assembled, tagged and embedded in the Chinese perspective within the logic of range of vision between here and there. The official rules and ideological conventions help to organize an unmanageable reality into news in China, thus the constructed picture of the world is likely to be reductive.

THE SMALL WORLD THROUGH A PARTIAL WINDOW

Although the economic reforms, external openness, and widespread use of telecommunications technology as well as the mounting attractiveness of the Internet in China have made it possible for foreign travels and greater exposure to alien media content, ideas, and information, for most Chinese people, the world beyond China's geographical horizons is largely out of sight and definitely out of reach. Being the medium that expansively saturates the country, television still counts as the most approachable bridge that links China with nations around the world. The hundreds of millions of viewers are the embodiment of the incredible specter of television in the daily life of Chinese society.

As the only national network in news broadcasting, CCTV has situated itself in a strategic position to regulate and mediate the volume and velocity of the one-way traffic for foreign stories to enter into China. The composite mosaic of the world's countries on CCTV news over time typifies how China as an observer checks out the lands far from its own immediate sphere of influence and relays their conditions in textual and visual forms to the Chinese people. In the process, the choice of hot spots or blind sites of the world's terrain does not appear to be random, leaving the end result of foreign news reporting in China to be predicated on elements of international might, regional relevance and practical needs. The corollary is that the reported news fabricates certain pictures of the world over other conjecturable ones. CCTV interprets as much what it observes as it has not.

A small number of countries and entities, notably the United States, Russia, the UN, Yugoslavia, Japan, Israel, PLO, and United Kingdom, dotted consistently on the CCTV news screen throughout the 1990s, creating a rather skewed, yet unambiguous, vantage of the world. It is an illustration of map that tinted the powerful nations in North America, western and eastern Europe, the Middle East, and East Asia with regard to their ability, might and standing to disturb the balance of local or global stability and prosperity. Countries in South Asia, Africa, as well as South and Central America were mostly either left out or delegated to obscurity in the news.

With a few nations and entities holding the central theater of foreign news on China's national television, they formed a distinctive network pattern in the respective regions that grouped other countries together. Two salient groupings centered around Russia and the former Soviet republics and key countries in the Middle East, such as Israel, PLO, Egypt, Jordan, Syria, and Lebanon. The connection among these countries or entities appears to be grounded one way or another in the international tension between the United States and Russia in the post-Cold War power division and the perennial confrontations in the Middle East that have been the world's powder kettle. Historically, China has long supported the Arab countries, particularly the PLO, in their struggle against the U.S.-backed Israel. This sort of concentration in the news constitutes a core form of interpretation providing a specific picture of the Middle East.

In the 1990s, CCTV news referred to the PLO as the Palestine Nation, not as a political entity, demonstrating the Chinese official recognition of its statehood when the PLO had not announced its establishment of a country and was not recognized as such by other nations. Although the PLO identity might be a single case among numerous stories of foreign identification on Chinese television, it was the epitome of China's unmistakable intent to inculcate a point of view in its news reporting in respect to how the world's geopolitical panorama was shaping up and where the individual countries could be placed vis-à-vis Beijing's own location in the global equation. The balance sheet had a typical Chinese imprint.

Like other countries in international communication, however, China attends to the unfamiliar reality in a predictable way: its eyes relentlessly watch over the places where the good, the bad and the ugly could be found. Above all, the world of foreign spectacles on CCTV news contrasts sharply with that of the domestic one regarding what and how events and issues were to be conceived and presented. It is a world that featured high-profile governmental officials and well-known organizations in diplomatic, political, and military activities. It is also a world that was more inclined to the spell of disasters, accidents, and social unrest than the land at home. Visually speaking, violence in the form of human conflicts and natural calamities interlaced through foreign news more habitually than domestic news in China.

Whether the two worlds—the peaceful and progressive China versus the rest of unsettling countries mired in a host of problematics— were indeed the way they were in reality, as portrayed on the Chinese television, was an epistemological question that could not be satisfactorily addressed by examining the news content alone. As a module in a wide-ranging communicative process, the media message is constrained by a country's political economy, social control, and cultural values. When comparable factors in international relations are introduced, the number of determinants of news production and presentation extends beyond reasonable computation. To attribute the news to a sheer function of propaganda in China is to commit reductionism in intellectual inquiry that often obfuscates more than illuminates the phenomenon under observation.

The divergence of images and dynamics of stories between domestic and foreign news in China nevertheless provide valuable clues with regard to how and why the mass media may contribute to the social construction of reality or the construction of social reality. The news is one of the building blocks that fortify the foundation on which social knowledge is ultimately forged, regardless of the content it may contain or the purpose it may serve. What is certain is that the news as social knowledge remains to be anchored in a frame that encodes a given border surrounded by what is achievable and allowable. It is, as Kuhn (1970) called it, a paradigm based on communal beliefs and anticipations prevailed currently in China. This Chinese communication mode can be best detected in foreign policy news coverage on CCTV.

WORLD MAKING AS CHINA SEES FIT

When foreign policy affairs are involved, the position and the ensuing codes of conduct for China in international communication change from those of an observer to those of a participant. In cross-national relations, no country can ever claim to be immune to the actions and reactions of other countries, no matter how big or small it is or whether it is democratic or authoritarian. Other than its own internal restructuring initiatives, China has since the late 1970s had to confront the escalating pressures from outside to adjust its ways of thinking and behaving towards the riveting reality of global realignment across a wide spectrum of political ideologies and national identities. It can no longer retreat to its own cocoon as it did during the heydays of the Cultural Revolution from 1966 to 1976.

The demise of Communism in eastern Europe and the breakup of former Soviet Union leave China as the last Communist stronghold that still adheres to the remnants of a failed sociopolitical experiment in name, although in reality it carries on its market economic reforms with a full thrust. More than ever before, China finds itself integrating steadily into the global marketplace and emerging nonchalantly as a formidable regional power, if not a world powerhouse in the making. Its worldview and the niche it carves out for itself, including how the country might respond to mutual and multiple relations, can be gauged through the news China brings to the attention of the Chinese people. The interplay between the news media and foreign policy affairs in China is not only descriptive, but also prescriptive.

In contradiction of foreign news in which China stands as a bystander, foreign policy news dictates that the world of Chinese external affairs and international relations be carefully sketched in order to further advance China's national interests and to safeguard its image as a accountable members in the family of nations (e.g., Schell & Shambaugh, 1999). Not surprisingly, coverage of Chinese foreign policy news on CCTV reveals a high level of ethnocentrism, looking at the domain of diplomatic transactions as the Middle Kingdom sees fit. One recurring scene is the reception of foreign delegates and visitors by the top Chinese leadership at the Zhongnanhai compound or the People's Hall in Beijing. It is the heart of China's central command. The manifest view in the news is polychromatic, but the latent perspective it conveys is relatively monochromatic.

If nothing else, the steady parade of dignitaries from overseas on Chinese national TV network legitimizes and reinforces China's foreign policy design to bolster its own standing as a world power. That image is ground, however, through a much smaller news prism in a shrinking global political platform. Throughout the 1990s, a very few select countries showed up time and again on CCTV news that more or less told of the direction to which China turned its foreign policy attention and the weight it assigned to the countries involved. By and large, the world as constructed in Chinese foreign policy news deviated significantly from that of foreign news. Nonetheless, its main characteristics disclosed a parallel concerted accentuation on the powerful, the elite or nearby countries that stressed China's long-term strategy in international affairs.

Again, the United States outdistanced all other countries on CCTV coverage of Chinese foreign affairs, with Japan, Russia, United Kingdom, the UN, and South Korea making up the core pack of nations that were unfailingly spotted on the national TV screen in the 1990s. At the macro-level, except for the United Nations, the five countries are located in regions that have been in the limelight of worldwide communication or bordered China's territories: North America, eastern and western Europe, and East Asia. Contrary to that in foreign news, Africa as a region received a relatively high proportion of coverage on CCTV, partially confirming Beijing's efforts to befriend countries in the Third World in Chinese foreign affairs activities. It dropped out of the CCTV news lineup when longitudinal coverage of individual countries from each region was used as a baseline for comparison.

There is little doubt that a majority of nations in Africa, the Middle East, Latin America, and South Asia had little bearing or significance as an object of news interest on China's national television network. Part of the reasons could certainly be attributed to the undeniable fact that events and issues of countries in the diplomatic arena are often represented unevenly by virtue of the geographical size, military might, political clout, and economic strength. The nature of foreign relations and their historical pertinence to China's sovereignty and national pride are also plausible explanations for why some countries or entities are preferred in the news over others.

As either primary or secondary countries or entities reported on CCTV in a diverse context and with varying frequencies, Taiwan and Hong Kong were two closely intertwined cases that allowed Chinese national television ideal opportunities to mold the definitions of situations based on China's calculation and specifications. They were overtly touted in CCTV's foreign affairs stories to assert Beijing's unwavering insistence that both were under China's sovereign jurisdiction and that the Chinese territorial integrity could not be violated or interfered with by foreign interests or their surrogates. In the case of Taiwan, it was often framed within the "one China" principle in the news that became nearly ritualistic in Chinese leaders' meetings with foreign heads of state or their representatives. Without any voice or challenge from Taiwan, the deliberate selection and expression of Taiwan as a part of China in the news give the constructed reality an unmistakable Chinese identity and a claim to legitimate jurisdiction over the island nation.

This form of reporting, although seemingly routine and innocuous, skillfully imparted a hegemonic scheme that, to a lesser degree, translated into the Hong Kong handover issue in which the transfer of governance from the British to the Chinese rule was couched as the triumph of nationalism and ultimate redemption over the Western intrusion and humiliation against China. Rarely did a foreign policy story concerning Hong Kong on CCTV before and after 1997 fall short to herald the ingenuity and supremacy of Beijing's blueprint to keep the Capitalist system in Hong Kong intact for 50 years and the Hong Kong residents' enthusiasm to embrace the motherland. For example, the exorbitant celebration of the first anniversary of Hong Kong's reversion to the Chinese rule as a special administrative region on CCTV news in 1998 proclaimed to the world the continuity and prosperity of life in the former British colony. It furnishes a Chinese image of reality that demonstrates a coherent body of knowledge.

Aside from circumspect facts, foreign policy news like that pertaining to Hong Kong and Taiwan was normally cast through a third party interviewed and then retold by CCTV's own correspondents. The intermediary comprised of ordinary people, experts, and officials who were sympathetic to China's sanctioned stance. A tenacious journalistic technique was to reiterate through translation the Chinese national policy via visiting delegations. Whether Chinese or foreign sources, however, they were seldom heard directly in their own voices on CCTV. Significantly missing in the news were officials from Hong Kong, Taiwan, or Western countries who might dispute Beijing's interpretations of relations among Hong Kong, Taiwan, and China.

Foreign policy news on CCTV is then a showground where China's diplomatic objectives and achievements are deliberately chronicled to steer the Chinese viewers toward a more rosy picture of the country's growing eminence among nations, whereas foreign news outlines a playground that leaves a telling impression of being unstable and volatile when China is not around as a contributor. In the company of great nations, the Chinese handling of foreign affairs news on television adds a strong flavor of confidence and freewill that breeds an intriguing spectacle not readily obtainable in either domestic or foreign stories. CCTV's coverage of Sino–American relations in the 1990s illustrates clearly this nuance of news reporting in China.

That the United States appeared as the most covered country in China follows a well documented pattern in the literature of international communication research. In a study of 38 countries in 1995, for instance, the United States was found to have "the unbeatable superstar status" in international news coverage among 23 nations across every region of the world (e.g., H. Wu, 2000, p. 126). It is a tribute to the U.S. preeminence in the global news flow and coverage from country to country. CCTV's dealing with the U.S.-related stories throughout the 1990s offers a fertile site for a kind of "thick description" in the intellectual exploration of news as text in specific context (e.g., Geertz, 1973).

THE UNITED STATES IN A PREFERRED CHINESE READING

For China, the United States is not simply a country among all countries that speckle across the world's vast geopolitical landscape, but rather a fearsome nation-state that had deeply entangled in Chinese domestic affairs (e.g., the Chinese civil war in the early 1940s) and in international politics against China (e.g., the U.S. foreign policy to contain and isolate Beijing) during the Cold War era since the 1950s and until the early 1970s. Whether willing or not, the U.S. news media became one of the weapons the United States used to block China's entry into the world community of nations or to denigrate the legitimacy and authority of Chinese Communist regime in and out of U.S. sphere of influences (e.g., Chang, 1993). On the other side of the equation, China has long learned how to use the mass media to "help build public support for a U.S.–PRC relationship—and to pressure the United States to accede to negotiating positions favorable to PRC interests" (Solomon, 1999, p. 113).

As a consequence of more than two decades of closed borders and narrowed vision, the highpolitics of relations between the United States and China inexorably instigated a journalistic deference to the governmental manipulation of news reporting in the two countries about each other. On the part of U.S. mass media, as Chang (1999, p. 39) observed, "the unchallenged forum and uncontested news channels resulted in a simplistic and one-dimensional reality of Sino-American relations" throughout the years before 1972 when President Nixon's historical trip to Beijing set up the stage for the eventual opening of China to the outside world. Since Beijing's open-door policy in the late 1970s, images of China in the U.S. news media have to some extent become less ideologically loaded and more detached from any explicit judgmental call or condensational references (e.g., Chang, 1993).

The same could be said of Chinese news portrayal of the United States during the first 20 years of the founding of the PRC. In the 1950s and 1960s, Beijing's distrust and antagonism toward earlier U.S. meddling of the Nationalist–Communist power struggle, the military tension in the Taiwan Strait, and international crises in Korea and Vietnam, coupled with the unchecked Chinese revolutionary fanaticism and rampant nationalism, all led to a political environment in China that was extremely hostile to the United States. Under these circumstances, the Chinese news media faithfully labeled the United States as an imperialist and the arch-enemy of China, reflecting not only the combative and provocative nature of the Beijing regime in its nascent years, but also the intense and diametrical discord between the Soviet Communist block and Western Capitalist camp.

Being the leader of the Capitalist world, the United States received invariable treatment in the Chinese national news media as a place where social injustice, moral decadence and financial anguish among the underprivileged or the non-mainstream in U.S. society and elsewhere grew out of the exploitation of the capitalist class and U.S. military expansion. In the journalistic eyes of Beijing's state apparatus, whatever Washington stood for in economic policies, social relations, cultural expressions, and international excursions invited troubles for other countries when they came into contact with the United States during the divisive Cold War era. It was not until the two countries embarked on the journey of normalization in the early 1980s that China began to re-evaluate its worldview vis-à-vis that of the United States and modify its rhetorical and news vocabularies toward the latter.

Despite China's behavioral turnaround, Chinese television seemed in the mid-1970s to pay no attention to the United States in the news, thanks to either its preoccupation with coverage of Third World countries or lack of interest in U.S.-related matters or both. One indirect evidence suggests that Chinese leaders "did not yet fully appreciate the potential of the 'new' medium of television" in foreign relations (Solomon, 1999, p. 114). By the mid-1980s, however, the United States had emerged as the chief source of country for foreign news on China's national television network. Unfortunately, earlier studies failed to probe the visual aspects of Chinese TV news to ascertain the quality and the quantity of U.S. stories on CCTV when China's economic reforms and openness were taking shape. The staggering growth of television and its wide-reaching penetration of Chinese market in the 1990s make it critical to unravel what, how, and why CCTV has steadfastly put the United States on top of its news lineup over time.

In international communication research, two types of content can be used to examine the delineation of any country in another country's news media: general reports and specific events (e.g., Rosengren, 1970). From a long-term point of view, general reports depict the country in a roughly broad stroke, highlighting some parts in greater detail while downplaying or leaving out other parts of reality to imagination. Conversely, the news of specific events zeros in on certain phenomenon that induces alertness and concerns as a result of natural cause or human action. A combined analysis of these two types of stories yields a more thorough comprehension of why countries become news across national borders the way they do. CCTV coverage of U.S. news in the 1990s in general and President Clinton's 1998 visit to China in particular consisted of all the ingredients for a close-up investigation.

On the Chinese national television network, the United States maintained an unmatched presence in the news that helped unveil the underlying logic of news reporting in China, particularly when Beijing's political interests were tied to those of Washington's. Depending on where China might place itself and what could be at stake, CCTV news typified the United States in two diverging molds. In the context of foreign news where China stood as an onlooker, the United States was typecast against a variety of backdrops that underlined, among other things, the dynamics of American economic life, diplomatic activities, and technological breakthroughs. All these stories were straight reports and most void of evaluative attachment. Behind the news as it was, however, lay a subtle depiction of the many faces of United States.

Of the blooms and glooms of U.S. society on CCTV, one judicious, yet notable, spot was the higher proportion of stories devoted to the failing (e.g., crimes and man-made accidents) and frailty (e.g., natural disasters) of the United States as a country when compared to all other nations covered over time in the 1990s. This chosen typification of the downside of the United States complements the upside of its vitality and domination on CCTV, denoting a preferred mode of reading of the United States in the news. In a cross-sectional observation, the subtlety embedded in the U.S. news could be easily lost to the China watchers due to the ostensibly scanty coverage of such category of stories. Within a comparative and long-term outlook, an attempt to counterbalance the glossy and to some extent rosy pictures of the United States on CCTV news has been gingerly put into place. It is no longer a blatant propagandistic finger-pointing, but rather a guarded disposition of criticism.

In foreign policy news on CCTV, the United States becomes a convenient vehicle to move the spotlight onto China in the theater of world politics. From the exchanges of official visits between the two countries to joint ventures in Sino–American relations, individuals, and companies alike from the U.S. side showed up on Chinese television news more frequently than actors from other countries throughout the 1990s. On many occasions, American visitors were shown well received by the top Chinese leadership on CCTV news. The essence of such reports is to articulate the importance attached to the event on the one hand and to gravitate public focus toward China's prevailing national engagement and policy direction on the other hand. The implicit message is that China stands as an important country to be reckoned with in international cooperation and global stability. Its approach to foreign policy, as Kissinger (2001) put it recently, "is skeptical and prudent" (p. 36).

President Clinton's summit meeting with Chinese President Jiang Zemin in June 1998 provided Beijing with a desirable political platform and an expedient journalistic site to exploit China's shoulder-to-shoulder standing with the United States in the world community of nations and to herald the independence and sovereign determination of Chinese foreign policy. Throughout the 9-day trip, the Sino–American spectacle was adroitly organized and covered on CCTV, giving away China's tenacity to package the news in a coordinated way that intended to maximize the publicity and diplomatic achievement for the Chinese leadership while making it friendlier for Clinton and his entourage to feel comfortable at home.

Both the reported and the unreported stories on Chinese television proceed on their prearranged trajectory that leaves an apparent trace to what China hopes to realize at the end. The surprised news conference and the feisty debate between Clinton and Jiang broadcast live on CCTV scored political points for Beijing among U.S. policymakers and China watchers. The bulk of the conference and the gist of the debate, however, vanished from the CCTV screen during the prime-time newscast on the same day, as if the first ever presidential debate over some sensitive topics such as human rights issues, Tiananmen Square incident, Tibet, and Taiwan between China and the United States never happened. So did Clinton's sexual escapade with Monica Lewinsky. There was no hint or trace of the sensational scandal that had the U.S. news media scrambling for every detail of the story. It is, by design, a conscious effort not to take up certain part of the reality deemed irrelevant or prejudicial to the Chinese interests.

In no small measure, the untold story or the unseen reality in the symbolic milieu of CCTV news carries as much weight as the narrative or the visible in China. What is included in the news is not simply a sequential recount of events or issues that transpire in the domestic or remote corners of the world, but rather a regimented mass communication project that builds on the raw information material to convey a specific Chinese point of view. As meaningful and celebrated as Clinton's state visit in China, the real story behind the Chinese news on national television is the golden opportunity and localized feasibility to pre-set the parameters beforehand and reshape the boundaries afterwards in Beijing's own terms, within which the event unfolds.

WHAT KIND OF CHINESE WINDOW ON THE WORLD?

Since China's economic reforms and openness in the late 1970s, the most compelling question about the structure and processes of Chinese mass communication has not been whether the news media would be affected by the fundamental shift in the state–market relationship, but rather how far they would be unleashed from the state domination and what the market might bring to upset the equation. A direct consequence of the interplay between the state retreat and the market advent is undeniably the emergence of a relatively open public sphere in China in which the world out there, along with all its political problems and social concerns, become more accessible, debatable, and rational.

Part of the transformation has resulted in the depoliticized and decentralized news media that have enjoyed greater leeways in organizational autonomy and more degree of freedom in journalistic practices. As far as newsgathering and reporting are concerned, unlike their predecessors in decades before the 1980s, the contemporary Chinese news media have moved away from the confines of narrow vision and rigid indoctrination based on the ideas and ideals of Communism utopia to a more broader view and pragmatic presentation of the world according to the logic of market economy. What kind of world is then presented to the Chinese public? If the longitudinal analysis of CCTV news is any guide, the answers seem to be mixed.

The indisputable fact is that the Chinese window on the world is at least ajar, if not as wide open as China observers may expect following Beijing's 20-year march to economic modernization and international opening. Underpinning the framework of China's window lies incompatible edifices between the state and the market that contribute to the conflicting and restrained functioning of the sole national television news network. At times, the prime-time news on CCTV is brave, confident, forthright, and professional to tell the story, whether domestic or foreign, "as is" without any trappings. But this is the exception, not the norm, however. Most of the times, CCTV news is guarded, ambivalent, and oblique in bringing the world to the attention of the Chinese viewers.

The real world is colorful and multidimensional. On the Chinese national television news, it tends to be black and white and reductional. From here to there, the world comes into view through different prisms that filter out some elements, while keeping others in the focal point. In the domestic setting, the news is largely anchored by central governmental officials in action, burgeoning institutions and ongoing social progress that assure a sense of normal, stable, and communal world. In the foreign context, the world is filled with news of a few powerful countries and hot spots, which projects a contested geopolitical landscape overshadowed by anomalies, uncertainty and volatility among nations. Only when Beijing enters into the scene does the world out there converge into a global civic arena where China takes the center stage. It is a world created with China's expectations and specifications.

For the consumer revolution and media commercialization that are sweeping through China, unless the state relinquishes its control of media ownership and guarantees freedom of the press, how much the Chinese people may be allowed to see the world in the news will remain in the purview of the powers that be. In the foreseeable future, the Chinese national television news will continue to take a pragmatic and calculated approach in constructing the social reality both at home and from abroad for the captive audiences. The constructed world is likely to be rooted in an authoritative and recognizable Chinese formulation that tends to reduce the complex reality to an orderable and meaningful news narrative. The social knowledge it produces is made possible by the prevailing collective experience and current orientation that the news media are positioned to construe through their ways of seeing, thinking and knowing in China.

APPENDIX: THE DATA AND CODING SCHEME

THE DATA

The empirical data on Chinese national television news are often hard to come by. There has never been any systematic and longitudinal analysis of actual video newscasts of the 7 p.m. national network news on CCTV before. Three sets of actual videotapes, each with nearly four consecutive weeks of the 30-minute daily newscasts, were collected: June 15 to July 15, 1992; December 7 to December 31, 1996; and June 15 to July 15, 1998. Because of missing or incomplete data, newscasts from the following days were excluded: June 20, 21, 27, 28, and July 7 in 1992 and June 21, 28, and July 9 and 12 in 1998. The three data sets included roughly equivalent sample size: 1992, 26 days; 1996, 25 days; and 1998, 27 days.

The first data set was supported by a research grant from the U.S. Information Agency (USIA) awarded to Tsan-Kuo Chang in 1992. The conclusions and interpretations presented in the book do not necessarily represent the views of USIA or of the U.S. government.

CODING SCHEME AND INTERCODER RELIABILITY

Each story was the coding unit, regardless of its length. Part of the coding scheme was based on Stevenson and Shaw (1984). The variables dealt with the general categories of when (e.g., temporal space), who (e.g., individuals or groups), what (e.g., events or issues), and ideas (e.g., common themes that ran through the events and issues) that would be most visible and identifiable on television news in China. To a large extent, they corresponded to the categories Gans (1979) used in his analysis of nation and society in news. In addition, the main thrust of each story was noted. Although they did not directly tap "knowledge about" per se, news stories on CCTV nevertheless constituted a kind of knowledge that articulated at a given point in time the scope of observable social practices, commitments, or problems.

All the stories were coded by three coders who were fluent in the Chinese language and understood the format of Chinese television news. The intercoder reliability coefficients (Holsti, 1969) for the first data set coded in 1992 were as follows: time of events/issues occurred, .92; type of news, .98; format of story, 1.0; placement of story, .98; attribution of news, .97; primary country involved, .96; secondary country involved, .98; geographical region, .98; main actors, .81; topics, .89; and focus of visual image, .93. The variable of "province/municipality" was added later with a coefficient of .99. The reliability tests of samples in the 1996 and 1998 data sets showed similar results, demonstrating the stability and reproducibility of the coding scheme.

For each story, the following variables were identified and recorded according to the range of values provided:

1. Story number:

2. Date of report: month/day/year

3. Date of events/issues occurred: Enter month/day/year. If unidentified, enter 999999 and code the time according to the categories in the next variable.

4. Time of events/issues occurred:
    1. Recently/this week
    2. Last week
    3. Last month
    4. Unidentified
    5. Today
    6. Yesterday
    7. Future

5. Type of news:
    1. *Domestic news*: News describes the activities of domestic individuals, groups or other entities in China. It does not involve any foreign country.
    2. *Home news abroad*: News describes mainly the activities of domestic individuals, groups, or other entities of China in a foreign country. It does not clearly involve any diplomatic activities or international relations with the host country.
    3. *Foreign news at home*: News describes the activities of foreign individuals, groups, or other entities in China. It does not clearly involve any diplomatic activities or international relations with China.
    4. *Foreign news abroad*: News describes the activities of foreign individuals, groups or other entities in any foreign country. It does not involve China.
    5. *Foreign relations/foreign policy news*: News deals with international relations and foreign policy concerning China. Both involve a foreign country or entity. Foreign policy refers to discrete governmental actions intended by the decision makers to influence the behavior of international actors. International relations concerns foreign relationships, such as joint ventures, trade and cultural exchanges, between China and at least one other country or foreign entity. It does not necessarily involve governmental activities.

6. Format of story:
    1. Anchor report/no video
    2. Domestic video report
    3. Foreign video report
    4. Live coverage
    5. Commentary

7. Placement of story: Order of news

8. Attribution of news:
    1. AFP
    2. AP
    3. Reuters
    4. UPI
    5. Xinhua News Agency
    6. Own correspondent or staff (including CCTV and other station)

      7. Other domestic medium
      8. Other foreign medium
      9. ITAR-TASS
     10. Other/unidentified
     11. Edited and reported by CCTV (foreign news only)

9. Primary country involved: News involving a foreign country; three-digit code for each country

10. Secondary country involved: News involving a foreign country; three-digit code for each country

11. Geographical region: News involving a foreign country.
      1. Africa
      2. Australia/New Zealand/Oceania
      3. Central America
      4. East Asia
      5. Eastern Europe/Russia
      6. Middle East
      7. North America
      8. South America
      9. South Asia
     10. Western Europe
     11. Nonapplicable

12. Main actors: Actors refer to primary individuals, groups or other entities that do things or are affected by events in a way that is essential to the story or comment. Actors may be individuals, plural or institutional. The main actor is the main subject of the story, usually the first mentioned. Nonhuman actors will be coded as others.
      1. Heads of state/government (including vice head)
      2. Ministers/cabinet members
      3. Diplomats/ambassadors
      4. Congressional or parliamentary members
      5. Provincial/state governmental members
      6. Local governmental members
      7. Political/party officials (within states)
      8. Interest groups (e.g., business, labor, peace groups)
      9. Public/public opinion (e.g., polls, other media, nonofficial individuals, etc.)
     10. Military/militia/security
     11. Courts
     12. UN/other international organizations
     13. Other/unidentifiable

13. Topics: The focus is on the main topic—what the story is mainly about. Each story is to be coded into one and only one main topic category.

    1. Diplomacy/government: Political activity between states/governments.

    2. Military/defense: Armed conflict or threat of; peace moves, negotiations, settlements; other, including arms deals, weapons, bases, exercises.

    3. Economic/trade/business: General description about the production, distribution, exchange, consumption of goods and services; other, including statistic index such as GNP, cost of living, inflation, output, sales, prices; agreements on trade, tariffs; other international trade, imports, exports, trade balance; capital investment, stock issues, state investments (not aid); stock exchange, share prices, dividends, profits.

    4. Education/arts/cultural activities: Academic matters, issues about schooling, teaching; high-level mental activities, including painting, sculpture, concert.

    5. Technology/science: Scientific research, projects, innovations, including natural and social sciences.

    6. Transportation/travel/tourism: Traffic, telecommunication, post services, trips for sightseeing.

    7. Social unrest: Internal conflicts, crises or violences, such as strikes, demonstrations, protests, coups, revolutions and assassination.

    8. Agriculture/forest: The work of producing crops and raising livestock; fishery, forestry.

    9. Social service/health: Hospitals, public health, medical research and innovation; family planning/abortion issues; other social services and social welfare matters.

    10. Sports: Athletic practice, competition, training, award.

    11. Entertainment: Activities for general amusement, such as popular music, movies/theaters, TV programs; show business.

    12. Politics (within states): Elections, campaigns, appointments, government changes; other political, including legislation, activities of political parties.

    13. Human interest/lifestyle: Odd happenings, animals, good deeds.

    14. Disasters/accidents: Damages caused by natural or human forces, such as floods, earthquakes, drought, car or airplane collision or crashes.

15. Crime/law: Acts that violate a law; police, judicial and penal activities; legal and court proceedings (e.g., claims for damages); other crime/legal issues.
16. Ecology/environment: Energy conservation; pollution; environmental ideas and policies.
17. Religion: Belief in and worship of God; a religious rite, code, sect; a philosophy of life.
18. Obituary: Death of prominent figures and their profile.
19. Other

14. Focus of visual image:
    1. Violence: The news pictures/TV films involve acts or deeds that lead to real or potential damage to propeties and human life.
    2. Nonviolence: The news pictures/TV films do not involve violent acts or deeds that lead to real or potential damage to properties and human life.
    3. Nonapplicable

15. Length of story: Time (seconds)

16. Province/Municipality: Enter the two-digit code below to indicate the main province or municipality involved in the domestic story. The province or municipality should be clearly identified either as the origin from which the story was reported or as the location in which the event occurred. Unless the municipal location, Beijing, is specifically mentioned, code those stories about the central government's activities as 99. If foreign, unclear, multiple or nonapplicable, enter 99.
    1. Anhui
    2. Beijing Municipality
    3. Fujian
    4. Gansu
    5. Guangdong
    6. Guangxi
    7. Guizhou
    8. Hainan
    9. Hebei
    10. Heilongjiang
    11. Henan
    12. Hubei
    13. Hunan
    14. Jiangsu

15. Jiangxi
16. Jilin
17. Liaoning
18. Neimonggol
19. Ningxia
20. Qinghai
21. Shandong
22. Shanghai Municipality
23. Shaanxi
24. Shanxi
25. Sichuan
26. Tianjin Municipality
27. Xinjiang
28. Xizang
29. Yunnan
30. Zhejiang
31. Hong Kong (before 1997 considered as foreign, but coded)
32. Chongqing Municipality

17. Text description of story: A brief text-string description of the specific subject of the story (e.g., "UN cease-fire in Bosnia," "MOFERT condemns MFN bill," "man invents new medicine").

REFERENCES

AC Nielson to introduce Beijing TV ratings service. (1998, December 22). *World Journal*, p. A8.

Adoni, H., & Mane, S. (1984). Media and the social construction of reality: Toward an integration of theory and research. *Communication Research, 11*, 323-340.

Alexander, J. C. (1981). The mass news media in systemic, historical, and comparative perspective. In E. Katz & T. Szeckso (Eds.), *Mass media and social change* (pp. 17-51). London: Sage.

Alford, R. R., & Friedland, R. (1985). *Powers of theory: Capitalism, the state, and democracy*. Cambridge: Cambridge University Press.

Altschull, J. H. (1995). *Agents of power: The media and public policy* (2nd ed.). New York: Longman.

Anderson, B. (1991). *Imagined communities*. London: Verso.

Associated Press. (2000, January 8). After long silence, devastation of '70 earthquake comes to light in China. *Star Tribune*, p. A7.

Associated Press. (2001, September 6). China nearing breakthrough deal with AOL, News Corp. *Star Tribune*, p. A6.

Authority still prohibits foreign capital to enter into radio and TV industries. (2001, March 25). *World Journal*, p. A8.

Ball-Rokeach, S., & Cantor, M. G. (Eds.). (1986). *Media, audience, and social structure*. Newbury Park, CA: Sage.

293

Bantz, C. R., McCorkle, S., & Baade, R. C. (1981). The news factory. In G. C. Wilhoit & H. de Bock (Eds.), *Mass communication review yearbook* (Vol. 2, pp. 366-389). Beverly Hills: Sage.

Barnes, B. (1988). *The nature of power.* Oxford: Polity Press.

Batscha, R. M. (1975). *Foreign affairs news and the broadcast journalist.* New York: Praeger.

Becker, J. (1992). Ideological bias in reporting China. In R. Porter (Ed.), *Reporting the news from China* (pp. 64-72). London: Royal Institute of International Affairs.

Beijing heightens control of propaganda media. (1999, January 22). *World Journal,* p. A1.

Beijing leadership pays increasing attention to western media. (2000, December 11). *World Journal,* p. A2.

Benavot, A., Cha, Y. K., Kamens, D., Meyer, J. W., & Wong, S. Y. (1991). Knowledge for the masses: World models and national curricula, 1920-1986. *American Sociological Review, 56,* 85-100.

Berger, P. L. (1991). *The capitalist revolution: Fifty propositions about prosperity, equality, & liberty.* New York: Basic Books.

Berger, P. L., & Luckmann, T. (1966). *The social construction of reality: A treatise in the sociology of knowledge.* New York: Anchor Books.

Bernstein, R. J. (1976). *The restructuring of social and political theory.* Philadelphia: The University of Pennsylvania Press.

Berry, N. O. (1990). *Foreign policy and the press: An analysis of The New York Times' coverage of U.S. foreign policy.* Westport, CT: Greenwood Press.

Bishop, R. L. (1989) *Qi Lai! Mobilizing one billion Chinese.* Ames: Iowa State University Press.

Black, E. (2000, January 19). Ambassador to U.S. rejects call for China to change. *Star Tribune,* p. A5.

Blau, P. M. (Ed.). (1975). *Approaches to the study of social structure.* New York: The Free Press.

Blumler, J. G., McLeod, J. M., & Rosengren, K. E. (Eds.). (1992). *Comparatively speaking: Communication and culture across space and time.* Newbury Park, CA: Sage.

Bo, W. (2000, January 5). News programs receiving highest ratings. *World Journal,* p. C15.

Boccardi, L. D. (1993). Redeploying a global journalistic army. *Media Studies Journal, 7,* 41-47.

Boulding, K. E. (1956). *The image: Knowledge in life and sociology.* Ann Arbor: The University of Michigan Press.

Bray, C. (1974). The media and foreign policy. *Foreign Policy, 16,* 109–125.

Brayne, M. (1992). Reporting the news from China: The problem of distance. In R. Porter (Ed.), *Reporting the news from China* (pp. 53–63). London: Royal Institute of International Affairs.

Breed, W. (1958). Mass communication and socio-cultural integration. *Social Forces, 37,* 109-116.

Cable TV networks fasten pace to integrate with telecommunications industry. (2000, January 18). *World Journal*, p. D4.

Cannon, T. (1990). Regions: Spatial inequality and regional policy. In T. Cannon & A. Jenkins (Eds.), *The geography of contemporary China: The impact of Deng Xiaoping's decade* (pp. 28–60). London: Routledge.

CCTV broadcast first condom commercial. (1999, November 29). *World Journal*, p. A9.

CCTV public service commercial on condom banned. (1999, December 2). *World Journal*, p. A7.

Central TV will broadcast first live court trial nationwide. (1998, July 8). *World Journal*, p. A8.

Chan, J. M. (1993). Commercialization without independence: Trends and tensions of media development in China. In J. Y. Cheng & M. Brosseau (Ed.), *China review 1993* (pp. 25.1-25.21). Hong Kong: The Chinese University Press.

Chan, J. M. (1994). Media internationalization in China: Processes and tensions. *Journal of Communication, 44,* 70-88.

Chan, J. M., & Lee, C. C. (1991). *Mass media and political transition: The Hong Kong press in China's orbit.* New York: Guilford Press.

Chang, T. K. (1993). *The news and China policy: The illusion of Sino-American relations, 1950-1984.* Norwood, NJ: Ablex.

Chang, T. K. (1998). All countries not created equal to be news: World system and international communication. *Communication Research, 25,* 528-563.

Chang, T. K. (1999). China from here and there. *Media Studies Journal, 13,* 32-39.

Chang, T. K., Chen, C. H., & Zhang, G. Q. (1993). Rethinking the mass propaganda model: Evidence from the Chinese regional press. *Gazette, 51,* 173-195.

Chang, T. K., Lau, T. Y., & Hao, X. (2000). From the United States with news and more: International flow, television coverage and the world system. *Gazette, 62,* 505-522.

Chang, T. K., Wang, J., & Chen, C. H. (1994). News as social knowledge in China: The changing worldview of Chinese national media. *Journal of Communication, 44,* 52-69.

Chang, T. K., Wang, J., & Chen, C. H. (1998). The social construction of international imagery in the post-cold war era: A comparative analysis of U.S. and Chinese national TV news. *Journal of Broadcasting & Electronic Media, 42,* 277–296.

Chang, W. H. (1989). *Mass media in China: The history and the future.* Ames: Iowa State University Press.

Cheek, T. (1989). Redefining propaganda: Debates on the role of journalism in post-Mao mainland China. *Issues and Studies, 25,* 15-24.

Chen, K. H. (1987). Changes of American news coverage in two Chinese newspapers: A comparison. In D. L. Paletz (Ed.), *Political communication research: Approaches, studies, assessments* (pp. 129-147). Norwood, NJ: Ablex.

Chen, Y. (1998). *Reviving the national soul: Communications and national integration in China's market economy era.* Unpublished doctoral thesis, Nanyang Technological University, Singapore.

China Broadcasting Yearbook (1996). Beijing: Beijing Broadcasting Institute Press.

China Broadcasting Yearbook (1997). Beijing: Beijing Broadcasting Institute Press.

China Broadcasting Yearbook (1998). Beijing: Beijing Broadcasting Institute Press.

China Broadcasting Yearbook (1999). Beijing: Beijing Broadcasting Institute Press.

China Broadcasting Yearbook (2000). Beijing: Beijing Broadcasting Institute Press.

China Statistical Yearbook (1996). Beijing: China Statistical Press.

China Statistical Yearbook (2000). Beijing: China Statistical Press.

Chinoy, M. (1999). *China live: People power and the television revolution.* Lanham, MD: Rowman & Littlefield.

Chu, G. C., & Ju, Y. A. (1992). *The Great Wall in ruins: Communication and cultural change in China.* Albany: State University of New York Press.

Chu, J. C. Y. (1978). People's Republic of China. In J. A. Lent (Ed.), *Broadcasting in Asia and the Pacific: A continental survey of radio and television* (pp. 21-41). Philadelphia: Temple University Press.

Chu, J. C. Y., & Fang, W. (1972). The training of journalists in Communist China. *Journalism Quarterly, 48,* 489-497.

Chu, L. L. (1994). Continuity and change in China's media reform. *Journal of Communication, 44,* 4-21.

Chu, L. L. (1978). Flow of international news on China's television. *The Asian Messenger, 3,* 38-43.

Chu, L. L. (1993). Coping with TV in China. *Media Development, 2,* 69-70.

Coggeshall, R. (1934). Diplomatic implications in international news. *Journalism Quarterly, 11,* 141–159.

Cohen, A. A., Adoni, H., & Bantz, C. R. (1990). *Social conflict and television news.* Newbury Park, CA: Sage.

Cohen, B. C. (1963). *The press and foreign policy.* Princeton, NJ: Princeton University Press.

Cunningham, P. J. (1999). Presidential and scandalous: Portraits of the United States in the Chinese media. *Media Studies Journal, 13,* 68-77.

Dahlgren, P., & Chakrapani, S. (1982). The Third World on TV news: Western ways of seeing the "other." In W.C. Adams (Ed.), *Television coverage of international affairs.* Norwood, NJ: Ablex.

Dant, T. (1991). *Knowledge, ideology and discourse: A sociological perspective*. London: Routledge.

Davis, D. (2000). *The consumer revolution in urban China*. Berkeley: University of California Press.

Davison, W. P., Shannon, D. R., & Yu, F. T. C. (1980). *News from abroad and the foreign policy public* (HEADLINE Series 250). New York: Foreign Policy Association.

Deng, Y. (1997, June 9). The big pinwheel garden at CCTV's Weihai film and TV base opens. *CCTV TV Guide*, p. 1.

Dennis, E. E., & Pease, E. C. (1993). Global news after the cold war. *Media Studies Journal, 7*, 9–11.

Ding, Z. Z. (1998). Decentralization and new central-local conflicts in China. *American Asian Review, 16*, 63-94.

Dorman, W. A., & Farhang, M. (1987). *The U.S. press and Iran*. Berkeley: University of California Press.

Douglass, P. F., & Bomer, K. (1932, July). The press as a factor in international relations. *The Annals of the American Academy of Political and Social Science*, pp. 241-272.

Edelman, M. (1988). *Constructing the political spectacle*. Chicago: The University of Chicago Press.

Edelman, M. (1992). Constructing the political spectacle. *Kettering Review*, 24–29.

Edelstein, A., & Liu, A. P. L. (1963). Anti-Americanism in Red China's People's Daily: A functional analysis. *Journalism Quarterly, 40*, 187-195

Ellman, M. (1986). Economic reform in China. *International Affairs, 62*, 423–442.

Epstein, E. J. (1973). *News from nowhere: Television and the news*. New York: Vintage Books.

First court case against Chinese journalism ended. (1999, September 3). *People's Daily*, internet edition (www.peopledaily.com.cn/zdxw/13/19990903/19990903132.html).

First live radio broadcast of Grammy Award in Beijing. (1999, February 25). *World Journal*, p. A8.

Fukuyama, F. (1992). *The end of history and the last man*. New York: Avon Books.

Fuzhou broadcast live court trial. (1999, March 13). *World Journal*, p. A9.

Galtung, J. (1990). Theory formation in social research: A plea for pluralism. In E. Oyen (Ed.), *Comparative methodology: Theory and practice in international social research* (pp. 96-112). London: Sage.

Galtung, J., & Ruge, M. (1981). Structuring and selecting news. In S. Cohen & J. Young (Eds.), *The manufacture of news: Social problems, deviance and the mass media* (pp. 52–63). London: Constable.

Gamson, W. A., Croteau, D., Hoynes, W., & Sasson, T. (1992). Media images and the social construction of reality. *Annual Review of Sociology, 18*, 373-93.

Gan, X. (1994). Debates contribute to the development of the journalistic science. *Journal of Communication, 44,* 38–51.

Gan, X. F. (1992). Debates conducive to the development of journalism science. In L. L. Chu & J. M. Chan (Eds.), *Communication and social development* (pp. 1-16). Hong Kong: Chinese University of Hong Kong.

Gan, X. F. (Ed.). (1993). *A dictionary of modern journalism.* Zhenzhou, China: Henan People's Publishing House.

Gans, H. J. (1979). *Deciding what's news: A study of CBS Evening News, NBC Nightly News, Newsweek and Time.* New York: Vintage Books.

Geertz, C. (1973). *The interpretation of cultures.* New York: Basic Books.

Gilder, G. (1990). Let a billion flowers bloom. In J. A. Dorn & W. Xi (Eds.), *Economic reform in China: Problems and prospects* (pp. 369–374). Chicago: University of Chicago Press.

Giles, R., & Synder, R. W. (1999). Covering China. *Media Studies Journal, 13,* 13–14.

Gitlin, T. (1980). *The whole world is watching: Mass media in the making & unmaking of the new left.* Berkeley: University of California Press.

Glasser, T. L. (1992). Professionalism and the derision of diversity: The case of the education of journalists. *Journal of Communication, 42,* 131-140.

Gomery, D. (1989). Media economics: Terms of analysis. *Critical Studies in Mass Communication, 6,* 43-60.

Goodman, R. I. (1990). Editorializing and favorableness of U.S. television news coverage of the People's Republic of China between 1972 and 1984. *Mass Communication Review, 17,* 14-19, 56.

Goodman, R. S. (1999). Prestige press coverage of US-China policy during the cold war's collapse and post-cold war years. *Gazette, 61,* 391-410.

Graber, D. A. (1993). *Mass media and American politics* (4th ed.). Washington, DC: CQ Press.

Graham-Yooll, A. (1993). New dawn for press freedom? A personal and prejudiced opinion. *Media Studies Journal, 7,* 21-27.

Greenberg, B. S., & Lau, T. Y. (1990). The revolution in journalism and communication education in the People's Republic of China. *Gazette, 45,* 19-31.

Griffin, M. (1992). Looking at TV news: Strategies for research. *Communication, 13,* 121-141.

Gruneau, R., & Hackett, R. A. (1990). The production of TV news. In J. Downing, A. Mohammadi, & A. Sreberny-Mohammadi (Eds.), *Questioning the media: A critical introduction* (pp. 281-295). Newbury Park, CA: Sage.

Gu, Y. L., & Zhang, N. (1998). Deng Xiaoping's theory and TV news reform. *Theoretical Frontier, 6,* 10-11.

Guo, L. (1999, September 15). Commercial websites should not carry news. *Guangming Daily*, internet edition (www.gmdaily. com.cn/19990915/gb/gm~18180~9~GM9-1509.html).

Guo, Z. Z. (1991). *A history of Chinese television*. Beijing: Chinese People's University Press.

Guo, Z. Z. (1994). Radio and broadcasting in market economy. *Journalism and Communication, 3*, 2-8.

Gwertzman, B. (1993). Memo to the *Times* foreign staff. *Media Studies Journal, 7*, 33-40.

Hallin, D. C. (1994). *We keep America on top of the world: Television journalism and the public sphere*. London: Routledge.

Hao, X., & Xu, X. (1997). Exploring between two worlds: China's journalism education. *Journalism & Mass Communication Educator, 52*, 35-47.

Hao, X., & Huang, Y. (1996). *Commercialization of broadcasting in China*. Paper presented to the Asia Media Information and Communication Center Silver Jubilee Conference, Singapore.

Hao, X., Huang, Y., & Zhang, K. (1998). Free market vs. political control in China: Convenience or contradiction? *Media Development, 1*, 35-38.

Harding, H. (1984). The study of Chinese politics: Toward a third generation of scholarship. *World Politics, 35*, 284-307.

Harris, P. (1974). Hierarchy and concentration in international news flow. *Politics, 9*, 159–165.

He, Z. (2000). Chinese Communist party press in a tug of war: A political-economic analysis of the Shenzhen Special Zone Daily. In C. C. Lee (Ed.), *Power, money, and the media: Communication patterns in greater China*. Evanston, IL: Northwestern University Press.

Herman, E. W., & Chomsky, N. (1988). *Manufacturing consent: The political economy of the mass media*. New York: Pantheon Books.

Hermann, C. F. (1972). Policy classification: A key to the comparative study of foreign policy. In J. N. Rosenau, V. Daivs, & M. A. East (Eds.), *The analysis of international politics* (pp. 58-79). New York: The Free Press.

Hester, A. (1973). Theoretical considerations in predicting volume and direction of international information flow. *Gazette, 19*, 239–247.

Heuvel, J. V. (1993). For the media, a brave (and scary) new world. *Media Studies Journal, 7*, 11-20.

High court requires enforcement of public trial system. (1999, March 11). *World Journal*, p. A7.

Hirsch, E. D., Jr. (1987). *Cultural literacy: What every American needs to know*. Boston: Houghton Mifflin.

Hoge, J. F., Jr. (1993). The end of predictability. *Media Studies Journal, 7*, 1-9.

Holsti, O. R. (1969). *Content analysis for the social sciences and humanities*. Reading, MA: Addison-Wesley.

Hong, J. (1997). Cultural relations between China and Taiwan. *Journal of Chinese Political Science, 3,* 1-25.

Hong, J. (1998). *The internationalization of television in China: The evolution of ideology, society, and media since the reform.* Westport, CT: Praeger.

Hong, J. H. (1993). China's TV program import 1958-1988: Towards the internationalization of television? *Gazette, 52,* 1-23.

Houn, F. (1961). *To change a nation: Propaganda and indoctrination in communist China.* New York: The Free Press.

Howkins, J. (1982). *Mass communication in China.* New York: Longman.

Hu, Y. (1985). *On the party's journalism work: Speech at the central secretariat meeting on February 8, 1985.* Beijing: People's Publishing House.

Huang, Y., & Yu, X. (1997). Broadcasting and politics: Chinese television in the Mao era, 1958-1976. *Historical Journal of Film, Radio and Television, 17,* 563-574.

Huang, Y. (1994). Peaceful evolution: The case of television reform in post-Mao China. *Media, Culture & Society, 16,* 217-241.

Huang, Y. (1995). Why China will not collapse. *Foreign Policy, 99,* 54-68.

Huang, Y. (1996). Why party media backfire? Television as the agent of social changes in post-Mao China—A case study of the Chinese TV series "River Elegy". *Journal of Radio and Television, 2,* 169-196.

Huang, Y., Hao, X., & Zhang, K. (1997). Challenges to government control of information in China. *Media Development, 2,* 17-22.

Jacobs, R. N. (2000). *Race, media and the crisis of civil society: From Watts to Rodney King.* Cambridge: Cambridge University Press.

Ji, B. (2001, May). Speech at the ceremony of the 20th National Award for TV Dramas. *Chinese TV,* pp. 2–7.

Jiang, H. (1995). *Chinese television and its transformation since 1978.* Unpublished master's thesis, City University of London, London.

Jiang, L. (2000, May 21). Chinese newspapers forming press groups to strengthen the ability to compete. *Mainland Affairs Weekly,* p. 1.

Jin, H. (2000, March 27). "To Speak the Truth" is expected to move into primetime slot. *World Journal,* p. C12.

Jin, L. (2000, October 21). Central TV introduces 24-hour English channel. *World Journal,* p. C6.

Jirik, J. (2001). *What is the state of the emperor's clothes? An investigation into the Chinese news as the mouthpiece of the party and government.* Unpublished paper, University of Texas at Austin.

Joint Economic Committee, Congress of the United States. (1978). *Chinese economy post-Mao* (Vol. 1). Washington, DC: U.S. Government Printing Office.

Joint Economic Committee, Congress of the United States. (1991). *China's economic dilemmas in the 1990s: The problems of reforms, modernization, and interdependence* (Vol. 1). Washington, DC: U.S. Government Printing Office.

Journalism and publishing industries under tight control of the authority. (1999, January 20). *World Journal*, p. A7.

Katz, E., & Wedell, G. (1977). *Broadcasting in the Third World: Promise and performance*. London: Macmillan.

Kenny, K. (1987). Photojournalism education growing in Chinese schools. *Journalism Educator, 42*, 19-21.

Kissinger, H. A. (2001, April 16). Face to face with China. *Newsweek*, pp. 36-37.

Kuhn, T. S. (1970). *The structure of scientific revolutions* (enlarged 2nd ed.). Chicago: The University of Chicago Press.

Kwang, M. (1996, September 27). Journalism tied to party and nation's destiny, says Jiang. *Straits Times*, p. 26.

Kwang, M. (1997, January 17). China to focus on structural reforms, more transparency. *Straits Times*, p. 2.

Larson, J. F. (1984). *Television's window on the world: International affairs coverage of the U.S. networks*. Norwood, NJ: Ablex.

Lau, T. Y. (1991). Audience preference of Chinese television: A content analysis of the letters to the editor in the Chinese Television Broadcasting Magazine, 1983–86. *Journal of Popular Culture, 24*, 161–176.

Lee, C. C. (1980). *Media imperialism reconsidered: The homogenizing of television culture*. Beverly Hills: Sage.

Lee, C. C. (1981). The United States as seen through the People's Daily. *Journal of Communication, 31*, 92-101.

Lee, C. C. (1982). Media images of America: A China case study. In L. E. Atwood, S. J. Bullion, & S. M. Murphy (Eds.), *International perspectives on news* (pp. 53-76). Carbondale: Southern Illinois University Press.

Lee, C. C. (1990a). Mass media: Of China, about China. In C. C. Lee (Ed.), *Voices of China: The interplay of politics and journalism*. New York: Guilford.

Lee, C. C. (Ed.). (1990b). *Voices of China: The interplay of politics and journalism*. New York: Guilford.

Lee, C. C. (Ed.). (1994). *China's media, media's China*. Boulder, CO: Westview Press.

Lee, C. C. (Ed.). (2000). *Money, power, and media: Communication patterns and bureaucratic control in cultural China*. Evanston, IL: Northwestern University Press.

Lee, P. S. N. (1994). Mass communication and national development in China: Media rules reconsidered. *Journal of Communication, 44*, 22-37.

Lee, P. S. N. (Ed.). (1997). *Telecommunications and development in China*. Cresskill, NJ: Hampton Press.

Lee, Y. L. (1981). Changing faces of China's press. *Asian Messenger, 5*, 32-35.

Li, B. (2000, April 7). Yang Weiguang and others criticized the three "too manys" of TV programs. *World Journal*, p. C12.

Li, C. H. (1998). *China: The consumer revolution*. Singapore: Wiley.

Li, H. (1999). Prospects of six industries in post-WTO China. *China Entrepreneur*, pp. 24–26.

Li, X. (1999, December 22). In the coming new century, what card do TV practitioners have to show? *World Journal*, p. C14.

Li, X. P. (1991). The Chinese television system and television news. *China Quarterly, 126*, 340-355.

Li, X., Liu, K., Xiong, L., Zhu, W., Han, S., Wu, J., Shi, A., & Wang, M. (1996). *The background of demonizing China*. Beijing: China Social Science Press.

Liebling, A. J. (1964). *The press*. New York: Ballantine Books.

Lin, C., & Salwen, M. (1986). Three press systems view Sino–U.S. normalization. *Journalism Quarterly, 63*, 360–362.

Lippmann, W. (1922). *Public opinion*. New York: The Free Press.

Liu, A. P. L. (1971). *Communications and national integration in Communist China*. Berkeley: University of California Press.

Liu, A. P. L. (1974). Control of public information and its effects on China's foreign affairs. *Asian Survey, 24*, 936–951.

Liu, H. (1999). Strive for a peaceful international environment. In O. Schell & D. Shambaugh (Eds.), *The China reader: The reform era* (pp. 459-470). New York: Vintage Books.

Liu, J. M. (1998). A general view on TV culture. *China Radio and TV Academic Journal, 1*, 17-21.

Liu, Y. L. (1994). A study of laws and regulations governing cable TV in China. *Journalism and Communication, 1*, 69-78.

Longino, H. E. (1990). *Science as social knowledge: Values and objectivity in scientific inquiry*. Princeton, NJ: Princeton University Press.

Lull, J. (1991). *China turned on: Television, reform, and resistance*. London: Routledge.

Luo, K. F. (1993, November). *The role of news media in promoting economic and trade development among mainland China, Taiwan and Hong Kong*. Paper presented at the Symposium on Journalism in Mainland China, Taiwan and Hong Kong, Hong Kong.

MacKinnon, S. R., & Friesen, O. (1987). *China reporting: An oral history of American journalism in the 1930s & 1940s*. Berkeley: University of California Press.

Malek, A. (Ed.). (1997). *News media & foreign relations: A multifaceted perspective*. Norwood, NJ: Ablex.

Mannheim, K. (1936). *Ideology and utopia: An introduction to the sociology of knowledge*. San Diego, CA: Harcourt Brace.

Mannheim, K. (1952). *Essays on the sociology of knowledge*. London: Routledge & Kegan Paul.

Masmoudi, M. (1979). The new world information order. *Journal of Communication, 29*, 172-185.

Matlock, J. (1993). The diplomat's view of the press and foreign policy. *Media Studies Journal, 7*, 49-57.

McLuhan, M. (1964). *Understanding the media: The extension of man*. New York: Mentor.

McManus, J. H. (1992). What kind of commodity is news? *Communication Research, 19*, 787-805.

McQuail, D. (1972). Introduction. In D. McQuail (Ed.), *Sociology of mass communications*. Harmondsworth: Penguin.

Merrill, J. C. (1983). *Global journalism: A survey of the world's mass media*. New York & London: Longman.

Merton, R. K. (1968). *Social theory and social structure* (enlarged ed.) New York: The Free Press.

Merton, R. K. (1973). *The sociology of science: Theoretical and empirical investigations*. Chicago: The University of Chicago Press.

Meyer, W. H. (1989). Global news flows: Dependency and neoimperialism. *Comparative Political Studies, 22*, 243-264.

Mickiewicz, E. (1999). *Changing channels: Television and the struggle for power in Russia* (revised and expanded ed.). Durham, NC: Duke University Press.

Mosco, V. (1988). Toward a theory of the state and telecommunications policy. *Journal of Communication, 38*, 107-124.

National Committee on United States–China Relations, Inc. (1998). *U.S. media coverage of China*. New York: National Committee on United States–China Relations.

Neuman, W. R., Just, M. R., & Crigler, A. N. (1992). *Common knowledge: News and the construction of political meaning*. Chicago: University of Chicago Press.

Officials still consider the media as propaganda mouthpiece of the party. (2000, January 5). *World Journal*, p. A7.

Oksenberg, M., & Tong, J. (March 1991). The evolution of central-provincial fiscal relations in China, 1971–1984: The formal system. *China Quarterly, 125*, 1–32.

Oliphant, C. A. (1964). The image of the United States projected by Beijing Review. *Journalism Quarterly, 41*, 416-420.

Pan, Z. D., & Chan, J. (1998). *Eroding the communist ideological domination: Changing modes of television and national integration in China*. Unpublished manuscript.

Park, R. E. (1955). *Society: Collective behavior, news and opinion, sociology and modern society*. Glencoe, IL: The Free Press.

Pei, X. (2001, March 11). News programs displaying various features. *World Journal*, p. C15.

Perlmutter, D. D. (1998). *Photojournalism and foreign policy: Icons of outrage in international crises*. Westport, CT: Praeger.

Plafker, T. (1999, March 5). Measuring academic freedom in China is more subtle than headlines portray. *The Chronicle of Higher Education*, pp. A47-48.

Polumbaum, J. (1990). The tribulations of China's journalists after a decade of reform. In C. C. Lee (Ed.), *Voices of China: The interplay of politics and journalism* (pp. 33-68). New York: Guilford.

Polumbaum, J. (1994). *Between propaganda and junk-food journalism: Exploratory terrains in mainland Chinese news coverage.* Paper presented at the annual conference of the Association for Education in Journalism and Mass Communication, Atlanta, GA.

Porter, R. (1992). Shaping China's news: Xinhua's Duiwaibu on the threshold of change. In R. Porter (Ed.), *Reporting the news from China* (pp. 1-15). London: Royal Institute of International Affairs.

Pye, L. W. (1978). Communication and Chinese political culture. *Asian Survey, 28,* 221-246.

Reston, J. B. (1967). *The artillery of the press: Its influence on American foreign policy.* New York: Harper & Row.

Robinson, D. C. (1981). Changing functions of mass media in the People's Republic of China. *Journal of Communication, 31,* 58–73.

Rogers, E. M., Zhao, X. Y., Pan, Z. D., Chen, M., & Beijing Journalists Assn. (1985). The Beijing audience survey. *Communication Research, 12,* 179–208.

Romano, C. (1986). The grisly truth about bare facts. In R. K. Manoff & M. Schudson (Eds.), *Reading the news* (pp. 38–78). New York: Pantheon Books.

Rosenblum, M. (1979). *Coups and earthquakes: Reporting the world for America.* New York: Harper & Row.

Rosengren, K. E. (1970). International news: Intra and extra media data. *Acta Sociologica, 13,* 96-109.

Rosengren, K. E. (1974). International news: Methods, data and theory. *Journal of Peace Research, 11,* 145–156.

Roshco, B. (1975). *Newsmaking.* Chicago: The University of Chicago Press.

Said, E. W. (1994). *Orientalism.* New York: Vintage Books.

Said, E. W. (1997). *Covering Islam: How the media and the experts determine how we see the rest of the world.* New York: Vintage Books.

Schell, O. (1987, Spring). Serving the people with advertising: Propaganda to P.R. in the new improved China. *Whole Earth Review,* 88-92.

Schell, O. (1988). *Discos and democracy: China in the throes of reform.* New York: Pantheon Books.

Schell, O., & Shambaugh, D. (Eds.). (1999). *The China reader: The reform era.* New York: Vintage Books

Schurmann, F. (1966). *Ideology and organization in Communist China.* Berkeley: University of California Press.

Seib, P. (1997). *Headline diplomacy: How news coverage affects foreign policy.* Westport, CT: Praeger.

Serfaty, S. (Ed.). (1990). *The media and foreign policy.* New York: St. Martin's Press.

Shambaugh, D. (1991). China in 1990: The year of damage control. *Asian Survey, 31,* 36–49.

Shanghai Satellite TV to begin 24-hour domestic and overseas broadcast. (1998, September 30). *World Journal*, p. A8.

Shao, Z. (1998, October 21). Live court broadcasts benefiting legal reform. *China Daily*, Internet edition (http://www.chinadaily.com.cn/cndydb/1998/10/d-298.j21.html).

Shi, T. Y. (1998). China's general condition determines the orientation of TV. *China Radio and TV Academic Journal, 3*, 42-45.

Shoemaker, P. J., with Mayfield, E. K. (1987). Building a theory of news content: A synthesis of current approaches. *Journalism Monographs, 103*, 1-36.

Shoemaker, P. J., & Reese, S. D. (1991). *Mediating the message: Theories of influences on mass media content*. New York: Longman.

Sigal, L. V. (1973). *Reporters and officials: The organization and politics of newsmaking*. Lexington, MA: Heath.

Sigal, L. V. (1986). Sources make the news. In R. K. Manoff & M. Schudson (Eds.), *Reading the news* (pp. 9–37). New York: Pantheon Books.

Smelser, N. J. (1976). *Comparative methods in the social sciences*. Englewood Cliffs, NJ: Prentice-Hall.

Solomon, R. H. (1999). *Chinese negotiating behavior: Pursuing interests through "old friends"*. Washington, DC: United States Institute of Peace Press.

Speech to the national conference on propaganda work. (1999, January 9). *Guangming Daily*, p. 1.

Speech to the national conference on propaganda work. (2000, January 12). *Guangming Daily*, p. 1.

Starck, K., & Yu, X. (1988). Loud thunder, small raindrops: The reform movement and press in China. *Gazette, 42*, 143-159.

Stevenson, R. L., & Shaw, D. L. (Eds.). (1984). *Foreign news and the new world information order*. Ames: Iowa State University.

Stowe, L. (1936). The press and international friction. *Journalism Quarterly, 13*, 1-6.

Subscription papers and party organs dividing the market equally. (1998, March 7). *World Journal*, p. A8.

Sun, J. Z. (1998). A speech at the national conference of department directors in charge of radio, film and television. *China Radio and TV Academic Journal, 2*, 6-11.

Sun, T., Chang, T. K., & Yu, G. (2001). Social structure, media system and audiences in China: Testing the uses and dependency model. *Mass Communication & Society, 4*, 199-217.

Sun, X. P. (1992). The functions and operation of news media in China during the new 10-year period. In L. L. Chu & J. M. Chan (Eds.), *Communication and societal development* (pp. 63-80). Hong Kong: The Chinese University of Hong Kong.

Sun, X. P. (1994). *New theories of journalism*. Beijing: Modern China Publishing House.

Sun, Y. M. (1993, November). *The progressive Chinese news media in reform.* Paper presented at the Symposium on Journalism in Mainland China, Taiwan and Hong Kong, Hong Kong.

Tefft, S. (1993). In Beijing, communism besieged. *Media Studies Journal, 7,* 59-64.

The Editors. (1993). Global news after the cold war. *Media Studies Journal, 7,* 11-19.

Tichenor, P. J., Donohue, G. A., & Olien, C. N. (1980). *Community conflict & the press.* Beverly Hills: Sage.

Trattner, J. H. (1982). Reporting foreign affairs. *Washington Quarterly, 5,* 103-111.

Tretiak, D. (1971). Is China preparing to "turn out"?: Changes in Chinese levels of attention to the international environment. *Asian Survey, 11,* 219–237.

Tuchman, G. (1978). *Making news: A study in the construction of reality.* New York: The Free Press.

Tunstall, J. (1992). Europe as world news leader. *Journal of Communication, 42,* 84-99.

TV and radio signals to reach every village by the end of the century. (1999, January 28). *Guangming Daily,* p. 2.

Undercover reporting of corrupted officials and scandalous behaviors. (1999, January 20). *World Journal,* p. A7.

Varis, T. (1984). The international flow of television programs. *Journal of Communication, 34,* 143–152.

Wang, J. (1993). *Structure is the message: An analysis of imported programs in the Chinese television menu, 1970-1990.* Unpublished master's thesis, University of Minnesota-Twin Cities.

Wang, J., & Chang, T. K. (1994, July). *Economic structure and Chinese TV programming: The flow of foreign programs into China, 1970-1990.* Paper presented at the 44th annual conference of the International Communication Association, Sydney, Australia.

Wang, J., & Chang, T. K. (1996). From class ideologue to state manager: TV programming and foreign imports in China, 1970-1990. *Journal of Broadcasting & Electronic Media, 40,* 196-207.

Wang, K., & Starck, K. (1972). Red China's external propaganda during Sino-U.S. rapprochement. *Journalism Quarterly, 49,* 674-678.

Wang, W. (2001, May). Random thoughts on improving the production of TV dramas promoting the key themes (leitmotif). *Chinese TV,* pp. 11–14.

Warren, J. (1988). Foreign and domestic news content of Chinese television. *Journal of Broadcasting & Electronic Media, 32,* 219-224.

Weber, M. (1949). *The methodology of the social sciences.* Glencoe, IL: The Free Press.

Wentworth, W. M. (1980). *Context and understanding: An inquiry into socialization theory.* New York: Elesevier.

White, L. T., III. (1990). All the news: Structure and politics in Shanghai's reform media. In C. C. Lee (Ed.), *Voices of China: The interplay of politics and journalism* (pp. 88–110). New York: Guilford.

Wildman, S., & Siwek, S. (1988). *International trade in film and television programs*. Cambridge, MA: Ballinger.

Wilke, J. (1987). Foreign news coverage and international news flow over three centuries. *Gazette, 39,* 147-180.

Williams, D. (1996). *Japan and the enemies of open political science*. London: Routledge.

Wong, S. R. (Ed.). (1990). *A collection of essays on the Constitution of the People's Republic of China*. Hong Kong: The Chinese University of Hong Kong Press.

Wu, H. D. (2000). Systemic determinants of international news coverage: A comparison of 38 countries. *Journal of Communication, 50,* 110-130.

Wu, X. X. (1997). The development of cable TV industry in China. In J. M. Chan, L. Chu, & Z. Pan (Eds.), *Mass communication and market economy* (pp. 53-64). Hong Kong: Lo Fung Learned Society.

Xiao, S. (1999, March 5). Television short-wave. *World Journal,* p. C7.

Xiong, L. (1998). *Dialogue across the Pacific*. Undocumented publication, pp. 11–13.

Yao, I. P. (1963). The New China News Agency: How it serves the party. *Journalism Quarterly, 40,* 83-86.

Yu, F. T. C. (1953). How the Chinese Reds transfer mass grievances into power. *Journalism Quarterly, 30,* 354-364.

Yu, F. T.C. (1964). *Mass persuasion in Communist China*. New York: Praeger.

Yu, J. (2000, April 21). With its earlier "king of broadcasting" status under challenge, Central TV undergoes comprehensive reforms. *World Journal,* p. C6.

Yu, J. L. (1989). *Rapid expansion and diffusion of television in China*. Unpublished doctoral dissertation, University of Washington, Seattle.

Yu, J. L. (1990). The structure and function of Chinese television, 1979-1989. In C.C. Lee (Ed.), *Voices of China: The interplay of politics and journalism* (pp. 69-87). New York: Guilford.

Yu, X. (1993, August). *Professionalization without guarantees: Changes of the Chinese press in post-1989 years*. Paper presented at the annual conference of the Association for Education in Journalism and Mass Communication, Kansas City, MO.

Yu, X. J., & Sears, A. (1996). "Localism" in Chinese media context: An examination of a closed circuit community cable system. *Journal of Broadcasting & Electronic Media, 40,* 208-226.

Zhang, M. (1999). Public images of the United States. In Y. Deng & F. L. Wang (Eds.), *In the eyes of the dragon* (pp. 141-157). Lanham, MD: Rowman & Littlefield.

Zhang, T. (1992). *A history of journalism of the People's Republic of China.* Beijing: Economic Daily Publishing House.

Zhang, X. (1993). The market versus the state: The Chinese press since Tiananmen. *Journal of International Affairs, 47,* 195-221.

Zhang, X. (1995). Radio, television and video industry. In *The state and trend of development in China, 1995-1996* (pp. 256-315). Beijing: Chinese Academy of Social Sciences Press.

Zhang, X. M. (1996). Chinese TV industry. In *The state and trend of development in China, 1995-1996* (pp. 283-315). Beijing: The Chinese Academy of Social Sciences Press.

Zhang, Y. (2000). From masses to audience: Changing media ideologies and practices in reform China. *Journalism Studies, 1,* 617–635.

Zhao, Y. (1998). *Media, market, and democracy in China: Between the party line and the bottom line.* Urbana: University of Illinois Press.

Zhao, Y. (2000). From commercialization to conglomeration: The transformation of the Chinese press within the orbit of the party state. *Journal of Communication, 50,* 3–26.

Zhao, Y. M. (1987). *A brief history of China's contemporary broadcasting.* Tianjin: China Broadcasting and Television Press.

Zheng, P. G. (1998). An analysis of TV program market. *China Radio and TV Academic Journal, 3,* 45-48.

Zhu, G. (2001, March 27). Six problems of TV drama production remain urgently to be solved. *World Journal,* p. C6.

Zi, M. (1998). The merits and demerits of current TV management (in Chinese). *China Radio and TV Academic Journal, 1,* 25-28.

AUTHOR INDEX

309

SUBJECT INDEX

A

ABC News, 234
  comparison with CCTV news, 239
  Good Morning America on, 241
A.C. Nielsen Media Research, 20
Actors on CCTV news
  domestic, 128-133, 150-151, 207-208, 269-271
  foreign, 173-175, 227-228, 232-234, 207-208, 272-274
  story length for domestic, 133-135
Advertising in China, 21, 31-32
  first TV, 20
  television, 14-15, 20-21, 50, 75, 82, 263, 268
Africa, 6, 24, 110, 167-171, 179, 182, 184, 199-201, 204-207, 273, 276
Albania, 5, 72, 76, 78, 171-172, 266
Algeria, 74, 80
American University, 214
Americas, 24
Angola, 171-172

Anhui, 145-146
AOL Time Warner, 25
Argentina, 24, 74, 171
Associated Press, 137
  Television News (APTN), 109, 184
Atlanta, 238
Australia, 5, 58, 74, 78, 165, 168-171, 196-197, 199-201, 189, 204-205, 207, 214, 250, 261
Azerbaijan, 171-172

B

BBC World Service, 157
Beijing No. 1 Intermediate People's Court, 30
Beijing People's Radio Station, 22
Beijing Television Station (BTS), 4-9, 62, 70, 136, 138
  coverage of United States, 221, 227
Beijing Television University, 19
Bosnia-Herzegovina, 171-172, 239
Brazil, 5, 74, 79-80, 171-172, 202-203
British Visnews services, 8, 88, 109
Brown, J., 241

315